The Photographic History
of The Civil War

TWO VOLUMES IN ONE.
The Decisive Battles

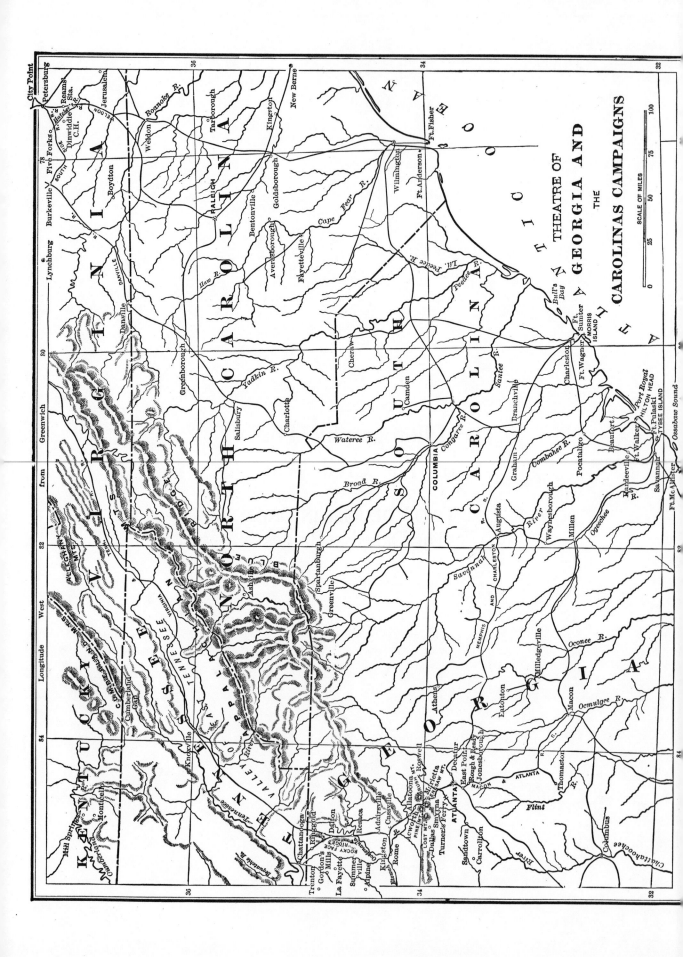

THEATRE OF
GEORGIA AND
THE
CAROLINAS CAMPAIGNS

SCALE OF MILES
0   25   50   75   100

1864—A SHOT THAT STARTLED WASHINGTON

After the shell whirled from the Confederate General Early's gun through the little house outside of Washington City, shortly before this photograph was taken in July, 1864, consternation spread throughout the North, and surprise the world over. A most audacious swoop down the Valley of Virginia, over the Potomac and across Maryland, had carried eight thousand seasoned veterans in gray to the very gates of Washington. A shot struck near President Lincoln himself at Fort Stevens. The capital was without sufficient trained defenders. Half a million Union soldiers were scattered south of the Potomac to the Gulf, but few remained north of the river when Early appeared after forced marches that tested the heroism of his devoted troops. Hastening on the afternoon of July 11th, two army corps arrived from Grant's army. Washington was saved; reluctantly the daring Confederates retreated, and abandoned their last invasion of the North.

The Photographic History
of The Civil War

Complete and Unabridged

TWO VOLUMES IN ONE.

Volume 2
*The Decisive Battles
The Cavalry

EDITOR

THEO. F. RODENBOUGH

Brigadier-General United States Army (Retired)

Contributors

THEO. F. RODENBOUGH
Brigadier-General United States Army
(Retired)

CHARLES D. RHODES
Captain, General Staff, United States
Army

HOLMES CONRAD
Major Cavalry Corps, Army of Northern
Virginia

JOHN A. WYETH, M.D., LL.D.
Captain Quirk's Scouts, Confederate
States Army

THE BLUE & GREY PRESS

PHOTOGRAPHIC HISTORY OF THE CIVIL WAR

Vol. 2
The Decisive Battles
The Cavalry

Two Volumes in One.

Copyright © 1987 by The Blue & Grey Press,
a division of Book Sales, Inc.
110 Enterprise Avenue
Secaucus, NJ 07094

Printed in the United States of America.

ISBN: 1-55521-199-2

PREFACE

THE introduction that follows from General Frederick Dent Grant is a simple statement of the large movements during the last year of the war in mass. In it the reader will find a concise summation of what follows in detail throughout the chapters of Volume III.

It is amazing to the non-military reader to find how simple was the direct cause for the tremendous results in the last year of the Civil War. It was the unification of the Federal army under Ulysses S. Grant. His son, in the pages that follow, repeats the businesslike agreement with President Lincoln which made possible the wielding of all the Union armies as one mighty weapon.

The structure of Volume II reflects the Civil War situation thus changed in May, 1864. No longer were battles to be fought here and there unrelated; but a definite movement was made by "GRANT VERSUS LEE" on the 4th of May, accompanied by "THE SIMULTANEOUS MOVEMENTS" of Butler, Sherman, and Sigel—all under the absolute control of the man who kept his headquarters near those of Meade, Commander of the Army of the Potomac.

Against such concentrated strokes the enfeebled Confederacy could not stand. Only the utter courage of leaders and soldiers innately brave, who were fighting for a cause they felt meant home no less than principle, prolonged the struggle during the tragic year ending with May, 1865.

CONTENTS

Contents

Part IV

FROM WAR TO PEACE
Henry W. Elson

Part V

ENGAGEMENTS OF THE CIVIL WAR FROM MAY, 1864, TO MAY, 1865
George L. Kilmer

———

PHOTOGRAPHIC DESCRIPTIONS THROUGHOUT VOLUME III
James Barnes

INTRODUCTION

By FREDERICK DENT GRANT
Major-General, U. S. A.

GENERAL ULYSSES S. GRANT AT CITY POINT IN 1864, WITH HIS
WIFE AND SON JESSE

INTRODUCTION

By Frederick Dent Grant
Major-General, United States Army

UPON being appointed lieutenant-general, and having assumed command of all the armies in the field, in March, 1864, General Grant had an interview with President Lincoln, during which interview Mr. Lincoln stated that procrastination on the part of commanders, and the pressure from the people of the North and from Congress, had forced him into issuing his series of military orders, some of which he *knew* were wrong, and all of which *may have been* wrong; that all he, the President, wanted, or had ever wanted, was some one who would take the responsibility of action, and would call upon him, as the Executive of the Government, for such supplies as were needed; the President pledging himself to use the full powers of the Government in rendering all assistance possible. General Grant assured the President that he would do the best he could with the means at hand, and would, as far as possible, avoid annoying the administration with unnecessary demands.

His first work was to inaugurate a plan of campaign for all the armies. During the first three years of the war, the various armies had acted independently—a condition which had enabled their enemies to reenforce each point of attack by drawing troops from points of inactivity.

Having this in view, General Grant planned to move all the armies at once. He looked upon the Army of the James as the left wing, the Army of the Potomac as the center, and the troops operating under General Sherman as the right wing; all other troops being considered as cooperative

[14]

columns. He believed that by moving the whole line at the same time the greatest number of troops practicable would be brought against the armed forces of his enemy, and would prevent them from using the same force to resist the efforts of the Union army, first at one point and then at another, and that, by continuously hammering against their armies, he would destroy both them and their sources of supply.

To carry out this idea, orders were given to the various commanders—on the 2d of April to Butler; on the 4th, to Sherman, and on the 9th, to Meade. In all these orders the same general ideas were expressed. To Butler he wrote:

"You will collect all the forces from your command that can be spared from garrison duty . . . to operate on the south side of James River, Richmond being your objective point."

To Sherman he wrote:

"It is my design, if the enemy keep quiet and allow me to take the initiative in the spring campaign, to work all the parts of the army together, and somewhat toward a common center. . . . You, I propose to move against Johnston's army, to break it up, and to get into the interior of the enemy's country as far as you can, inflicting all the damage you can against their war resources."

To Meade he wrote:

"Lee's army will be your objective point. Wherever Lee goes, there you will go also."

Thus it will be seen that General Grant's plan with reference to the movements of the Army of the Potomac was similar to that of Napoleon in the Russian campaign, while his plan in reference to the whole army much resembles the plan adopted by the Allies in their campaign against France in 1813–14.

When these movements began, the situation was about as follows: In the possession of the Union was all the territory north of a line beginning at Fortress Monroe, following the Chesapeake Bay to the Potomac River, up that river to near

Washington, the northern border of Virginia as far as Harper's Ferry, covered by the Army of the Potomac; across the mountains into West Virginia, to the headwaters of the Holston River in Tennessee, down that river and the Tennessee to Chattanooga, and thence along the Memphis and Charleston Railroad to the Mississippi, which was also in Union hands. All south of that line was in the hands of the Confederates, except a few stations along the sea coast, the possession of which assisted in the blockade.

Most of the opposing troops which were east of the Mississippi had been concentrated into the armies commanded by Lee and Johnston; that commanded by Lee facing the Army of the Potomac and guarding Richmond, while that of Johnston was at Dalton, in the northern part of Georgia, facing Sherman and defending Atlanta, a great railroad center and a point of concentration of supplies for the Confederate troops, wherever they were stationed, east of the Mississippi River. Richmond and the armies under Lee and Johnston were the main objectives of the campaign.

General Grant, as commander of the Union armies, placed himself with the Army of the Potomac, where the greatest opposition was to be expected, and where he considered his personal presence would be of the greatest value, and whence he exercised general supervision over the movements of all the armies.

The main movements being against Lee and Johnston, all other troops were directed to cooperate with the main armies. The movements of detached bodies would compel the Confederates either to detach largely for the protection of his supplies and lines of communication, or else to lose them altogether.

Everything being prepared, orders were given for the start, and all the armies were on the move by the 6th of May, with what results the chapters that follow will tell the reader in detail.

Early on the morning of the 4th of May, 1864, the Army of the Potomac moved out of its camp near Culpeper Court House and, heading toward Richmond, crossed the Rapidan at Germanna and Ely's fords and entered the Wilderness. At the same time the Army of the James moved from Fortress Monroe up the James River, landing on the south side of the James near City Point, threatening Petersburg. The army in the Shenandoah valley had already started, and Sherman was about to move.

As the Army of the Potomac was marching through the Wilderness it was attacked by Lee, who had moved from his fortifications at Mine Run. The head of Lee's column met the Army of the Potomac near the Wilderness Tavern, and the struggle for military supremacy in the field began. This battle, locally known as "The Wilderness," had by the 7th of May spread along the entire line of the Federal armies, and was raging from the Atlantic Ocean to the Mississippi valley. Columns of men were engaged in battle on the James River, in the Wilderness, in the Shenandoah valley, and in northern Georgia. In a few days the question was to be determined whether the North or the South possessed the military mastery of the continent. The decision of this struggle is told in detail by the chapters which follow.

From now on the tactics of Lee and Johnston were defensive, and they awaited the assaults of the Union armies behind fortifications. The Union center attacked and maneuvered, always by the left flank, while the right wing maneuvered generally by the right flank. One flank movement after another forced the Confederates out of position after position, until their main armies were thrown back to near the James River, to Staunton, Virginia, and to the Etowah River, Georgia. In the East, the great battle of Cold Harbor was fought, and a sudden flank movement to the left was made, the crossing of the James effected, and the carrying of the outer lines of Petersburg, which city, with Richmond, was immediately laid under siege. The junction of the armies of the James and of the Potomac now took place, and from this time on they together formed the left wing of the Union armies. The column in the Shenandoah valley had penetrated to near Staunton and Lynchburg, in Virginia; but their ammunition becoming almost exhausted, especially that for artillery, the army had to move over the mountains toward the Kanawha valley, thus leaving the Shenandoah valley open for General Early to pass through in making raids on the North; while the right wing of the Union army pushed its way on through northern Georgia to the Chattahoochee River, which it crossed, and moved toward Atlanta. The first phase of the great campaign was thus ended, and the second phase now opens before us.

As already described, the Shenandoah valley was left open to raids by Southern troops into the North, and so able a man as General Lee did not miss such an opportunity. A portion of the Confederates within the strong entrenchments of Petersburg and Richmond were detached under General Early, who marched down the Shenandoah, crossed the Potomac, and entered Maryland, penetrating as far as Washington, for the defense of which city two corps were detached from the right wing. They succeeded in saving the national capital and in driving Early's forces to the north and west, and took up the line of the Monocacy. Sheridan was given the command of the Federal defense. He soon placed himself in the valley of the Shenandoah, where his army now became the center of the Union line.

The second phase was the adoption of the policy to keep the Confederate armies within the besieged cities, Richmond, Petersburg, and Atlanta, and actively to engage the outside troops, to drive all the smaller bands to the south, to devastate the country from which supplies were drawn, and, as far as possible, to destroy the troops that gathered these supplies. In these movements the most active and most effective column was the Army of the Shenandoah, which soon sent the oppos-

ing force, as Sheridan expressed it, "whirling through Winchester," annihilated two armies gathered to protect the Valley, and destroyed all the war supplies it contained.

In the meantime, the Confederate Government, finding that it was losing so much ground by its defensive policy, relieved Johnston, an officer of great ability, who was commanding at Atlanta. Hood was placed in charge of that wing of the army. He immediately assumed the offensive and attacked the Army of the Tennessee on the 22d of July, but was defeated and thrown back, with great losses, into his works at Atlanta.

Sherman soon followed Hood's lead by making another flank movement, which caused the fall of the city, the Confederates evacuating the place and moving to the west and north, threatening Sherman's line of supplies. Sherman followed Hood for a while, but it was soon decided to detach part of the troops under him, to concentrate them at Nashville, in Tennessee, so as to prevent an invasion of the North by Hood's army, and to abandon the lines of supplies to the rear; and then for Sherman to push on to the sea, cutting through Georgia, living off the country, and destroying as far as possible the store houses from which the army in Richmond gathered its food.

Hood followed one of the detachments from Sherman's army, and penetrated as far north as Nashville, where, in December, the decisive battle of Nashville was fought. This relieved the country in the rear of the line from menace, and one might say that the Confederacy was limited to the segment of a circle the circumference of which would pass through Richmond, Petersburg, Savannah, Atlanta, and Nashville. The policy maintained was continually to reduce the size of this circle until the Confederacy was crushed.

Sherman turned north, marching through the Carolinas. Part of the troops that had fought at Nashville under Thomas

were sent to Wilmington, under Schofield, after the fall of Fort Fisher. Sheridan's troopers were pressed forward up the Shenandoah Valley, to cross over to the headwaters of the James River, and down that stream to join the armies of the Potomac and of the James in front of Richmond and Petersburg. Stoneman moved from east Tennessee into the Virginias. The circle was contracted and the Confederacy was pressed on every side. This constituted the second phase of the great campaign, and the grand finale was about to be enacted.

As soon as Sheridan reached the Army of the Potomac, his troops were placed on the left of that army, to attack the remaining lines of communication between Richmond and the South. This forced the Confederates to detach large numbers of troops from their works, and, while thus weakened, the Army of the Potomac assaulted and carried the lines in front of Petersburg on the 2d of April, 1865. The fall of the fortifications around Petersburg opened to the Union armies all the lines of communication which the Confederates had to the south from Richmond, and forced the evacuation of that city. A race was begun by the Confederates to get beyond the Army of the Potomac and Sheridan's troopers, to join Johnston, and so possibly to overpower Sherman's army. Sheridan succeeded in heading Lee off and in forcing him from the railroad, where his supplies were, while parts of the armies of the Potomac and the James followed and pressed Lee's army in the rear, until the 9th of April, when he was nearly surrounded at Appomattox Court House and his position was such that he was forced to surrender.

With the fall of Richmond and Petersburg and the surrender of Lee, the main prop of the Confederacy was broken, and all that was now necessary was to gather in the other Southern armies. As further resistance was useless, these armies asked for terms, which were granted, and thus ended the third and last phase of the great campaign.

PART I
GRANT VERSUS LEE

THE BATTLES IN
THE WILDERNESS

WRECKAGE OF TREES AND MEN, AS THEY FELL IN THE DENSE FOREST—VICTIMS OF THE MONTH'S
ADVANCE THAT COST 40,000 UNION DEAD AND WOUNDED

ULYSSES S. GRANT

GENERAL–IN–CHIEF OF THE FEDERAL ARMY IN 1865.
BORN 1822; WEST POINT 1843; DIED 1885.

ROBERT E. LEE

GENERAL-IN-CHIEF OF THE CONFEDERATE ARMY IN 1865.
BORN 1807; WEST POINT 1829; DIED 1870.

GRANT'S FIRST MOVE AGAINST LEE

ADVANCE OF THE ARMY OF THE POTOMAC, MAY 5, 1864

The gleaming bayonets that lead the winding wagons mark the first lunge of one champion against another—the Federal military arm stretching forth to begin the "continuous hammering" which Grant had declared was to be his policy. By heavy and repeated blows he had vanquished Pemberton, Bragg, and every Southern general that had opposed him. Soon he was to be face to face with Lee's magnificent veterans, and here above all other places he had chosen to be in person. Profiting by the experience of Halleck, he avoided Washington. Sherman pleaded in vain with him to "come out West." Grant had recognized the most difficult and important task to be the destruction of Lee's army, and therefore had determined "to fight it out on this line." The Army of the Potomac was but one body of the 533,447 Federal

PONTOONS AT GERMANNA FORD ON THE RAPIDAN

BEGINNING THE "SIMULTANEOUS MOVEMENT" TO END THE WAR

troops set in motion by the supreme word of Grant at the beginning of May, 1864. East and West, the concentrated forces were to participate as much as possible in one simultaneous advance to strike the vitals of the Confederacy. The movements of Sherman, Banks, Sigel, and Butler were intended to be direct factors in the efficiency of his own mighty battering on the brave front of Lee's army. All along the line from the Mississippi to the Atlantic there was to be coöperation so that the widely separated armies of the South would have their hands full of fighting and could spare no reenforcements to each other. But it took only a few weeks to convince Grant that in Robert E. Lee, he had met more than his match in strategy. Sigel and Butler failed him at New Market and Drewry's Bluff. The simultaneous movement crumbled.

LEE'S MEN

The faces of the veterans in this photograph of 1864 reflect more forcibly than volumes of historical essays, the privations and the courage of the ragged veterans in gray who faced Grant, with Lee as their leader. They did not know that their struggle had already become unavailing; that no amount of perseverance and devotion could make headway against the resources, determination, and discipline of the Northern armies, now that they had become concentrated and wielded by a master of men like Grant. But Grant was as yet little more than a name to the armies of the East. His successes had been won on Western fields—Donelson, Vicksburg, Chattanooga. It was not yet known that the Army of the Potomac under the new general-in-chief was to prove irresistible. So these faces reflect perfect confidence.

CONFEDERATE SOLDIERS IN VIRGINIA, 1864

Though prisoners when this picture was taken—a remnant of Grant's heavy captures during May and June, when he sent some ten thousand Confederates to Coxey's Landing, Virginia, as a result of his first stroke against Lee—though their arms have been taken from them, though their uniforms are anything but "uniform," their hats partly the regulation felt of the Army of Northern Virginia, partly captured Federal caps, and partly nondescript—yet these ragged veterans stand and sit with the dignity of accomplishment. To them, "Marse Robert" is still the general unconquerable, under whom inferior numbers again and again have held their own, and more; the brilliant leader under whom every man gladly rushes to any assault, however impossible it seems, knowing that every order will be made to count.

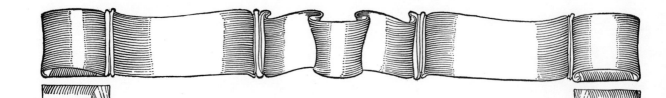

THE BATTLE IN THE WILDERNESS

The volunteers who composed the armies of the Potomac and Northern Virginia were real soldiers now, inured to war, and desperate in their determination to do its work without faltering or failure. This fact—this change in the temper and *morale* of the men on either side—had greatly simplified the tasks set for Grant and Lee to solve. They knew their men. They knew that those men would stand against anything, endure slaughter without flinching, hardship without complaining, and make desperate endeavor without shrinking. The two armies had become what they had not been earlier in the contest, *perfect instruments of war*, that could be relied upon as confidently as the machinist relies upon his engine scheduled to make so many revolutions per minute at a given rate of horse-power, and with the precision of science itself.—*George Cary Eggleston, in "The History of the Confederate War."*

AFTER the battle of Gettysburg, Lee started for the Potomac, which he crossed with some difficulty, but with little interruption from the Federals, above Harper's Ferry, on July 14, 1863. The thwarted invader of Pennsylvania wished to get to the plains of Virginia as quickly as possible, but the Shenandoah was found to be impassable. Meade, in the mean time, had crossed the Potomac east of the Blue Ridge and seized the principal outlets from the lower part of the Valley. Lee, therefore, was compelled to continue his retreat up the Shenandoah until Longstreet, sent in advance with part of his command, had so blocked the Federal pursuit that most of the Confederate army was able to emerge through Chester Gap and move to Culpeper Court House. Ewell marched through Thornton's Gap and by the 4th of August practically the whole Army of Northern Virginia was south of the Rapidan, prepared to dispute the crossing of that river. But Meade, continuing his flank pursuit, halted at

[28]

THE COMING OF THE STRANGER GRANT

Hither, to Meade's headquarters at Brandy Station, came Grant on March 10, 1864. The day before, in Washington, President Lincoln handed him his commission, appointing him Lieutenant-General in command of all the Federal forces. His visit to Washington convinced him of the wisdom of remaining in the East to direct affairs, and his first interview with Meade decided him to retain that efficient general in command of the Army of the Potomac. The two men had known each other but slightly from casual meetings during the Mexican War. "I was a stranger to most of the Army of the Potomac," said Grant, "but Meade's modesty and willingness to serve in any capacity impressed me even more than had his victory at Gettysburg." The only prominent officers Grant brought on from the West were Sheridan and Rawlins.

Culpeper Court House, deeming it imprudent to attempt the Rapidan in the face of the strongly entrenched Confederates. In the entire movement there had been no fighting except a few cavalry skirmishes and no serious loss on either side.

On the 9th of September, Lee sent Longstreet and his corps to assist Bragg in the great conflict that was seen to be inevitable around Chattanooga. In spite of reduced strength, Lee proceeded to assume a threatening attitude toward Meade, and in October and early November there were several small but severe engagements as the Confederate leader attempted to turn Meade's flank and force him back to the old line of Bull Run. On the 7th of November, Sedgwick made a brilliant capture of the redoubts on the Rappahannock, and Lee returned once more to his old position on the south side of the Rapidan. This lay between Barnett's Ford, near Orange Court House (Lee's headquarters), and Morton's Ford, twenty miles below. Its right was also protected by entrenchments along the course of Mine Run. Against these, in the last days of November, Meade sent French, Sedgwick, and Warren. It was found impossible to carry the Confederate position, and on December 1st the Federal troops were ordered to recross the Rapidan. In this short campaign the Union lost sixteen hundred men and the Confederacy half that number. With the exception of an unsuccessful cavalry raid against Richmond, in February, nothing disturbed the existence of the two armies until the coming of Grant.

In the early months of 1864, the Army of the Potomac lay between the Rapidan and the Rappahannock, most of it in the vicinity of Culpeper Court House, although some of the troops were guarding the railroad to Washington as far as Bristoe Station, close to Manassas Junction. On the south side of the Rapidan, the Army of Northern Virginia was, as has been seen, securely entrenched. The Confederates' ranks were thin and their supplies were scarce; but the valiant spirit which had characterized the Southern hosts in former battles

ON THE WAY TO THE FRONT

The Streets of Culpeper, Virginia, in March, 1864. After Grant's arrival, the Army of the Potomac awoke to the activity of the spring campaign. One of the first essentials was to get the vast transport trains in readiness to cross the Rapidan. Wagons were massed by thousands at Culpeper, near where Meade's troops had spent the winter. The work of the teamsters was most arduous; wearied by long night marches—nodding, reins in hand, for lack of sleep—they might at any moment be suddenly attacked in a bold attempt to capture or destroy their precious freight. When the arrangements were completed, each wagon bore the corps badge, division color, and number of the brigade it was to serve. Its contents were also designated, together with the branch of the service for which it was intended. While loaded, the wagons must keep pace with the army movements whenever possible in order to be parked at night near the brigades to which they belonged.

still burned fiercely within their breasts, presaging many desperate battles before the heel of the invader should tread upon their cherished capital, Richmond, and their loved cause, the Confederacy.

Within the camp religious services had been held for weeks in succession, resulting in the conversion of large numbers of the soldiers. General Lee was a religious man. The influence of the awakening among the men in the army during this revival was manifest after the war was over, when the soldiers had gone back to civil life, under conditions most trying and severe. To this spiritual frame of mind may be credited, perhaps, some of the remarkable feats accomplished in subsequent battles by the Confederate army.

On February 29, 1864, the United States Congress passed a law reviving the grade of lieutenant-general, the title being intended for Grant, who was made general-in-chief of the armies of the United States. Grant had come from his victorious battle-grounds in the West, and all eyes turned to him as the chieftain who should lead the Union army to success. On the 9th of March he received his commission. He now planned the final great double movement of the war. Taking control of the whole campaign against Lee, but leaving the Army of the Potomac under Meade's direct command, he chose the strongest of his corps commanders, W. T. Sherman, for the head of affairs in the West. Grant's immediate objects were to defeat Lee's army and to capture Richmond, the latter to be accomplished by General Butler and the Army of the James; Sherman's object was to crush Johnston, to seize that important railroad center, Atlanta, Georgia, and, with Banks' assistance, to open a way between the Atlantic coast and Mobile, on the Gulf, thus dividing the Confederacy north and south, as the conquest of the Mississippi had parted it east and west. It was believed that if either or both of these campaigns were successful, the downfall of the Confederacy would be assured.

BELLE PLAIN, WHERE THE WAGON–TRAINS STARTED

In Grant's advance through the desolate tract guarded by Lee's veterans, extending for ten miles along the south bank of the Rapidan and for fifteen miles to the southward, he was unable to gather a particle of forage. His train of wagons in single file would have stretched from the Rapidan to Richmond. Never was a quartermaster's corps better organized than that of the Army of the Potomac in 1864. General Rufus Ingalls, Chief Quartermaster, managed his department with the precision of clockwork. The wagons, as fast as emptied, were returned to the base to be reloaded. Nevertheless within a week the losses of this well-equipped Army of the Potomac in the Wilderness campaign made dreadful reading. But with grim determination Grant wrote on May 11, 1864: "I am now sending back to Belle Plain all my wagons for a fresh supply of provisions and ammunition, and I propose to fight it out on this line if it takes all summer."

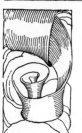

On a recommendation of General Meade's, the Army of the Potomac was reorganized into three corps instead of the previous five. The Second, Fifth, and Sixth corps were retained, absorbing the First and Third.

Hancock was in command of the Second; Warren, the Fifth; and Sedgwick, the Sixth. Sheridan was at the head of the cavalry. The Ninth Corps acted as a separate army under Burnside, and was now protecting the Orange and Alexandria Railroad. As soon as Meade had crossed the Rapidan, Burnside was ordered to move promptly, and he reached the battlefield of the Wilderness on the morning of May 6th. On May 24th his corps was assigned to the Army of the Potomac. The Union forces, including the Ninth Corps, numbered about one hundred and eighteen thousand men.

The Army of Northern Virginia consisted of three corps of infantry, the First under Longstreet, the Second under Ewell, and the Third under A. P. Hill, and a cavalry corps commanded by Stuart. A notable fact in the organization of the Confederate army was the few changes made in commanders. The total forces under Lee were about sixty-two thousand.

After assuming command, Grant established his headquarters at Culpeper Court House, whence he visited Washington once a week to consult with President Lincoln and the Secretary of War. He was given full authority, however, as to men and movements, and worked out a plan of campaign which resulted in a series of battles in Virginia unparalleled in history. The first of these was precipitated in a dense forest, a wilderness, from which the battle takes its name.

Grant decided on a general advance of the Army of the Potomac upon Lee, and early on the morning of May 4th the movement began by crossing the Rapidan at several fords below Lee's entrenched position, and moving by his right flank. The crossing was effected successfully, the line of march taking part of the Federal troops over a scene of defeat in the

CAMP IS BROKEN—THE ARMY ADVANCES

To secure for Grant the fullest possible information about Lee's movements was the task of General Sharp, Chief of the Secret Service of the Army, whose deserted headquarters at Brandy Station, Va., in April, 1864, are shown in this photograph. Here are the stalls built for the horses and the stockade for prisoners. The brick fireplace that had lent its cheer to the general's canvas house is evidence of the comforts of an army settled down for the respite of winter. Regretfully do soldiers exchange all this for forced marches and hard fighting; and to the scouts, who precede an army, active service holds a double hazard. Visitors to Federal camps often wondered at soldiers in Confederate gray chatting or playing cards with the men in blue and being allowed to pass freely. These were Federal spies, always in danger of being captured and summarily shot, not only by the Confederates, but in returning and attempting to regain their own lines.

previous spring. One year before, the magnificent Army of the Potomac, just from a long winter's rest in the encampment at Falmouth on the north bank of the Rappahannock, had met the legions of the South in deadly combat on the battlefield of Chancellorsville. And now Grant was leading the same army, whose ranks had been freshened by new recruits from the North, through the same field of war.

By eight o'clock on the morning of the 4th the various rumors as to the Federal army's crossing the Rapidan received by Lee were fully confirmed, and at once he prepared to set his own army in motion for the Wilderness, and to throw himself across the path of his foe. Two days before he had gathered his corps and division commanders around him at the signal station on Clark's Mountain, a considerable eminence south of the Rapidan, near Robertson's Ford. Here he expressed the opinion that Grant would cross at the lower fords, as he did, but nevertheless Longstreet was kept at Gordonsville in case the Federals should move by the Confederate left.

The day was oppressively hot, and the troops suffered greatly from thirst as they plodded along the forest aisles through the jungle-like region. The Wilderness was a maze of trees, underbrush, and ragged foliage. Low-limbed pines, scrub-oaks, hazels, and chinkapins interlaced their branches on the sides of rough country roads that lead through this labyrinth of desolation. The weary troops looked upon the heavy tangles of fallen timber and dense undergrowth with a sense of isolation. Only the sounds of the birds in the trees, the rustling of the leaves, and the passing of the army relieved the heavy pall of solitude that bore upon the senses of the Federal host.

The forces of the Northern army advanced into the vast no-man's land by the roads leading from the fords. In the afternoon, Hancock was resting at Chancellorsville, while Warren posted his corps near the Wilderness Tavern, in which General Grant established his headquarters. Sedgwick's corps

THE "GRAND CAMPAIGN" UNDER WAY—THE DAY BEFORE THE BATTLE

Pontoon-Bridges at Germanna Ford, on the Rapidan. Here the Sixth Corps under Sedgwick and Warren's Fifth Corps began crossing on the morning of May 4, 1864. The Second Corps, under Hancock, crossed at Ely's Ford, farther to the east. The cavalry, under Sheridan, was in advance. By night the army, with the exception of Burnside's Ninth Corps, was south of the Rapidan, advancing into the Wilderness. The Ninth Corps (a reserve of twenty thousand men) remained temporarily north of the Rappahannock, guarding railway communications. On the wooden pontoon-bridge the rear-guard is crossing while the pontonniers are taking up the canvas bridge beyond. The movement was magnificently managed; Grant believed it to be a complete surprise, as Lee had offered no opposition. That was yet to come. In the baffling fighting of the Wilderness and Spotsylvania Court House, Grant was to lose a third of his superior number, arriving a month later on the James with a dispirited army that had left behind 54,926 comrades in a month.

had followed in the track of Warren's veterans, but was ordered to halt near the river crossing, or a little south of it. The cavalry, as much as was not covering the rear wagon trains, was stationed near Chancellorsville and the Wilderness Tavern. That night the men from the North lay in bivouac with little fear of being attacked in this wilderness of waste, where military maneuvers would be very difficult.

Two roads—the old Orange turnpike and the Orange plank road—enter the Wilderness from the southwest. Along these the Confederates moved from their entrenched position to oppose the advancing hosts of the North. Ewell took the old turnpike and Hill the plank road. Longstreet was hastening from Gordonsville. The troops of Longstreet, on the one side, and of Burnside, on the other, arrived on the field after exhausting forced marches.

The locality in which the Federal army found itself on the 5th of May was not one that any commander would choose for a battle-ground. Lee was more familiar with its terrible features than was his opponent, but this gave him little or no advantage. Grant, having decided to move by the Confederate right flank, could only hope to pass through the desolate region and reach more open country before the inevitable clash would come. But this was not to be. General Humphreys, who was Meade's chief of staff, says in his "Virginia Campaign of 1864 and 1865": "So far as I know, no great battle ever took place before on such ground. But little of the combatants could be seen, and its progress was known to the senses chiefly by the rising and falling sounds of a vast musketry fire that continually swept along the lines of battle, many miles in length, sounds which at times approached to the sublime."

As Ewell, moving along the old turnpike on the morning of May 5th, came near the Germanna Ford road, Warren's corps was marching down the latter on its way to Parker's store, the destination assigned it by the orders of the day. This meeting precipitated the battle of the Wilderness.

THE TANGLED BATTLEFIELD

The Edge of the Wilderness, May 5, 1864. Stretching away to the westward between Grant's army and Lee's lay no-man's-land—the Wilderness. Covered with a second-growth of thicket, thorny underbrush, and twisted vines, it was an almost impassable labyrinth, with here and there small clearings in which stood deserted barns and houses, reached only by unused and overgrown farm roads. The Federal advance into this region was not a surprise to Lee, as Grant supposed. The Confederate commander had caused the region to be carefully surveyed, hoping for the precise opportunity that Grant was about to give him. At the very outset of the campaign he could strike the Federals in a position where superior numbers counted little. If he could drive Grant beyond the Rappahannock—as he had forced Pope, Burnside and Hooker before him—says George Cary Eggleston (in the "History of the Confederate War"), "loud and almost irresistible would have been the cry for an armistice, supported (as it would have been) by Wall Street and all Europe."

Meade learned the position of Ewell's advance division and ordered an attack. The Confederates were driven back a mile or two, but, re-forming and reenforced, the tide of battle was turned the other way. Sedgwick's marching orders were sending him to the Wilderness Tavern on the turnpike. He was on his way when the battle began, and he now turned to the right from the Germanna Ford road and formed several of his divisions on Warren's right. The presence of Hill on the plank road became known to Meade and Grant, about eight in the morning. Hancock, at Chancellorsville, was too far away to check him, so Getty's division of Sedgwick's corps, on its way to the right, was sent over the Brock road to its junction with the plank road for the purpose of driving Hill back, if possible, beyond Parker's store.

Warren and Sedgwick began to entrench themselves when they realized that Ewell had effectively blocked their progress. Getty, at the junction of the Brock and the Orange plank roads, was likewise throwing up breastworks as fast as he could. Hancock, coming down the Brock road from Chancellorsville, reached him at two in the afternoon and found two of A. P. Hill's divisions in front. After waiting to finish his breastworks, Getty, a little after four o'clock, started, with Hancock supporting him, to carry out his orders to drive Hill back. Hancock says: "The fighting became very fierce at once. The lines of battle were exceedingly close, the musketry continuous and deadly along the entire line. . . . The battle raged with great severity and obstinacy until about 8 P.M. without decided advantage to either party." Here, on the Federal left, and in this desperate engagement, General Alexander Hays, one of Hancock's brigade commanders, was shot through the head and killed.

The afternoon had worn away with heavy skirmishing on the right. About five o'clock Meade made another attempt on Ewell's forces. Both lines were well entrenched, but the Confederate artillery enfiladed the Federal positions. It was after

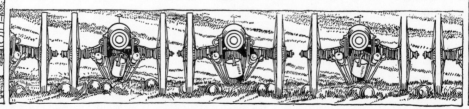

WHERE EWELL'S CHARGE SURPRISED GRANT

A photograph of Confederate breastworks raised by Ewell's men a few months before, while they fought in the Wilderness, May 5, 1864. In the picture we see some of the customary breastworks which both contending armies threw up to strengthen their positions. These were in a field near the turnpike in front of Ewell's main line. The impracticable nature of the ground tore the lines on both sides into fragments; as they swept back and forth, squads and companies strove fiercely with one another, hand-to-hand. Grant had confidently expressed the belief to one of his staff officers that there was no more advance left in Lee's army. He was surprised to learn on the 5th that Ewell's Corps was marching rapidly down the Orange turnpike to strike at Sedgwick and Warren, while A. P. Hill, with Longstreet close behind, was pushing forward on the Orange plank-road against Hancock.

dark when General Seymour of Sedgwick's corps finally withdrew his brigade, with heavy loss in killed and wounded.

When the battle roar had ceased, the rank and file of the Confederate soldiers learned with sorrow of the death of one of the most dashing brigade leaders in Ewell's corps, General John M. Jones. This fighting was the preliminary struggle for position in the formation of the battle-lines of the two armies, to secure the final hold for the death grapple. The contestants were without advantage on either side when the sanguinary day's work was finished.

Both armies had constructed breastworks and were entrenched very close to each other, front to front, gathered and poised for a deadly spring. Early on the morning of May 6th Hancock was reenforced by Burnside, and Hill by Longstreet.

Grant issued orders, through Meade, for a general attack by Sedgwick, Warren, and Hancock along the entire line, at five o'clock on the morning of the 6th. Fifteen minutes before five the Confederates opened fire on Sedgwick's right, and soon the battle was raging along the whole five-mile front. It became a hand-to-hand contest. The Federals advanced with great difficulty. The combatants came upon each other but a few paces apart. Soldiers on one side became hopelessly mixed with those of the other.

Artillery played but little part in the battle of the Wilderness. The cavalry of the two armies had one indecisive engagement on the 5th. The next day both Custer and Gregg repulsed Hampton and Fitzhugh Lee in two separate encounters, but Sheridan was unable to follow up the advantage. He had been entrusted with the care of the wagon trains and dared not take his cavalry too far from them. The battle was chiefly one of musketry. Volley upon volley was poured out unceasingly; screaming bullets mingled with terrific yells in the dense woods. The noise became deafening, and the wounded and dying lying on the ground among the trees made a scene of indescribable horror. Living men rushed in to take

LEE GIVES BLOW FOR BLOW

Another view of Ewell's advanced entrenchments — the bark still fresh where the Confederates had worked with the logs. In the Wilderness, Lee, ever bold and aggressive, executed one of the most brilliant maneuvers of his career. His advance was a sudden surprise for Grant, and the manner in which he gave battle was another. Grant harbored the notion that his adversary would act on the defensive, and that there would be opportunity to attack the Army of Northern Virginia only behind strong entrenchments. But in the Wilderness, Lee's veterans, the backbone of the South's fighting strength, showed again their unquenchable spirit of aggressiveness. They came forth to meet Grant's men on equal terms in the thorny thickets. About noon, May 5th, the stillness was broken by the rattle of musketry and the roar of artillery, which told that Warren had met with resistance on the turnpike and that the battle had begun. Nearly a mile were Ewell's men driven back, and then they came magnificently on again, fighting furiously in the smoke-filled thickets with Warren's now retreating troops. Sedgwick, coming to the support of Warren, renewed the conflict. To the southward on the plank road, Getty's division, of the Sixth Corps, hard pressed by the forces of A. P. Hill, was succored by Hancock with the Second Corps, and together these commanders achieved what seemed success. It was brief; Longstreet was close at hand to save the day for the Confederates.

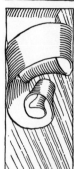

the places of those who had fallen. The missiles cut branches from the trees, and saplings were mowed down as grass in a meadow is cut by a scythe. Bloody remnants of uniforms, blue and gray, hung as weird and uncanny decorations from remaining branches.

The story of the Federal right during the morning is easily told. Persistently and often as he tried, Warren could make no impression on the strongly entrenched Ewell—nor could Sedgwick, who was trying equally hard with Wright's division of his corps. But with Hancock on the left, in his entrenchments on the Brock road, it was different. The gallant and heroic charges here have elicited praise and admiration from friend and foe alike. At first, Hill was forced back in disorder, and driven in confusion a mile and a half from his line. The Confederates seemed on the verge of panic and rout. From the rear of the troops in gray came the beloved leader of the Southern host, General Lee. He was astride his favorite battle-horse, and his face was set in lines of determination. Though the crisis of the battle for the Confederates had arrived, Lee's voice was calm and soft as he commanded, "Follow me," and then urged his charger toward the bristling front of the Federal lines. The Confederate ranks were electrified by the brave example of their commander. A ragged veteran who had followed Lee through many campaigns, leaped forward and caught the bridle-rein of the horse. "We won't go on until you go back," cried the devoted warrior. Instantly the Confederate ranks resounded with the cry, "Lee to the rear! Lee to the rear!" and the great general went back to safety while his soldiers again took up the gage of battle and plunged into the smoke and death-laden storm. But Lee, by his personal presence, and the arrival of Longstreet, had restored order and courage in the ranks, and their original position was soon regained.

The pursuit of the Confederates through the dense forest had caused confusion and disorganization in Hancock's corps.

TREES IN THE TRACK OF THE IRON STORM

The Wilderness to the north of the Orange turnpike. Over ground like this, where men had seldom trod before, ebbed and flowed the tide of trampling thousands on May 5 and 6, 1864. Artillery, of which Grant had a superabundance, was well-nigh useless, wreaking its impotent fury upon the defenseless trees. Even the efficacy of musketry fire was hampered. Men tripping and falling in the tangled underbrush arose bleeding from the briars to struggle with an adversary whose every movement was impeded also. The cold steel of the bayonet finished the work which rifles had begun. In the terrible turmoil of death the hopes of both Grant and Lee were doomed to disappointment. The result was a victory for neither. Lee, disregarding his own safety, endeavored to rally the disordered ranks of A. P. Hill, and could only be persuaded to retire by the pledge of Longstreet that his advancing force would win the coveted victory. Falling upon Hancock's flank, the fresh troops seemed about to crush the Second Corps, as Jackson's men had crushed the Eleventh the previous year at Chancellorsville. But now, as Jackson, at the critical moment, had fallen by the fire of his own men, so Longstreet and his staff, galloping along the plank road, were mistaken by their own soldiers for Federals and fired upon. A minie-ball struck Longstreet in the shoulder, and he was carried from the field, feebly waving his hat that his men might know that he was not killed. With him departed from the field the life of the attack.

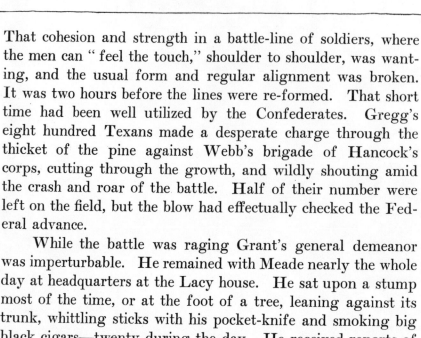

That cohesion and strength in a battle-line of soldiers, where the men can "feel the touch," shoulder to shoulder, was wanting, and the usual form and regular alignment was broken. It was two hours before the lines were re-formed. That short time had been well utilized by the Confederates. Gregg's eight hundred Texans made a desperate charge through the thicket of the pine against Webb's brigade of Hancock's corps, cutting through the growth, and wildly shouting amid the crash and roar of the battle. Half of their number were left on the field, but the blow had effectually checked the Federal advance.

While the battle was raging Grant's general demeanor was imperturbable. He remained with Meade nearly the whole day at headquarters at the Lacy house. He sat upon a stump most of the time, or at the foot of a tree, leaning against its trunk, whittling sticks with his pocket-knife and smoking big black cigars—twenty during the day. He received reports of the progress of the battle and gave orders without the least evidence of excitement or emotion. "His orders," said one of his staff, "were given with a spur," implying instant action. On one occasion, when an officer, in great excitement, brought him the report of Hancock's misfortune and expressed apprehension as to Lee's purpose, Grant exclaimed with some warmth: "Oh, I am heartily tired of hearing what Lee is going to do. Go back to your command and try to think what we are going to do ourselves."

Several brigades of Longstreet's troops, though weary from their forced march, were sent on a flanking movement against Hancock's left, which demoralized Mott's division and caused it to fall back three-quarters of a mile. Longstreet now advanced with the rest of his corps. The dashing leader, while riding with Generals Kershaw and Jenkins at the head of Jenkins' brigade on the right of the Southern battle array, was screened by the tangled thickets from the view of his own troops, flushed with the success of brilliant flank movement.

THE GRAVEYARD OF THREE CAMPAIGNS

As this photograph was taken, May 12, 1864, the dead again were being brought to unhappy Fredericksburg, where slept thousands that had fought under Burnside and Hooker. Now, once more, the sad cavalcade is arriving, freighted still more heavily. The half-ruined homes, to which some of the dwellers had returned, for the third time become temporary hospitals. It was weeks before the wounded left. The Wilderness brought death's woe to 2,246 Northern homes, and Spotsylvania added its 2,725 more. At the South, mourning for lost ones was not less widespread. As a battle, the fighting at close quarters in the Wilderness was indecisive; as a slaughter, it proved that the deadly determination on both sides was equal. Grant, as he turned his face in anguish away from the passing trains of dead and wounded, had learned a bitter lesson—not only as to the fighting blood of his new command but also of that of the foe he had come to crush.

Suddenly the passing column was seen indistinctly through an opening and a volley burst forth and struck the officers. When the smoke lifted Longstreet and Jenkins were down—the former seriously wounded, and the latter killed outright. As at Chancellorsville a year before and on the same battleground, a great captain of the Confederacy was shot down by his own men, and by accident, at the crisis of a battle. Jackson lingered several days after Chancellorsville, while Longstreet recovered and lived to fight for the Confederacy till the surrender at Appomattox. General Wadsworth, of Hancock's corps, was mortally wounded during the day, while making a daring assault on the Confederate works, at the head of his men.

During the afternoon, the Confederate attack upon Hancock's and Burnside's forces, which constituted nearly half the entire army, was so severe that the Federal lines began to give way. The combatants swayed back and forth; the Confederates seized the Federal breastworks repeatedly, only to be repulsed again and again. Once, the Southern colors were placed on the Union battlements. A fire in the forest, which had been burning for hours, and in which, it is estimated, about two hundred of the Federal wounded perished, was communicated to the timber entrenchments, the heat and smoke driving into the faces of the men on the Union side, and compelling them in some places to abandon the works. Hancock made a gallant and heroic effort to re-form his lines and push the attack, and, as he rode along the lines, his inspiring presence elicited cheer upon cheer from the men, but the troops had exhausted their ammunition, the wagons were in the rear, and as night was approaching, further attack was abandoned. The contest ended on the lines where it began.

Later in the evening consternation swept the Federal camp when heavy firing was heard in the direction of Sedgwick's corps, on the right. The report was current that the entire Sixth Corps had been attacked and broken. What had happened was a surprise attack by the Confederates,

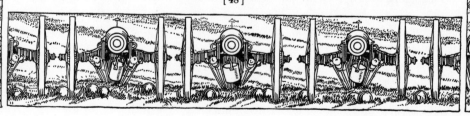

A LOSS IN "EFFECTIVE STRENGTH"—WOUNDED AT FREDERICKSBURG

Federal wounded in the Wilderness campaign, at Fredericksburg. Grant lost 17.3 per cent. of his numbers engaged in the two days' battles of the Wilderness alone. Lee's loss was 18.1 per cent. More than 24,000 of the Army of the Potomac and of the Army of Northern Virginia lay suffering in those uninhabited thickets. There many of them died alone, and some perished in the horror of a forest fire on the night of May 5th. The Federals lost many gallant officers, among them the veteran Wadsworth. The Confederates lost Generals Jenkins and Jones, killed, and suffered a staggering blow in the disabling of Longstreet. The series of battles of the Wilderness and Spotsylvania campaigns were more costly to the Federals than Antietam and Gettysburg combined.

commanded by General John B. Gordon, on Sedgwick's right flank, Generals Seymour and Shaler with six hundred men being captured. When a message was received from Sedgwick that the Sixth Corps was safe in an entirely new line, there was great rejoicing in the Union camp.

Thus ended the two days' fighting of the battle of the Wilderness, one of the greatest struggles in history. It was Grant's first experience in the East, and his trial measure of arms with his great antagonist, General Lee. The latter returned to his entrenchments and the Federals remained in their position. The first clash had been undecisive. While Grant had been defeated in his plan to pass around Lee, yet he had made a new record for the Army of the Potomac, and he was not turned from his purpose of putting himself between the Army of Northern Virginia and the capital of the Confederacy. During the two days' engagement, there were ten hours of actual fighting, with a loss in killed and wounded of about seventeen thousand Union and nearly twelve thousand Confederates, nearly three thousand men sacrificed each hour. It is the belief of some military writers that Lee deliberately chose the Wilderness as a battle-ground, as it would effectually conceal great inferiority of force, but if this be so he seems to have come to share the unanimous opinions of the generals of both sides that its difficulties were unsurmountable, and within his entrenchments he awaited further attack. It did not come.

The next night, May 7th, Grant's march by the Confederate right flank was resumed, but only to be blocked again by the dogged determination of the tenacious antagonist, a few miles beyond, at Spotsylvania. Lee again anticipated Grant's move. It is not strange that the minds of these two men moved along the same lines in military strategy, when we remember they were both military experts of the highest order, and were now working out the same problem. The results obtained by each are told in the story of the battle of Spotsylvania.

PART I
GRANT VERSUS LEE

SPOTSYLVANIA AND THE BLOODY ANGLE

QUARLES' MILL, NORTH ANNA RIVER—THE GOAL AFTER
SPOTSYLVANIA

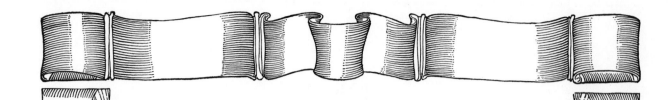

THE BATTLE OF SPOTSYLVANIA COURT HOUSE

But to Spotsylvania history will accord the palm, I am sure, for having furnished an unexampled muzzle-to-muzzle fire; the longest roll of incessant, unbroken musketry; the most splendid exhibition of individual heroism and personal daring by large numbers, who, standing in the freshly spilt blood of their fellows, faced for so long a period and at so short a range the flaming rifles as they heralded the decrees of death. This heroism was confined to neither side. It was exhibited by both armies, and in that hand-to-hand struggle for the possession of the breastworks it seemed almost universal. It would be commonplace truism to say that such examples will not be lost to the Republic.—*General John B. Gordon, C.S.A., in "Reminiscences of the Civil War."*

IMMEDIATELY after the cessation of hostilities on the 6th of May in the Wilderness, Grant determined to move his army to Spotsylvania Court House, and to start the wagon trains on the afternoon of the 7th. Grant's object was, by a flank move, to get between Lee and Richmond. Lee foresaw Grant's purpose and also moved his cavalry, under Stuart, across the opponent's path. As an illustration of the exact science of war we see the two great military leaders racing for position at Spotsylvania Court House. It was revealed later that Lee had already made preparations on this field a year before, in anticipation of its being a possible battleground.

Apprised of the movement of the Federal trains, Lee, with his usual sagacious foresight, surmised their destination. He therefore ordered General R. H. Anderson, now in command of Longstreet's corps, to march to Spotsylvania Court House at three o'clock on the morning of the 8th. But the smoke and flames from the burning forests that surrounded

SPOTSYLVANIA COURT HOUSE

WHERE GRANT WANTED TO "FIGHT IT OUT"

For miles around this quaint old village-pump surged the lines of two vast contending armies, May 8–12, 1864. In this picture of only a few months later, the inhabitants have returned to their accustomed quiet, although the reverberations of battle have hardly died away. But on May 7th Generals Grant and Meade, with their staffs, had started toward the little courthouse. As they passed along the Brock Road in the rear of Hancock's lines, the men broke into loud hurrahs. They saw that the movement was still to be southward. But chance had caused Lee to choose the same objective. Misinterpreting Grant's movement as a retreat upon Fredericksburg, he sent Longstreet's corps, now commanded by Anderson, to Spotsylvania. Chance again, in the form of a forest fire, drove Anderson to make, on the night of May 7th, the march from the Wilderness that he had been ordered to commence on the morning of the 8th. On that day, while Warren was contending with the forces of Anderson, Lee's whole army was entrenching on a ridge around Spotsylvania Court House. "Accident," says Grant, "often decides the fate of battle." But this "accident" was one of Lee's master moves.

Anderson's camp in the Wilderness made the position untenable, and the march was begun at eleven o'clock on the night of the 7th. This early start proved of inestimable value to the Confederates. Anderson's right, in the Wilderness, rested opposite Hancock's left, and the Confederates secured a more direct line of march to Spotsylvania, several miles shorter than that of the Federals. The same night General Ewell at the extreme Confederate left was ordered to follow Anderson at daylight, if he found no large force in his front. This order was followed out, there being no opposing troops, and the corps took the longest route of any of Lee's troops. General Ewell found the march exhausting and distressing on account of the intense heat and dust and smoke from the burning forests.

The Federal move toward Spotsylvania Court House was begun after dark on the 7th. Warren's corps, in the lead, took the Brock road behind Hancock's position and was followed by Sedgwick, who marched by way of Chancellorsville. Burnside came next, but he was halted to guard the trains. Hancock, covering the move, did not start the head of his command until some time after daylight. When Warren reached Todd's Tavern he found the Union cavalry under Merritt in conflict with Fitzhugh Lee's division of Stuart's cavalry. Warren sent Robinson's division ahead; it drove Fitzhugh Lee back, and, advancing rapidly, met the head of Anderson's troops. The leading brigades came to the assistance of the cavalry; Warren was finally repulsed and began entrenching. The Confederates gained Spotsylvania Court House.

Throughout the day there was continual skirmishing between the troops, as the Northerners attempted to break the line of the Confederates. But the men in gray stood firm. Every advance of the blue was repulsed. Lee again blocked the way of Grant's move. The Federal loss during the day had been about thirteen hundred, while the Confederates lost fewer men than their opponents.

MEADE AND SEDGWICK—BEFORE THE ADVANCE THAT BROUGHT SEDGWICK'S
DEATH AT SPOTSYLVANIA

To the right of General Meade, his chief and friend, stands Major-General John Sedgwick, commanding
the Sixth Army Corps. He wears his familiar round hat and is smiling. He was a great tease; evidently
the performances of the civilian who had brought his new-fangled photographic apparatus into camp suggested a joke. A couple of months later, on the 9th of May, Sedgwick again was jesting—before Spotsylvania Court House. McMahon of his staff had begged him to avoid passing some artillery exposed to
the Confederate fire, to which Sedgwick had playfully replied, "McMahon, I would like to know who
commands this corps, you or I?" Then he ordered some infantry before him to shift toward the right.
Their movement drew the fire of the Confederates. The lines were close together; the situation tense. A
sharpshooter's bullet whistled—Sedgwick fell. He was taken to Meade's headquarters. The Army of
the Potomac had lost another corps commander, and the Union a brilliant and courageous soldier.

The work of both was now the construction of entrenchments, which consisted of earthworks sloping to either side, with logs as a parapet, and between these works and the opposing army were constructed what are known as abatis, felled trees, with the branches cut off, the sharp ends projecting toward the approaching forces.

Lee's entrenchments were of such character as to increase the efficiency of his force. They were formed in the shape of a huge V with the apex flattened, forming a salient angle against the center of the Federal line. The Confederate lines were facing north, northwest, and northeast, the corps commanded by Anderson on the left, Ewell in the center, and Early on the right, the latter temporarily replacing A. P. Hill, who was ill. The Federals confronting them were Burnside on the left, Sedgwick and Warren in the center, and Hancock on the right.

The day of the 9th was spent in placing the lines of troops, with no fighting except skirmishing and some sharpshooting. While placing some field-pieces, General Sedgwick was hit by a sharpshooter's bullet and instantly killed. He was a man of high character, a most competent commander, of fearless courage, loved and lamented by the army. General Horatio G. Wright succeeded to the command of the Sixth Corps.

Early on the morning of the 10th, the Confederates discovered that Hancock had crossed the Po River in front of his position of the day before and was threatening their rear. Grant had suspected that Lee was about to move north toward Fredericksburg, and Hancock had been ordered to make a reconnaissance with a view to attacking and turning the Confederate left. But difficulties stood in the way of Hancock's performance, and before he had accomplished much, Meade directed him to send two of his divisions to assist Warren in making an attack on the Southern lines. The Second Corps started to recross the Po. Before all were over Early made

THE APEX OF THE BATTLEFIELD

McCool's house, within the "Bloody Angle." The photographs were taken in 1864, shortly after the struggle of Spotsylvania Court House, and show the old dwelling as it was on May 12th, when the fighting was at flood tide all round it; and below, the Confederate entrenchments near that blood-drenched spot. At a point in these Confederate lines in advance of the McCool house, the entrenchments had been thrown forward like the salient of a fort, and the wedge-shaped space within them was destined to become renowned as the "Bloody Angle." The position was defended by the famous "Stonewall Division" of the Confederates under command of General Edward Johnson. It was near the scene of Upton's gallant charge on the 10th. Here at daybreak on May 12th the divisions of the intrepid Barlow and Birney, sent forward by Hancock, stole a march upon the unsuspecting Confederates. Leaping over the breastworks the Federals were upon them and the first of the terrific hand-to-hand conflicts that marked the day began. It ended in victory for Hancock's men, into whose hands fell 20 cannon, 30 standards and 4,000 prisoners, "the best division in the Confederate army."

CONFEDERATE ENTRENCHMENTS NEAR "BLOODY ANGLE"

Flushed with success, the Federals pressed on to Lee's second line of works, where Wilcox's division of the Confederates held them until reënforcements sent by Lee from Hill and Anderson drove them back. On the Federal side the Sixth Corps, with Upton's brigade in the advance, was hurried forward to hold the advantage gained. But Lee himself was on the scene, and the men of the gallant Gordon's division, pausing long enough to seize and turn his horse, with shouts of "General Lee in the rear," hurtled forward into the conflict. In five separate charges by the Confederates the fighting came to close quarters. With bayonets, clubbed muskets, swords and pistols, men fought within two feet of one another on either side of the entrenchments at "Bloody Angle" till night at last left it in possession of the Federals. None of the fighting near Spotsylvania Court House was inglorious. On the 10th, after a day of strengthening positions on both sides, young Colonel Emory Upton of the 121st New York, led a storming party of twelve regiments into the strongest of the Confederate entrenchments. For his bravery Grant made him a brigadier-general on the field.

a vigorous assault on the rear division, which did not escape without heavy loss. In this engagement the corps lost the first gun in its most honorable career, a misfortune deeply lamented by every man in the corps, since up to this moment it had long been the only one in the entire army which could make the proud claim of never having lost a gun or a color.

But the great event of the 10th was the direct assault upon the Confederate front. Meade had arranged for Hancock to take charge of this, and the appointed hour was five in the afternoon. But Warren reported earlier that the opportunity was most favorable, and he was ordered to start at once. Wearing his full uniform, the leader of the Fifth Corps advanced at a quarter to four with the greater portion of his troops. The progress of the valiant Northerners was one of the greatest difficulty, owing to the dense wood of low cedartrees through which they had to make their way. Longstreet's corps behind their entrenchments acknowledged the advance with very heavy artillery and musket fire. But Warren's troops did not falter or pause until some had reached the abatis and others the very crest of the parapet. A few, indeed, were actually killed inside the works. All, however, who survived the terrible ordeal were finally driven back with heavy loss. General James C. Rice was mortally wounded.

To the left of Warren, General Wright had observed what he believed to be a vulnerable spot in the Confederate entrenchments. Behind this particular place was stationed Doles' brigade of Georgia regiments, and Colonel Emory Upton was ordered to charge Doles with a column of twelve regiments in four lines. The ceasing of the Federal artillery at six o'clock was the signal for the charge, and twenty minutes later, as Upton tells us, "at command, the lines rose, moved noiselessly to the edge of the wood, and then, with a wild cheer and faces averted, rushed for the works. Through a terrible front and flank fire the column advanced quickly, gaining the parapet. Here occurred a deadly hand-to-hand

UNION ARTILLERY MASSING
FOR THE ADVANCE THAT
EWELL'S ATTACK DELAYED
THAT SAME AFTERNOON

BEVERLY HOUSE, MAY 18, 1864

The artillery massing in the meadow gives to this view the interest of an impending tragedy. In the foreground the officers, servants, and orderlies of the headquarters mess camp are waiting for the command to strike their tents, pack the wagons, and move on. But at the very time this photograph was taken they should have been miles away. Grant had issued orders the day before that should have set these troops in motion. However, the Confederate General Ewell had chosen the 18th to make an attack on the right flank. It not only delayed the departure but forced a change in the intended positions of the division as they had been contemplated by the commander-in-chief. Beverly House is where General Warren pitched his headquarters after Spotsylvania, and the spectator is looking toward the battlefield that lies beyond the distant woods. After Ewell's attack, Warren again found himself on the right flank, and at this very moment the main body of the Federal army is passing in the rear of him. The costly check at Spotsylvania, with its wonderful display of fighting on both sides, had in its apparently fruitless results called for the display of all Grant's gifts as a military leader. It takes but little imagination to supply color to this photograph; it is full of it—full of the movement and detail of war also. It is springtime; blossoms have just left the trees and the whole country is green and smiling, but the earth is scarred by thousands of trampling feet and hoof-prints. Ugly ditches cross the landscape; the débris of an army marks its onsweep from one battlefield to another.

conflict. The enemy, sitting in their pits with pieces upright, loaded, and with bayonets fixed ready to impale the first who should leap over, absolutely refused to yield the ground. The first of our men who tried to surmount the works fell, pierced through the head by musket-balls. Others, seeing the fate of their comrades, held their pieces at arm's length and fired downward, while others, poising their pieces vertically, hurled them down upon their enemy, pinning them to the ground. . . . The struggle lasted but a few seconds. Numbers prevailed, and like a resistless wave, the column poured over the works, quickly putting *hors de combat* those who resisted and sending to the rear those who surrendered. Pressing forward and expanding to the right and left, the second line of entrenchments, its line of battle, and a battery fell into our hands. The column of assault had accomplished its task."

The Confederate line had been shattered and an opening made for expected support. This, however, failed to arrive. General Mott, on the left, did not bring his division forward as had been planned and as General Wright had ordered. The Confederates were reenforced, and Upton could do no more than hold the captured entrenchments until ordered to retire. He brought twelve hundred prisoners and several stands of colors back to the Union lines; but over a thousand of his own men were killed or wounded. For gallantry displayed in this charge, Colonel Upton was made brigadier-general.

The losses to the Union army in this engagement at Spotsylvania were over four thousand. The loss to the Confederates was probably two thousand.

During the 11th there was a pause. The two giant antagonists took a breathing spell. It was on the morning of this date that Grant penned the sentence, " I propose to fight it out on this line if it takes all summer," to his chief of staff, General Halleck.

During this time Sheridan, who had brought the cavalry

THE ONES WHO NEVER CAME BACK

These are some of the men for whom waiting women wept—the ones who never came back. They belonged to Ewell's Corps, who attacked the Federal lines so gallantly on May 18th. There may be some who will turn from this picture with a shudder of horror, but it is no morbid curiosity that will cause them to study it closely. If pictures such as this were familiar everywhere there would soon be an end of war. We can realize money by seeing it expressed in figures; we can realize distances by miles, but some things in their true meaning can only be grasped and impressions formed with the seeing eye. Visualizing only this small item of the awful cost—the cost beside which money cuts no figure—an idea can be gained of what war is. Here is a sermon in the cause of universal peace. The handsome lad lying with outstretched arms and clinched fingers is a mute plea. Death has not disfigured him—he lies in an attitude of relaxation and composure. Perhaps in some Southern home this same face is pictured in the old family album, alert and full of life and hope, and here is the end. Does there not come to the mind the insistent question, "Why?" The Federal soldiers standing in the picture are not thinking of all this, it may be true, but had they meditated in the way that some may, as they gaze at this record of death, it would be worth their while. One of the men is apparently holding a sprig of blossoms in his hand. It is a strange note here.

up to a state of great efficiency, was making an expedition to the vicinity of Richmond. He had said that if he were permitted to operate independently of the army he would draw Stuart after him. Grant at once gave the order, and Sheridan made a detour around Lee's army, engaging and defeating the Confederate cavalry, which he greatly outnumbered, on the 11th of May, at Yellow Tavern, where General Stuart, the brilliant commander of the Confederate cavalry, was mortally wounded.

Grant carefully went over the ground and decided upon another attack on the 12th. About four hundred yards of clear ground lay in front of the sharp angle, or salient, of Lee's lines. After the battle this point was known as the "Bloody Angle," and also as "Hell's Hole." Here Hancock was ordered to make an attack at daybreak on the 12th. Lee had been expecting a move on the part of Grant. On the evening of the 10th he sent to Ewell this message: "It will be necessary for you to reestablish your whole line to-night. . . . Perhaps Grant will make a night attack, as it was a favorite amusement of his at Vicksburg."

Through rain and mud Hancock's force was gotten into position within a few hundred yards of the Confederate breastworks. He was now between Burnside and Wright. At the first approach of dawn the four divisions of the Second Corps, under Birney, Mott, Barlow, and Gibbon (in reserve) moved noiselessly to the designated point of attack. Without a shot being fired they reached the Confederate entrenchments, and struck with fury and impetuosity a mortal blow at the point where least expected, on the salient, held by General Edward Johnson of Ewell's corps. The movement of the Federals was so swift and the surprise so complete, that the Confederates could make practically no resistance, and were forced to surrender.

The artillery had been withdrawn from the earthworks occupied by Johnson's troops on the previous night, but

DIGGING A LONELY GRAVE—AFTER SPOTSYLVANIA

If we should take out the grim reminder of war's horrors, the dead man on the litter with the stiff upturned arms, we should have a charming picture of a little Virginia farm, a cozy little house with its blossoming peach trees in the garden and the big Chinaberry tree shading the front yard. But within a stone's throw lie scores of huddled heaps distressing to gaze upon. Only a few hours before they had been living, breathing, fighting men; for here occurred Ewell's fierce attack on the 18th of May. The little farm belonged to a widow by the name of Allsop, and the garden and the ground back of the barns and outbuildings became a Confederate cemetery. Soldiers grow callous to the work of putting friends and foemen to rest for the last long sleep. Evidently this little squad of the burying detail have discovered that this man is an officer, and

JUST "ONE OF EWELL'S MEN"

instead of putting him in the long trench where his comrades rest with elbows touching in soldierly alignment, they are giving him a grave by himself. Down at a fence corner on the Allsop farm they found the dead Confederate of the smaller photograph. He was of the never-surrender type, this man in the ragged gray uniform, one of the do or die kind that the bullets find most often. Twice wounded before his dauntless spirit left him was this gallant fellow; with a shattered leg that he had tied about hastily with a cotton shirt, he still fought on, firing from where he lay until he could see no longer, and he fell back and slowly bled to death from the ghastly wound in the shoulder. There was no mark on him to tell his name; he was just one of Ewell's men, and became merely a number on the tally sheet that showed the score of the game of war.

developments had led to an order to have it returned early in the morning. It was approaching as the attack was made. Before the artillerymen could escape or turn the guns upon the Federals, every cannon had been captured. General Johnson with almost his whole division, numbering about three thousand, and General Steuart, were captured, between twenty and thirty colors, and several thousand stands of arms were taken. Hancock had already distinguished himself as a leader of his soldiers, and from his magnificent appearance, noble bearing, and courage had been called "Hancock the Superb," but this was the most brilliant of his military achievements.

Pressing onward across the first defensive line of the Confederates, Hancock's men advanced against the second series of trenches, nearly half a mile beyond. As the Federals pushed through the muddy fields they lost all formation. They reached close to the Confederate line. The Southerners were prepared for the attack. A volley poured into the throng of blue, and General Gordon with his reserve division rushed forward, fighting desperately to drive the Northerners back. As they did so General Lee rode up, evidently intending to go forward with Gordon. His horse was seized by one of the soldiers, and for the second time in the campaign the cry arose from the ranks, "Lee to the rear!" The beloved commander was led back from the range of fire, while the men, under the inspiration of his example, rushed forward in a charge that drove the Federals back until they had reached the outer line of works. Here they fought stubbornly at deadly range. Neither side was able to force the other back. But Gordon was not able to cope with the entire attack. Wright and Warren both sent some of their divisions to reenforce Hancock, and Lee sent all the assistance possible to the troops struggling so desperately to restore his line at the salient.

Many vivid and picturesque descriptions of this fighting at the angle have been written, some by eye-witnesses, others by able historians, but no printed page, no cold type can

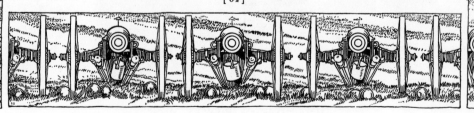

IN ONE LONG BURIAL TRENCH

It fell to the duty of the First Massachusetts Heavy Artillery of General Tyler's division to put under ground the men they slew in the sharp battle of May 18th, and here they are near Mrs. Allsop's barn digging the trench to hide the dreadful work of bullet and shot and shell. No feeling of bitterness exists in moments such as these. What soldier in the party knows but what it may be his turn next to lie beside other lumps of clay and join his earth-mother in this same fashion in his turn. But men become used to work of any kind, and these men digging up the warm spring soil, when their labor is concluded, are neither oppressed nor nerve-shattered by what they have seen and done. They have lost the power of experiencing sensation. Senses become numbed in a measure; the value of life itself from close and constant association with death is minimized almost to the vanishing point. In half an hour these very men may be singing and laughing as if war and death were only things to be expected, not reasoned over in the least.

ONE OF THE FEARLESS CONFEDERATES

convey to the mind the realities of that terrible conflict. The results were appalling. The whole engagement was practically a hand-to-hand contest. The dead lay beneath the feet of the living, three and four layers deep. This hitherto quiet spot of earth was devastated and covered with the slain, weltering in their own blood, mangled and shattered into scarcely a semblance of human form. Dying men were crushed by horses and many, buried beneath the mire and mud, still lived. Some artillery was posted on high ground not far from the apex of the salient, and an incessant fire was poured into the Confederate works over the Union lines, while other guns kept up an enfilade of canister along the west of the salient.

The contest from the right of the Sixth to the left of the Second Corps was kept up throughout the day along the whole line. Repeatedly the trenches had to be cleared of the dead. An oak tree twenty-two inches in diameter was cut down by musket-balls. Men leaped upon the breastworks, firing until shot down.

The battle of the "angle" is said to have been the most awful in duration and intensity in modern times. Battle-line after battle-line, bravely obeying orders, was annihilated. The entrenchments were shivered and shattered, trunks of trees carved into split brooms. Sometimes the contestants came so close together that their muskets met, muzzle to muzzle, and their flags almost intertwined with each other as they waved in the breeze. As they fought with the desperation of madmen, the living would stand on the bodies of the dead to reach over the breastworks with their weapons of slaughter. Lee hurled his army with unparalleled vigor against his opponent five times during the day, but each time was repulsed. Until three o'clock the next morning the slaughter continued, when the Confederates sank back into their second line of entrenchments, leaving their opponents where they had stood in the morning.

All the fighting on the 12th was not done at the "Bloody Angle." Burnside on the left of Hancock engaged Early's

BETHEL CHURCH—WAITING FOR ORDERS

The couriers lounging around the church door will soon be galloping away with orders; for it is the 23d of May, and, the afternoon before, Burnside, with his Ninth Corps, arrived and took up his headquarters here, within ten miles of the North Anna. In the "sidling" movement, as the Confederate soldiers called it, begun by Grant on May 19th, the corps of Hancock and Warren were pressing forward to Guiney's Station through a strange country, over roads unknown to them, while the corps of Burnside and Wright were still demonstrating against the Confederates at Spotsylvania. Here was an opportunity for Lee to take the initiative, and with his whole force either attack Wright and Burnside, or, pushing forward by the Telegraph Road, strike Hancock alone, or at most Hancock and Warren. But Lee, fearing perhaps to risk a general contest, remained strictly on the defensive, moving his troops out along the Telegraph Road to make sure of keeping between his adversary and Richmond. Meanwhile, Burnside, followed by Wright, marched on the evening of the 21st, and next day came up with Grant's headquarters at Guiney's Station. Here he found Grant sitting on the porch, reading the despatch that told of Sherman's capture of Kingston, Georgia, and his crossing of the Etowah River. Burnside was ordered forward to Bethel Church and thence to Ox Ford, on the North Anna, there on the 24th to be held in check by Lee's faultless formation.

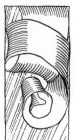
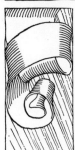

troops and was defeated, while on the other side of the salient Wright succeeded in driving Anderson back.

The question has naturally arisen why that " salient " was regarded of such vital importance as to induce the two chief commanders to force their armies into such a hand-to-hand contest that must inevitably result in unparalleled and wholesale slaughter. It was manifest, however, that Grant had shown generalship in finding the weak point in Lee's line for attack. It was imperative that he hold the gain made by his troops. Lee could ill afford the loss resistance would entail, but he could not withdraw his army during the day without disaster.

The men on both sides seemed to comprehend the gravity of the situation, that it was a battle to the death for that little point of entrenchment. Without urging by officers, and sometimes without officers, they fell into line and fought and bled and died in myriads as though inspired by some unseen power. Here men rushed to their doom with shouts of courage and eagerness.

The pity of it all was manifested by the shocking scene on that battlefield the next day. Piles of dead lay around the " Bloody Angle," a veritable " Hell's Hole " on both sides of the entrenchments, four layers deep in places, shattered and torn by bullets and hoofs and clubbed muskets, while beneath the layers of dead, it is said, there could be seen quivering limbs of those who still lived.

General Grant was deeply moved at the terrible loss of life. When he expressed his regret for the heavy sacrifice of men to General Meade, the latter replied, " General, we can't do these little tricks without heavy losses." The total loss to the Union army in killed, wounded, and missing at Spotsylvania was nearly eighteen thousand. The Confederate losses have never been positively known, but from the best available sources of information the number has been placed at not less than fifteen thousand. Lee's loss in high officers was very

THE REDOUBT THAT LEE LET GO

This redoubt covered Taylor's Bridge, but its flanks were swept by artillery and an enfilading fire from rifle-pits across the river. Late in the evening of the 23d, Hancock's corps, arriving before the redoubt, had assaulted it with two brigades and easily carried it. During the night the Confederates from the other side made two attacks upon the bridge and finally succeeded in setting it afire. The flames were extinguished by the Federals, and on the 24th Hancock's troops crossed over without opposition. The easy crossing of the Federals here was but another example of Lee's favorite rule to let his antagonist attack him on the further side of a stream. Taylor's Bridge could easily have been held by Lee for a much longer time, but its ready abandonment was part of the tactics by which Grant was being led into a military dilemma. In the picture the Federal soldiers confidently hold the captured redoubt, convinced that the possession of it meant that they had driven Lee to his last corner.

severe, the killed including General Daniel and General Perrin, while Generals Walker, Ramseur, R. D. Johnston, and McGowan were severely wounded. In addition to the loss of these important commanders, Lee was further crippled in efficient commanders by the capture of Generals Edward Johnson and Steuart. The Union loss in high officers was light, excepting General Sedgwick on the 9th. General Webb was wounded, and Colonel Coon, of the Second Corps, was killed.

Lee's forces had been handled with such consummate skill as to make them count one almost for two, and there was the spirit of devotion for Lee among his soldiers which was indeed practically hero-worship. All in all, he had an army, though shattered and worn, that was almost unconquerable. Grant found that ordinary methods of war, even such as he had experienced in the West, were not applicable to the Army of Northern Virginia. The only hope for the Union army was a long-drawn-out process, and with larger numbers, better kept, and more often relieved, Grant's army would ultimately make that of Lee's succumb, from sheer exhaustion and disintegration.

The battle was not terminated on the 12th. During the next five days there was a continuous movement of the Union corps to the east which was met by a corresponding readjustment of the Confederate lines. After various maneuvers, Hancock was ordered to the point where the battle was fought on the 12th, and on the 18th and 19th, the last effort was made to break the lines of the Confederates. Ewell, however, drove the Federals back and the next day he had a severe engagement with the Union left wing, while endeavoring to find out something of Grant's plans.

Twelve days of active effort were thus spent in skirmishing, fighting, and countermarching. In the last two engagements the Union losses were nearly two thousand, which are included in those before stated. It was decided to abandon the attempt to dislodge Lee from his entrenchments, and to move

COPYRIGHT, 1911, REVIEW OF REVIEWS CO.

"WALK YOUR HORSES"

ONE OF THE GRIM JOKES OF WAR

AS PLAYED AT

CHESTERFIELD BRIDGE, NORTH ANNA

The sign posted by the local authorities at Taylor's bridge, where the Telegraph Road crosses the North Anna, was "Walk your horses." The wooden structure was referred to by the military as Chesterfield bridge. Here Hancock's Corps arrived toward evening of May 23d, and the Confederate entrenchments, showing in the foreground, were seized by the old "Berry Brigade." In the heat of the charge the Ninety-third New York carried their colors to the middle of the bridge, driving off the Confederates before they could destroy it. When the Federals began crossing next day they had to run the gantlet of musketry and artillery fire from the opposite bank. Several regiments of New York heavy artillery poured across the structure at the double-quick with the hostile shells bursting about their heads. When Captain Sleeper's Eighteenth Massachusetts battery began crossing, the Confederate cannoneers redoubled their efforts to blow up the ammunition by well-aimed shots. Sleeper passed over only one piece at a time in order to diminish the target and enforce the observance of the local law by walking his horses! The Second Corps got no further than the ridge beyond, where Lee's strong V formation held it from further advance.

to the North Anna River. On the 20th of May the march was resumed. The men had suffered great hardships from hunger, exposure, and incessant action, and many would fall asleep on the line of march.

On the day after the start, Hancock crossed the Mattapony River at one point and Warren at another. Hancock was ordered to take position on the right bank and, if practicable, to attack the Confederates wherever found. By the 22d, Wright and Burnside came up and the march proceeded. But the vigilant Lee had again detected the plans of his adversary.

Meade's army had barely started in its purpose to turn the Confederates' flank when the Southern forces were on the way to block the army of the North. As on the march from the Wilderness to Spotsylvania, Lee's troops took the shorter route, along main roads, and reached the North Anna ahead of the Federals. Warren's corps was the first of Meade's army to arrive at the north bank of the river, which it did on the afternoon of May 23d. Lee was already on the south bank, but Warren crossed without opposition. No sooner had he gotten over, however, than he was attacked by the Confederates and a severe but undecisive engagement followed. The next morning (the 24th) Hancock and Wright put their troops across at places some miles apart, and before these two wings of the army could be joined, Lee made a brilliant stroke by marching in between them, forming a wedge whose point rested on the bank, opposite the Union center, under Burnside, which had not yet crossed the river.

The Army of the Potomac was now in three badly separated parts. Burnside could not get over in sufficient strength to reenforce the wings, and all attempts by the latter to aid him in so doing met with considerable disaster. The loss in these engagements approximated two thousand on each side.

On the 25th, Sheridan and his cavalry rejoined the army. They had been gone since the 9th and their raid was most

WHERE GRANT FOUND OUT HIS MISTAKE

At those white tents above Quarles' Mill dam sits Grant, at his "General Headquarters" on the 24th of May, and he has found out too late that Lee has led him into a trap. The Army of Northern Virginia had beaten him in the race for the North Anna, and it was found strongly entrenched on the south side of the stream. The corps of Warren and Wright had crossed at Jericho Mills a mile above Quarles' Mill, and Hancock's crossing had been effected so easily at the wooden bridge just below Quarles' Mill. Grant had reenforced both wings of his army before he discovered that it was divided. Lee's lines stretched southward in the form of a V, with the apex resting close to the river. The great strategist had folded back his flanks to let in Grant's forces on either side. This and the following pictures form a unique series of illustrations in panorama of the futile crossing of the North Anna by the Federals.

THE UNDISPUTED CROSSING
AT NORTH ANNA

These pictures show the pontoon-bridge laid for the crossing of the corps of Warren and Wright at Jericho Ford, about four miles farther upstream than the Chesterfield or Taylor's bridge. The Federals met with no opposition at this crossing, their sharpshooters being able to keep off the Confederates, while the pontonniers were at work. In the two upper pictures the old Jericho Mill stands on the north bank. On the eminence above it is the Gentry house and other dwellings, past which the ammunition-train is winding down the road to the crossing. Warren's Fifth Corps was soon to need its ammunition. The infantry were all across by 4:30 in the afternoon of May 23d and, advancing over the ground seen in the lower picture, formed their lines on the edge of a wood half a mile beyond the south bank. The artillery was posted on the ridge. Before Warren could get into position Lee sent the whole of Hill's Corps against him. A brigade of Cutler's division was forced back, but after some sharp fighting the Confederates were driven back into their trenches, leaving many killed and wounded, and five hundred prisoners.

THE REAR-GUARD

Thus the Federals held the approaches to their pontoon-bridge at Jericho Mill during the sultry days of May (24–26) while Grant was making up his mind that Lee's position could not be successfully attacked. The corps of Warren and Wright have all crossed the bridge, followed by the wagon-trains. Guards have been posted on either bank. The felled timber on the north bank was cut so as to allow the Federal reserve artillery to command the bridge. At either end sit two sentinels ready to challenge perfunctorily any straggler who may pass. The rest of the men have stacked arms and given themselves up to idleness, stretching their improvised shelters to shield them from the broiling sun. One man by the old mill is bathing his feet, weary with the long march.

THE CAPTURED REDAN AND THE BRIDGE

Across this insecure foot-bridge Hancock's troop had to pass in the attack on the Confederate works which commanded Taylor's bridge on the North Anna. A tongue of land formed by the junction of Long Creek with the larger stream was the position chosen for the redan which is seen topping the ridge in the upper picture. Birney's division advanced across the bare and barren plain of the little peninsula, and pressing across the shaky little foot-bridge at the double-quick, swept up the sharp height seen in the picture above, while three sections of Tidball's battery covered the assault of Pierce and Egan. As their line approached, the Confederates abandoned the redan and fled. The Federals, digging footholds in the parapet with their bayonets, clambered up and planted their colors. In taking the lower picture the camera was placed within the Confederate works looking toward the ground over which the Federals approached. The fresh earthworks in the foreground were hastily thrown up to strengthen the redan, which was originally built during the Chancellorsville campaign.

WHERE THE BATTLE–LINE WENT OVER

On the pontoon-bridge in the lower picture crossed Smyth's division of the Second Corps on the morning of May 24th. Forming in line of battle on the south bank, they advanced and carried the Confederate works that commanded Taylor's or the Chesterfield bridge above. The Confederates at once brought up reënforcements and attacked Smyth, who, also reenforced, held his position during a furious rain-storm until dark. Until the pontoons were laid, Grant could not get his army across the North Anna in sufficient force to make the attack he contemplated. The lower picture shows one of the two pontoon-bridges laid below Taylor's bridge so that its defenders could be driven off and the Federal troops enabled to use it. The railroad bridge below Taylor's had been destroyed, but still farther downstream was an old foot-bridge. A short distance above here the pontoons were laid. They can be seen in the upper picture beyond the pontonniers in the foreground, who are at work strengthening the foot-bridge so that it, too, can be used for the passage of the troops that were to retreat from the embarrassing predicament into which Lee had lured them.

successful. Besides the decisive victory over the Confederate cavalry at Yellow Tavern, they had destroyed several depots of supplies, four trains of cars, and many miles of railroad track. Nearly four hundred Federal prisoners on their way to Richmond had been rescued from their captors. The dashing cavalrymen had even carried the first line of work around Richmond, and had made a detour down the James to communicate with General Butler. Grant was highly satisfied with Sheridan's performance. It had been of the greatest assistance to him, as it had drawn off the whole of the Confederate cavalry, and made the guarding of the wagon trains an easy matter.

But here, on the banks of the North Anna, Grant had been completely checkmated by Lee. He realized this and decided on a new move, although he still clung to his idea of turning the Confederate right. The Federal wings were withdrawn to the north side of the river during the night of May 26th and the whole set in motion for the Pamunkey River at Hanovertown. Two divisions of Sheridan's cavalry and Warren's corps were in advance. Lee lost no time in pursuing his great antagonist, but for the first time the latter was able to hold his lead. Along the Totopotomoy, on the afternoon of May 28th, infantry and cavalry of both armies met in a severe engagement in which the strong position of Lee's troops again foiled Grant's purpose. The Union would have to try at some other point, and on the 31st Sheridan's cavalry took possession of Cold Harbor. This was to be the next battle-ground.

PART I
GRANT VERSUS LEE

———

COLD HARBOR

———

WAITING THE WORD FOR THE COLD HARBOR FLANKING MARCH
—UNION TROOPS REPULSED AT THE NORTH ANNA

COPYRIGHT, 1911, PATRIOT PUB.

TEN MINUTES WITH GENERAL GRANT, JUNE 2, 1864—THE FIRST SCENE

As the General-in-Chief of all the Federal armies sits smoking with his back to the smaller tree, two extraordinary things are happening: Grant is arriving at the tremendous decision to "fight it out" that cost him ten thousand men the next morning; and the enterprising photographer with the Union army has climbed upstairs in the little roadside meeting house (Bethesda Church, on the way to Cold Harbor), and is photographing the scene again and again. The result is a veritable "moving picture" series of Grant in the field— an opportunity without a parallel to witness the acting of history itself. The informal consultation which the pictures reveal was as near a council of war as Grant ever came.

TEN MINUTES WITH GENERAL GRANT—THE SECOND AND THIRD SCENES

It is due to the courtesy of General Horace Porter, himself an actor in these three scenes as a member of Grant's staff, that so many participants in the historic episode can here be identified. In the first picture (on the facing page) General Porter himself sits reading a newspaper on Grant's right, and on his left is General Rawlins, his chief of staff, next to Colonel Ely S. Parker. General Grant impassively listens to the report that Colonel Bowers, his adjutant-general, is reading as he stands inside the circle to the right of the picture. In the second picture (immediately above) the General-in-Chief has arisen and walked to the left, where he leans over General Meade's shoulder and consults his map. In front of them a newly arrived officer bends forward, receiving orders or reporting. Colonel Parker has passed his newspaper to another officer. The rest of the group center their looks upon Grant. Soldiers from the Third Division of the Fifth Army Corps, whose

wagons are passing, stop and gaze at the men in whose hands their lives are held. At last, in the third picture, the General-in-Chief has made up his mind. He is back in his original seat and is writing out his orders. The problem has been a painful one; on the one side his conviction that his "hammering policy" is the right one; on the other the heated protest of Northern press and public against what seemed so extravagant a waste of human life. The question was, as General Porter later wrote: "Whether to attempt to crush Lee's army on the north side of the James, with the prospect, in case of success, of driving him into Richmond, capturing the city, perhaps without a siege, and putting the Confederate Government to flight; or to move the Union army south of the James without giving battle and transfer the field of operations to the vicinity of Petersburg. It was a nice question of judgment." Grant's judgment was to fight; the result, Cold Harbor.

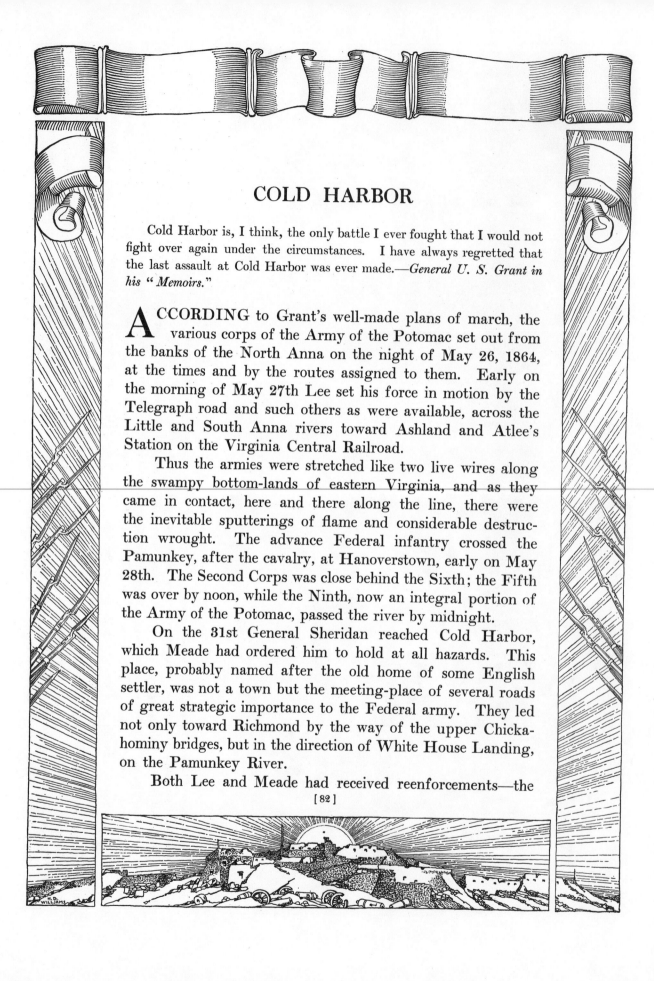

COLD HARBOR

Cold Harbor is, I think, the only battle I ever fought that I would not fight over again under the circumstances. I have always regretted that the last assault at Cold Harbor was ever made.—General U. S. Grant in his " Memoirs."

ACCORDING to Grant's well-made plans of march, the various corps of the Army of the Potomac set out from the banks of the North Anna on the night of May 26, 1864, at the times and by the routes assigned to them. Early on the morning of May 27th Lee set his force in motion by the Telegraph road and such others as were available, across the Little and South Anna rivers toward Ashland and Atlee's Station on the Virginia Central Railroad.

Thus the armies were stretched like two live wires along the swampy bottom-lands of eastern Virginia, and as they came in contact, here and there along the line, there were the inevitable sputterings of flame and considerable destruction wrought. The advance Federal infantry crossed the Pamunkey, after the cavalry, at Hanoverstown, early on May 28th. The Second Corps was close behind the Sixth; the Fifth was over by noon, while the Ninth, now an integral portion of the Army of the Potomac, passed the river by midnight.

On the 31st General Sheridan reached Cold Harbor, which Meade had ordered him to hold at all hazards. This place, probably named after the old home of some English settler, was not a town but the meeting-place of several roads of great strategic importance to the Federal army. They led not only toward Richmond by the way of the upper Chickahominy bridges, but in the direction of White House Landing, on the Pamunkey River.

Both Lee and Meade had received reenforcements—the

[82]

READY FOR THE ADVANCE THAT LEE DROVE BACK

Between these luxuriant banks stretch the pontoons and bridges to facilitate the rapid crossing of the North Anna by Hancock's Corps on May 24th.   Thus was completed the passage to the south of the stream of the two wings of the Army of the Potomac.   But when the center under Burnside was driven back and severely handled at Ox Ford, Grant immediately detached a brigade each from Hancock and Warren to attack the apex of Lee's wedge on the south bank of the river, but the position was too strong to justify the attempt.   Then it dawned upon the Federal general-in-chief that Lee had cleaved the Army of the Potomac into two separated bodies.   To reënforce either wing would require two crossings of the river, while Lee could quickly march troops from one side to the other within his impregnable wedge.   As Grant put it in his report, " To make a direct attack from either wing would cause a slaughter of our men that even success would not justify."

former by Breckinridge, and the scattered forces in western Virginia, and by Pickett and Hoke from North Carolina. From Bermuda Hundred where General Butler was "bottled up"—to use a phrase which Grant employed and afterward regretted—General W. F. Smith was ordered to bring the Eighteenth Corps of the Army of the James to the assistance of Meade, since Butler could defend his position perfectly well with a small force, and could make no headway against Beauregard with a large one. Grant had now nearly one hundred and fourteen thousand troops and Lee about eighty thousand.

Sheridan's appearance at Cold Harbor was resented in vain by Fitzhugh Lee, and the next morning, June 1st, the Sixth Corps arrived, followed by General Smith and ten thousand men of the Eighteenth, who had hastened from the landing-place at White House. These took position on the right of the Sixth, and the Federal line was promptly faced by Longstreet's corps, a part of A. P. Hill's, and the divisions of Hoke and Breckinridge. At six o'clock in the afternoon Wright and Smith advanced to the attack, which Hoke and Kershaw received with courage and determination. The Confederate line was broken in several places, but before night checked the struggle the Southerners had in some degree regained their position. The short contest was a severe one for the Federal side. Wright lost about twelve hundred men and Smith one thousand.

The following day the final dispositions were made for the mighty struggle that would decide Grant's last chance to interpose between Lee and Richmond. Hancock and the Second Corps arrived at Cold Harbor and took position on the left of General Wright. Burnside, with the Ninth Corps, was placed near Bethesda Church on the road to Mechanicsville, while Warren, with the Fifth, came to his left and connected with Smith's right. Sheridan was sent to hold the lower Chickahominy bridges and to cover the road to White House,

IMPROVISED BREASTWORKS

The End of the Gray Line at Cold Harbor. Here at the extreme left of the Confederate lines at Cold Harbor is an example of the crude protection resorted to by the soldiers on both sides in advance or retreat. A momentary lull in the battle was invariably employed in strengthening each position. Trees were felled under fire, and fence rails gathered quickly were piled up to make possible another stand. The space between the lines at Cold Harbor was so narrow at many points as to resemble a road, encumbered with the dead and wounded. This extraordinary proximity induced a nervous alertness which made the troops peculiarly sensitive to night alarms; even small parties searching quietly for wounded comrades might begin a panic. A few scattering shots were often enough to start a heavy and continuous musketry fire and a roar of artillery along the entire line. It was a favorite ruse of the Federal soldiers to aim their muskets carefully to clear the top of the Confederate breastworks and then set up a great shout. The Confederates, deceived into the belief that an attack was coming, would spring up and expose themselves to the well-directed volley which thinned their ranks.

which was now the base of supplies. On the Southern side Ewell's corps, now commanded by General Early, faced Burnside's and Warren's. Longstreet's corps, still under Anderson, was opposite Wright and Smith, while A. P. Hill, on the extreme right, confronted Hancock. There was sharp fighting during the entire day, but Early did not succeed in getting upon the Federal right flank, as he attempted to do.

Both armies lay very close to each other and were well entrenched. Lee was naturally strong on his right, and his left was difficult of access, since it must be approached through wooded swamps. Well-placed batteries made artillery fire from front and both flanks possible, but Grant decided to attack the whole Confederate front, and word was sent to the corps commanders to assault at half-past four the following morning.

The hot sultry weather of the preceding days had brought much suffering. The movement of troops and wagons raised clouds of dust which settled down upon the sweltering men and beasts. But five o'clock on the afternoon of June 2d brought the grateful rain, and this continued during the night, giving great relief to the exhausted troops.

At the hour designated the Federal lines moved promptly from their shallow rifle-pits toward the Confederate works. The main assault was made by the Second, Sixth, and Eighteenth corps. With determined and firm step they started to cross the space between the opposing entrenchments. The silence of the dawning summer morning was broken by the screams of musket-ball and canister and shell. That move of the Federal battle-line opened the fiery furnace across the intervening space, which was, in the next instant, a Vesuvius, pouring tons and tons of steel and lead into the moving human mass. From front, from right and left, artillery crashed and swept the field, musketry and grape hewed and mangled and mowed down the line of blue as it moved on its approach.

COLD HARBOR

The battle of Cold Harbor on June 3d was the third tremendous engagement of Grant's campaign against Richmond within a month. It was also his costliest onset on Lee's veteran army. Grant had risked much in his change of base to the James in order to bring him nearer to Richmond and to the friendly hand which Butler with the Army of the James was in a position to reach out to him. Lee had again confronted him, entrenching himself but six miles from the outworks of Richmond, while the Chickahominy cut off any further flanking movement. There was nothing to do but fight it out, and Grant ordered an attack all along the line. On June 3d he hurled the Army of the Potomac against the inferior numbers of Lee, and in a brave assault upon the Confederate entrenchments, lost ten thousand men in twenty minutes.

Grant's assault at Cold Harbor was marked by the gallantry of General Hancock's division and of the brigades of Gibbon and Barlow, who

WHERE TEN THOUSAND FELL

FEDERAL CAMP AT COLD HARBOR AFTER THE BATTLE

on the left of the Federal line charged up the ascent in their front upon the concentrated artillery of the Confederates; they took the position and held it for a moment under a galling fire, which finally drove them back, but not until they had captured a flag and three hundred prisoners. The battle was substantially over by half-past seven in the morning, but sullen fighting continued throughout the day. About noontime General Grant, who had visited all the corps commanders to see for himself the positions gained and what could be done, concluded that the Confederates were too strongly entrenched to be dislodged and ordered that further offensive action should cease. All the next day the dead and wounded lay on the field uncared for while both armies warily watched each other. The lower picture was taken during this weary wait. Not till the 7th was a satisfactory truce arranged, and then all but two of the wounded Federals had died. No wonder that Grant wrote, "I have always regretted that the last assault at Cold Harbor was ever made."

The three corps of the Federal army had gotten in some places as near as thirty yards to the main Confederate entrenchments, but to carry them was found impossible. The whole line was ordered to lie down, and shelter from the deadly fire was sought wherever it could be found. The advance had occupied less than ten minutes, and before an hour had passed the greater part of the fighting was over. Meade, at headquarters, was quickly made aware that each corps commander had a serious grievance against his neighbor, and, strange to say, the complaints were all phrased alike. General McMahon in "Battles and Leaders of the Civil War" explains this curious state of affairs:

"Each corps commander reported and complained to General Meade that the other corps commanders, right or left, as the case might be, failed to protect him from enfilading fire by silencing batteries in their respective fronts; Smith, that he could go no farther until Wright advanced upon his left; Hancock, that it was useless for him to attempt a further advance until Wright advanced upon his right; Wright, that it was impossible for him to move until Smith and Hancock advanced to his support on his right and left to shield him from the enemy's enfilade. These despatches necessarily caused mystification at headquarters. . . . The explanation was simple enough, although it was not known until reconnaissance had been made. The three corps had moved upon diverging lines, each directly facing the enemy in its immediate front, and the farther each had advanced the more its flank had become exposed."

Not yet understanding the real state of affairs Meade continued to issue orders to advance. To do so was now beyond human possibility. The men could only renew the fire from the positions they had gained. General Smith received a verbal order from Meade to make another assault, and he flatly refused to obey. It was long past noon, and after Grant was cognizant of the full situation, that

THE FORCES AT LAST JOIN HANDS

Charles City Court House on the James River, June 14, 1864. It was with infinite relief that Grant saw the advance of the Army of the Potomac reach this point on June 14th. His last flanking movement was an extremely hazardous one. More than fifty miles intervened between him and Butler by the roads he would have to travel, and he had to cross both the Chickahominy and the James, which were unbridged. The paramount difficulty was to get the Army of the Potomac out of its position before Lee, who confronted it at Cold Harbor. Lee had the shorter line and better roads to move over and meet Grant at the Chickahominy, or he might, if he chose, descend rapidly on Butler and crush him before Grant could unite with him. "But," says Grant, "the move had to be made, and I relied upon Lee's not seeing my danger as I saw it." Near the old Charles City Court House the crossing of the James was successfully accomplished, and on the 14th Grant took steamer and ran up the river to Bermuda Hundred to see General Butler and direct the movement against Petersburg, that began the final investment of that city.

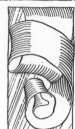

Meade issued orders for the suspension of all further offensive operations.

A word remains to be said as to fortunes of Burnside's and Warren's forces, which were on the Federal right. Generals Potter and Willcox of the Ninth Corps made a quick capture of Early's advanced rifle-pits and were waiting for the order to advance on his main entrenchments, when the order of suspension arrived. Early fell upon him later in the day but was repulsed. Warren, on the left of Burnside, drove Rodes' division back and repulsed Gordon's brigade, which had attacked him. The commander of the Fifth Corps reported that his line was too extended for further operations and Birney's division was sent from the Second Corps to his left. But by the time this got into position the battle of Cold Harbor was practically over.

After the day's conflict the field presented a scene that was indescribable. It showed war in all its horror. It is even painful to attempt a record of the actual facts, so appalling was the loss and the suffering. The groans and the moaning of the wounded during the night were heart-breaking. For three days many unfortunate beings were left lying, uncared for, where they fell. It was almost certain death to venture outside of the entrenchments. Where the heaviest assaults occurred the ground was literally covered with the dead and dying, and nearly all of them were Federal soldiers. Volunteers who offered to go to their relief were in peril of being shot, yet many went bravely out in the face of the deadly fire, to bring in their wounded comrades.

On the 5th, the Second Corps was extended to the Chickahominy, and the Fifth Corps was ordered to the rear of Cold Harbor. The Eighteenth Corps was placed along the Matadequin. Lee threatened attack on the 6th and 7th, but he soon desisted and retired to his entrenchments.

The losses to the Federal army in this battle and the engagements which preceded it were over seventeen thousand,

BACK TO THE OLD BASE

White House Landing, on the Pamunkey River, bustles with life in June, 1864. Once more, just before the battle of Cold Harbor, McClellan's old headquarters at the outset of the Peninsula Campaign of '62 springs into great activity. River steamers and barges discharge their cargoes for the army that is again endeavoring to drive Lee across the Chickahominy and back upon Richmond. Grant's main reliance was upon the inexhaustible supplies which lay at the command of the North. He knew well that the decimated and impoverished South could not long hold out against the "hammering" which the greater abundance of Federal money and men made it possible for him to keep up. Hence, without haste but without rest, he attacked Lee upon every occasion and under all conditions, aware that his own losses, even if the greater, could be made up, while those of his antagonist could not. He believed that this was the surest and speediest way to end the war, and that all told it would involve the least sacrifice of blood and treasure.

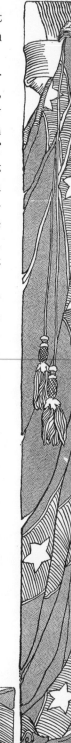

while the Confederate loss did not exceed one-fifth of that number. Grant had failed in his plan to destroy Lee north of the James River, and saw that he must now cross it.

Thirty days had passed in the campaign since the Wilderness and the grand total in losses to Grant's army in killed, wounded, and missing was 54,929. The losses in Lee's army were never accurately given, but they were very much less in proportion to the numerical strength of the two armies. If Grant had inflicted punishment upon his foe equal to that suffered by the Federal forces, Lee's army would have been practically annihilated. But, as matters stood, after the battle of Cold Harbor, with reenforcements to the Confederate arms and the comparatively small losses they had sustained, Lee's army stood on the field of this last engagement almost as large as it was at the beginning of the campaign.

For nearly twelve days the two armies lay within their entrenchments on this field, while the Federal cavalry was sent to destroy the railroad communications between Richmond and the Shenandoah valley and Lynchburg. One writer says that during this time sharpshooting was incessant, and "no man upon all that line could stand erect and live an instant." Soldiers whose terms of service had expired and were ordered home, had to crawl on their hands and knees through the trenches to the rear. No advance was attempted during this time by the Confederates, but every night at nine o'clock the whole Confederate line opened fire with musket and cannon. This was done by Lee in apprehension of the possible withdrawal by night of Grant's army.

The Federal general-in-chief had decided to secure Petersburg and confront Lee once more. General Gillmore was sent by Butler, with cavalry and infantry, on June 10th to make the capture, but was unsuccessful. Thereupon General Smith and the Eighteenth Corps were despatched to White House Landing to go forward by water and reach Petersburg before Lee had time to reenforce it.

PART II
THE SIMULTANEOUS MOVEMENTS

———

DREWRY'S BLUFF
IMPREGNABLE

———

IN BATTERY DANTZLER—CONFEDERATE GUN COMMANDING
THE RIVER AFTER BUTLER'S REPULSE ON LAND

PORT DARLING

Charles Francis Adams, who, as a cavalry officer, served in Butler's campaign, compares Grant's maneuvers of 1864 to Napoleon's of 1815. While Napoleon advanced upon Wellington it was essential that Grouchy should detain Blucher. So Butler was to eliminate Beauregard while Grant struck at Lee. With forty thousand men, he was ordered to land at Bermuda Hundred, seize and hold City Point as a future army base, and advance upon Richmond by way of Petersburg, while Grant meanwhile engaged Lee farther north. Arriving at Broadway Landing, seen in the lower picture, Butler put his army over the Appomattox on pontoons, occupied City Point, May 4th, and advanced within three miles of Petersburg, May 9th. The city might have been easily taken by a vigorous move, but Butler delayed until Beauregard arrived with a hastily gathered army and decisively defeated the Federals at Drewry's Bluff, May 10th. Like Grouchy, Butler failed.

THE MASKED BATTERY

WHERE BUTLER'S TROOPS CROSSED — BROADWAY LANDING ON THE APPOMATTOX

BUTLER "BOTTLED UP"

Butler, after his disastrous repulse at Drewry's Bluff, threw up strong entrenchments across the neck of the bottle-shaped territory which he occupied between the Appomattox and the James. That was exactly what Beauregard wanted, and the Confederate general immediately constructed field works all along Butler's front, effectually closing the neck of this "bottle." Here Butler remained in inactivity till the close of the war. He built the elaborate signal tower seen in the picture so that he could observe all the operations of the Confederates, although he could make no move against any of them. Generals Gilmore and "Baldy" Smith both urged upon Butler the laying of pontoons across the Appomattox in order to advance on Petersburg, the key to Richmond. But Butler curtly replied that he would build no bridges for West Pointers to retreat over.

BUTLER'S SIGNAL TOWER

THE LOOKOUT

THE THIRTEENTH NEW YORK HEAVY ARTILLERY IDLING IN WINTER QUARTERS AT BERMUDA HUNDRED

THE IMPASSABLE JAMES RIVER

The gun is in Confederate Battery Brooke—another of the defenses on the James constructed after Butler was bottled up. Here in 1865 the gunners were still at their posts guarding the water approach to Richmond. The Federals had not been able to get up the river since their first unsuccessful effort in 1862, when the hastily constructed Fort Darling at Drewry's Bluff baffled the *Monitor* and the *Galena*. Battery Brooke was situated above Dutch Gap, the narrow neck of Farrar's Island, where Butler's was busily digging his famous canal to enable the Federal gunboats to get by the obstructions he himself had caused to be sunk in the river. Even the canal proved a failure, for when the elaborate ditch was finished under fire from the Confederate batteries above, the dam was unskilfully blown up and remained an effective barrier against the passage of vessels.

AN ADVANCE DEFENSE OF RICHMOND

This Confederate gun at Battery Dantzler swept the James at a point where the river flows due south around Farrar's Island. "But-ler's Campaign" consisted merely of an advance by land up the James to Drewry's Bluff and inglorious retreat back again. Far from threatening Richmond, it enabled the Confederates to construct strong river defenses below Fort Darling on the James to hold in check the Federal fleet and assist in keeping the neck of Butler's "bottle" tightly closed. The guns at Battery Dantzler controlled the river at Trent's Reach. In a straight line from Drewry's Bluff to City Point it was but nine miles, but the James flows in a suc-cession of curves and bends at all angles of the compass, around steep bluffs, past swamp and meadow-land, making the route by water a journey of thirty miles. If the Federal gunboats could have passed their own obstructions and the Confederate torpedoes, they would still have been subjected to the fire of Battery Dantzler from their rear in attempting to reach Richmond.

ABOVE DUTCH GAP—A GUN THAT MOCKED THE FEDERALS

This huge Confederate cannon in one of the batteries above Dutch Gap bore on the canal that was being dug by the Federals. Away to the south stretches the flat and swampy country, a complete protection against hostile military operations. The Confederate cannoneers amused themselves by dropping shot and shell upon the Federal colored regiments toiling on Butler's canal. Aside from the activity of the diggers, the Army of the James had nothing to do.

PART II
THE SIMULTANEOUS MOVEMENTS

TO ATLANTA

SHERMAN'S MEN IN THE ATLANTA TRENCHES

THE MAN WHO DEFINED WAR

William Tecumseh Sherman and his staff. Leaning carelessly on the breach of the gun stands General William Tecumseh Sherman at the close of one of the war's most brilliant and successful campaigns which his military genius had made possible. The old slouch hat does not indicate that the general is holding a triumphant review of his army, but the uniform is as near full dress as Sherman ever came. "He hated fine clothes," says General Rodenbough, "and endured hardships with as much fortitude as any of his men."

In the upper picture rises the precipitous height of Rocky Face as Sherman saw it on May 7, 1864. His troops under Thomas had moved forward along the line of the railroad, opening the great Atlanta campaign on schedule time. Looking down into the gorge called Buzzard's Roost, through which the railroad passes, Sherman could see swarms of Confederate troops, the road filled with obstructions, and hostile batteries crowning the cliffs on either side. He knew that his antagonist, Joe Johnston, here confronted him in force. But it was to be a campaign of brilliant flanking movements, and Sherman sat quietly down to wait till the trusty McPherson should execute the first one.

BUZZARD'S ROOST, GEORGIA, MAY 7, 1864

In the lower picture, drawn up on dress parade, stands one of the finest fighting organizations in the Atlanta campaign. This regiment won its spurs in the first Union victory in the West at Mill Springs, Kentucky, January 19, 1862. There, according to the muster-out roll, "William Blake, musician, threw away his drum and took a gun." The spirit of this drummer boy of Company F was the spirit of all the troops from Minnesota. A Georgian noticed an unusually fine body of men marching by, and when told that they were a Minnesota regiment, said, "I didn't know they had any troops up there." But the world was to learn the superlative fighting qualities of the men from the Northwest. Sherman was glad to have all he could get of them in this great army of one hundred thousand veterans.

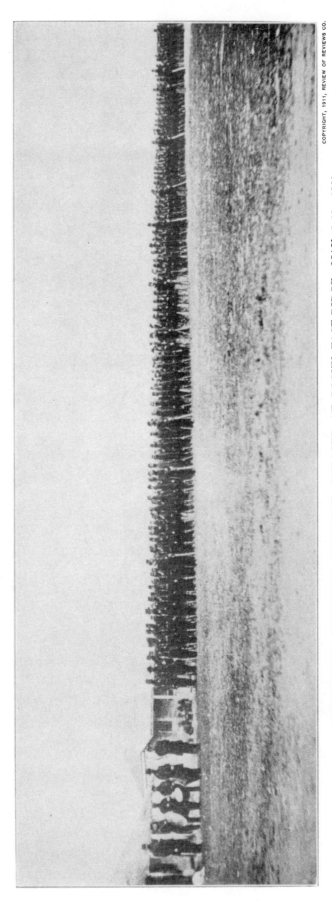

THE SECOND MINNESOTA INFANTRY—ENGAGED AT ROCKY FACE RIDGE, MAY 8-11, 1864

A REGIMENT THAT CHARGED UP KENESAW—THE ONE HUNDRED AND TWENTY-FIFTH OHIO

These are some of the men who charged upon the slopes of Kenesaw Mountain, Sherman's stumbling-block in his Atlanta campaign. They belonged to Company M of the One Hundred and Twenty-fifth Ohio, in the brigade led by the daring General Harker, Newton's division, Second Corps. Johnston had drawn up his forces on the Kenesaw Mountains along a line stronger, both naturally and by fortification, than the Union position at Gettysburg. But for the same reason that Lee attacked Little Round Top, Sherman, on June 27, 1864, ordered an assault on the southern slope of Little Kenesaw. The Federal forces did not pause, in spite of a terrific fire from the breastworks, till they gained the edge of the felled trees. There formations were lost; men struggled over trunks and through interlaced boughs. Before the concentrated fire of artillery and musketry they could only seek shelter behind logs and boulders. General Harker, already famous for his gallantry, cheered on his men, but as he was rushing forward he fell mortally wounded.

KENESAW MOUNTAIN IN 1864

Sherman's Stumbling Block. Thus the rugged height of Kenesaw Mountain rose in the distance to the sight of Sherman's advancing army in the middle of June, 1864. The men knew the ground, for most of them had marched over it the year before in the Chickamauga campaign. Now to its difficulties were added the strong entrenchments of Johnston's army and the batteries posted on the heights, which must be surmounted before Atlanta, the coveted goal, could be reached. But the Federals also knew that under "Old Tecumseh's" watchful eye they had flanked Johnston's army out of one strong position after another, and in little over a month had advanced nearly a hundred miles through "as difficult country as was ever fought over by civilized armies." But there was no flinching when the assaulting columns fought their way to the summit on June 27th.

TO ATLANTA

Johnston was an officer who, by the common consent of the military men of both sides, was reckoned second only to Lee, if second, in the qualities which fit an officer for the responsibility of great commands. . . . He practised a lynx-eyed watchfulness of his adversary, tempting him constantly to assault his entrenchments, holding his fortified positions to the last moment, but choosing that last moment so well as to save nearly every gun and wagon in the final withdrawal, and always presenting a front covered by such defenses that one man in the line was, by all sound military rules, equal to three or four in the attack. In this way he constantly neutralized the superiority of force his opponent wielded, and made his campaign from Dalton to the Chattahoochee a model of defensive warfare. It is Sherman's glory that, with a totally different temperament, he accepted his adversary's game, and played it with a skill that was finally successful, as we shall see.—*Major-General Jacob D. Cox, U.S.V., in "Atlanta."*

THE two leading Federal generals of the war, Grant and Sherman, met at Nashville, Tennessee, on March 17, 1864, and arranged for a great concerted double movement against the two main Southern armies, the Army of Northern Virginia and the Army of Tennessee. Grant, who had been made commander of all the Federal armies, was to take personal charge of the Army of the Potomac and move against Lee, while to Sherman, whom, at Grant's request, President Lincoln had placed at the head of the Military Division of the Mississippi, he turned over the Western army, which was to proceed against Johnston.

It was decided, moreover, that the two movements were to be simultaneous and that they were to begin early in May. Sherman concentrated his forces around Chattanooga on the Tennessee River, where the Army of the Cumberland had

IN THE FOREFRONT—GENERAL RICHARD W. JOHNSON AT GRAYSVILLE

On the balcony of this little cottage at Graysville, Georgia, stands General Richard W. Johnson, ready to advance with his cavalry division in the vanguard of the direct movement upon the Confederates strongly posted at Dalton. Sherman's cavalry forces under Stoneman and Garrard were not yet fully equipped and joined the army after the campaign had opened. General Richard W. Johnson's division of Thomas' command, with General Palmer's division, was given the honor of heading the line of march when the Federals got in motion on May 5th. The same troops (Palmer's division) had made the same march in February, sent by Grant to engage Johnston at Dalton during Sherman's Meridian campaign. Johnson was a West Pointer; he had gained his cavalry training in the Mexican War, and had fought the Indians on the Texas border. He distinguished himself at Corinth, and rapidly rose to the command of a division in Buell's army. Fresh from a Confederate prison, he joined the Army of the Cumberland in the summer of 1862 to win new laurels at Stone's River, Chickamauga, and Missionary Ridge. His sabers were conspicuously active in the Atlanta campaign; and at the battle of New Hope Church on May 28th Johnson himself was wounded, but recovered in time to join Schofield after the fall of Atlanta and to assist him in driving Hood and Forrest out of Tennessee. For his bravery at the battle of Nashville he was brevetted brigadier-general, U. S. A., December 16, 1864, and after the war he was retired with the brevet of major-general.

spent the winter, and where a decisive battle had been fought some months before, in the autumn of 1863. His army was composed of three parts, or, more properly, of three armies operating in concert. These were the Army of the Tennessee, led by General James B. McPherson; the Army of Ohio, under General John M. Schofield, and the Army of the Cumberland, commanded by General George H. Thomas. The last named was much larger than the other two combined. The triple army aggregated the grand total of ninety-nine thousand men, six thousand of whom were cavalrymen, while four thousand four hundred and sixty belonged to the artillery. There were two hundred and fifty-four heavy guns.

Soon to be pitted against Sherman's army was that of General Joseph E. Johnston, which had spent the winter at Dalton, in the State of Georgia, some thirty miles southeast of Chattanooga. It was by chance that Dalton became the winter quarters of the Confederate army. In the preceding autumn, when General Bragg had been defeated on Missionary Ridge and driven from the vicinity of Chattanooga, he retreated to Dalton and stopped for a night's rest. Discovering the next morning that he was not pursued, he there remained. Some time later he was superseded by General Johnston.

By telegraph, General Sherman was apprised of the time when Grant was to move upon Lee on the banks of the Rapidan, in Virginia, and he prepared to move his own army at the same time. But he was two days behind Grant, who began his Virginia campaign on May 4th. Sherman broke camp on the 6th and led his legions across hill and valley, forest and stream, toward the Confederate stronghold. Nature was all abloom with the opening of a Southern spring and the soldiers, who had long chafed under their enforced idleness, now rejoiced at the exhilarating journey before them, though their mission was to be one of strife and bloodshed.

Johnston's army numbered about fifty-three thousand,

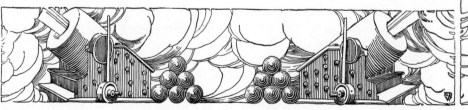

BEGINNING THE FIRST FLANK MOVEMENT

In the upper picture, presented through the kindness of General G. P. Thruston, are the headquarters of General Thomas at Ringgold, Georgia, May 5, 1864. On that day, appointed by Grant for the beginning of the "simultaneous movements" he had planned to carry out in 1864, General Sherman rode out the eighteen miles from Chattanooga to Ringgold with his staff, about half a dozen wagons, and a single company of Ohio sharpshooters. A small company of irregular Alabama cavalry acted as couriers. Sherman's mess establishment was less bulky than that of any of his brigade commanders. "I wanted to set the example," he says, "and gradually to convert all parts of that army into a mobile machine willing and able to start at a minute's notice and to subsist on the scantiest food." On May 7th, General Thomas moved in force to Tunnel Hill to begin the turning of Johnston's flank.

TUNNEL HILL, GA., BEYOND WHICH JOHNSTON OCCUPIED A STRONG POSITION . . BUZZARD'S ROOST GAP

and was divided into two corps, under the respective commands of Generals John B. Hood and William J. Hardee. But General Polk was on his way to join them, and in a few days Johnston had in the neighborhood of seventy thousand men. His position at Dalton was too strong to be carried by a front attack, and Sherman was too wise to attempt it. Leaving Thomas and Schofield to make a feint at Johnston's front, Sherman sent McPherson on a flanking movement by the right to occupy Snake Creek Gap, a mountain pass near Resaca, which is about eighteen miles below Dalton.

Sherman, with the main part of the army, soon occupied Tunnel Hill, which faces Rocky Face Ridge, an eastern range of the Cumberland Mountains, north of Dalton, on which a large part of Johnston's army was posted. The Federal leader had little or no hope of dislodging his great antagonist from this impregnable position, fortified by rocks and cliffs which no army could scale while under fire. But he ordered that demonstrations be made at several places, especially at a pass known as Rocky Face Gap. This was done with great spirit and bravery, the men clambering over rocks and across ravines in the face of showers of bullets and even of masses of stone hurled down from the heights above them. On the whole they won but little advantage.

During the 8th and 9th of May, these operations were continued, the Federals making but little impression on the Confederate stronghold. Meanwhile, on the Dalton road there was a sharp cavalry fight, the Federal commander, General E. M. McCook, having encountered General Wheeler. McCook's advance brigade under Colonel La Grange was defeated and La Grange was made prisoner.

Sherman's chief object in these demonstrations, it will be seen, was so to engage Johnston as to prevent his intercepting McPherson in the latter's movement upon Resaca. In this Sherman was successful, and by the 11th he was giving his whole energy to moving the remainder of his forces by the

RESACA—FIELD OF THE FIRST HEAVY FIGHTING

The chips are still bright and the earth fresh turned, in the foreground where are the Confederate earthworks such as General Joseph E. Johnston had caused to be thrown up by the Negro laborers all along his line of possible retreat. McPherson, sent by Sherman to strike the railroad in Johnston's rear, got his head of column through Snake Creek Gap on May 9th, and drove off a Confederate cavalry brigade which retreated toward Dalton, bringing to Johnston the first news that a heavy force of Federals was already in his rear. McPherson, within a mile and a half of Resaca, could have walked into the town with his twenty-three thousand men, but concluded that the Confederate entrenchments were too strongly held to assault. When Sherman arrived he found that Johnston, having the shorter route, was there ahead of him with his entire army strongly posted. On May 15th, "without attempting to assault the fortified works," says Sherman, "we pressed at all points, and the sound of cannon and musketry rose all day to the dignity of a battle." Its havoc is seen in the shattered trees and torn ground in the lower picture.

THE WORK OF THE FIRING AT RESACA

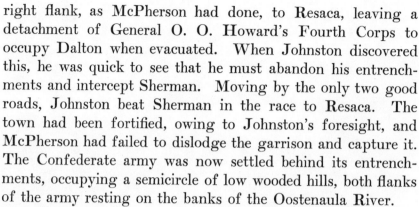

right flank, as McPherson had done, to Resaca, leaving a detachment of General O. O. Howard's Fourth Corps to occupy Dalton when evacuated. When Johnston discovered this, he was quick to see that he must abandon his entrenchments and intercept Sherman. Moving by the only two good roads, Johnston beat Sherman in the race to Resaca. The town had been fortified, owing to Johnston's foresight, and McPherson had failed to dislodge the garrison and capture it. The Confederate army was now settled behind its entrenchments, occupying a semicircle of low wooded hills, both flanks of the army resting on the banks of the Oostenaula River.

On the morning of May 14th, the Confederate works were invested by the greater part of Sherman's army and it was evident that a battle was imminent. The attack was begun about noon, chiefly by the Fourteenth Army Corps under Palmer, of Thomas' army, and Judah's division of Schofield's. General Hindman's division of Hood's corps bore the brunt of this attack and there was heavy loss on both sides. Later in the day, a portion of Hood's corps was massed in a heavy column and hurled against the Federal left, driving it back. But at this point the Twentieth Army Corps under Hooker, of Thomas' army, dashed against the advancing Confederates and pushed them back to their former lines.

The forenoon of the next day was spent in heavy skirmishing, which grew to the dignity of a battle. During the day's operations a hard fight for a Confederate lunette on the top of a low hill occurred. At length, General Butterfield, in the face of a galling fire, succeeded in capturing the position. But so deadly was the fire from Hardee's corps that Butterfield was unable to hold it or to remove the four guns the lunette contained.

With the coming of night, General Johnston determined to withdraw his army from Resaca. The battle had cost each army nearly three thousand men. While it was in progress, McPherson, sent by Sherman, had deftly marched around

ANOTHER RETROGRADE MOVEMENT OVER THE ETOWAH BRIDGE

The strong works in the pictures, commanding the railroad bridge over the Etowah River, were the fourth fortified position to be abandoned by Johnston within a month. Pursued by Thomas from Resaca, he had made a brief stand at Kingston and then fallen back steadily and in superb order into Cassville. There he issued an address to his army announcing his purpose to retreat no more but to accept battle. His troops were all drawn up in preparation for a struggle, but that night at supper with Generals Hood and Polk he was convinced by them that the ground occupied by their troops was untenable, being enfiladed by the Federal artillery. Johnston, therefore, gave up his purpose of battle, and on the night of May 20th put the Etowah River between himself and Sherman and retreated to Allatoona Pass, shown in the lower picture.

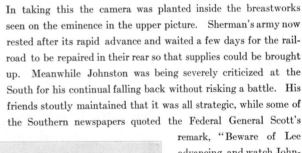

In taking this the camera was planted inside the breastworks seen on the eminence in the upper picture. Sherman's army now rested after its rapid advance and waited a few days for the railroad to be repaired in their rear so that supplies could be brought up. Meanwhile Johnston was being severely criticized at the South for his continual falling back without risking a battle. His friends stoutly maintained that it was all strategic, while some of the Southern newspapers quoted the Federal General Scott's remark, "Beware of Lee advancing, and watch Johnston at a stand; for the devil himself would be defeated in the attempt to whip him retreating." But General Jeff C. Davis, sent by Sherman, took Rome on May 17th and destroyed valuable mills and foundries. Thus began the accomplishment of one of the main objects of Sherman's march.

ALLATOONA PASS IN THE DISTANCE

Johnston's left with the view of cutting off his retreat south by seizing the bridges across the Oostenaula, and at the same time the Federal cavalry was threatening the railroad to Atlanta which ran beyond the river. It was the knowledge of these facts that determined the Confederate commander to abandon Resaca. Withdrawing during the night, he led his army southward to the banks of the Etowah River. Sherman followed but a few miles behind him. At the same time Sherman sent a division of the Army of the Cumberland, under General Jeff. C. Davis, to Rome, at the junction of the Etowah and the Oostenaula, where there were important machine-shops and factories. Davis captured the town and several heavy guns, destroyed the factories, and left a garrison to hold it.

Sherman was eager for a battle in the open with Johnston and on the 17th, near the town of Adairsville, it seemed as if the latter would gratify him. Johnston chose a good position, posted his cavalry, deployed his infantry, and awaited combat. The Union army was at hand. The skirmishing for some hours almost amounted to a battle. But suddenly Johnston decided to defer a conclusive contest to another time.

Again at Cassville, a few days later, Johnston drew up the Confederate legions in battle array, evidently having decided on a general engagement at this point. He issued a spirited address to the army: " By your courage and skill you have repulsed every assault of the enemy. . . . You will now turn and march to meet his advancing columns. . . . I lead you to battle." But, when his right flank had been turned by a Federal attack, and when two of his corps commanders, Hood and Polk, advised against a general battle, Johnston again decided on postponement. He retreated in the night across the Etowah, destroyed the bridges, and took a strong position among the rugged hills about Allatoona Pass, extending south to Kenesaw Mountain.

Johnston's decision to fight and then not to fight was a

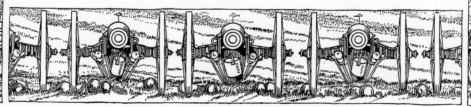

ENTRENCHMENTS HELD BY THE CONFEDERATES AGAINST HOOKER ON MAY 25TH

These views of the battlefield of New Hope Church, in Georgia, show the evidences of the sharp struggle at this point that was brought on by Sherman's next attempt to flank Johnston out of his position at Allatoona Pass. The middle picture gives mute witness to the leaden storm that raged among the trees during that engagement. In the upper and lower pictures are seen the

THE CANNONADED FOREST

entrenchments which the Confederates had hastily thrown up and which resisted Hooker's assaults on May 25th. For two days each side strengthened its position; then on the 28th the Confederates made a brave attack upon General McPherson's forces as they were closing up to this new position. The Confederates were repulsed with a loss of two thousand.

ANOTHER POSITION OF THE CONFEDERATES AT NEW HOPE CHURCH

cause for grumbling both on the part of his army and of the inhabitants of the region through which he was passing. His men were eager to defend their country, and they could not understand this Fabian policy. They would have preferred defeat to these repeated retreats with no opportunity to show what they could do.

Johnston, however, was wiser than his critics. The Union army was larger by far and better equipped than his own, and Sherman was a master-strategist. His hopes rested on two or three contingencies—that he might catch a portion of Sherman's army separated from the rest; that Sherman would be so weakened by the necessity of guarding the long line of railroad to his base of supplies at Chattanooga, Nashville, and even far-away Louisville, as to make it possible to defeat him in open battle, or, finally, that Sherman might fall into the trap of making a direct attack while Johnston was in an impregnable position, and in such a situation he now was.

Not yet, however, was Sherman inclined to fall into such a trap, and when Johnston took his strong position at and beyond Allatoona Pass, the Northern commander decided, after resting his army for a few days, to move toward Atlanta by way of Dallas, southwest of the pass. Rations for a twenty days' absence from direct railroad communication were issued to the Federal army. In fact, Sherman's railroad connection with the North was the one delicate problem of the whole movement. The Confederates had destroyed the iron way as they moved southward; but the Federal engineers, following the army, repaired the line and rebuilt the bridges almost as fast as the army could march.

Sherman's movement toward Dallas drew Johnston from the slopes of the Allatoona Hills. From Kingston, the Federal leader wrote on May 23d, " I am already within fifty miles of Atlanta." But he was not to enter that city for many weeks, not before he had measured swords again and again with his great antagonist. On the 25th of May, the two great

PINE MOUNTAIN, WHERE POLK, THE FIGHTING BISHOP OF THE CONFEDERACY, WAS KILLED

The blasted pine rears its gaunt height above the mountain slope, covered with trees slashed down to hold the Federals at bay; and here, on June 14, 1864, the Confederacy lost a commander, a bishop, and a hero. Lieut.-General Leonidas Polk, commanding one of Johnston's army corps, with Johnston himself and Hardee, another corps commander, was studying Sherman's position at a tense moment of the latter's advance around Pine Mountain. The three Confederates stood upon the rolling height, where the center of Johnston's army awaited the Federal attack. They could see the columns in blue pushing east of them; the smoke and rattle of musketry as the pickets were driven in; and the bustle with which the Federal advance guard felled trees and constructed trenches at their very feet. On the lonely height the three figures stood conspicuous. A Federal order was given the artillery to open upon any men in gray who looked like officers reconnoitering the new position. So, while Hardee was pointing to his comrade and his chief the danger of one of his divisions which the Federal advance was cutting off, the bishop-general was struck in the chest by a cannon shot. Thus the Confederacy lost a leader of unusual influence. Although a bishop of the Episcopal Church, Polk was educated at West Point. When he threw in his lot with the Confederacy, thousands of his fellow-Louisianians followed him. A few days before the battle of Pine Mountain, as he and General Hood were riding together, the bishop was told by his companion that he had never been received into the communion of a church and was begged that the rite might be performed. Immediately Polk arranged the ceremony. At Hood's headquarters, by the light of a tallow candle, with a tin basin on the mess table for a baptismal font, and with Hood's staff present as witnesses, all was ready. Hood, "with a face like that of an old crusader," stood before the bishop. Crippled by wounds at Gaines' Mill, Gettysburg, and Chickamauga, he could not kneel, but bent forward on his crutches. The bishop, in full uniform of the Confederate army, administered the rite. A few days later, by a strange coincidence, he was approached by General Johnston on the same errand, and the man whom Hood was soon to succeed was baptized in the same simple manner. Polk, as Bishop, had administered his last baptism, and as soldier had fought his last battle; for Pine Mountain was near.

LIEUT.-GEN. LEONIDAS POLK, C.S.A.

armies were facing each other near New Hope Church, about four miles north of Dallas. Here, for three or four days, there was almost incessant fighting, though there was not what might be called a pitched battle.

Late in the afternoon of the first day, Hooker made a vicious attack on Stewart's division of Hood's corps. For two hours the battle raged without a moment's cessation, Hooker being pressed back with heavy loss. During those two hours he had held his ground against sixteen field-pieces and five thousand infantry at close range. The name "Hell Hole" was applied to this spot by the Union soldiers.

On the next day there was considerable skirmishing in different places along the line that divided the two armies. But the chief labor of the day was throwing up entrenchments, preparatory to a general engagement. The country, however, was ill fitted for such a contest. The continuous succession of hills, covered with primeval forests, presented little opportunity for two great armies, stretched out almost from Dallas to Marietta, a distance of about ten miles, to come together simultaneously at all points.

A severe contest occurred on the 27th, near the center of the battle-lines, between General O. O. Howard on the Federal side and General Patrick Cleburne on the part of the South. Dense and almost impenetrable was the undergrowth through which Howard led his troops to make the attack. The fight was at close range and was fierce and bloody, the Confederates gaining the greater advantage.

The next day Johnston made a terrific attack on the Union right, under McPherson, near Dallas. But McPherson was well entrenched and the Confederates were repulsed with a serious loss. In the three or four days' fighting the Federal loss was probably twenty-four hundred men and the Confederate somewhat greater.

In the early days of June, Sherman took possession of the town of Allatoona and made it a second base of supplies,

IN THE HARDEST FIGHT OF THE CAMPAIGN—THE ONE–HUNDRED–AND–TWENTY–FIFTH OHIO

During the dark days before Kenesaw it rained continually, and Sherman speaks of the peculiarly depressing effect that the weather had upon his troops in the wooded country. Nevertheless he must either assault Johnston's strong position on the mountain or begin again his flanking tactics. He decided upon the former, and on June 27th, after three days' preparation, the assault was made. At nine in the morning along the Federal lines the furious fire of musketry and artillery was begun, but at all points the Confederates met it with determined courage and in great force. McPherson's attacking column, under General Blair, fought its way up the face of little Kenesaw but could not reach the summit. Then the courageous troops of Thomas charged up the face of the mountain and planted their colors on the very parapet of the Confederate works. Here General Harker, commanding the brigade in which fought the 125th Ohio, fell mortally wounded, as did Brigadier-General Daniel McCook, and also General Wagner.

FEDERAL ENTRENCHMENTS AT THE FOOT OF KENESAW MOUNTAIN

after repairing the railroad bridge across the Etowah River. Johnston swung his left around to Lost Mountain and his right extended beyond the railroad—a line ten miles in length and much too long for its numbers. Johnston's army, however, had been reenforced, and it now numbered about seventy-five thousand men. Sherman, on June 1st, had nearly one hundred and thirteen thousand men and on the 8th he received the addition of a cavalry brigade and two divisions of the Seventeenth Corps, under General Frank P. Blair, which had marched from Alabama.

So multifarious were the movements of the two great armies among the hills and forests of that part of Georgia that it is impossible for us to follow them all. On the 14th of June, Generals Johnston, Hardee, and Polk rode up the slope of Pine Mountain to reconnoiter. As they were standing, making observations, a Federal battery in the distance opened on them and General Polk was struck in the chest with a Parrot shell. He was killed instantly.

General Polk was greatly beloved, and his death caused a shock to the whole Confederate army. He was a graduate of West Point; but after being graduated he took orders in the church and for twenty years before the war was Episcopal Bishop of Louisiana. At the outbreak of the war he entered the field and served with distinction to the moment of his death.

During the next two weeks there was almost incessant fighting, heavy skirmishing, sparring for position. It was a wonderful game of military strategy, played among the hills and mountains and forests by two masters in the art of war. On June 23d, Sherman wrote, " The whole country is one vast fort, and Johnston must have full fifty miles of connected trenches. . . . Our lines are now in close contact, and the fighting incessant. . . . As fast as we gain one position, the enemy has another all ready."

Sherman, conscious of superior strength, was now anxious for a real battle, a fight to the finish with his antagonist.

THOMAS' HEADQUARTERS NEAR MARIETTA DURING THE FIGHTING OF
THE FOURTH OF JULY

This is a photograph of Independence Day, 1864. As the sentries and staff officers stand outside the sheltered tents, General Thomas, commanding the Army of the Cumberland, is busy; for the fighting is fierce
to-day. Johnston has been outflanked from Kenesaw and has fallen back eastward until he is actually
farther from Atlanta than Sherman's right flank. Who will reach the Chattahoochee first? There, if anywhere, Johnston must make his stand; he must hold the fords and ferries, and the fortifications that, with
the wisdom of a far-seeing commander, he has for a long time been preparing. The rustic work in the photograph, which embowers the tents of the commanding general and his staff, is the sort of thing that Civil
War soldiers had learned to throw up within an hour after pitching camp.

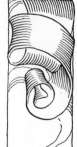

But Johnston was too wily to be thus caught. He made no false move on the great chessboard of war. At length, the impatient Sherman decided to make a general front attack, even though Johnston, at that moment, was impregnably entrenched on the slopes of Kenesaw Mountain. This was precisely what the Confederate commander was hoping for.

The desperate battle of Kenesaw Mountain occurred on the 27th of June. In the early morning hours, the boom of Federal cannon announced the opening of a bloody day's struggle. It was soon answered by the Confederate batteries in the entrenchments along the mountain side, and the deafening roar of the giant conflict reverberated from the surrounding hills. About nine o'clock the Union infantry advance began. On the left was McPherson, who sent the Fifteenth Army Corps, led by General John A. Logan, directly against the mountain. The artillery from the Confederate trenches in front of Logan cut down his men by hundreds. The Federals charged courageously and captured the lower works, but failed to take the higher ridges.

The chief assault of the day was by the Army of the Cumberland, under Thomas. Most conspicuous in the attack were the divisions of Newton and Davis, advancing against General Loring, successor of the lamented Polk. Far up on a ridge at one point, General Cleburne held a line of breastworks, supported by the flanking fire of artillery. Against this a vain and costly assault was made.

When the word was given to charge, the Federals sprang forward and, in the face of a deadly hail of musket-balls and shells, they dashed up the slope, firing as they went. Stunned and bleeding, they were checked again and again by the withering fire from the mountain slope; but they re-formed and pressed on with dauntless valor. Some of them reached the parapets and were instantly shot down, their bodies rolling into the Confederate trenches among the men who had slain them, or back down the hill whence they had come. General

THE CHATTAHOOCHEE BRIDGE

"One of the strongest pieces of field fortification I ever saw"—this was Sherman's characterization of the entrenchments that guarded the railroad bridge over the Chattahoochee on July 5th. A glimpse of the bridge and the freshly-turned earth in 1864 is given by the upper picture. At this river Johnston made his final effort to hold back Sherman from a direct attack upon Atlanta. If Sherman could get successfully across that river, the Confederates would be compelled to fall back behind the defenses of the city, which was the objective of the campaign. Sherman perceived at once the futility of trying to carry by assault this strongly garrisoned position. Instead, he made a feint at crossing the river lower down, and simultaneously went to work in earnest eight miles north of the bridge. The lower picture shows the canvas pontoon boats as perfected by Union engineers in 1864. A number of these were stealthily set up and launched by Sherman's Twenty-third Corps near the mouth of Soap Creek, behind a ridge. Byrd's brigade took the defenders of the southern bank completely by surprise. It was short work for the Federals to throw pontoon bridges across and to occupy the coveted spot in force.

INFANTRY AND ARTILLERY CROSSING ON BOATS MADE OF PONTOONS

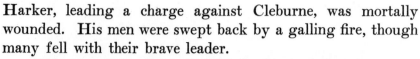

Harker, leading a charge against Cleburne, was mortally wounded. His men were swept back by a galling fire, though many fell with their brave leader.

This assault on Kenesaw Mountain cost Sherman three thousand men and won him nothing. Johnston's loss probably exceeded five hundred. The battle continued but two and a half hours. It was one of the most recklessly daring assaults during the whole war period, but did not greatly affect the final result of the campaign.

Under a flag of truce, on the day after the battle, the men of the North and of the South met on the gory field to bury their dead and to minister to the wounded. They met as friends for the moment, and not as foes. It was said that there were instances of father and son, one in blue and the other in gray, and brothers on opposite sides, meeting one another on the bloody slopes of Kenesaw. Tennessee and Kentucky had sent thousands of men to each side in the fratricidal struggle and not infrequently families had been divided.

Three weeks of almost incessant rain fell upon the struggling armies during this time, rendering their operations disagreeable and unsatisfactory. The camp equipage, the men's uniforms and accouterments were thoroughly saturated with rain and mud. Still the warriors of the North and of the South lived and fought on the slopes of the mountain range, intent on destroying each other.

Sherman was convinced by his drastic repulse at Kenesaw Mountain that success lay not in attacking his great antagonist in a strong position, and he resumed his old tactics. He would flank Johnston from Kenesaw as he had flanked him out of Dalton and Allatoona Pass. He thereupon turned upon Johnston's line of communication with Atlanta, whence the latter received his supplies. The movement was successful, and in a few days Kenesaw Mountain was deserted.

Johnston moved to the banks of the Chattahoochee,

Johnston's parrying of Sherman's mighty strokes was "a model of defensive warfare," declares one of Sherman's own division commanders, Jacob D. Cox. There was not a man in the Federal army from Sherman down that did not rejoice to hear that Johnston had been superseded by Hood on July 17th. Johnston, whose mother was a niece of Patrick Henry, was fifty-seven years old, cold in manner, measured and accurate in speech. His dark firm face, surmounted by a splendidly intellectual forehead, betokened the experienced and cautious soldier. His dismissal was one of the political mistakes which too often hampered capable leaders on both sides. His Fabian policy in Georgia was precisely the same as that which was winning fame against heavy odds for Lee in Virginia.

GENERAL JOSEPH EGGLESTON
JOHNSTON, C. S. A.
BORN 1809; WEST POINT 1829; DIED 1891

LIEUTENANT–GENERAL
JOHN B. HOOD, C. S. A.
BORN 1831; WEST POINT 1853; DIED 1879

The countenance of Hood, on the other hand, indicates an eager, restless energy, an impetuosity that lacked the poise of Sherman, whose every gesture showed the alertness of mind and soundness of judgment that in him were so exactly balanced. Both Schofield and McPherson were classmates of Hood at West Point, and characterized him to Sherman as "bold even to rashness and courageous in the extreme." He struck the first offensive blow at Sherman advancing on Atlanta, and wisely adhered to the plan of the battle as it had been worked out by Johnston just before his removal. But the policy of attacking was certain to be finally disastrous to the Confederates.

Sherman following in the hope of catching him while crossing the river. But the wary Confederate had again, as at Resaca, prepared entrenchments in advance, and these were on the north bank of the river. He hastened to them, then turned on the approaching Federals and defiantly awaited attack. But Sherman remembered Kenesaw and there was no battle.

The feints, the sparring, the flanking movements among the hills and forests continued day after day. The immediate aim in the early days of July was to cross the Chattahoochee. On the 8th, Sherman sent Schofield and McPherson across, ten miles or more above the Confederate position. Johnston crossed the next day. Thomas followed later.

Sherman's position was by no means reassuring. It is true he had, in the space of two months, pressed his antagonist back inch by inch for more than a hundred miles and was now almost within sight of the goal of the campaign— the city of Atlanta. But the single line of railroad that connected him with the North and brought supplies from Louisville, five hundred miles away, for a hundred thousand men and twenty-three thousand animals, might at any moment be destroyed by Confederate raiders.

The necessity of guarding the Western and Atlantic Railroad was an ever-present concern with Sherman. Forrest and his cavalry force were in northern Mississippi waiting for him to get far enough on the way to Atlanta for them to pounce upon the iron way and tear it to ruins. To prevent this General Samuel D. Sturgis, with eight thousand troops, was sent from Memphis against Forrest. He met him on the 10th of June near Guntown, Mississippi, but was sadly beaten and driven back to Memphis, one hundred miles away. The affair, nevertheless, delayed Forrest in his operations against the railroad, and meanwhile General Smith's troops returned to Memphis from the Red River expedition, somewhat late according to the schedule but eager to join Sherman in the advance on Atlanta. Smith, however, was directed to

PEACH–TREE CREEK, WHERE HOOD HIT HARD

Counting these closely clustered Federal graves gives one an idea of the overwhelming onset with Hood become the aggressor on July 20th. Beyond the graves are some of the trenches from which the Federals were at first irresistibly driven. In the background flows Peach-Tree Creek, the little stream that gives its name to the battlefield. Hood, impatient to signalize his new responsibility by a stroke that would at once dispel the gloom at Richmond, had posted his troops behind strongly fortified works on a ridge commanding the valley of Peach-Tree Creek about five miles to the north of Atlanta. Here he awaited the approach of Sherman. As the Federals were disposing their lines and entrenching before this position, Hood's eager eyes detected a gap in their formation and at four o'clock in the afternoon hurled a heavy force against it. Thus he proved his reputation for courage, but the outcome showed the mistake. For a brief interval Sherman's forces were in great peril. But the Federals under Newton and Geary rallied and held their ground, till Ward's division in a brave counter-charge drove the Confederates back. This first effort cost Hood dear. He abandoned his entrenchments that night, leaving on the field five hundred dead, one thousand wounded, and many prisoners. Sherman estimated the total Confederate loss at no less than five thousand. That of the Federals was fifteen hundred.

PALISADES AND *CHEVAUX-DE-FRISE* GUARDING ATLANTA

At last Sherman is before Atlanta. The photograph shows one of the keypoints in the Contederate defense, the fort at the head of Marietta Street, toward which the Federal lines were advancing from the northwest. The old Potter house in the background, once a quiet, handsome country seat, is now surrounded by bristling fortifications, palisades, and double lines of *chevaux-de-frise*. Atlanta was engaged in the final grapple with the force that was to overcome her. Sherman has fought his way past Kenesaw and across the Chattahoochee, through a country which he describes as "one vast fort," saying that "Johnston must have at least fifty miles of connected trenches with abatis and finished batteries." Anticipating that Sherman might drive him back upon Atlanta, Johnston had constructed, during the winter, heavily fortified positions all the way from Dalton. During his two months in retreat the fortifications at Atlanta had been strengthened to the utmost. What he might have done behind them was never to be known.

AFTER THE SHARPSHOOTING IN POTTER'S HOUSE

One gets a closer look at Potter's house in the background opposite. It was occupied by sharpshooters in the skirmishing and engagements by which the investing lines were advanced. So the Federals made it a special target for their artillery. After Atlanta fell, nearly a ton of shot and shell was found in the house. The fort on Marietta Street, to the northwest of the city, was the first of the inner defenses to be encountered as Sherman advanced quickly on July 21st, after finding that Hood had abandoned his outer line at Peach-Tree Creek. The vicinity of the Potter house was the scene of many vigorous assaults and much brave resistance throughout the siege. Many another dwelling in Atlanta suffered as badly as this one in the clash of arms. During Sherman's final bombardment the city was almost laid in ruins. Even this was not the end, for after the occupation Captain Poe and his engineers found it necessary, in laying out the new fortifications, to destroy many more buildings throughout the devastated town.

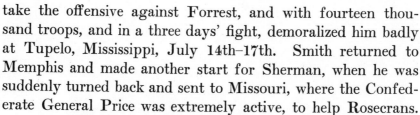

take the offensive against Forrest, and with fourteen thousand troops, and in a three days' fight, demoralized him badly at Tupelo, Mississippi, July 14th–17th. Smith returned to Memphis and made another start for Sherman, when he was suddenly turned back and sent to Missouri, where the Confederate General Price was extremely active, to help Rosecrans.

To avoid final defeat and to win the ground he had gained had taxed Sherman's powers to the last degree and was made possible only through his superior numbers. Even this degree of success could not be expected to continue if the railroad to the North should be destroyed. But Sherman must do more than he had done; he must capture Atlanta, this Richmond of the far South, with its cannon foundries and its great machine-shops, its military factories, and extensive army supplies. He must divide the Confederacy north and south as Grant's capture of Vicksburg had split it east and west.

Sherman must have Atlanta, for political reasons as well as for military purposes. The country was in the midst of a presidential campaign. The opposition to Lincoln's re-election was strong, and for many weeks it was believed on all sides that his defeat was inevitable. At least, the success of the Union arms in the field was deemed essential to Lincoln's success at the polls. Grant had made little progress in Virginia and his terrible repulse at Cold Harbor, in June, had cast a gloom over every Northern State. Farragut was operating in Mobile Bay; but his success was still in the future.

The eyes of the supporters of the great war-president turned longingly, expectantly, toward General Sherman and his hundred thousand men before Atlanta. "Do something—something spectacular—save the party and save the country thereby from permanent disruption!" This was the cry of the millions, and Sherman understood it. But withal, the capture of the Georgia city may have been doubtful but for the fact that at the critical moment the Confederate President made a decision that resulted, unconsciously, in a decided

THE ARMY'S FINGER–TIPS—PICKETS BEFORE ATLANTA

A Federal picket post on the lines before Atlanta. This picture was taken shortly before the battle of July 22d. The soldiers are idling about unconcerned at exposing themselves; this is on the "reserve post." Somewhat in advance of this lay the outer line of pickets, and it would be time enough to seek cover if they were driven in. Thus armies feel for each other, stretching out first their sensitive fingers—the pickets. If these recoil, the skirmishers are sent forward while the strong arm, the line of battle, gathers itself to meet the foe. As this was an inner line, it was more strongly fortified than was customary with the pickets. But the men of both sides had become very expert in improvising field-works at this stage of the war. Hard campaigning had taught the veterans the importance to themselves of providing such protection, and no orders had to be given for their construction. As soon as a regiment gained a position desirable to hold, the soldiers would throw up a strong parapet of dirt and logs in a single night. In order to spare the men as much as possible, Sherman ordered his division commanders to organize pioneer detachments out of the Negroes that escaped to the Federals. These could work at night.

service to the Union cause. He dismissed General Johnston and put another in his place, one who was less strategic and more impulsive.

Jefferson Davis did not agree with General Johnston's military judgment, and he seized on the fact that Johnston had so steadily retreated before the Northern army as an excuse for his removal. On the 18th of July, Davis turned the Confederate Army of Tennessee over to General John B. Hood. A graduate of West Point of the class of 1853, a classmate of McPherson, Schofield, and Sheridan, Hood had faithfully served the cause of the South since the opening of the war. He was known as a fighter, and it was believed that he would change the policy of Johnston to one of open battle with Sherman's army. And so it proved.

Johnston had lost, since the opening of the campaign at Dalton, about fifteen thousand men, and the army that he now delivered to Hood consisted of about sixty thousand in all.

While Hood was no match for Sherman as a strategist, he was not a weakling. His policy of aggression, however, was not suited to the circumstances—to the nature of the country—in view of the fact that Sherman's army was far stronger than his own.

Two days after Hood took command of the Confederate army he offered battle. Sherman's forces had crossed Peach Tree Creek, a small stream flowing into the Chattahoochee, but a few miles from Atlanta, and were approaching the city. They had thrown up slight breastworks, as was their custom, but were not expecting an attack. Suddenly, however, about four o'clock in the afternoon of July 20th, an imposing column of Confederates burst from the woods near the position of the Union right center, under Thomas. The Federals were soon at their guns. The battle was short, fierce, and bloody. The Confederates made a gallant assault, but were pressed back to their entrenchments, leaving the ground covered with dead and wounded. The Federal loss in the battle

THE SCENE OF McPHERSON'S DEATH

Near the tree seen in the upper picture the brave and wise McPherson, one of Sherman's best generals, was killed, July 22d. On the morning of that day, McPherson, in excellent spirits, rode up with his staff to Sherman's headquarters at the Howard House. The night before his troops had gained a position on Leggett's Hill, from which they could look over the Confederate parapets into Atlanta. McPherson explained to Sherman that he was planting batteries to knock down a large foundry which the position commanded. Sitting down on the steps of the porch, the two generals discussed the chances of battle and agreed that they ought to be unusually cautious. McPherson said that his old classmate Hood, though not deemed much of a scholar at West Point, was none the less brave and determined. Walking down the road the two comrades in arms sat down at the foot of a tree and examined the Federal positions on a map. Suddenly the sound of battle broke upon their ears and rose to the volume of a general engagement. McPherson, anxious about his newly gained position, called for his horse and rode off. Reaching the battlefield he sent one orderly after another to bring up troops, and then riding alone through the woods to gain another part of the field, ran directly into a Confederate skirmish line. Upon his refusal to surrender a volley brought him lifeless to the ground. The battle of Atlanta, on July 22d, was Hood's second attempt to repel Sherman's army that was rapidly throwing its cordon around the city to the north and threatening to cut his rail communication with Augusta to the eastward. To prevent this, it was imperative that the hill gained by McPherson should be retaken, and Hood thought he saw his opportunity in the thinly extended Federal line near this position. His abandoned entrenchments near Peach-Tree Creek were but a ruse to lure Sherman on into advancing incautiously. Sherman and McPherson had so decided when Hood began to strike. McPherson's prompt dispositions saved the day at the cost of his life. A skilful soldier, tall and handsome, universally liked and respected by his comrades, he was cut off in his prime at the age of thirty-six.

DÉBRIS FROM THE BATTLE OF ATLANTA

of Peach Tree Creek was placed at over seventeen hundred, the Confederate loss being much greater. This battle had been planned by Johnston before his removal, but he had been waiting for the strategic moment to fight it.

Two days later, July 22d, occurred the greatest engagement of the entire campaign—the battle of Atlanta. The Federal army was closing in on the entrenchments of Atlanta, and was now within two or three miles of the city. On the night of the 21st, General Blair, of McPherson's army, had gained possession of a high hill on the left, which commanded a view of the heart of the city. Hood thereupon planned to recapture this hill, and make a general attack on the morning of the 22d. He sent General Hardee on a long night march around the extreme flank of McPherson's army, the attack to be made at daybreak. Meantime, General Cheatham, who had succeeded to the command of Hood's former corps, and General A. P. Stewart, who now had Polk's corps, were to engage Thomas and Schofield in front and thus prevent them from sending aid to McPherson.

Hardee was delayed in his fifteen-mile night march, and it was noon before he attacked. At about that hour Generals Sherman and McPherson sat talking near the Howard house, which was the Federal headquarters, when the sudden boom of artillery from beyond the hill that Blair had captured announced the opening of the coming battle. McPherson quickly leaped upon his horse and galloped away toward the sound of the guns. Meeting Logan and Blair near the railroad, he conferred with them for a moment, when they separated, and each hastened to his place in the battle-line. McPherson sent aides and orderlies in various directions with despatches, until but two were still with him. He then rode into a forest and was suddenly confronted by a portion of the Confederate army under General Cheatham. " Surrender," was the call that rang out. But he wheeled his horse as if to flee, when he was instantly shot dead, and the horse galloped back riderless.

COPYRIGHT, 1911, PATRIOT PUB. CO.

THE FINAL BLOW TO THE CONFEDERACY'S SOUTHERN STRONGHOLD

It was Sherman's experienced railroad wreckers that finally drove Hood out of Atlanta. In the picture the rails heating red-hot amid the flaming bonfires of the ties, and the piles of twisted débris show vividly what Sherman meant when he said their "work was done with a will." Sherman saw that in order to take Atlanta without terrific loss he must cut off all its rail communications. This he did by "taking the field with our main force and using it against the communications of Atlanta instead of against its intrench- ments." On the night of August 25th he moved with practically his entire army and wagon-trains loaded with fifteen days' rations. By the morning of the 27th the whole front of the city was deserted. The Confederates concluded that Sherman was in retreat. Next day they found out their mistake, for the Federal army lay across the West Point Railroad while the soldiers began wrecking it. Next day they were in motion toward the railroad to Macon, and General Hood began to understand that a colossal raid was in progress. After the occupation, when this picture was taken, Sherman's men completed the work of destruction.

 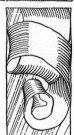

The death of the brilliant, dashing young leader, James B McPherson, was a great blow to the Union army. But thirty-six years of age, one of the most promising men in the country, and already the commander of a military department. McPherson was the only man in all the Western armies whom Grant, on going to the East, placed in the same military class with Sherman.

Logan succeeded the fallen commander, and the battle raged on. The Confederates were gaining headway. They captured several guns. Cheatham was pressing on, pouring volley after volley into the ranks of the Army of the Tennessee, which seemed about to be cut in twain. A gap was opening. The Confederates were pouring through. General Sherman was present and saw the danger. Calling for Schofield to send several batteries, he placed them and poured a concentrated artillery fire through the gap and mowed down the advancing men in swaths. At the same time, Logan pressed forward and Schofield's infantry was called up. The Confederates were hurled back with great loss. The shadows of night fell—and the battle of Atlanta was over. Hood's losses exceeded eight thousand of his brave men, whom he could ill spare. Sherman lost about thirty-seven hundred.

The Confederate army recuperated within the defenses of Atlanta—behind an almost impregnable barricade. Sherman had no hope of carrying the city by assault, while to surround and invest it was impossible with his numbers. He determined, therefore, to strike Hood's lines of supplies. On July 28th, Hood again sent Hardee out from his entrenchments to attack the Army of the Tennessee, now under the command of General Howard. A fierce battle at Ezra Church on the west side of the city ensued, and again the Confederates were defeated with heavy loss.

A month passed and Sherman had made little progress toward capturing Atlanta. Two cavalry raids which he organized resulted in defeat, but the two railroads from the

THE RUIN OF HOOD'S RETREAT—DEMOLISHED CARS AND ROLLING-MILL

On the night of August 31st, in his headquarters near Jonesboro, Sherman could not sleep. That day he had defeated the force sent against him at Jonesboro and cut them off from returning to Atlanta. This was Hood's last effort to save his communications. About midnight sounds of exploding shells and what seemed like volleys of musketry arose in the direction of Atlanta. The day had been exciting in that city. Supplies and ammunition that Hood could carry with him were being removed; large quantities of provisions were being distributed among the citizens, and as the troops marched out they were allowed to take what they could from the public stores. All that remained was destroyed. The noise that Sherman heard that night was the blowing up of the rolling-mill and of about a hundred cars and six engines loaded with Hood's abandoned ammunition. The picture shows the Georgia Central Railroad east of the town.

SHERMAN'S MEN IN THE ABANDONED DEFENSES

At last Sherman's soldiers are within the Confederate fortifications which held them at bay for a month and a half. This is Confederate Fort D, to the southwest of the city, and was incorporated in the new line of defenses which Sherman had laid out preparatory to holding Atlanta as a military post. In the left background rises the new Federal fort, No. 7. The General himself felt no such security as these soldiers at ease seem to feel. His line of communications was long, and the Confederates were threatening it aggressively.

IN POSSESSION OF THE GOAL

This Confederate fort was to the west of Peach-Tree Street, and between it and the Chatta-nooga Railroad. Here, four hundred miles from his base, Sherman, having accomplished in four months what he set out to do, rested his army. Had Johnston's skill been opposed to him till the end, the feat would hardly have been so quickly performed. Hood's impetuous bravery had made it difficult and costly enough, but Sherman's splendid army, in the hands of its aggressive leader, had faced the intrepid assaults and won.

south into Atlanta were considerably damaged. But, late in August, the Northern commander made a daring move that proved successful. Leaving his base of supplies, as Grant had done before Vicksburg, and marching toward Jonesboro, Sherman destroyed the Macon and Western Railroad, the only remaining line of supplies to the Confederate army.

Hood attempted to block the march on Jonesboro, and Hardee was sent with his and S. D. Lee's Corps to attack the Federals, while he himself sought an opportunity to move upon Sherman's right flank. Hardee's attack failed, and this necessitated the evacuation of Atlanta. After blowing up his magazines and destroying the supplies which his men could not carry with them, Hood abandoned the city, and the next day, September 2d, General Slocum, having succeeded Hooker, led the Twentieth Corps of the Federal army within its earthen walls. Hood had made his escape, saving his army from capture. His chief desire would have been to march directly north on Marietta and destroy the depots of Federal supplies, but a matter of more importance prevented. Thirty-four thousand Union prisoners were confined at Andersonville, and a small body of cavalry could have released them. So Hood placed himself between Andersonville and Sherman.

In the early days of September the Federal hosts occupied the city toward which they had toiled all the summer long. At East Point, Atlanta, and Decatur, the three armies settled for a brief rest, while the cavalry, stretched for many miles along the Chattahoochee, protected their flanks and rear. Since May their ranks had been depleted by some twenty-eight thousand killed and wounded, while nearly four thousand had fallen prisoners, into the Confederates' hands.

It was a great price, but whatever else the capture of Atlanta did, it ensured the reelection of Abraham Lincoln to the presidency of the United States. The total Confederate losses were in the neighborhood of thirty-five thousand, of which thirteen thousand were prisoners.

PART II
THE SIMULTANEOUS MOVEMENTS

THE LAST CONFLICTS
IN THE SHENANDOAH

THE CAPITOL IN WAR TIME

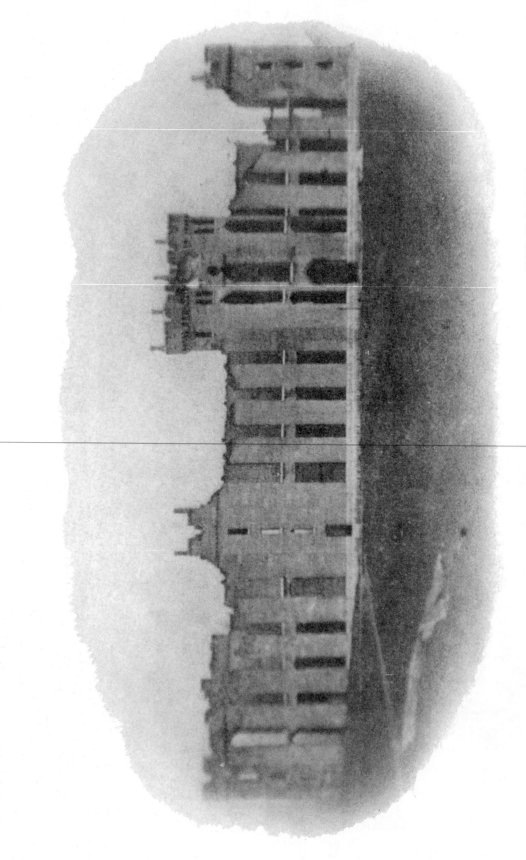

WAR'S WRECKAGE IN THE SHENANDOAH VALLEY

Ruins of the Virginia Military Institute at Lexington, after Hunter's raid in 1864. The picture shows the blackened walls of the leading Virginia military institution after General Hunter's raid through the valley in the early summer of 1864. The "V. M. I." meant much to the people of Virginia. It was in this well-known school that "Stonewall" Jackson had served for ten years as a professor before the outbreak of the war. The cadets of the "V. M. I." had fought like veterans in a body under Breckinridge in the battle with Sigel at New Market. Possibly it was because of the school's contributions to the Confederate cause that General Hunter ordered it to be burned. At any rate, he seems to have acted solely on his own responsibility in the matter. General Grant never approved of the unnecessary destruction of schools, churches, and private property. Retaliatory movements had an important part in the operations of General Early during the remainder of the summer. Such scenes undoubtedly spurred his footsore soldiers in their march.

A CONFEDERATE REPRISAL ON PENNSYLVANIA SOIL

Chambersburg as McCausland left it. As a reprisal for Hunter's raid in the Shenandoah Valley, the Confederate General McCausland burned the town of Chambersburg, in the Cumberland Valley of Pennsylvania. One high-minded and courageous officer in Mc-Causland's command—Colonel William E. Peters, of Virginia—refused to obey the order to apply the torch. A year before, on the march to Gettysburg, General Lee had issued in the very town of Chambersburg his famous "General Order No. 73," in which he ex-horted his troops to abstain from "any unnecessary or wanton injury to private property," and General Gordon is authority for the statement that the burning of Chambersburg by his subordinate was a great shock to General Lee's sensibilities. It seems inevitable that war should leave in its train such tottering walls and roofless homes.

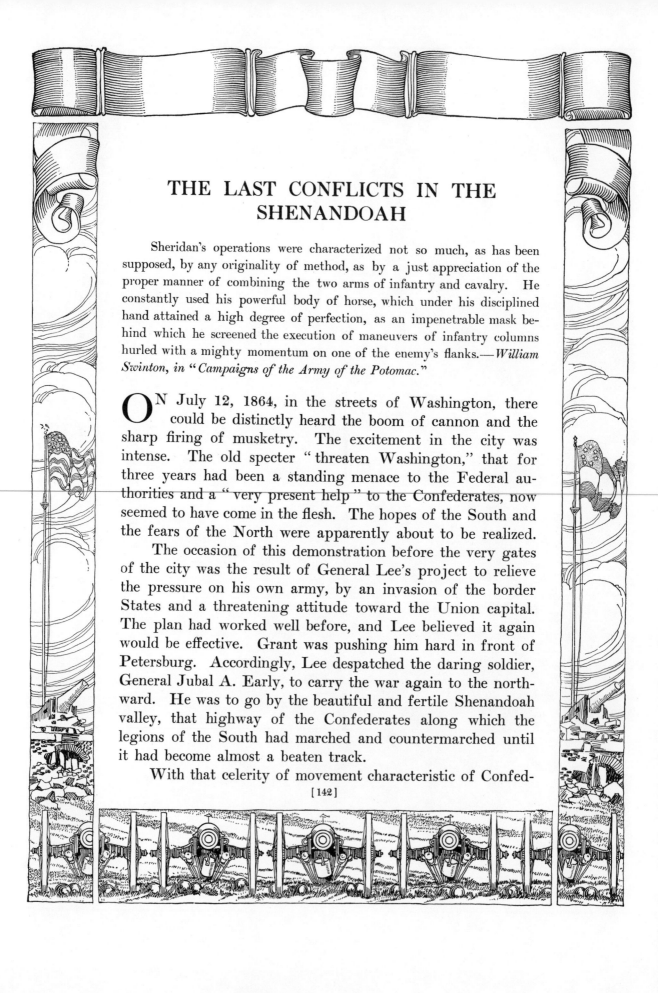

THE LAST CONFLICTS IN THE SHENANDOAH

Sheridan's operations were characterized not so much, as has been supposed, by any originality of method, as by a just appreciation of the proper manner of combining the two arms of infantry and cavalry. He constantly used his powerful body of horse, which under his disciplined hand attained a high degree of perfection, as an impenetrable mask behind which he screened the execution of maneuvers of infantry columns hurled with a mighty momentum on one of the enemy's flanks.—*William Swinton, in "Campaigns of the Army of the Potomac."*

ON July 12, 1864, in the streets of Washington, there could be distinctly heard the boom of cannon and the sharp firing of musketry. The excitement in the city was intense. The old specter "threaten Washington," that for three years had been a standing menace to the Federal authorities and a "very present help" to the Confederates, now seemed to have come in the flesh. The hopes of the South and the fears of the North were apparently about to be realized.

The occasion of this demonstration before the very gates of the city was the result of General Lee's project to relieve the pressure on his own army, by an invasion of the border States and a threatening attitude toward the Union capital. The plan had worked well before, and Lee believed it again would be effective. Grant was pushing him hard in front of Petersburg. Accordingly, Lee despatched the daring soldier, General Jubal A. Early, to carry the war again to the northward. He was to go by the beautiful and fertile Shenandoah valley, that highway of the Confederates along which the legions of the South had marched and countermarched until it had become almost a beaten track.

With that celerity of movement characteristic of Confed-

THE CAPITOL AT WASHINGTON IN 1863

When the Capitol at Washington was threatened by the Confederate armies, it was still an unfinished structure, betraying its incompleteness to every beholder. This picture shows the derrick on the dome. It is a view of the east front of the building and was taken on July 11, 1863. Washington society had not been wholly free from occasional "war scares" since the withdrawal of most of the troops whose duty it had been to guard the city. Early's approach in July, 1864, found the Nation's capital entirely unprotected. Naturally there was a flutter throughout the peaceable groups of non-combatants that made up the population of Washington at that time, as well as in official circles. There were less than seventy thousand people living in the city in 1864, a large proportion of whom were in some way connected with the Government.

erate marches, General Early prepared to sweep from the valley the fragmentary bodies of Union troops there collected. Less than a week after receiving his commission, he encountered the forces of General Hunter at Lynchburg, Virginia. There was some skirmishing, but Hunter, who did not have enough ammunition to sustain a real battle, returned westward. For three days Early's barefoot, half-clad soldiers followed the retreating columns of Hunter until the latter had safely filed his men through the passes of the Blue Ridge Mountains and into the Kanawha valley.

The Shenandoah valley was now uncovered, but not as Lee had expected. Believing that if Hunter were defeated he would retreat down the Valley, Early had been instructed to follow him into Maryland. But the Federal general had gone in the other direction, and southwestern Virginia had thereby been placed in great danger. The question was, how to draw Hunter from his new position. To pursue him further would have been a difficult task for Early. So it was decided to carry out the plans for a march into Maryland, in the hope of luring Hunter from his lair. So Early turned to the north with his seventeen thousand troops, and marching under the steady glare of a July sun, two weeks later, his approach was the signal for the Union troops at Martinsburg, under Sigel, to fall back across the Potomac to Maryland Heights. The road to Washington was thus blocked at Harper's Ferry, where Early intended to cross. He therefore was compelled to get over at Shepherdstown, while Breckenridge engaged Sigel at Harper's Ferry. Once across the river, Early's scouting parties quickly destroyed miles of the Baltimore and Ohio Railroad, cut the embankments and locks of the Chesapeake and Ohio Canal, levied contributions upon the citizens of Hagerstown and Frederick, and pushed their tattered ranks of gray in the direction of the Federal capital. On the 9th of July, the advance lines of the Confederate force came to the banks of the Monocacy, where they

PROTECTING LOCOMOTIVES FROM THE CONFEDERATE RAIDER

The United States railroad photographer, Captain A. J. Russell, labeled this picture of 1864: "Engines stored in Washington to prevent their falling into Rebel hands in case of a raid on Alexandria." Here they are, almost under the shadow of the Capitol dome (which had just been completed). This was one of the precautions taken by the authorities at Washington, of which the general public knew little or nothing at the time. These photographs are only now revealing official secrets recorded fifty years ago.

ONE OF WASHINGTON'S DEFENDERS

Heavy artillery like this was of comparatively little use in repulsing such an attack as Early might be expected to make. Not only were these guns hard to move to points of danger, but in the summer of '64 there were no trained artillerists to man them. Big as they were, they gave Early no occasion for alarm.

found General Lew Wallace posted, with eight thousand men, half of Early's numbers, on the eastern side of that stream, to contest the approach of the Southern troops.

The battle was brief but bloody; the Confederates, crossing the stream and climbing its slippery banks, hurled their lines of gray against the compact ranks of blue. The attack was impetuous; the repulse was stubborn. A wail of musketry rent the air and the Northern soldiers fell back to their second position. Between the opposing forces was a narrow ravine through which flowed a small brook. Across this stream the tide of battle rose and fell. Its limpid current was soon crimsoned by the blood of the dead and wounded. Wallace's columns, as did those of Early, bled, but they stood. The result of the battle for a time hung in the balance. Then the Federal lines began to crumble. The retreat began, some of the troops in order but the greater portion in confusion, and the victorious Confederates found again an open way to Washington.

Now within half a dozen miles of the city, with the dome of the Capitol in full view, the Southern general pushed his lines so close to Fort Stevens that he was ready to train his forty pieces of artillery upon its walls.

General Augur, in command of the capital's defenses, hastily collected what strength in men and guns he could. Heavy artillery, militia, sailors from the navy yard, convalescents, Government employees of all kinds were rushed to the forts around the city. General Wright, with two divisions of the Sixth Corps, arrived from the camp at Petersburg, and Emory's division of the Nineteenth Corps came just in time from New Orleans. This was on July 11th, the very day on which Early appeared in front of Fort Stevens. The Confederate had determined to make an assault, but the knowledge of the arrival of Wright and Emory caused him to change his mind. He realized that, if unsuccessful, his whole force would be lost, and he concluded to return. Nevertheless, he spent the 12th of July in threatening the city. In the middle of

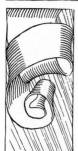

ENTRANCE TO WASHINGTON FROM THE SOUTH—THE FAMOUS "CHAIN BRIDGE"

The sentry and vedette guarding the approach to Washington suggest one reason why Early did not make his approach to the capital from the Virginia side of the Potomac. A chain of more than twenty forts protected the roads to Long Bridge (shown below), and there was no way of marching troops into the city from the south, excepting over such exposed passages. Most of the troops left for the defense of the city were on the Virginia side. Therefore Early wisely picked out the northern outposts as the more vulnerable. Long Bridge was closely guarded at all times, like Chain Bridge and the other approaches, and at night the planks of its floor were removed.

LONG BRIDGE AND THE CAPITOL ACROSS THE BROAD POTOMAC

the afternoon General Wright sent out General Wheaton with Bidwell's brigade of Getty's division, and Early's pickets and skirmishers were driven back a mile.

This small engagement had many distinguished spectators. Pond in "The Shenandoah Valley" thus describes the scene: "On the parapet of Fort Stevens stood the tall form of Abraham Lincoln by the side of General Wright, who in vain warned the eager President that his position was swept by the bullets of sharpshooters, until an officer was shot down within three feet of him, when he reluctantly stepped below. Sheltered from the line of fire, Cabinet officers and a group of citizens and ladies, breathless with excitement, watched the fortunes of the fight."

Under cover of night the Confederates began to retrace their steps and made their way to the Shenandoah, with General Wright in pursuit. As the Confederate army was crossing that stream, at Snicker's Ferry, on the 18th, the pursuing Federals came upon them. Early turned, repulsed them, and continued on his way to Winchester, where General Averell, from Hunter's forces, now at Harper's Ferry, attacked them with his cavalry and took several hundred prisoners, two days later. The Union troops under Wright returned to the defenses of Washington.

The Confederate army now became a shuttlecock in the game of war, marching and countermarching up and down, in and across, the valley of the Shenandoah, in military maneuvers, with scarcely a day of rest. This fruitful valley was to be the granary for its supplies. From it, as a base of operations, Early would make his frequent forays—a constant menace to the peace of the authorities at Washington.

General Crook was sent up the Valley after him, but at Kernstown, near Winchester, on July 24th, he met a disastrous defeat and made his way to the north side of the Potomac. Early, now in undisputed possession of the Valley, followed him to Martinsburg and sent his cavalry across the

COPYRIGHT, 1911, REVIEW OF REVIEWS CO.

GENERAL JUBAL A. EARLY, THE CONFED-ERATE RAIDER WHO THREATENED WASHINGTON

"My bad old man," as General Lee playfully called him, was forty-eight years of age when he made the brilliant Valley campaign of the summer of 1864, which was halted only by the superior forces of Sheridan. A West Point graduate and a veteran of the Mexican War, Early became, after the death of Jackson, one of Lee's most efficient subordinates. He was alert, aggressive, resourceful. His very eccentricities, perhaps, made him all the more successful as a commander of troops in the field. "Old Jube's" caustic wit and austere ways made him a terror to stragglers, and who shall say that his fluent, forcible profanity did not endear him to men who were accustomed to like roughness of speech?

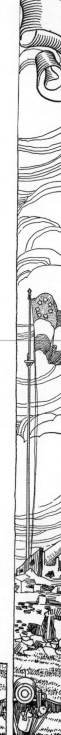

border river. With a bold movement General McCausland swept into Chambersburg and demanded a ransom of war. Compliance was out of the question and the torch was applied to the town, which in a short time was reduced to ashes. General Averell dashed in pursuit of McCausland and forced him to recross the Potomac.

The Federal authorities were looking for a "man of the hour"—one whom they might pit against the able and strategic Early. Such a one was found in General Philip Henry Sheridan, whom some have called the "Marshal Ney of America." He was selected by General Grant, and his instructions were to drive the Confederates out of the Valley and to make it untenable for any future military operations.

It was a magnificent setting for military genius. The men, the armies, and the beautiful valley combined to make it one of the great strategic campaigns of the war. The Union forces comprising the Army of the Shenandoah, as it was afterward called, amounted to about twenty-seven thousand men; the Confederates, to about twenty thousand. There was over a month of preliminary skirmishing and fighting. Cavalry raiders from both armies were darting hither and thither. Sheridan pushed up the Valley and fell back again toward the Potomac. Early followed him, only to retreat in turn toward Winchester, Sheridan now being pursuer. Both generals were watching an opportunity to strike. Both seemed anxious for battle, but both were sparring for the time and place to deliver an effective blow.

The middle of September found the Confederate forces centered about Winchester, and the Union army was ten miles distant, with the Opequon between them. At two o'clock on the morning of September 19th, the Union camp was in motion, preparing for marching orders. At three o'clock the forward movement was begun, and by daylight the Federal advance had driven in the Confederate pickets. Emptying into the Opequon from the west are two converging streams,

A HOUSE NEAR WASHINGTON STRUCK BY ONE OF EARLY'S SHELLS

The arrival of Grant's trained veterans in July, 1864, restored security to the capital city after a week of fright. The fact that shells had been thrown into the outskirts of the city gave the inhabitants for the first time a realizing sense of immediate danger. This scene is the neighborhood of Fort Stevens, on the Seventh Street road, not far from the Soldiers' Home, where President Lincoln was spending the summer. The campaign for his reëlection had begun and the outlook for his success and that of his party seemed at this moment as dubious as that for the conclusion of the war. Grant had weakened his lines about Richmond in order to protect Washington, while Lee had been able to detach Early's Corps for the brilliant Valley Campaign, which saved his Shenandoah supplies.

forming a triangle with the Winchester and Martinsburg pike as a base.

The town of Winchester is situated on this road, and was therefore at the bottom of the triangle. Before the town, the Confederate army stretched its lines between the two streams. The Union army would have to advance from the apex of the triangle, through a narrow ravine, shut in by thickly wooded hills and gradually emerging into an undulating valley. At the end of the gorge was a Confederate outwork, guarding the approach to Winchester. Both generals had the same plan of battle in mind. Sheridan would strike the Confederate center and right. Early was willing he should do this, for he planned to strike the Union right, double it back, get between Sheridan's army and the gorge, and thus cut off its retreat.

It took time for the Union troops to pass through the ravine, and it was late in the forenoon before the line of battle was formed. The attack and defense were alike obstinate. Upon the Sixth Corps and Grover's division of the Nineteenth Corps fell the brunt of the battle, since they were to hold the center while the Army of West Virginia, under General Crook, would sweep around them and turn the position of the opposing forces. The Confederate General Ramseur, with his troops, drove back the Federal center, held his ground for two hours, while the opposing lines were swept by musketry and artillery from the front, and enfiladed by artillery. Many Federal prisoners were taken.

By this time, Russell's division of the Sixth Corps emerged from the ravine. Forming in two lines, it marched quickly to the front. About the same time the Confederates were also being reenforced. General Rodes plunged into the fight, making a gallant attack and losing his life. General Gordon, with his columns of gray, swept across the summit of the hills and through the murky clouds of smoke saw the steady advance of the lines of blue. One of Russell's brigades struck the Confederate flank, and the Federal line was reestablished. As the

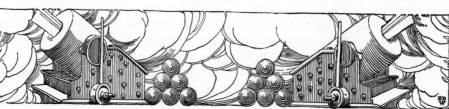

THE FIRST CONNECTICUT HEAVY ARTILLERY, ASSIGNED TO THE DEFENSE OF WASHINGTON

When Early approached Washington from the north, in 1864, the crack artillery companies, like that represented in the photograph (the First Connecticut Heavy), had all left the city to its fate. In the spring of 1862, as this picture was taken, just before the beginning of McClellan's Peninsula Campaign, Colonel Tyler was in the act of examining a despatch at the sally-port of Fort Richardson, Arlington Heights, Virginia. During the first two years of the war the Government devoted a great part of its energies to the development of a strong line of fortifications around the capital city, on both sides of the Potomac. Washington's nearness to the Confederate lines made such precautions necessary. The political significance of a possible capture of the national capital by the Confederates was fully appreciated. The retaining of large bodies of troops for the protection of Washington was a fixed policy during 1861 and 1862, as the first commander of the Army of the Potomac knew to his sorrow. As the war wore on, the increasing need of troops for the investment of Richmond, coupled with the apparent security of the capital, led to a reversal of that policy. Washington was practically abandoned, in a military sense, save for the retention of a few regiments of infantry, including a very small proportion of men who had seen actual fighting, and the forts were garrisoned chiefly by raw recruits.

division moved forward to do this General Russell fell, pierced through the heart by a piece of shell.

The Fifth Maine battery, galloping into the field, unlimbered and with an enfilading storm of canister aided in turning the tide. Piece by piece the shattered Union line was picked up and reunited. Early sent the last of his reserves into the conflict to turn the Union right. Now ensued the fiercest fighting of the day. Regiment after regiment advanced to the wood only to be hurled back again. Here it was that the One hundred and fourteenth New York left its dreadful toll of men. Its position after the battle could be told by the long, straight line of one hundred and eighty-five of its dead and wounded.

It was three o'clock in the afternoon; the hour of Early's repulse had struck. To the right of the Union lines could be heard a mighty yell. The Confederates seemed to redouble their fire. The shivering lightning bolts shot through the air and the volleys of musketry increased in intensity. Then, across the shell-plowed field, came the reserves under General Crook. Breasting the Confederate torrent of lead, which cut down nine hundred of the reserves while crossing the open space, they rushed toward the embattled lines of the South.

At the same moment, coming out of the woods in the rear of the Federals, were seen the men of the Nineteenth Corps under General Emory, who had for three hours been lying in the grass awaiting their opportunity. The Confederate bullets had been falling thick in their midst with fatal certainty. They were eager for action. Rushing into the contest like madmen, they stopped at nothing. From two sides of the wood the men of Emory and Crook charged simultaneously. The Union line overlapped the Confederate at every point and doubled around the unprotected flanks. The day for the Southerners was irretrievably lost. They fell back toward Winchester in confusion. As they did so, a great uproar was heard on the pike road. It was the Federal cavalry under

[154]

WHERE LINCOLN WAS UNDER FIRE

This is Fort Stevens (originally known as Fort Massachusetts), north of Washington, near the Soldiers' Home, where President Lincoln had his summer residence. It was to this outpost that Early's troops advanced on July 12, 1864. In the fighting of that day Lincoln himself stood on the ramparts, and a surgeon who stood by his side was wounded. These works were feebly garrisoned, and General Gordon declared in his memoirs that when the Confederate troops reached Fort Stevens they found it untenanted. This photograph was taken after the occupation of the fort by Company F of the Third Massachusetts Artillery.

General Torbert sweeping up the road, driving the Confederate troopers before them. The surprised mass was pressed into its own lines. The infantry was charged and many prisoners and battle-flags captured.

The sun was now sinking upon the horizon, and on the ascending slopes in the direction of the town could be seen the long, dark lines of men following at the heels of the routed army. Along the crest of the embattled summit galloped a force of cavalrymen, which, falling upon the disorganized regiments of Early, aided, in the language of Sheridan, " to send them whirling through Winchester." The Union pursuit continued until the twilight had come and the shadows of night screened the scattered forces of Early from the pursuing cavalrymen. The battle of Winchester, or the Opequon, had been a bloody one—a loss of five thousand on the Federal side, and about four thousand on the Confederate.

By daylight of the following morning the victorious army was again in pursuit. On the afternoon of that day, it caught up with the Confederates, who now turned at bay at Fisher's Hill to resist the further approach of their pursuers. The position selected by General Early was a strong one, and his antagonist at once recognized it as such. The valley of the Shenandoah at this point is about four miles wide, lying between Fisher's Hill and Little North Mountain. General Early's line extended across the entire valley, and he had greatly increased his already naturally strong position. His army seemed safe from attack. From the summit of Three Top Mountain, his signal corps informed him of every movement of the Union army in the valley below. General Sheridan's actions indicated a purpose to assault the center of the Confederate line. For two days he continued massing his regiments in that direction, at times even skirmishing for position. General Wright pushed his men to within seven hundred yards of the Southern battle-line. While this was going on in full view of the Confederate general and his army, another movement was being executed

WAR DEPARTMENT OFFICIALS AND CLERKS IN WAR–TIME

Non-combatants of this type formed the main reliance of the authorities against Early's veterans in July, 1864. The forces available, prior to the arrival of the Sixth and Nineteenth Corps from Grant's army, are summarized by General Barnard thus: "The effective forces were 1,819 infantry, 1,834 artillery, and 63 cavalry north of the Potomac, and 4,064 infantry, 1,772 artillery, and 51 cavalry south thereof. There were besides, in Washington and Alexandria, about 3,900 effectives and about 4,400 (six regiments) of Veteran Reserves. The foregoing constitute a total of about 20,400 men. Of that number, however, but 9,600, mostly perfectly raw troops, constituted the garrison of the defenses. Of the other troops, a considerable portion were unavailable, and the whole would form but an inefficient force for service on the lines."

which even the vigilant signal officers on Three Top Mountain had not observed.

On the night of September 20th, the troops of General Crook were moved into the timber on the north bank of Cedar Creek. All during the next day, they lay concealed. That night they crossed the stream and the next morning were again hidden by the woods and ravines. At five o'clock on the morning of the 22d, Crook's men were nearly opposite the Confederate center. Marching his men in perfect silence, by one o'clock he had arrived at the left and front of the unsuspecting Early. By four o'clock he had reached the east face of Little North Mountain, to the left and rear of the Confederates. While the movement was being made, the main body of the Federal army was engaging the attention of the Confederates in front. Just before sundown, Crook's men plunged down the mountain side, from out of the timbered cover. The Confederates were quick to see that they had been trapped. They had been caught in a pocket and there was nothing for them to do except to retreat or surrender. They preferred the former, which was, according to General Gordon, "first stubborn and slow, then rapid, then—a rout."

After the battle of Fisher's Hill the pursuit still continued. The Confederate regiments re-formed, and at times would stop and contest the approach of the advancing cavalrymen. By the time the Union infantry would reach the place, the retreating army would have vanished. Torbert had been sent down Luray Valley in pursuit of the Confederate cavalry, with the hope of scattering it and seizing New Market in time to cut off the Confederate retreat from Fisher's Hill. But at Milford, in a narrow gorge, General Wickham held Torbert and prevented the fulfilment of his plan; and General Early's whole force was able to escape. Day after day this continued until Early had taken refuge in the Blue Ridge in front of Brown's Gap. Here he received reenforcements. Sheridan in the mean time had gone into camp at Harrisonburg, and for

A MARYLAND VILLAGE ON THE LINE OF EARLY'S RETREAT

This is a winter scene in Poolesville, a typical village in this part of Maryland, overrun for the last time by Confederate armies in the summer of 1864. Early passed through the place on his second day's march from Washington, closely pursued by General Wright's force of Federals. After Early had made good his escape and threatened to levy heavy toll on the defenseless communities of Maryland and Pennsylvania if he were not vigorously opposed, Grant selected Sheridan for the task of clearing the Valley of Confederates and finally destroying its value as a source of supplies for Lee's army. Sheridan waited until Early had been seriously weakened before he assaulted him; but when he struck, the blows were delivered with tremendous energy. The battles of the Opequon, Fisher's Hill, and Cedar Creek (the latter made memorable by Read's famous poem, "Sheridan's Ride"), drove Early back to New Market and wholly broke the Confederate power in that part of Virginia. This photograph (loaned by Mr. George A. Brackett, of Annapolis), was taken when the Eighth Minnesota held it, in the winter of 1862.

some time the two armies lay watching each other. The Federals were having difficulty in holding their lines of supply.

With the Valley practically given up by Early, Sheridan was anxious to stop here. He wrote to Grant, " I think the best policy will be to let the burning of the crops in the Valley be the end of the campaign, and let some of this army go somewhere else." He had the Petersburg line in mind. Grant's consent to this plan reached him on October 5th, and the following day he started on his return march down the Shenandoah. His cavalry extended across the entire valley. With the unsparing severity of war, his men began to make a barren waste of the region. The October sky was overcast with clouds of smoke and sheets of flame from the burning barns and mills.

As the army of Sheridan proceeded down the Valley, the undaunted cavaliers of Early came in pursuit. His horsemen kept close to the rear of the Union columns. On the morning of October 9th, the cavalry leader, Rosser, who had succeeded Wickham, found himself confronted by General Custer's division, at Tom's Brook. At the same time the Federal general, Wesley Merritt, fell upon the cavalry of Lomax and Johnson on an adjacent road. The two Union forces were soon united and a mounted battle ensued. The fight continued for two hours. There were charges and countercharges. The ground being level, the maneuvering of the squadrons was easy. The clink of the sabers rang out in the morning air. Both sides fought with tenacity. The Confederate center held together, but its flanks gave way. The Federals charged along the whole front, with a momentum that forced the Southern cavalrymen to flee from the field. They left in the hands of the Federal troopers over three hundred prisoners, all their artillery, except one piece, and nearly every wagon the Confederate cavalry had with them.

The Northern army continued its retrograde movement, and on the 10th crossed to the north side of Cedar Creek. Early's army in the mean time had taken a position at the

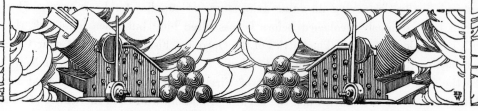

ONE OF CHAMBERSBURG'S QUIET STREETS

The invasion of Pennsylvania had only a minor part in the plan of Early's campaign, which in a month's time had accomplished two important results: It had restored to Lee free access to the rich supplies which the Shenandoah Valley could furnish, and it had caused Grant to withdraw from his operations at Petersburg a strong force for the protection of Washington. The cavalry raid in Pennsylvania was planned as retaliation for Hunter's operations in the Shenandoah. Early succeeded in holding the "Valley of Virginia" (Shenandoah) until the concentration of Sheridan's forces compelled his retirement. Then the "Valley" finally became eliminated as an avenue of danger to Washington.

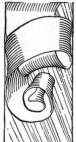

wooded base of Fisher's Hill, four miles away. The Sixth Corps started for Washington, but the news of Early at Fisher's Hill led to its recall. The Union forces occupied ground that was considered practically unassailable, especially on the left, where the deep gorge of the Shenandoah, along whose front rose the bold Massanutten Mountain, gave it natural protection.

The movements of the Confederate army were screened by the wooded ravines in front of Fisher's Hill, while, from the summit of the neighboring Three Top Mountain, its officers could view, as in a panorama, the entire Union camp. Seemingly secure, the corps of Crook on the left of the Union line was not well protected. The keen-eyed Gordon saw the weak point in the Union position. Ingenious plans to break it down were quickly made.

Meanwhile, Sheridan was summoned to Washington to consult with Secretary Stanton. He did not believe that Early proposed an immediate attack, and started on the 15th, escorted by the cavalry, and leaving General Wright in command. At Front Royal the next day word came from Wright enclosing a message taken for the Confederate signal-flag on Three Top Mountain. It was from Longstreet, advising Early that he would join him and crush Sheridan. The latter sent the cavalry back to Wright, and continued on to Washington, whence he returned at once by special train, reaching Winchester on the evening of the 18th.

Just after dark on October 18th, a part of Early's army under the command of General John B. Gordon, with noiseless steps, moved out from their camp, through the misty, autumn night. The men had been stripped of their canteens, in fear that the striking of them against some object might reveal their movements. Orders were given in low whispers. Their path followed along the base of the mountain—a dim and narrow trail, upon which but one man might pass at a time. For seven miles this sinuous line made its way through the dark

CHAMBERSBURG—A LANDMARK IN EARLY'S INVASION OF THE NORTH

After withdrawing from Washington, in July, 1864, Early sent a cavalry expedition under General McCausland to invade Pennsylvania. Chambersburg, in the Cumberland Valley, which was burned by McCausland's orders, marked the limit of the northward advance in this remarkable campaign. Early's force of ten thousand men had been detached from Lee's army of defense around Richmond on June 12th, had driven Hunter out of the Shen-andoah, and (after marching the length of that valley) had crossed the Potomac, forced back Lew Wallace with his six thousand Federals at the Monocacy, and camped within sight of the capitol's dome at Washington. Much of this marching had been at the rate of twenty miles a day, and at one time half of the command had been shoeless. The dash and endurance of the troops shone as bright as the leadership displayed by Early.

gorge, crossing the Shenandoah, and at times passing within four hundred yards of the Union pickets.

It arrived at the appointed place, opposite Crook's camp on the Federal right, an hour before the attack was to be made. In the shivering air of the early morning, the men crouched on the river bank, waiting for the coming of the order to move forward. At last, at five o'clock, it came. They plunged into the frosty water of the river, emerged on the other side, marched in "double quick," and were soon sounding a reveille to the sleeping troops of Sheridan. The minie balls whizzed and sang through the tents. In the gray mists of the dawn the legions of the South looked like phantom warriors, as they poured through the unmanned gaps. The Northerners sprang to arms. There was a bloody struggle in the trenches. Their eyes saw the flames from the Southern muskets; the men felt the breath of the hot muzzles in their faces, while the Confederate bayonets were at their breasts. There was a brief struggle, then panic and disorganization. Only a quarter of an hour of this yelling and struggling, and two-thirds of the Union army broke like a mill-dam and poured across the fields, leaving their accouterments of war and the stiffening bodies of their comrades. Rosser, with the cavalry, attacked Custer and assisted Gordon.

Meanwhile, during these same early morning hours, General Early had himself advanced to Cedar Creek by a more direct route. At half-past three o'clock his men had come in sight of the Union camp-fires. They waited under cover for the approach of day. At the first blush of dawn and before the charge of Gordon, Early hurled his men across the stream, swept over the breastworks, captured the batteries and turned them upon the unsuspecting Northerners. The Federal generals tried to stem the impending disaster. From the east of the battlefield the solid lines of Gordon were now driving the fugitives of Crook's corps by the mere force of momentum. Aides were darting hither and thither, trying to reassemble the

GENERAL PHILIP H. SHERIDAN IN THE SHENANDOAH CAMPAIGN

Two generations of schoolboys in the Northern States have learned the lines beginning, "Up from the south at break of day." This picture represents Sheridan in 1864, wearing the same hat that he waved to rally his soldiers on that famous ride from "Winchester, twenty miles away." As he reined up his panting horse on the turnpike at Cedar Creek, he received salutes from two future Presidents of the United States. The position on the left of the road was held by Colonel Rutherford B. Hayes, who had succeeded, after the rout of the Eighth Corps in the darkness of the early morning, in rallying some fighting groups of his own brigade; while on the right stood Major William McKinley, gallantly commanding the remnant of his fighting regiment—the Twenty-sixth Ohio.

crumbling lines. The Nineteenth Corps, under Emory, tried to hold its ground; for a time it fought alone, but after a desperate effort to hold its own, it, too, melted away under the scorching fire. The fields to the rear of the army were covered with wagons, ambulances, stragglers, and fleeing soldiers.

The Sixth Corps now came to the rescue. As it slowly fell to the rear it would, at times, turn to fight. At last it found a place where it again stood at bay. The men hastily gathered rails and constructed rude field-works. At the same time the Confederates paused in their advance. The rattle of musketry ceased. There was scarcely any firing except for the occasional roar of a long-range artillery gun. The Southerners seemed willing to rest on their well-earned laurels of the morning. In the language of the successful commander, it was "glory enough for one day."

But the brilliant morning victory was about to be changed to a singular afternoon defeat. During the morning's fight, when the Union troops were being rapidly overwhelmed with panic, Rienzi, the beautiful jet-black war-charger, was bearing his master, the commander of the Federal army, to the field of disaster. Along the broad valley highway that leads from Winchester, General Sheridan had galloped to where his embattled lines had been reduced to a flying mob. While riding leisurely away from Winchester about nine o'clock he had heard unmistakable thunder-peals of artillery. Realizing that a battle was on in the front, he hastened forward, soon to be met, as he crossed Mill Creek, by the trains and men of his routed army, coming to the rear with appalling rapidity.

News from the field told him of the crushing defeat of his hitherto invincible regiments. The road was blocked by the retreating crowds as they pressed toward the rear. The commander was forced to take to the fields, and as his steed, flecked with foam, bore him onward, the disheartened refugees greeted him with cheers. Taking off his hat as he rode, he cried, "We will go back and recover our camps." The words

SHERIDAN'S CAVALRY IN THE SHENANDOAH—GENERAL TORBERT AND HIS STAFF

Sheridan appointed General Alfred T. A. Torbert Chief of Cavalry of the Army of the Shenandoah in August, 1864. General Torbert had been a regular army officer and was now a major-general of volunteers. This photograph was taken in 1864, on the vine-covered veranda of a Virginia mansion occupied as headquarters. In all the operations in the Valley during September and October, Sheridan made such good use of the cavalry that this branch of the service leaped into prominence, and received a goodly share of the praise for eliminating the Valley of Virginia from the field of war.

seemed to inspire the demoralized soldiers. Stragglers fell into line behind him; men turned to follow their magnetic leader back to the fight.

Vaulting his horse over the low barricade of rails, he dashed to the crest of the field. There was a flutter along the battle-line. The men from behind their protecting wall broke into thunderous cheers. From the rear of the soldiers there suddenly arose, as from the earth, a line of the regimental flags, which waved recognition to their leader. Color-bearers reassembled. The straggling lines re-formed. Early made another assault after one o'clock, but was easily repulsed.

It was nearly four o'clock when the order for the Federal advance was given. General Sheridan, hat in hand, rode in front of his infantry line that his men might see him. The Confederate forces now occupied a series of wooded crests. From out of the shadow of one of these timbered coverts, a column of gray was emerging. The Union lines stood waiting for the impending crash. It came in a devouring succession of volleys that reverberated into a deep and sullen roar. The Union infantry rose as one man and passed in among the trees. Not a shot was heard. Then, suddenly, there came a screaming, humming rush of shell, a roar of musketry mingling with the yells of a successful charge. Again the firing ceased, except for occasional outbursts. The Confederates had taken a new position and reopened with a galling fire. General Sheridan dashed along the front of his lines in personal charge of the attack. Again his men moved toward the lines of Early's fast thinning ranks. It was the final charge. The Union cavalry swept in behind the fleeing troops of Early and sent, again, his veteran army "whirling up the Valley."

The battle of Cedar Creek was ended; the tumult died away. The Federal loss had been about fifty-seven hundred; the Confederate over three thousand. Fourteen hundred Union prisoners were sent to Richmond. Never again would the gaunt specter of war hover over Washington.

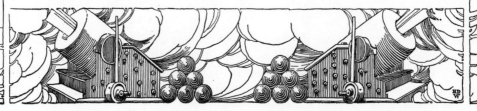

PART III
CLOSING IN

CHARLESTON, THE UNCAPTURED PORT

CONFEDERATE GARRISON COOKING DINNER
IN RUINED SUMTER—1864

MAKING SAND–BAGS INSIDE FORT SUMTER IN 1864

The story of how these photographs in unconquered Sumter were secured is a romance in itself. No one, North or South, can escape a thrill at the knowledge that several of them were actually taken in the beleaguered port by George S. Cook, the Confederate photographer. This adventurous spirit was one of the enterprising and daring artists who are now and then found ready when and where great events impend. He had risked his life in 1863, taking photographs of the Federal fleet as it was bombarding Sumter. The next year, while the magnificent organization of the Northern armies was closing in day by day; while the stores and homes and public buildings of Charleston were crumbling into pitiful ruins under the bombardment; while shoes and clothing and food were soaring to unheard-of prices in the depreciated Confederate currency, Cook still ingeniously secured his precious chemicals from the New York firm of Anthony & Co., which, curiously enough, was the same that supplied Brady. Cook's method was to smuggle his chemicals through as quinine! It is only the most fortunate of chances that preserved these photographs of the Confederates defending Charleston through the nearly half century which elapsed between their taking and the publication of the PHOTOGRAPH HISTORY. Editors of the work traveled thousands of miles and wrote thousands of letters in the search for such photographs. Of the priceless examples and specimens, several are here reproduced. How rare such pictures are may be judged by the fact that some of the men prominent and active in the circles of Confederate veterans, together with families of former Confederate generals and leaders, were unable to lay their hands on any such pictures. The natural disappointment in the South at the end of the war was such that photographers were forced to destroy all negatives, just as owners destroyed all the objects that might serve as souvenirs or relics of the terrible struggle, thinking, for the moment at least, that they could not bear longer the strain of brooding over the tragedy. Constant ferreting, following up clues, digging in dusty garrets amid relics buried generations ago, interviews with organizations like the Daughters of the Confederacy (to the Charleston chapter of which acknowledgment must be made for the picture of the Charleston Zouaves)—only after such exertions did it become possible to show on these pages the countenances and bearing and drill of the men who held Charleston against the ever-increasing momentum of the Northern power.

THE TOTTERING WALLS OF THE FORT SHORED UP

THE CONFEDERATE CAMP WASHINGTON. LOCKED IN ON THE SANDY BEACH NEAR SULLIVAN INLET
WHERE THE SOUTH CAROLINA WARRIORS MAINTAINED THEIR MILITARY POST FOR FOUR YEARS

CHARLESTON'S FAMOUS ZOUAVE CADETS DRILLING AT CASTLE PINCKNEY

REMAINS OF THE CIRCULAR CHURCH AND "SECESSION HALL,"
WHERE SOUTH CAROLINA DECIDED TO LEAVE THE UNION

"Prodigies of talent, audacity, intrepidity, and perseverance were exhibited in the attack, as in the defense of the city, which will assign to the siege of Charleston an exceptional place in military annals." Thus spoke the expert of the French *Journal of Military Science* in 1865, only a few months after this attack and defense had passed into history. Charleston was never captured. It was evacuated only after Sherman's advance through the heart of South Carolina had done what over five hundred and fifty-seven days of continuous attack and siege by the Federal army and navy could not do—make it untenable. When, on the night of February 17, 1865, Captain H. Huguenin, lantern in hand, made his last silent rounds of the deserted fort and took the little boat for shore, there ended the four years' defense of Fort Sumter, a feat of war unsurpassed in ancient or modern times—eclipsing (says an English military critic) "such famous passages as Sale's defense of Jellalabad against the Afghans and Havelock's obdurate tenure of the residency at Lucknow." Charleston with its defenses—Forts Sumter, Moultrie, Wagner, and Castle Pinckney from the sea and the many batteries on the land side—was the heart of the Confederacy,

and some of the most vigorous efforts of the Federal forces were made to capture it. Though "closed in" upon more than once, it never surrendered. But beleaguered it certainly was, in the sternest sense of the word. It is a marvel how the photographer, Cook, managed to get his supplies past the Federal army on one side and the Federal blockading fleet on the other. Yet there he remained at his post, catching with his lens the ruins of the uncaptured fort and the untaken city in 1864. How well he made these pictures may be seen on the pages preceding and the lower picture opposite. They furnish a glimpse into American history that most people—least of all the Confederate veterans themselves—never expected to enjoy. Those who actually knew what it was to be besieged in Petersburg, invaded in Georgia, starved in Tennessee, or locked up by a blockading fleet—such veterans have been astonished to find these authenticated photographs of the garrison beleaguered in the most important of Southern ports.

ON "THE BATTERY," CHARLESTON'S SPACIOUS PROMENADE

INSIDE FORT MOULTRIE—LOOKING EASTWARD

OUTSIDE FORT JOHNSON—SUMTER IN THE DISTANCE

GRIM-VISAGED WAR ALONG THE PALMETTO SHORE-LINE OF CHARLESTON HARBOR

THE DESOLATE INTERIOR OF SUMTER IN SEPTEMBER, 1863, AFTER THE GUNS OF THE FEDERAL FLEET
HAD BEEN POUNDING IT FOR MANY WEEKS

IN CHARLESTON AFTER THE BOMBARDMENT

So long as the Confederate flag flew over the ramparts of Sumter, Charleston remained the one stronghold of the South that was firmly held. That flag was never struck. It was lowered for an evacuation, not a surrender. The story of Charleston's determined resistance did not end in triumph for the South, but it did leave behind it a sunset glory, in which the valor and dash of the Federal attack is paralleled by the heroism and self-sacrifice of the Confederate defense, in spite of wreck and ruin.

PART III
CLOSING IN

THE INVESTMENT
OF PETERSBURG

ON GRANT'S CITY POINT RAILROAD—A NEW KIND
OF SIEGE GUN

WHERE THE PHOTOGRAPHER "DREW FIRE"

June 21, 1864, is the exact date of the photograph that made this picture and those on the three following pages. A story goes with them, told by one of the very men pictured here. As he looked at it forty-six years later, how vividly the whole scene came back to him! This is Battery B, First Pennsylvania Light Artillery, known as Cooper's Battery of the Fifth Corps, under General G. K. Warren. On the forenoon of this bright June day, Brady, the photographer, drove his light wagon out to the entrenchments. The Confederates lay along the sky-line near where rose the ruined chimney of a house belonging to a planter named Taylor. Approaching Captain Cooper, Brady politely asked if he could take a picture of the battery, when just about to fire. At the command, from force of habit, the men jumped to their positions. Hardly a face was turned toward the camera. They might be oblivious of its existence. The cannoneer rams home a charge. The gunner "thumbs the vent"—but "our friend the enemy" just over the hill observes the movement,

THE MAN WHO REMEMBERED

and, thinking it means business, opens up. Away goes Brady's horse, scattering chemicals and plates. The gun in the foreground is ready to send a shell across the open ground, but Captain Cooper reserves his fire. Brady, seeing his camera is uninjured, recalls his assistant and takes the other photographs, moving his instrument a little to the rear. And the man who saw it then, sees it all again to-day just as it was. He is even able to pick out many of the men by name. Their faces come back to him. Turning the page, may be seen Captain James H. Cooper, leaning on his sword, and Lieutenant Alcorn, on the extreme right. In the photograph above is Lieutenant Miller, back of the gun. Lieutenant James A. Gardner was the man who saw all this, and in the picture on the preceding page he appears seated on the trail of the gun to the left in the act of sighting the gun. The other officers shown in this picture were no longer living when, in 1911, he described the actors in the drama that the glass plate had preserved forty-six years.

JUST AS THE CAMERA CAUGHT THEM

General Warren's Corps had arrived in front of Petersburg on the 17th of June, 1864, and Battery B of the First Pennsylvania Light Artillery was put into position near the Avery house. Before them the Confederates were entrenched, with Beauregard in command. On the 17th, under cover of darkness, the Confederates fell back to their third line, just visible beyond the woods to the left in the first picture. Early the next morning Battery B was advanced to the line of entrenchments shown above, and a sharp interchange of artillery fire took place in the afternoon. So busy were both sides throwing up entrenchments and building forts and lunettes that there had been very little interchange of compliments in the way of shells or bullets at this point until Photographer Brady's presence and the gathering of men of Battery B at their posts called forth the well-pointed salute. Men soon became accustomed to artillery

THE MAN WHO REMEMBERED

and shell-fire. It was not long before Battery D was advanced from the position shown above to that held by the Confederates on the 21st of June, and there Fort Morton was erected, and beyond the line of woods the historic Fort Stedman, the scene of some of the bloodiest fighting before Petersburg. If you look closely at the second photograph, you will perceive a man in civilian clothes; Lieutenant Gardner (standing just back of the man with the haversack) thinks that this is Mr. Brady himself. There are fifteen people in this picture whom Lieutenant Gardner, of this battery, recognized after a lapse of forty-six years and can recall by name. There may be more gallant Pennsylvanians who, on studying this photograph, will see themselves and their comrades, surviving and dead, as once they fought on the firing-line.

"WHERE IS GRANT?"

This heavy Federal battery looks straight across the low-lying country to Petersburg. Its spires show in the distance. The smiling country is now to be a field of blood and suffering. For Grant's army, unperceived, has swung around from Cold Harbor, and "the Confederate cause was lost when Grant crossed the James," declared the Southern General Ewell. It was a mighty and a masterful move, practicable only because of the tremendous advantages the Federals held in the undisputed possession of the waterways, the tremendous fleet of steamers, barges, and river craft that made a change of base and transportation easy. Petersburg became the objective of the great army under Grant. His movements to get there had not been heralded; they worked like well-oiled machinery. "Where is Grant?" frantically asked Beauregard of Lee. The latter, by his despatches, shows that he could not answer with any certainty. In fact, up to the evening of the 13th of June, when the Second Corps, the advance of the Army of the Potomac, reached

HEAVY ARTILLERY JUST ARRIVED BEFORE PETERSBURG—1864

the north bank of the James, Lee could not learn the truth. By midnight of the 15th, bridges were constructed, and following the Second Corps, the Ninth began to cross. But already the Fifth and Sixth Corps and part of the Army of the James were on their way by water from White House to City Point. The Petersburg campaign had begun. Lee's army drew its life from the great fields and stock regions south and southwest of Richmond. With the siege of Petersburg, the railroad center of the state, this source of supply was more and more cut off, until six men were made to live on the allowance first given to each separate Southern soldier. Outnumbered three to one in efficient men, with the cold of winter coming on and its attendant hardships in prospect, no wonder the indomitable Southern bravery was tried to the utmost. Sherman was advancing. The beginning of the end was near.

THE BUSIEST PLACE IN DIXIE

City Point, just after its capture by Butler. From June, 1864, until April, 1865, City Point, at the juncture of the Appomattox and the James, was a point of entry and departure for more vessels than any city of the South including even New Orleans in times of peace. Here landed supplies that kept an army numbering, with fighting force and supernumeraries, nearly one hundred and twenty thousand well-supplied, well-fed, well-contented, and well-munitioned men in the field. This was the marvelous base —safe from attack, secure from molestation. It was meals and money that won at Petersburg, the bravery of full stomachs and warm-clothed bodies against the desperation of starved and shivering out-numbered men. A glance at this picture tells the story. There is no need of rehearsing charges, counter-charges, mines, and counter-mines. Here lies the reason—Petersburg had to fall. As we look back with a retro-spective eye on this scene of plenty and abundance, well may the American heart be proud that only a few miles away were men of their own blood enduring the hardships that the defenders of Petersburg suffered in the last campaign of starvation against numbers and plenty.

THE TEEMING WHARVES

No signs of warfare, no marching men or bodies lying on the blood-soaked sward, are needed to mark this as a war-time photograph. No laboring boss would have fallen into the position of the man on the top of the embankment. Four years in uniform has marked this fellow; he has caught the eye of the camera and drawn up at "Attention," shoulders back, heels together, and arms hanging at his side. There is no effect of posing, no affectation here; he stands as he has been taught to stand. He is a soldier. No frowning cannon could suggest the military note more clearly. Just beyond the point to the left, above the anchorage and the busy wharves, are General Grant's headquarters at City Point. From here it was but a few minutes' ride on the rough military rail-

SUPPLIES FOR AN ARMY—BELOW, AN ENGINE OF THE U. S. MILITARY RAILROAD

way to where the one hundred and ten thousand fighting men lay entrenched with the sixty-six thousand veterans in gray opposed to them. A warship lying where these vessels lie could drop a 12-inch shell into Petersburg in modern days. From here President Lincoln set out to see a grand review and witnessed a desperate battle. Here General Sherman, fresh from his victorious march from Atlanta to the sea, came up in the little gunboat *Bat* to visit Grant. During the last days, when to the waiting world peace dawned in sight, City Point, to all intents and purposes, was the National Capital, for from here President Lincoln held communication with his Cabinet officers, and replied to Stanton's careful injunctions "to take care of himself" with the smiling assurance that he was in the hands of Grant and the army.

A MOVABLE MENACE

The 17,000-pound mortar, "Dictator," was run on a flat-car from point to point on a curve of the railroad track along the bank of
the Appomattox.   It was manned and served before Petersburg, July 9–31, 1864, by Company G, First Connecticut Artillery, during
its stay.   When its charge of fourteen pounds of powder was first fired, the car broke under the shock; but a second car was prepared

THE RAILROAD MORTAR

by the engineers, strengthened by additional beams, tied strongly by iron rods and covered with iron-plating. This enabled the "Dictator" to be used at various points, and during the siege it fired in all forty-five rounds—nineteen of which were fired during the battle of the Crater. It was given at last a permanent emplacement near Battery No. 4—shown on the following pages.

THE DICTATORS OF THE "DICTATOR"

Here are the men who did the thinking for the great mortar that rests so stolidly in the midst of the group. They are its cabinet ministers, artillerymen every one, versed in the art of range-finding and danger-angles, of projectory arcs and the timing of shell-fuses. In the front line the two figures from left to right are Colonel H. L. Abbott, First Connecticut Heavy Artillery, and General H. J. Hunt, Chief of Artillery. In the second, or rear line, also from left to right, the first is Captain F. A. Pratt; second (just behind Colonel Abbott), Captain E. C. Dow; fourth (just behind and to General Hunt's left), Major T. S. Trumbull.

A PERMANENT POSITION

THE RAILROAD GUN'S EXECUTIVE COMMITTEE

These nine men are the executive committee that controlled the actions of the great mortar, and a glance at them shows that they were picked men for the job—men in the prime of life, brawny and strong—they were the slaves of their pet monster. Some shots from this gun went much farther than they were ever intended, carrying their fiery trails over the Confederate entrenchments and exploding within the limits of the town itself, over two and a quarter miles. The roar of the explosion carried consternation to all within hearing. In the lower picture is the great mortar resting in the position it occupied longest, near Battery No. 4.

POINTED TOWARD PETERSBURG

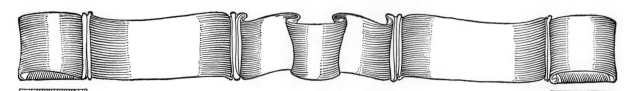

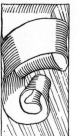

THE INVESTMENT OF PETERSBURG

The cause was lost, but the end was not yet. The noble Army of Northern Virginia, once, twice conqueror of empire, must bite the dust before its formidable adversary.—*Lieutenant-General James Longstreet, C.S.A., in "From Manassas to Appomattox."*

THE disastrous failure of the Union army on the sanguinary battlefield of Cold Harbor, in June, 1864, destroyed Grant's last chance to turn the Confederate right flank north of Richmond. He could still try to turn Lee's left and invest Richmond from the north, but this would not have interfered with the lines of supply over the James River and the railroads from the South and West. The city could have resisted for an indefinite time. If Richmond were to fall, it must be besieged from the south.

The movement from Cold Harbor began after dark on June 12th, and Meade's whole army was safely over the James River at Wilcox's Landing by midnight on the 16th of June. The little city of Petersburg is situated twenty-one miles south of Richmond on the southern bank of the Appomattox, a small stream threading its way through the Virginia tidewater belt, almost parallel with the James, into which it flows. In itself the town was of little value to either army. But it was the doorway to Richmond from the south. Three railroads from Southern points converged here. To reach the Confederate capital, Petersburg must first be battered down. At this time the town ought not to have been difficult to capture, for its defenses were but weak entrenchments, and they were not formidably manned. General Smith, who reached Bermuda Hundred by water, with his corps, on the night of the 14th, was ordered by Butler, under instructions from Grant, to move on Petersburg at daylight.

THE DIGGERS AT PETERSBURG—1864

There was not a day during the whole of the nine months' siege of Petersburg that pick and shovel were idle. At first every man had to turn to and become for the nonce a laborer in the ditches. But in an army of one hundred and ten thousand men, in the maintenance of camp discipline, there were always soldier delinquents who for some infringement of military rules or some neglected duty were sentenced to extra work under the watchful eye of an officer and an armed sentry. Generally, these small punishments meant six to eight hours' digging, and here we see a group of Federal soldiers thus employed. They are well within the outer chain of forts, near where the military road joins the Weldon & Petersburg Railroad. The presence of the camera man has given them a moment's relaxation.

The Confederate forces at Petersburg were now commanded by General Beauregard. He had conjectured what Grant's plans might be, and in order to prevent the capture of the town and enable him to hold Butler at Bermuda Hundred, he called on Lee for immediate reenforcement. But the latter, not yet convinced that Grant was not moving on Richmond, sent only Hoke's division. On the day after Meade began to move his army toward the James, Lee left the entrenchments at Cold Harbor. Keeping to the right and rear of the Union lines of march, by the morning of the 16th, he had thrown a part of his force to the south side of the James, and, by the evening of the 18th, the last of the regiments had united with those of Beauregard, and the two great opposing armies were once more confronting each other—this time for a final settlement of the issue at arms. The Union army outnumbered that of the Confederates, approximately, two to one.

The contest for Petersburg had already begun. For two days the rapidly gathering armies had been combating with each other. On June 15th, General Smith pushed his way toward the weakly entrenched lines of the city. General Beauregard moved his men to an advanced line of rifle-pits. Here the initial skirmish occurred. The Confederates were driven to the entrenched works of Petersburg, and not until evening was a determined attack made upon them. At this time Hancock, " The Superb," came on the field. Night was falling but a bright moon was shining, and the Confederate redoubts, manned by a little over two thousand men, might have been carried by the Federals. But Hancock, waiving rank, yielded to Smith in command. No further attacks were made and a golden opportunity for the Federals was lost.

By the next morning the Confederate trenches were beginning to fill with Hoke's troops. The Federal attack was not made until afternoon, when the fighting was severe for three hours, and some brigades of the Ninth Corps assisted the Second and Eighteenth. The Confederates were driven back

MAHONE, "THE HERO OF THE CRATER"

General William Mahone, C. S. A. It was through the promptness and valor of General Mahone that the Southerners, on July 30, 1864, were enabled to turn back upon the Federals the disaster threatened by the hidden mine. On the morning of the explosion there were but eighteen thousand Confederates left to hold the ten miles of lines about Petersburg. Everything seemed to favor Grant's plans for the crushing of this force. Immediately after the mine was sprung, a terrific cannonade was opened from one hundred and fifty guns and mortars to drive back the Confederates from the breach, while fifty thousand Federals stood ready to charge upon the panic-stricken foe. But the foe was not panic-stricken long. Colonel McMaster, of the Seventeenth South Carolina, gathered the remnants of General Elliott's brigade and held back the Federals massing at the Crater until General Mahone arrived at the head of three brigades. At once he prepared to attack the Federals, who at that moment were advancing to the left of the Crater. Mahone ordered a counter-charge. In his inspiring presence it swept with such vigor that the Federals were driven back and dared not risk another assault. At the Crater, Lee had what Grant lacked—a man able to direct the entire engagement.

some distance and made several unsuccessful attempts during the night to recover their lost ground. Before the next noon, June 17th, the battle was begun once more. Soon there were charges and countercharges along the whole battle-front. Neither side yielded. The gray and blue lines surged back and forth through all the afternoon. The dusk of the evening was coming on and there was no prospect of a cessation of the conflict. The Union troops were pressing strongly against the Confederates. There was a terrible onslaught, which neither powder nor lead could resist. A courier, dashing across the field, announced to Beauregard the rout of his army. Soon the panic-stricken Confederate soldiers were swarming in retreat. The day seemed to be irreparably lost. Then, suddenly in the dim twilight, a dark column was seen emerging from the wooded ravines to the rear, and General Gracie, with his brigade of twelve hundred gallant Alabamians, plunged through the smoke, leapt into the works, and drove out the Federals. Now the battle broke out afresh, and with unabated fury continued until after midnight.

Early on the morning of the 18th, a general assault was ordered upon the whole Confederate front. The skirmishers moved forward but found the works, where, on the preceding day, such desperate fighting had occurred, deserted. During the night, Beauregard had successfully made a retrograde movement. He had found the old line too long for the number of his men and had selected a shorter one, from five hundred to one thousand yards to the rear, that was to remain the Confederate wall of the city during the siege. But there were no entrenchments here and the weary battle-worn soldiers at once set to work to dig them, for the probable renewal of the contest. In the darkness and through the early morning hours, the men did with whatever they could find as tools—some with their bayonets, or split canteens, while others used their hands. This was the beginning of those massive works that defied the army of Grant before Petersburg for nearly a year. By noon

WHAT EIGHT THOUSAND POUNDS OF POWDER DID

The Crater, torn by the mine within Elliott's Salient. At dawn of July 30, 1864, the fifty thousand Federal troops waiting to make a charge saw a great mass of earth hurled skyward like a water-spout. As it spread out into an immense cloud, scattering guns, carriages, timbers, and what were once human beings, the front ranks broke in panic; it looked as if the mass were descending upon their own heads. The men were quickly rallied; across the narrow plain they charged, through the awful breach, and up the heights beyond to gain Cemetery Ridge. But there were brave fighters on the other side still left, and delay among the Federals enabled the Confederates to rally and re-form in time to drive the Federals back down the steep sides of the Crater. There, as they struggled amidst the horrible débris, one disaster after another fell upon them. Huddled together, the mass of men was cut to pieces by the canister poured upon them from well-planted Confederate batteries. At last, as a forlorn hope, the colored troops were sent forward; and they, too, were hurled back into the Crater and piled upon their white comrades.

of that day they had assumed quite a defensive character. Again the Federals attempted to break the Confederate line. All during the afternoon, regiments were hurled against the newly made works. Artillery bombarded here and there with but little effect. At times the attacking force would come within thirty yards of the entrenchments, only to recoil. Night came, and in front of the trenches the ranks of the Union dead lay thickly strewn.

During these four days, divisions and batteries were being added to both armies, and when the Union assault was successfully repulsed in the twilight hours of June 18, 1864, those two grim adversaries, Grant and Lee, stood in full battle array—this time for the final combat. The siege of Petersburg began the next day.

It was a beautiful June Sabbath. There was only the occasional boom of some great gun as it thundered along the Appomattox, or the fretful fire of picket musketry, to break the stillness. But it was not a day of rest. With might and main the two armies busily plied with pick and spade and axe.

In an incredibly short time, as if by magic, impregnable bastioned works began to loom about Petersburg. More than thirty miles of frowning redoubts, connected with extended breastworks, strengthened by mortar batteries and field-works of every description, lined the fields near the Appomattox. In front were abatis—bushy entanglements and timber slashings. Bomb-proofs and parapets completed these cordons of offense and defense—the one constructed to keep the Federals out; the other to keep the Confederates in. So formidable were the works, that only twice during the siege was there any serious attempt made by either army upon the entrenchments of the other, and both assaults were failures.

It was Grant's purpose to extend his lines to the south and west, until they would finally envelop Lee's right flank, and then strike at the railroads, upon which the Confederate army and Richmond depended for supplies. On June 21st, two corps,

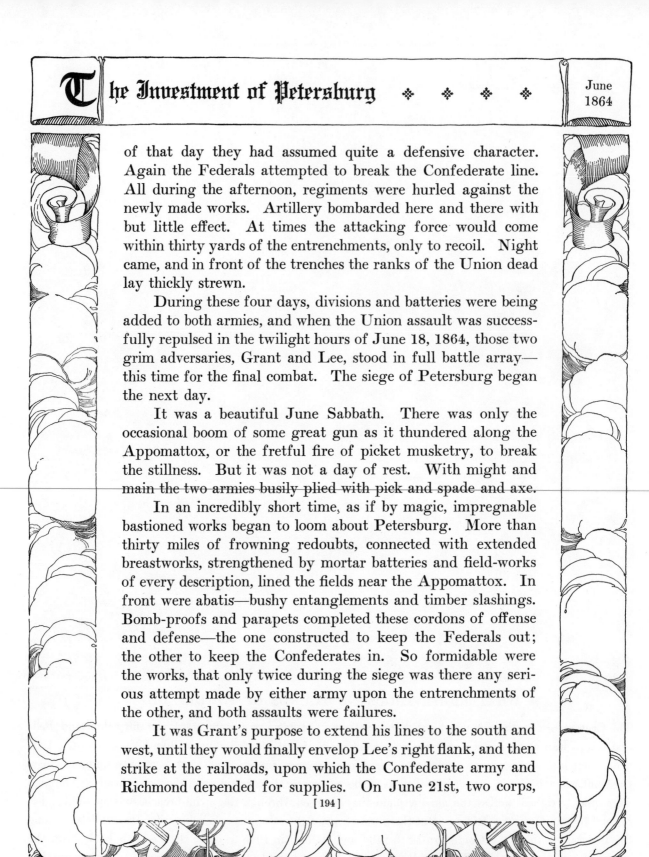

COLORED TROOPS AFTER THE DISASTER OF THE MINE

On July 30, 1864, at the exploding of the hidden mine under Elliott's salient, the strong Confederate fortification opposite. The plan of the mine was conceived by Colonel Henry Pleasants and approved by Burnside, whose Ninth Corps, in the assaults of June 17th and 18th, had pushed their advance position to within 130 yards of the Confederate works. Pleasants had been a mining engineer and his regiment, the Forty-eighth Pennsylvania, was composed mainly of miners from the coal regions. The work was begun on June 25th and prosecuted under the greatest difficulties. In less than a month Pleasants had the main gallery, 510.8 feet long, the left lateral gallery, 37 feet long, and the right lateral gallery, 38 feet long, all completed. While

FORT MORTON, BEFORE PETERSBURG

finishing the last gallery, the right one, the men could hear the Confederates working in the fortification above them, trying to locate the mine, of which they had got wind. It was General Burnside's plan that General Edward Ferrero's division of colored troops should head the charge when the mine should be sprung. The black men were kept constantly on drill and it was thought, as they had not seen any very active service, that they were in better condition to lead the attack than any of the white troops. In the upper picture are some of the colored troops drilling and idling in camp after the battle of the Crater, in which about three hundred of their comrades were lost. The lower picture shows the entrenchments at Fort Morton, whence they sallied forth.

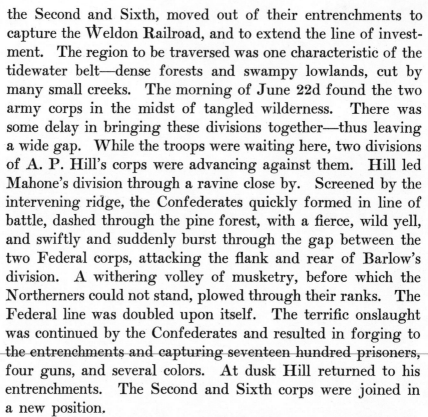

the Second and Sixth, moved out of their entrenchments to capture the Weldon Railroad, and to extend the line of investment. The region to be traversed was one characteristic of the tidewater belt—dense forests and swampy lowlands, cut by many small creeks. The morning of June 22d found the two army corps in the midst of tangled wilderness. There was some delay in bringing these divisions together—thus leaving a wide gap. While the troops were waiting here, two divisions of A. P. Hill's corps were advancing against them. Hill led Mahone's division through a ravine close by. Screened by the intervening ridge, the Confederates quickly formed in line of battle, dashed through the pine forest, with a fierce, wild yell, and swiftly and suddenly burst through the gap between the two Federal corps, attacking the flank and rear of Barlow's division. A withering volley of musketry, before which the Northerners could not stand, plowed through their ranks. The Federal line was doubled upon itself. The terrific onslaught was continued by the Confederates and resulted in forging to the entrenchments and capturing seventeen hundred prisoners, four guns, and several colors. At dusk Hill returned to his entrenchments. The Second and Sixth corps were joined in a new position.

At the same time the cavalry, under General James H. Wilson, including Kautz's division, started out to destroy the railroads. The Confederate cavalry leader, General W. H. F. Lee, followed closely, and there were several sharp engagements. The Union cavalry leader succeeded, however, in destroying a considerable length of track on both the Weldon and South Side railroads between June 22d and 27th. Then he turned for the works at Petersburg, but found it a difficult task. The woods were alive with Confederates. Infantry swarmed on every hand. Cavalry hung on the Federals' flanks and rear at every step. Artillery and wagon trains were being captured constantly. During the entire night of June 28th, the Union troopers were constantly

AN OASIS IN THE DESERT OF WAR

Throughout all the severe fighting south of Petersburg the Aiken house and its inhabitants remained un-harmed, their safety respected by the combatants on both sides. The little farmhouse near the Weldon Railroad between the lines of the two hostile armies was remembered for years by many veterans on both sides. When Grant, after the battle of the Crater, began to force his lines closer to the west of Petersburg the Weldon Railroad became an objective and General Warren's command pushed forward on August 18, 1864, and after a sharp fight with the Confederates, established themselves in an advance position near Ream's Station. Three gallant assaults by the Confederates on the three succeeding days failed to dis-lodge the Federals. In these engagements the tide of battle ebbed and flowed through the woods and through thickets of vine and underbrush more impenetrable even than the "Wilderness."

harassed on every hand. They fell back in every direction. The two divisions became separated and, driven at full speed in front of the Confederate squadrons, became irreparably broken, and when they finally reached the Union lines—the last of them on July 2d—it was in straggling parties in wretched plight.

On June 25th, Sheridan returned from his raid on the Virginia Central Railroad. He had encountered Hampton and Fitzhugh Lee at Trevilian Station on June 11th, and turned back after doing great damage to the Railroad. His supply of ammunition did not warrant another engagement.

Now ensued about five weeks of quiet during which time both generals were strengthening their fortifications. However, the Federals were covertly engaged in an undertaking that was destined to result in a conspicuous failure. While the Northern soldiers were enduring the rays of a blistering July sun behind the entrenchments, one regiment was delving underneath in the cool, moist earth. It was the Forty-eighth Pennsylvania regiment of the Ninth Corps, made up mostly of miners from the upper Schuylkill coal-district of Pennsylvania. From June 25th until July 23d, these men were boring a tunnel from the rear of the Union works to a point underneath the Confederate fortifications. Working under the greatest difficulties, with inadequate tools for digging, and hand-barrows made out of cracker boxes, in which to carry away the earth, there was excavated in this time a passage-way five hundred and ten feet in length, terminating in left and right lateral galleries, thirty-seven and thirty-eight feet respectively. Into these lateral galleries eight thousand pounds of gunpowder were packed and tamped, and a fuse attached. On July 28th, everything was ready for the match to be applied and for the gigantic upheaval, sure to follow.

Grant, in order to get a part of Lee's army away, had sent Hancock's corps and two divisions of cavalry north of the James, as if he might attack Richmond. The ruse was successful. Preparations were then completed to fire the mine,

THE SAFE END OF THE MOVING BATTERY

The Federals were not the first to use a gun mounted on railway trucks. In the defense of Richmond during the Seven Days' and at the attack on Savage's Station the Confederates had mounted a field-piece on a flat-car and it did severe damage to the Federal camps. But they possessed no such formidable armored truck as this. Propelled by man-power, no puffing locomotive betrayed its whereabouts; and as it rolled along the tracks, firing a shot from time to time, it must have puzzled the Confederate outposts. This was no clumsy experimental toy, but a land gunboat on wheels, armored with iron-plating, backed by massive beams.

At the Globe Tavern General Warren made his headquarters after the successful advance of August 18th, and from here he directed the maneuvers by which the Federal lines to the westward of Petersburg were drawn closer and closer to cut off the last of Confederate communications. The country hereabout was the theater of constant activities on both sides during the autumn, and skirmishing between the hostile forces was kept up far into November. The old tavern was the very center of war's alarms. Yet the junior officers of the staff were not wholly deprived of amenities, since the Aiken house near by domiciled no less than seven young ladies, a fact that guaranteed full protection to the family during the siege. A strong safeguard was encamped within the garden railing to protect the house from intrusion by stragglers.

THE GLOBE TAVERN, WELDON RAILROAD

tear a gap in the Confederate works, and rush the Union troops into the opening. A division of colored soldiers, under General Ferrero, was selected and thoroughly drilled to lead the charge. Everything was in readiness for a successful attack, but at the last moment the colored division was replaced by the First Division of the Ninth Corps, under General Ledlie. The explosion was to take place at half-past three on the morning of July 30th. The appointed time had come. Everything required was in its place, ready to perform its part. Less than four hundred feet in front were the Confederate works, and directly beneath them were four tons of powder waiting to perform their deadly work.

Then the Federals applied the match. The fuse sputtered as the consuming flame ate its way to the magazines within the tunnel. The men waited in breathless suspense. In another moment the earth would be rent by the subterranean upheaval. Minute after minute passed. The delay was unbearable. Something must have gone wrong. A gallant sergeant of the Forty-eighth Pennsylvania, Henry Rees by name, volunteered to enter the gallery and find out why the fuse had failed. It had parted within fifty feet of the powder. Rees returned for materials to resplice the fuse, and on the way out met Lieutenant Jacob Douty. The two men made the necessary repairs; the fire was again applied, and then—at twenty minutes to five —the ground underneath trembled as if by an earthquake, a solid mass of earth shot two hundred feet into the air, and a flame of fire burst from the vent as from a new-born volcano. Smoke rose after the ascending column. There in mid-air, earth, cannon, timbers, sand-bags, human beings, smoke, and fire, hung suspended an instant, and bursting asunder, fell back into and around the smoking crater where three hundred Confederates had met their end.

When the cloud of smoke had cleared away, the waiting troops of Ledlie charged, Colonel Marshall at the head of the Second Brigade, leading the way. They came to an immense

FEDERAL FIGHTERS AT REAMS' STATION

These men of Barlow's First division of the Second Corps, under command of Brigadier-General Nelson A. Miles, gallantly repulsed the second and third attacks by the Confederates upon Reams' Station, where Hancock's men were engaged in destroying the Weldon Railroad on August 24, 1864. In the upper picture is seen Company D of the famous "Clinton Guard," as the Sixty-first New York Infantry called itself. The picture was taken at Falmouth in April, 1863, and the trim appearance of the troops on dress parade indicates nothing of the heavy losses they sustained when at Fredericksburg, led by Colonel Miles, they fought with distinguished bravery against Jackson's men. Not only the regiment but its officers attained renown, for the regiment had the honor to be commanded by able soldiers. First, Francis C. Barlow was its colonel, then Nelson A. Miles, then Oscar A. Broady, and lastly George W. Scott.

opening, one hundred and seventy feet long, sixty feet wide, and thirty feet deep. They climbed the rim, looked down into the pit at the indescribable horrors, and then plunged into the crater. Here, they huddled in inextricable confusion. The two brigades poured in until the yawning pit was crowded with the disorganized mass. All semblance of organization vanished. In the confusion, officers lost power to recognize, much less to control, their own troops. A regiment climbed the slope, but finding that no one was following, went back to the crater.

The stunned and paralyzed Confederates were not long in grasping the situation. Batteries were soon planted where they could sweep the approach to the crater. This cut off the possibility of retreat. Then into the pit itself poured a stream of wasting fire, until it had become a veritable slaughter-house. Into this death-trap, the sun was sending down its shafts until it became as a furnace. Attempts were made to pass around the crater and occupy Cemetery Hill, which had been the objective of the Federals. But the withering fire prevented. The colored troops, who had been originally trained to lead in the charge, now tried to save the day. They passed by the side of the crater and started for the crest of the hill. They had not gone far when the Confederates delivered a countercharge that broke their ranks.

The Confederates were being rapidly reenforced. At eight o'clock Mahone's division of Georgians and Virginians swept onto the field, to the scene of the conflict. They had been hidden from view until they were almost ready for the charge. The Federals, seeing the intended attack, made ready to resist it. Lieutenant-Colonel Bross of the Twenty-ninth Colored regiment sprang upon the edge of the crater with the Union flag in his hand and was quickly struck down. The men began to scramble out after him, but before a line could be formed the Confederates were on them, and the Federals were driven back into the pit, already overflowing with the living and the dead. Huge missiles from Confederate mortars

FORT MAHONE—"FORT DAMNATION"

RIVES' SALIENT

TRAVERSES AGAINST CROSS–FIRE

GRACIE'S SALIENT, AND OTHER FORTS ALONG THE TEN MILES OF DEFENSES

Dotted with formidable fortifications such as these, Confederate works stretched for ten miles around Petersburg. Fort Mahone was situated opposite the Federal Fort Sedgwick at the point where the hostile lines converged most closely after the battle of the Crater. Owing to the constant cannonade which it kept up, the Federals named it Fort Damnation, while Fort Sedgwick, which was no less active in reply, was known to the Confederates as Fort Hell. Gracie's salient, further north on the Confederate line, is notable as the point in front of which General John B. Gordon's gallant troops moved to the attack on Fort Stedman, the last desperate effort of the Confederates to break through the Federal cordon. The views of Gracie's salient show the French form of *chevaux-de-frise*, a favorite protection against attack much employed by the Confederates.

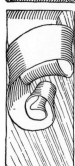

rained into the awful chasm. The muskets left by the retreating Federals were thrown like pitchforks among the huddled troops. The shouts, the explosions, the screams, and groans added to the horror of the carnage. The clay in the pit was drenched with the blood of the dead and dying. The Southerners pushed in from both sides of the crater, forming a cordon of bayonets about it. The third and final charge was made, about two in the afternoon, and the bloody fight at the crater was ended as the brigade commanders followed Burnside's order to withdraw to the Federal lines. Both of Ledlie's brigade commanders were captured in the crater. The total Federal loss in this disastrous affair was over thirty-nine hundred, of whom all but one hundred were in the Ninth Corps. The Confederates lost about one thousand.

Now came a season of comparative quiet about Petersburg, except for the strategic maneuverings of the Federals who were trying to find weak places in the Confederate walls. On August 18th, however, Grant sent General Warren to capture the Weldon Railroad. Desperate fighting was to be expected, for this was one of the important routes along which supplies came to the Confederate capital. The Federal forces moved out quietly from their camp, but the alert Beauregard was ready for them. By the time Warren had reached the railroad, near the Globe Tavern, four miles from Petersburg, he was met by a force under Heth which at once drove him back. Rallying his troops, Warren entrenched on the railroad.

The fight was renewed on the next day, when, strongly reenforced by Lee, the Confederates burst suddenly upon the Federals. Mahone thrust his gallant division through the Federal skirmish line and then turned and fought from the rear, while another division struck the right wing. The Union force was soon in confusion; more than two thousand were taken prisoners, including General Joseph Hayes, and but for the arrival of the Ninth Corps, the field would have been lost. Two days later, Lee again attacked the position by massing

THE DEFENDERS' COUNTER–MINE

The sinister burrow opens within the Confederate Fort Mahone, seen more fully at the top of the preceding page. Fort Sedgwick, directly opposite Fort Mahone, had been originally captured from the Confederates and its defenses greatly strengthened. So galling did its fire become, and so important was its position to the Confederates, that early in the siege they planned to lay a mine in order to regain it and perhaps break through the Federal lines and raise the siege. The distance across the intervening plain was but fifteen hundred feet. The Confederates ran their main gallery somewhat more than a third of this distance before finally abandoning it, the difficulties of the undertaking having proved too great. This fort was named after General William Mahone, who was conspicuously engaged in the defense of Petersburg, and whose gallant conduct at the explosion of the Federal mine under Elliott's salient saved the day to the Confederates. Weak as were the defenses of Petersburg in comparison with the strong investing works of the Federals, they withstood all assaults during nine months except when Elliott's salient was captured during the battle of the Crater.

WHERE GORDON'S MEN ATTACKED, FORT STEDMAN

At Fort Stedman was directed the gallant onslaught of Gordon's men that resulted so disastrously for the Confederates on the 25th of March. For no troops could stand the heavy artillery and musketry fire directed on them from both flanks and from the rear at daylight. What was left of this brave division, shattered and broken, drifted back to their own line. It was the forlorn hope of Lee's beleaguered army. Fort McGilvery was less than one-half a mile from the Appomattox River, just north of the City

THE POWDER MAGAZINE AT FORT McGILVERY

Point Railroad, at the extreme right of the Federal line. It was one of the earliest forts completed, being built in July, 1864. Fort Morton, named after Major St. Clair Morton, killed by a sharpshooter's bullet in July, 1864, was renowned as the place from which the mine was dug and from which the disastrous attempt to break through the Confederate lines was made on July 30th. Fort Morton lay almost in the center of the most active portion of the lines, and was about a mile south of Fort Stedman.

FORT MORTON, OPPOSITE THE CRATER

A POSITION OF COMPLETE DEFENSE, FORT MEIKLE

THE SWEEPING LINES OF FORT SEDGWICK

Almost every one of the forts in the long Federal line was named after some gallant officer who had lost his life in action. They might have been termed the memorial forts. The almost circular entrenchment, strengthened by logs and sandbags and defended by the formidable abatis of tree trunks, was named after Lieutenant-Colonel George W. Meikle, of the Twentieth Indiana Volunteers. From the position shown we are looking directly into Petersburg. Military observers have conceded that the fortifications surrounding Petersburg were the most remarkable of any in the world. Before the end of October, 1864, the Army of the Potomac occupied a formidable cordon of defenses that stretched for more than thirty-two miles, and comprised thirty-six forts and fifty batteries. For years succeeding the war excursions were run from New York and from all parts of the country to this historic ground. It took three days to complete the tour. Then most of the forts were in the condition in which we see them pictured here.

FORT RICE, AS THE CONFEDERATES SAW IT

thirty guns and pouring volley after volley of fierce fire into the ranks of blue. The Union lines stood firm and returned the fire. Finally, the fighting Mahone, with his matchless band, was brought to turn the tide. The attack was made with his usual impetuousness, but the blue-clad riflemen withstood the terrific charge, and the serried ranks of Mahone fell back. The Weldon Railroad was lost to the Confederacy.

Hancock, who had returned from the north side of the James, proceeded to destroy the road, without hindrance, until three days later, August 25th, when General A. P. Hill made his appearance and Hancock retreated to some hastily built breastworks at Ream's Station. The Confederate attack was swift and terrific. The batteries broke the Union lines. The men were panic-stricken and were put to flight. Hancock tried in vain to rally his troops, but for once this splendid soldier, who had often seen his men fall but not fail, was filled with agony at the rout of his soldiers. Their rifle-pits had been lost, their guns captured and turned upon them. Finally, General Nelson A. Miles succeeded in rallying a few men, formed a new line and, with the help of some dismounted cavalry, partly regained their former position. The night came on and, under cover of darkness, Hancock withdrew his shattered columns.

The two great opposing armies had now come to a deadlock. For weeks they lay in their entrenchments, each waiting for the other to move. Each knew that it was an almost hopeless task to assail the other's position. At the end of September, General Ord, with the Eighteenth Corps, and General Birney, with the Tenth, captured Fort Harrison north of the James, securing a vantage-point for threatening Richmond. The Union line had been extended to within three miles of the South Side Railroad, and on October 27th, practically the whole Army of the Potomac was put in motion to secure this other avenue of transportation to Richmond. After severe fighting for one day the attempt was given up, and the Union troops returned to the entrenchments in front of Petersburg.

PART III

CLOSING IN

SHERMAN'S FINAL CAMPAIGNS

WAITING FOR THE MARCH TO THE SEA

After the capture of Atlanta, says Sherman, "all the army, officers and men, seemed to relax more or less and sink into a condition of idleness." All but the engineers! For it was their task to construct the new lines of fortifications surveyed by General Poe so that the city could be held by a small force while troops were detached in pursuit of Hood. The railroad lines and bridges along the route by which the army had come had to be repaired so that the sick and wounded and prisoners could be sent back to Chattanooga and the army left free of encumbrances before undertaking the march to the sea. In the picture, their work practically done, the men of the First Michigan Engineers are idling about the old salient of the Confederate lines southeast of Atlanta near which their camp

CAMP OF THE FIRST MICHIGAN ENGINEERS AT ATLANTA, AUTUMN, 1864

was pitched. The organization was the best known and one of the most efficient of the Michigan regiments. It was composed almost entirely of mechanics and trained engineers and mustered eighteen hundred strong. The work of these men dotted the whole theater of war in the West. The bridges and trestles of their making, if combined, would have to be measured by the mile, and many of them were among the most wonderful feats of military engineering. The First Michigan Engineers could fight, too, for a detachment of them under Colonel Innes at Stone's River successfully defended the army trains from an attack by Wheeler's cavalry. The march to the sea could not have been made without these men.

[c]

THE LAST TRAIN WAITING

This series of three photographs, taken a few minutes apart, tells the story of Sherman's order evicting the inhabitants of Atlanta, September, 1864. A train of cars stands empty beside the railroad station. But in the second picture piles of household effects appear on some of the cars. This disordered embarkation takes little time; the wagon train advancing in the first picture has not yet passed the camera. By the time the shutter clicked for the bottom photograph, every car was heaped with household effects—bedding and pitiful packages of a dozen kinds. Unfortunate owners dangle their feet from the cars;

others, white-bonnetted women in the group, cluster 'around their chairs and other belongings not yet shipped. The last train of refugees was ready to leave Atlanta. Sherman outlined very clearly his reasons for ordering the evacuation of the city by its inhabitants. He wrote on September 17, 1864: "I take the ground that Atlanta is a conquered place, and I propose to use it purely for our own military purposes, which are inconsistent with its habitation by the families of a brave people. I am shipping them *all*, and by next Wednesday the town will be a real military town, with no women boring me every order I give."

CHATTELS APPEAR ON TOP OF THE CARS

THE CARS PILED HIGH WITH HOUSEHOLD GOODS—THE LAST TRAIN OF INHABITANTS READY
TO LEAVE ATLANTA

THE END OF THE RAILROAD DEPOT

The crumpled wreck is hardly recognizable as the same spacious train-shed that sheltered such human activities as those pictured opposite, yet this is the Atlanta depot. But such destruction was far from the wanton outrage that it naturally seemed to those whose careers it rudely upset. As early as September, Sherman, with Atlanta on his hands, had deemed it essential for the prosecutions of his movements and the end of the war that the city should be turned into a military post. So he determined "to remove the entire civil population, and to deny to all civilians from the rear the expected profits of civil trade. This was to avoid the necessity of a heavy garrison to hold the position, and prevent the crippling of the armies in the fields as heretofore by 'detachments' to guard and protect the interests of a hostile population." The railroad station, as the heart of the modern artery of business, was second in importance only to the buildings and institutions of the Confederate government itself, as a subject for elimination.

SHERMAN'S FINAL CAMPAIGNS

I only regarded the march from Atlanta to Savannah as a "shift of base," as the transfer of a strong army, which had no opponent, and had finished its then work, from the interior to a point on the sea coast, from which it could achieve other important results. I considered this march as a means to an end, and not as an essential act of war. Still, then as now, the march to the sea was generally regarded as something extraordinary, something anomalous, something out of the usual order of events; whereas, in fact, I simply moved from Atlanta to Savannah, as one step in the direction of Richmond, a movement that had to be met and defeated, or the war was necessarily at an end.—*General W. T. Sherman, in his "Memoirs."*

THE march to the sea, in which General William T. Sherman won undying fame in the Civil War, is one of the greatest pageants in the world's warfare—as fearful in its destruction as it is historic in its import. But this was not Sherman's chief achievement; it was an easy task compared with the great campaign between Chattanooga and Atlanta through which he had just passed. "As a military accomplishment it was little more than a grand picnic," declared one of his division commanders, in speaking of the march through Georgia and the Carolinas.

Almost immediately after the capture of Atlanta, Sherman, deciding to remain there for some time and to make it a Federal military center, ordered all the inhabitants to be removed. General Hood pronounced the act one of ingenious cruelty, transcending any that had ever before come to his notice in the dark history of the war. Sherman insisted that his act was one of kindness, and that Johnston and Hood themselves had done the same—removed families from their homes—in other places. The decision was fully carried out.

THE ATLANTA BANK BEFORE THE MARCH TO THE SEA

As this photograph was taken, the wagons stood in the street of Atlanta ready to accompany the Federals in their impending march to the sea. The most interesting thing is the bank building on the corner, completely destroyed, although around it stand the stores of merchants entirely untouched. Evidently there had been here faithful execution of Sherman's orders to his engineers—to destroy all buildings and property of a public nature, such as factories, foundries, railroad stations, and the like; but to protect as far as possible strictly private dwellings and enterprises. Those of a later generation who witnessed the growth of Atlanta within less than half a century after this photograph was taken, and saw tall office-buildings and streets humming with industry around the location in this photograph, will find in it an added fascination.

Many of the people of Atlanta chose to go southward, others to the north, the latter being transported free, by Sherman's order, as far as Chattanooga.

Shortly after the middle of September, Hood moved his army from Lovejoy's Station, just south of Atlanta, to the vicinity of Macon. Here Jefferson Davis visited the encampment, and on the 22d he made a speech to the homesick Army of Tennessee, which, reported in the Southern newspapers, disclosed to Sherman the new plans of the Confederate leaders. These involved nothing less than a fresh invasion of Tennessee, which, in the opinion of President Davis, would put Sherman in a predicament worse than that in which Napoleon found himself at Moscow. But, forewarned, the Federal leader prepared to thwart his antagonists. The line of the Western and Atlantic Railroad was more closely guarded. Divisions were sent to Rome and to Chattanooga. Thomas was ordered to Nashville, and Schofield to Knoxville. Recruits were hastened from the North to these points, in order that Sherman himself might not be weakened by the return of too many troops to these places.

Hood, in the hope of leading Sherman away from Atlanta, crossed the Chattahoochee on the 1st of October, destroyed the railroad above Marietta and sent General French against Allatoona. It was the brave defense of this place by General John M. Corse that brought forth Sherman's famous message, "Hold out; relief is coming," sent by his signal officers from the heights of Kenesaw Mountain, and which thrilled the North and inspired its poets to eulogize Corse's bravery in verse. Corse had been ordered from Rome to Allatoona by signals from mountain to mountain, over the heads of the Confederate troops, who occupied the valley between. Reaching the mountain pass soon after midnight, on October 5th, Corse added his thousand men to the nine hundred already there, and soon after daylight the battle began. General French, in command of the Confederates, first

"TUNING UP"—A DAILY DRILL IN THE CAPTURED FORT

Here Sherman's men are seen at daily drill in Atlanta. This photograph has an interest beyond most war pictures, for it gives a clear idea of the soldierly bearing of the men that were to march to the sea. There was an easy carelessness in their appearance copied from their great commander, but they were never allowed to become slouchy. Sherman was the antithesis of a martinet, but he had, in the Atlanta campaign, molded his army into the "mobile machine" that he desired it to be, and he was anxious to keep the men up to this high pitch of efficiency for the performance of still greater deeds. No better disciplined army existed in the world at the time Sherman's "bummers" set out for the sea.

summoned Corse to surrender, and, receiving a defiant answer, opened with his guns. Nearly all the day the fire was terrific from besieged and besiegers, and the losses on both sides were very heavy.

During the battle Sherman was on Kenesaw Mountain, eighteen miles away, from which he could see the cloud of smoke and hear the faint reverberation of the cannons' boom. When he learned by signal that Corse was there and in command, he said, "If Corse is there, he will hold out; I know the man." And he did hold out, and saved the stores at Allatoona, at a loss of seven hundred of his men, he himself being among the wounded, while French lost more than a thousand.

General Hood continued to move northward to Resaca and Dalton, passing over the same ground on which the two great armies had fought during the spring and summer. He destroyed the railroads, burned the ties, and twisted the rails, leaving greater havoc, if possible, in a country that was already a wilderness of desolation. For some weeks Sherman followed Hood in the hope that a general engagement would result. But Hood had no intention to fight. He went on to the banks of the Tennessee opposite Florence, Alabama. His army was lightly equipped, and Sherman, with his heavily burdened troops, was unable to catch him. Sherman halted at Gaylesville and ordered Schofield, with the Twenty-third Corps, and Stanley, with the Fourth Corps, to Thomas at Nashville.

Sherman thereupon determined to return to Atlanta, leaving General Thomas to meet Hood's appearance in Tennessee. It was about this time that Sherman fully decided to march to the sea. Some time before this he had telegraphed to Grant: "Hood . . . can constantly break my roads. I would infinitely prefer to make a wreck of the road . . . send back all my wounded and worthless, and, with my effective army, move through Georgia, smashing things to the sea." Grant thought it best for Sherman to destroy Hood's army

CUTTING LOOSE FROM THE BASE, NOVEMBER 12TH

"On the 12th of November the railroad and telegraph communications with the rear were broken and the army stood detached from all friends, dependent on its own resources and supplies," writes Sherman. Meanwhile all detachments were marching rapidly to Atlanta with orders to break up the railroad en route and "generally to so damage the country as to make it untenable to the enemy." This was a necessary war measure. Sherman, in a home letter written from Grand Gulf, Mississippi, May 6, 1863, stated clearly his views regarding the destruction of property. Speaking of the wanton havoc wrought on a fine plantation in the path of the army, he added: "It is done, of course, by the accursed stragglers who won't fight but hang behind and disgrace our cause and country. Dr. Bowie had fled, leaving everything on the approach of our troops. Of course, devastation marked the whole path of the army, and I know all the principal officers detest the infamous practice as much as I do. Of course, I expect and do take corn, bacon, ham, mules, and everything to support an army, and don't object much to the using of fences for firewood, but this universal burning and wanton destruction of private property is not justified in war."

first, but Sherman insisted that his plan would put him on the offensive rather than the defensive. He also believed that Hood would be forced to follow him. Grant was finally won to the view that if Hood moved on Tennessee, Thomas would be able to check him. He had, on the 11th of October, given permission for the march. Now, on the 2d of November, he telegraphed Sherman at Rome: "I do not really see that you can withdraw from where you are to follow Hood without giving up all we have gained in territory. I say, then, go on as you propose." It was Sherman, and not Grant or Lincoln, that conceived the great march, and while the march itself was not seriously opposed or difficult to carry out, the conception and purpose were masterly.

Sherman moved his army by slow and easy stages back to Atlanta. He sent the vast army stores that had collected at Atlanta, which he could not take with him, as well as his sick and wounded, to Chattanooga, destroyed the railroad to that place, also the machine-shops at Rome and other places, and on November 12th, after receiving a final despatch from Thomas and answering simply, "Despatch received—all right," the last telegraph line was severed, and Sherman had deliberately cut himself off from all communication with the Northern States. There is no incident like it in the annals of war. A strange event it was, as Sherman observes in his memoirs. "Two hostile armies marching in opposite directions, each in the full belief that it was achieving a final and conclusive result in a great war."

For the next two days all was astir in Atlanta. The great depot, round-house, and machine-shops were destroyed. Walls were battered down; chimneys pulled over; machinery smashed to pieces, and boilers punched full of holes. Heaps of rubbish covered the spots where these fine buildings had stood, and on the night of November 15th the vast débris was set on fire. The torch was also applied to many places in the business part of the city, in defiance of the strict orders of

THE BUSTLE OF DEPARTURE FROM ATLANTA

Sherman's men worked like beavers during their last few days in Atlanta. There was no time to be lost; the army was gotten under way with that precision which marked all Sherman's movements. In the upper picture, finishing touches are being put to the railroad, and in the lower is seen the short work that was made of such public buildings as might be of the slightest use in case the Confederates should recapture the town. As far back as Chattanooga, while plans for the Atlanta campaign were being formed, Sherman had been revolving a subsequent march to the sea in case he was successful. He had not then made up his mind whether it should be in the direction of Mobile or Savannah, but his Meridian campaign, in Mississippi, had convinced him that the march was entirely feasible, and gradually he worked out in his mind its masterly details. At seven in the morning on November 16th, Sherman rode out along the Decatur road, passed his marching troops, and near the spot where his beloved McPherson had fallen, paused for a last look at the city. "Behind us," he says, "lay Atlanta, smouldering and in ruins, the black smoke rising high in air and hanging like a pall over the ruined city." All about could be seen the glistening gun-barrels and white-topped wagons, "and the men marching steadily and rapidly with a cheery look and swinging pace." Some regimental band struck up "John Brown," and the thousands of voices of the vast army joined with a mighty chorus in song. A feeling of exhilaration pervaded the troops. This marching into the unknown held for them the allurement of adventure, as none but Sherman knew their destination. But as he worked his way past them on the road, many a group called out, "Uncle Billy, I guess Grant is waiting for us at Richmond." The devil-may-care spirit of the troops brought to Sherman's mind grave thoughts of his own responsibility. He knew that success would be regarded as a matter of course, but should he fail the march would be set down as "the wild adventure of a crazy fool." He had no intention of marching directly to Richmond, but from the first his objective was the seacoast, at Savannah or Port Royal, or even Pensacola, Florida.

RUINS IN ATLANTA

Captain Poe, who had the work of destruction in charge.
The court-house and a large part of the dwellings escaped
the flames.

Preparations for the great march were made with extreme care. Defective wagons and horses were discarded; the
number of heavy guns to be carried along was sixty-five, the
remainder having been sent to Chattanooga. The marching
army numbered about sixty thousand, five thousand of whom
belonged to the cavalry and eighteen hundred to the artillery.
The army was divided into two immense wings, the Right,
the Army of the Tennessee, commanded by General O. O.
Howard, and consisting of the Fifteenth and Seventeenth
corps, and the Left, the Army of Georgia, by General Henry
W. Slocum, composed the Fourteenth and Twentieth corps.
Sherman himself was in supreme command. There were
twenty-five hundred wagons, each drawn by six mules; six
hundred ambulances, with two horses each, while the heavy
guns, caissons, and forges were each drawn by eight horses.
A twenty days' supply of bread, forty of coffee, sugar, and
salt was carried with the army, and a large herd of cattle was
driven on foot.

In Sherman's general instructions it was provided that
the army should march by four roads as nearly parallel as
possible, except the cavalry, which remained under the direct
control of the general commanding. The army was directed
"to forage liberally on the country," but, except along the
roadside, this was to be done by organized foraging parties
appointed by the brigade commanders. Orders were issued
forbidding soldiers to enter private dwellings or to commit
any trespass. The corps commanders were given the option
of destroying mills, cotton-gins, and the like, and where the
army was molested in its march by the burning of bridges,
obstructing the roads, and so forth, the devastation should be
made "more or less relentless, according to the measure of
such hostility." The cavalry and artillery and the foraging

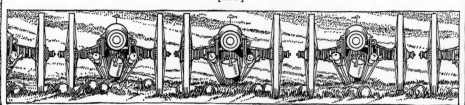

THE GUNS THAT SHERMAN TOOK ALONG

In Hood's hasty evacuation of Atlanta many of his guns were left behind. These 12-pounder Napoleon bronze field-pieces have been gathered by the Federals from the abandoned fortifications, which had been equipped entirely with field artillery, such as these. It was an extremely useful capture for Sherman's army, whose supply of artillery had been somewhat limited during the siege, and still further reduced by the necessity to fortify Atlanta. On the march to the sea Sherman took with him only sixty-five field-pieces. The Negro refugees in the lower picture recall an embarrassment of the march to the sea. "Negroes of all sizes" flocked in the army's path and stayed there, a picturesque procession, holding tightly to the skirts of the army which they believed had come for the sole purpose of setting them free. The cavalcade of Negroes soon became so numerous that Sherman became anxious for his army's sustenance, and finding an old gray-haired black at Covington, Sherman explained to him carefully that if the Negroes continued to swarm after the army it would fail in its purpose and they would not get their freedom. Sherman believed that the old man spread this news to the slaves along the line of march, and in part saved the army from being overwhelmed by the contrabands.

NEGROES FLOCKING IN THE ARMY'S PATH

parties were permitted to take horses, mules, and wagons from the inhabitants without limit, except that they were to discriminate in favor of the poor. It was a remarkable military undertaking, in which it was intended to remove restrictions only to a sufficient extent to meet the requirements of the march. The cavalry was commanded by General Judson Kilpatrick, who, after receiving a severe wound at Resaca, in May, had gone to his home on the banks of the Hudson, in New York, to recuperate, and, against the advice of his physician, had joined the army again at Atlanta.

On November 15th, most of the great army was started on its march, Sherman himself riding out from the city next morning. As he rode near the spot where General McPherson had fallen, he paused and looked back at the receding city with its smoking ruins, its blackened walls, and its lonely, tenantless houses. The vision of the desperate battles, of the hope and fear of the past few months, rose before him, as he tells us, "like the memory of a dream." The day was as perfect as Nature ever gives. The men were hilarious. They sang and shouted and waved their banners in the autumn breeze. Most of them supposed they were going directly toward Richmond, nearly a thousand miles away. As Sherman rode past them they would call out, "Uncle Billy, I guess Grant is waiting for us at Richmond." Only the commanders of the wings and Kilpatrick were entrusted with the secret of Sherman's intentions. But even Sherman was not fully decided as to his objective—Savannah, Georgia, or Port Royal, South Carolina—until well on the march.

There was one certainty, however—he was fully decided to keep the Confederates in suspense as to his intentions. To do this the more effectually he divided his army at the start, Howard leading his wing to Gordon by way of McDonough as if to threaten Macon, while Slocum proceeded to Covington and Madison, with Milledgeville as his goal. Both were secretly instructed to halt, seven days after starting, at Gor-

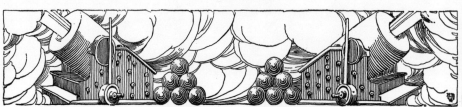

The task of General Hardee in defending Savannah was one of peculiar difficulty. He had only eighteen thousand men, and he was uncertain where Sherman would strike. Some supposed that Sherman would move at once upon Charleston, but Hardee argued that the Union army would have to establish a new base of supplies on the seacoast before attempting to cross the numerous deep rivers and swamps of South Carolina. Hardee's task therefore was to hold Savannah just as long as possible, and then to withdraw northward to unite with the troops which General Bragg was assembling, and with the detachments scattered at this time over the Carolinas. In protecting his position around Savannah, Fort McAllister was of prime importance, since it commanded the Great Ogeechee River in such a way as to prevent the approach of the Federal fleet,

THE DEFENDER OF SAVANNAH

Sherman's dependence for supplies. It was accordingly manned by a force of two hundred under command of Major G. W. Anderson, provided with fifty days' rations for use in case the work became isolated. This contingency did not arrive. About noon of December 13th, Major Anderson's men saw troops in blue moving about in the woods. The number increased. The artillery on the land side of the fort was turned upon them as they advanced from one position to another, and sharpshooters picked off some of their officers. At half-past four o'clock, however, the long-expected charge was made from three different directions, so that the defenders, too few in number to hold the whole line, were soon overpowered. Hardee now had to consider more narrowly the best time for withdrawing from the lines at Savannah.

COPYRIGHT, 1911, PATRIOT PUB. CO.

FORT McALLISTER—THE LAST BARRIER TO THE SEA

FROM SAVANNAH'S ROOF–TOPS—1865

No detailed maps, no written description, could show better than these clear and beautiful photographs the almost impregnable position of the city.   For miles the higher ground on which it was possible to build lay on the south bank of the river.   From only one direction, the westward, could Savannah be approached without difficult feats of engineering, and here the city was guarded along the lines of the Georgia Central Railroad by strong entrenchments, held by General Hardee's men.   Sherman perceived that a frontal attack would not only be costly but effort thrown away, and determined that after he had taken Fort McAllister he would make a combination with the naval forces and invest the city from all sides.   The march to the sea would not be completed until such a combination had been effected.   On the evening of the 12th Sherman held consultation with General Howard and with General Hazen

OVER THE IMPASSABLE MARSHES

of the Fifteenth Corps. The latter received orders from Sherman in person to march down the right bank of the Ogeechee and to assault and carry Fort McAllister by storm. He was well informed as to the latter's defenses and knew that its heavier batteries pointed seaward, but that it was weak if attacked from the rear. General Hardee's brave little force of 10,000 were soon to hear the disheartening news that they were outflanked, that McAllister had fallen, and that Sherman and Admiral Dahlgren, in command of the fleet in Ossabaw Sound, were in communication. This was on the 13th of December, 1864, but it was not until nine days later that Sherman was able to send his historic despatch to President Lincoln that began with: "I beg to present you, as a Christmas gift, the City of Savannah."

[c]

don and Milledgeville, the latter the capital of Georgia, about a hundred miles to the southeast. These two towns were about fifteen miles apart.

General Hood and General Beauregard, who had come from the East to assist him, were in Tennessee, and it was some days after Sherman had left Atlanta that they heard of his movements. They realized that to follow him would now be futile. He was nearly three hundred miles away, and not only were the railroads destroyed, but a large part of the intervening country was utterly laid waste and incapable of supporting an army. The Confederates thereupon turned their attention to Thomas, who was also in Tennessee, and was the barrier between Hood and the Northern States.

General Sherman accompanied first one corps of his army and then another. The first few days he spent with Davis' corps of Slocum's wing. When they reached Covington, the negroes met the troops in great numbers, shouting and thanking the Lord that "deliverance" had come at last. As Sherman rode along the streets they would gather around his horse and exhibit every evidence of adoration.

The foraging parties consisted of companies of fifty men. Their route for the day in which they obtained supplies was usually parallel to that of the army, five or six miles from it. They would start out before daylight in the morning, many of them on foot; but when they rejoined the column in the evening they were no longer afoot. They were astride mules, horses, in family carriages, farm wagons, and mule carts, which they packed with hams, bacon, vegetables, chickens, ducks, and every imaginable product of a Southern farm that could be useful to an army.

In the general orders, Sherman had forbidden the soldiers to enter private houses; but the order was not strictly adhered to, as many Southern people have since testified. Sherman declares in his memoirs that these acts of pillage and violence were exceptional and incidental. On one occasion Sherman

WATERFRONT AT SAVANNAH, 1865

Savannah was better protected by nature from attack by land or water than any other city near the Atlantic seaboard. Stretching to the north, east, and southward lay swamps and morasses through which ran the river-approach of twelve miles to the town. Innumerable small creeks separated the marshes into islands over which it was out of the question for an army to march without first building roads and bridging miles of waterways. The Federal fleet had for months been on the blockade off the mouth of the river, and Savannah had been closed to blockade runners since the fall of Fort Pulaski in April, 1862. But obstructions and powerful batteries held the river, and Fort McAllister, ten miles to the south, on the Ogeechee, still held the city safe in its guardianship.

FORT McALLISTER, THAT HELD THE FLEET AT BAY

saw a man with a ham on his musket, a jug of molasses under his arm, and a big piece of honey in his hand. As the man saw that he was observed by the commander, he quoted audibly to a comrade, from the general order, "forage liberally on the country." But the general reproved him and explained that foraging must be carried on only by regularly designated parties.

It is a part of military history that Sherman's sole purpose was to weaken the Confederacy by recognized means of honorable warfare; but it cannot be denied that there were a great many instances, unknown to him, undoubtedly, of cowardly hold-ups of the helpless inhabitants, or ransacking of private boxes and drawers in search of jewelry and other family treasure. This is one of the misfortunes of war—one of war's injustices. Such practices always exist even under the most rigid discipline in great armies, and the jubilation of this march was such that human nature asserted itself in the license of warfare more than on most other occasions. General Washington met with similar situations in the American Revolution. The practice is never confined to either army in warfare.

Opposed to Sherman were Wheeler's cavalry, and a large portion of the Georgia State troops which were turned over by General G. W. Smith to General Howell Cobb. Kilpatrick and his horsemen, proceeding toward Macon, were confronted by Wheeler and Cobb, but the Federal troopers drove them back into the town. However, they issued forth again, and on November 21st there was a sharp engagement with Kilpatrick at Griswoldville. The following day the Confederates were definitely checked and retreated.

The night of November 22d, Sherman spent in the home of General Cobb, who had been a member of the United States Congress and of Buchanan's Cabinet. Thousands of soldiers encamped that night on Cobb's plantation, using his fences for camp-fire fuel. By Sherman's order, everything on the

THE FIFTEEN MINUTES' FIGHT

Across these ditches at Fort McAllister, through entangling abatis, over palisading, the Federals had to fight every inch of their way against the Confederate garrison up to the very doors of their bomb-proofs, before the defenders yielded on December 13th. Sherman had at once perceived that the position could be carried only by a land assault. The fort was strongly protected by ditches, palisades, and plentiful abatis; marshes and streams covered its flanks, but Sherman's troops knew that shoes and clothing and abundant rations were waiting for them just beyond it, and had any of them been asked if they could take the fort their reply would have been in the words of the poem: "Ain't we simply got to take it?" Sherman selected for the honor of the assault General Hazen's second division of the Fifteenth Corps, the same which he himself had commanded at Shiloh and Vicksburg. Gaily the troops crossed the bridge on the morning of the 13th. Sherman was watching anxiously through his glass late in the afternoon when a Federal steamer came up the river and signaled the query: "Is Fort McAllister taken?" To which Sherman sent reply: "Not yet, but it will be in a minute." At that instant Sherman saw Hazen's troops emerge from the woods before the fort, "the lines dressed as on parade, with colors flying." Immediately dense clouds of smoke belching from the fort enveloped the Federals. There was a pause; the smoke cleared away, and, says Sherman, "the parapets were blue with our men." Fort McAllister was taken.

plantation movable or destructible was carried away next day,
or destroyed. Such is the price of war.

By the next night both corps of the Left Wing were
at Milledgeville, and on the 24th started for Sandersville.
Howard's wing was at Gordon, and it left there on the day
that Slocum moved from Milledgeville for Irwin's Cross-
roads. A hundred miles below Milledgeville was a place called
Millen, and here were many Federal prisoners which Sherman
greatly desired to release. With this in view he sent Kilpatrick toward Augusta to give the impression that the army was
marching thither, lest the Confederates should remove the prisoners from Millen. Kilpatrick had reached Waynesboro when
he learned that the prisoners had been taken away. Here he
again encountered the Confederate cavalry under General
Wheeler. A sharp fight ensued and Kilpatrick drove Wheeler
through the town toward Augusta. As there was no further
need of making a feint on Augusta, Kilpatrick turned back
toward the Left Wing. Wheeler quickly followed and at
Thomas' Station nearly surrounded him, but Kilpatrick cut his
way out. Wheeler still pressed on and Kilpatrick chose a good
position at Buck Head Creek, dismounted, and threw up breastworks. Wheeler attacked desperately, but was repulsed, and
Kilpatrick, after being reenforced by a brigade from Davis'
corps, joined the Left Wing at Louisville.

On the whole, the great march was but little disturbed by
the Confederates. The Georgia militia, probably ten thousand in all, did what they could to defend their homes and
their firesides; but their endeavors were futile against the vast
hosts that were sweeping through the country. In the skirmishes that took place between Atlanta and the sea the militia
was soon brushed aside. Even their destroying of bridges and
supplies in front of the invading army checked its progress
but for a moment, as it was prepared for every such emergency.
Wheeler, with his cavalry, caused more trouble, and engaged
Kilpatrick's attention a large part of the time. But even he

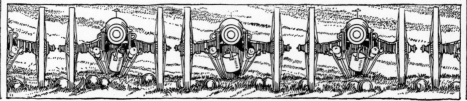

A BIG GUN AT FORT McALLISTER

Fort McAllister is at last in complete possession of the Federals, and a group of the men who had charged over these ramparts has arranged itself before the camera as if in the very act of firing the great gun that points seaward across the marshes, toward Ossabaw Sound. There is one very peculiar thing proved by this photograph—the gun itself is almost in a fixed position as regards range and sweep of fire. Instead of the elevating screw to raise or depress the muzzle, there has been substituted a block of wood wedged with a heavy spike, and the narrow pit in which the gun carriage is sunk admits of it being turned but a foot or so to right or left. It evidently controlled one critical point in the river, but could not have been used in lending any aid to the repelling of General Hazen's attack. The officer pointing with outstretched arm is indicating the very spot at which a shell fired from his gun would fall. The men in the trench are artillerymen of General Hazen's division of the Fifteenth Corps; their appearance in their fine uniforms, polished breastplates and buttons, proves that Sherman's men could not have presented the ragged appearance that they are often pictured as doing in the war-time sketches. That Army and Navy have come together is proved also by the figure of a marine from the fleet, who is standing at "Attention" just above the breach of the gun. Next, leaning on his saber, is a cavalryman, in short jacket and chin-strap.

did not seriously retard the irresistible progress of the legions of the North.

The great army kept on its way by various routes, covering about fifteen miles a day, and leaving a swath of destruction, from forty to sixty miles wide, in its wake. Among the details attendant upon the march to the sea was that of scientifically destroying the railroads that traversed the region. Battalions of engineers had received special instruction in the art, together with the necessary implements to facilitate rapid work. But the infantry soon entered this service, too, and it was a common sight to see a thousand soldiers in blue standing beside a stretch of railway, and, when commanded, bend as one man and grasp the rail, and at a second command to raise in unison, which brought a thousand railroad ties up on end. Then the men fell upon them, ripping rail and tie apart, the rails to be heated to a white heat and bent in fantastic shapes about some convenient tree or other upright column, the ties being used as the fuel with which to make the fires. All public buildings that might have a military use were burned, together with a great number of private dwellings and barns, some by accident, others wantonly. This fertile and prosperous region, after the army had passed, was a scene of ruin and desolation.

As the army progressed, throngs of escaped slaves followed in its trail, "from the baby in arms to the old negro hobbling painfully along," says General Howard, "negroes of all sizes, in all sorts of patched costumes, with carts and broken-down horses and mules to match." Many of the old negroes found it impossible to keep pace with the army for many days, and having abandoned their homes and masters who could have cared for them, they were left to die of hunger and exposure in that naked land.

After the Ogeechee River was crossed, the character of the country was greatly changed from that of central Georgia. No longer were there fertile farms, laden with their Southern

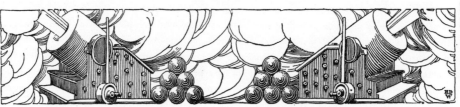

THE SPOILS OF VICTORY

THE TROOPS THAT MARCHED

TO THE SEA

BECOME DAY–LABORERS

Here are the men that marched to the sea doing their turn as day-laborers, gleefully trundling their wheelbarrows, gathering up everything of value in Fort McAllister to swell the size of Sherman's "Christmas present." Brigadier-General W. B. Hazen, after his men had successfully stormed the stubbornly defended fort, reported the capture of twenty-four pieces of ordnance, with their equipment, forty tons of ammunition, a month's supply of food for the garrison, and the small arms of the command. In the upper picture the army engineers are busily at work removing a great 48-pounder 8-inch Columbiad that had so long repelled the Federal fleet. There is always work enough and to spare for the engineers both before and after the capture of a fortified position. In the wheelbarrows is a harvest of shells and torpedoes. These deadly instruments of destruction had been relied upon by the Confederates to protect the land approach to Fort McAllister, which was

much less strongly defensible on that side than at the waterfront. While Sherman's army was approaching Savannah one of his officers had his leg blown off by a torpedo buried in the road and stepped on by his horse. After that Sherman set a line of Confederate prisoners across the road to march ahead of the army, and no more torpedoes were found. After the capture of Fort McAllister the troops set to work gingerly scraping about wherever the ground seemed to have been disturbed, trying to find and remove the dangerous hidden menaces to life. At last the ground was rendered safe and the troops settled down to the occupation of Fort McAllister where the bravely fighting little Confederate garrison had held the key to Savannah. The city was the first to fall of the Confederacy's Atlantic seaports, now almost locked from the outside world by the blockade. By the capture of Fort McAllister, which crowned the march to the sea, Sherman had numbered the days of the war. The fall of the remaining ports was to follow in quick succession, and by Washington's Birthday, 1865, the entire coast-line was to be in possession of the Federals.

SHERMAN'S TROOPS DISMANTLING FORT McALLISTER

harvests of corn and vegetables, but rather rice plantations and great pine forests, the solemn stillness of which was broken by the tread of thousands of troops, the rumbling of wagon-trains, and by the shouts and music of the marching men and of the motley crowd of negroes that followed.

Day by day Sherman issued orders for the progress of the wings, but on December 2d they contained the decisive words, " Savannah." What a tempting prize was this fine Southern city, and how the Northern commander would add to his laurels could he effect its capture! The memories cling-ing about the historic old town, with its beautiful parks and its magnolia-lined streets, are part of the inheritance of not only the South, but of all America. Here Oglethorpe had bartered with the wild men of the forest, and here, in the days of the Revolution, Count Pulaski and Sergeant Jasper had given up their lives in the cause of liberty.

Sherman had partially invested the city before the middle of December; but it was well fortified and he refrained from assault. General Hardee, sent by Hood from Tennessee, had command of the defenses, with about fifteen thousand men. And there was Fort McAllister on the Ogeechee, protecting the city on the south. But this obstruction to the Federals was soon removed. General Hazen's division of the Fifteenth Corps was sent to capture the fort. At five o'clock in the afternoon of the 13th Hazen's men rushed through a shower of grape, over abatis and hidden torpedoes, scaled the parapet and captured the garrison. That night Sherman boarded the *Dandelion*, a Union vessel, in the river, and sent a message to the outside world, the first since he had left Atlanta.

Henceforth there was communication between the army and the Federal squadron, under the command of Admiral Dahlgren. Among the vessels that came up the river there was one that was received with great enthusiasm by the sol-diers. It brought mail, tons of it, for Sherman's army, the accumulation of two months. One can imagine the eagerness

With much foresight, General Hardee had not waited for Sherman's approach, but before the Federal forces could prevent, had marched out with his force with the intention of joining Johnston. There were in the neighborhood of some twenty thousand inhabitants in the city of Savannah when Sherman took possession, and the man who had made a Christmas present of their city to Lincoln had no easy task before him to preserve order and to meet the many claims made upon his time by the responsibilities of city government. But Sherman regarded the war as practically over and concluded that he would make it optional with the citizens and their families to remain in the city under a combination of military and civil government, or rejoin their friends in Augusta or the still unsurrendered but beleaguered town of Charleston. After consulting with Dr. Arnold, the Mayor, the City Council was assembled and authorized to take charge generally of the interests of those who remained. About two hundred of the families of men still fighting in the Confederate army were sent by steamer under a flag of truce to Charleston, but the great majority preferred to remain

DESTRUCTION THAT FOLLOWED WAR

RUINS AT SAVANNAH, 1865

in Savannah. During the night before the Federal occupation, fires had broken out and a scene of chaos had resulted. There is no doubt that Sherman had destroyed vast amounts of Confederate stores, that he had torn up railway tracks and burned stations, and that his army had subsisted on what supplies it could gather from the country through which it had passed, but in the bitter feelings of the times, rumors scattered by word of mouth and repeated by newspapers as deliberate accusations had gone to the extreme in stating the behavior of his army. Yet, nevertheless, many Confederate officers still in the field confided their families to Sherman's keeping and left them in their city homes. Cotton was contraband and although the Confederates sought to destroy it, as was just and proper, at Savannah thirty-one bales of cotton became a prize to the army. The newspapers were not suppressed entirely and two were allowed to be published, although under the closest censorship. But as we look at the ruins of fine houses and desolated homes we begin to appreciate more fully Sherman's own solemn declaration that "War is Hell."

with which these war-stained veterans opened the longed-for letters and sought the answer to the ever-recurring question, "How are things at home?"

Sherman had set his heart on capturing Savannah; but, on December 15th, he received a letter from Grant which greatly disturbed him. Grant ordered him to leave his artillery and cavalry, with infantry enough to support them, and with the remainder of his army to come by sea to Virginia and join the forces before Richmond. Sherman prepared to obey, but hoped that he would be able to capture the city before the transports would be ready to carry him northward.

He first called on Hardee to surrender the city, with a threat of bombardment. Hardee refused. Sherman hesitated to open with his guns because of the bloodshed it would occasion, and on December 21st he was greatly relieved to discover that Hardee had decided not to defend the city, that he had escaped with his army the night before, by the one road that was still open to him, which led across the Savannah River into the Carolinas. The stream had been spanned by an improvised pontoon bridge, consisting of river-boats, with planks from city wharves for flooring and with old car-wheels for anchors. Sherman immediately took possession of the city, and on December 22d he sent to President Lincoln this message: "I beg to present to you, as a Christmas gift, the city of Savannah, with one hundred and fifty heavy guns and plenty of ammunition, and also about twenty-five thousand bales of cotton." As a matter of fact, over two hundred and fifty guns were captured, and thirty-one thousand bales of cotton. General Hardee retreated to Charleston.

Events in the West now changed Grant's views as to Sherman's joining him immediately in Virginia. On the 16th of December, General Thomas accomplished the defeat and utter rout of Hood's army at Nashville. In addition, it was found that, owing to lack of transports, it would take at least two months to transfer Sherman's whole army by sea. There-

HOMEWARD BOUND

Wagon-trains leaving Savannah. Here the wagon-trains of the victorious army are ready just outside of Savannah for the march northward. The troops, in high glee and splendid condition, again abundantly supplied with food and clothes, are impatient to be off. But a difficult country confronts them—a land of swollen streams and nearly tropical swamps like that in the lower photograph, picturesque enough, but "bad going" for teams. Near this the Fifteenth Corps passed on its way to Columbia. It is typical of the spongy ground over which the army must pass, building causeways and corduroying roads. Sherman himself rated this homeward march as a greater achievement than his much-sung "Atlanta to the Sea."

THE CAPTURED CAPITAL OF SOUTH CAROLINA

This striking photograph of Columbia will stir the memory of many a veteran. One recalls marching through the two small gates in the fence with his comrades. He points out the broken wagon wheels and old iron pipe in the foreground, and explains that they are the remains of dummy cannon which the Confederates had constructed and mounted there as Sherman's army approached. There were some real cannon in the town, however, and in a window of one of the houses one of these had been mounted and opened on the Federals, who had to bring up one of their own small guns before they could dislodge the men bravely defending Columbia.

RUINS OF THE UNFINISHED COURTHOUSE AT COLUMBIA

On the 16th of February Sherman was opposite Columbia. A few shells had been thrown into the city, but it was never under bombardment. But on the morning of the 17th the mayor had come out to surrender the city, and before the troops had entered a high wind was carrying about flakes of cotton that had in some manner become ignited. With the aid of an old fire-engine the soldiers endeavored to put out the conflagration, but much property was destroyed. In the afternoon the wind moderated and the fire was controlled.

THE CONGAREE RIVER BRIDGE

THE EMPTY PRISON

THE PRESBYTERIAN LECTURE-ROOM

HUNT'S HOUSE

FREIGHT DEPOT, SOUTH CAROLINA RAILROAD

THE CATHOLIC CONVENT

AS COLUMBIA LOOKED AFTER SHERMAN'S ARMY PASSED, IN 1865

HOME OF STATE SURGEON-GENERAL GIBBS

THE LUTHERAN CHURCH

EVANS AND COGGSWELL'S PRINTING SHOP

DESERTED MAIN STREET

THE METHODIST EPISCOPAL CHURCH, WASHINGTON STREET

THE SOUTH CAROLINA RAILROAD OFFICES

WHAT WAR BROUGHT TO THE CAPITAL OF SOUTH CAROLINA

[c]

fore, it was decided that Sherman should march through the Carolinas, destroying the railroads in both States as he went. A little more than a month Sherman remained in Savannah. Then he began another great march, compared with which, as Sherman himself declared, the march to the sea was as child's play. The size of his army on leaving Savannah was practically the same as when he left Atlanta—sixty thousand. It was divided into two wings, under the same commanders, Howard and Slocum, and was to be governed by the same rules. Kilpatrick still commanded the cavalry. The march from Savannah averaged ten miles a day, which, in view of the conditions, was a very high average. The weather in the early part of the journey was exceedingly wet and the roads were well-nigh impassable. Where they were not actually under water the mud rendered them impassable until corduroyed. Moreover, the troops had to wade streams, to drag themselves through swamps and quagmires, and to remove great trees that had been felled across their pathway.

The city of Savannah was left under the control of General J. G. Foster, and the Left Wing of Sherman's army under Slocum moved up the Savannah River, accompanied by Kilpatrick, and crossed it at Sister's Ferry. The river was overflowing its banks and the crossing, by means of a pontoon bridge, was effected with the greatest difficulty. The Right Wing, under Howard, embarked for Beaufort, South Carolina, and moved thence to Pocotaligo, near the Broad River, whither Sherman had preceded it, and the great march northward was fairly begun by February 1, 1865.

Sherman had given out the word that he expected to go to Charleston or Augusta, his purpose being to deceive the Confederates, since he had made up his mind to march straight to Columbia, the capital of South Carolina.

The two wings of the army were soon united and they continued their great march from one end of the State of South Carolina to the other. The men felt less restraint in devas-

THE MEN WHO LIVED OFF THE COUNTRY—HEADQUARTERS GUARD ON THE MARCH THROUGH
NORTH CAROLINA

These men have not been picked out by the photographer on account of their healthy and well-fed appearance; they are just average samples of what the units of Sherman's army looked like as they pressed on toward Fayetteville and the last battle in the Carolinas, Bentonville, where General Johnston made a brave stand before falling back upon Raleigh. The men of the march to the sea were champions in covering ground. The condition of the roads did not seem to stop them, nor the fact that they had to fight as they pressed on. During the forced march to Bentonville the right wing, under General Howard, marched twenty miles, almost without a halt, skirmishing most of the way.

tating the country and despoiling the people than they had
felt in Georgia. The reason for this, given by Sherman and
others, was that there was a feeling of bitterness against South
Carolina as against no other State. It was this State that
had led the procession of seceding States and that had fired
on Fort Sumter and brought on the great war. No doubt
this feeling, which pervaded the army, will account in part for
the reckless dealing with the inhabitants by the Federal soldiery. The superior officers, however, made a sincere effort
to restrain lawlessness.

On February 17th, Sherman entered Columbia, the mayor
having come out and surrendered the city. The Fifteenth
Corps marched through the city and out on the Camden road,
the remainder of the army not having come within two miles
of the city. On that night Columbia was in flames. The conflagration spread and ere the coming of the morning the best
part of the city had been laid in ashes.

Before Sherman left Columbia he destroyed the machine-
shops and everything else which might aid the Confederacy.
He left with the mayor one hundred stand of arms with which
to keep order, and five hundred head of cattle for the destitute.

As Columbia was approached by the Federals, the occupation of Charleston by the Confederates became more and
more untenable. In vain had the governor of South Carolina
pleaded with President Davis to reenforce General Hardee,
who occupied the city. Hardee thereupon evacuated the historic old city—much of which was burned, whether by design
or accident is not known—and its defenses, including Fort
Sumter, the bombardment of which, nearly four years before,
had precipitated the mighty conflict, were occupied by Colonel
Bennett, who came over from Morris Island.

On March 11th, Sherman reached Fayetteville, North
Carolina, where he destroyed a fine arsenal. Hitherto, Sherman's march, except for the annoyance of Wheeler's cavalry,
had been but slightly impeded by the Confederates. But

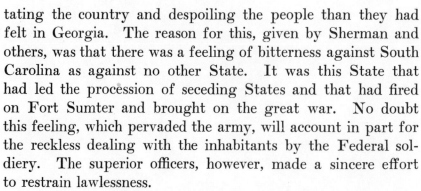

COLOR–GUARD OF THE EIGHTH MINNESOTA—WITH SHERMAN WHEN JOHNSTON SURRENDERED

The Eighth Minnesota Regiment, which had joined Sherman on his second march, was with him when Johnston's surrender wrote "Finis" to the last chapter of the war, April 27, 1865. In Bennett's little farmhouse, near Durham's Station, N. C., were begun the negotiations between Johnston and Sherman which finally led to that event. The two generals met there on April 17th; it was a highly dramatic moment, for Sherman had in his pocket the cipher message just received telling of the assassination of Lincoln.

THE END OF THE MARCH—BENNETT'S FARMHOUSE

henceforth this was changed. General Joseph E. Johnston, his old foe of Resaca and Kenesaw Mountain, had been recalled and was now in command of the troops in the Carolinas. No longer would the streams and the swamps furnish the only resistance to the progress of the Union army.

The first engagement came at Averysboro on March 16th. General Hardee, having taken a strong position, made a determined stand; but a division of Slocum's wing, aided by Kilpatrick, soon put him to flight, with the loss of several guns and over two hundred prisoners.

The battle of Bentonville, which took place three days after that of Averysboro, was more serious. Johnston had placed his whole army, probably thirty-five thousand men, in the form of a V, the sides embracing the village of Bentonville. Slocum engaged the Confederates while Howard was hurried to the scene. On two days, the 19th and 20th of March, Sherman's army fought its last battle in the Civil War. But Johnston, after making several attacks, resulting in considerable losses on both sides, withdrew his army during the night, and the Union army moved to Goldsboro. The losses at Bentonville were: Federal, 1,604; Confederate, 2,348.

At Goldsboro the Union army was reenforced by its junction with Schofield, who had come out of the West with over twenty-two thousand men from the army of Thomas in Tennessee. But there was little need of reenforcement. Sherman's third great march was practically over. As to the relative importance of the second and third, Sherman declares in his memoirs, he would place that from Atlanta to the sea at one, and that from Savannah through the Carolinas at ten.

Leaving his army in charge of Schofield, Sherman went to City Point, in Virginia, where he had a conference with General Grant and President Lincoln, and plans for the final campaign were definitely arranged. He returned to Goldsboro late in March, and, pursuing Johnston, received, finally, on April 26th the surrender of his army.

PART III
CLOSING IN

NASHVILLE—THE END
IN TENNESSEE

GUARDING THE CUMBERLAND—WHERE THOMAS WATCHED
FOR HOOD AT THE NASHVILLE BRIDGE

FORT NEGLEY,

THE IMPOSING DEFENSE

OF NASHVILLE

Perched on a hill overlooking Nashville stood Fort Negley—a large, complex citadel ready for action at any time. Though it was little called upon, its very aspect would have caused an enemy much reflection ere deciding to attack. Within the work were two casemates (one of which is shown in the fine photograph above) covered with railroad iron and made bomb-proof with earth. Fort Negley was designed and built on the German polygonal system early in 1862 and was regarded as satisfying the most exacting of the Old World standards as an up-to-date fortification. By the middle of November, 1864, with Sherman well on his march to the sea, the struggle in middle Tennessee had reached a crisis. Hood had invaded the State and Thomas had confided to Schofield the task of checking the Southern army. Thomas himself sent out his couriers and drew in all the available Federal forces to Nashville. There he meant to give battle to Hood when the Confederate leader, racing Schofield, should reach the State capital. The dramatic running fight between Hood and Schofield from Columbia to Nashville is graphically described in the accompanying text.

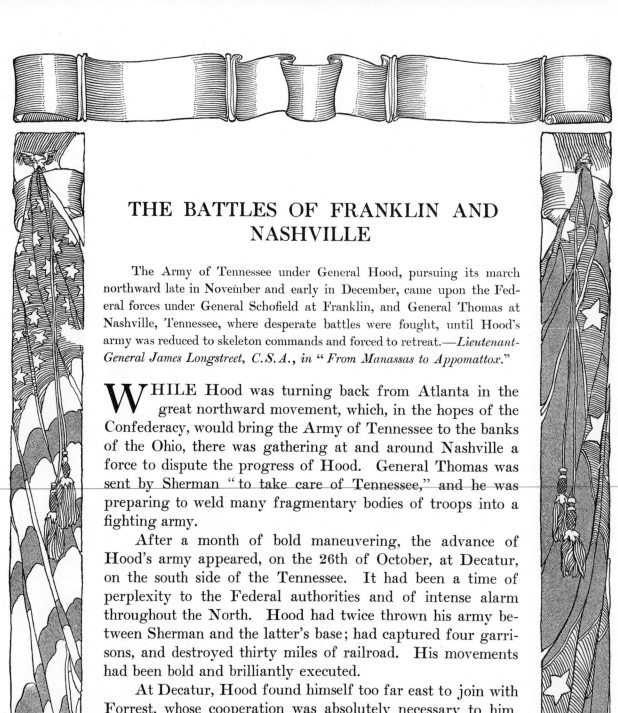

THE BATTLES OF FRANKLIN AND NASHVILLE

The Army of Tennessee under General Hood, pursuing its march northward late in November and early in December, came upon the Federal forces under General Schofield at Franklin, and General Thomas at Nashville, Tennessee, where desperate battles were fought, until Hood's army was reduced to skeleton commands and forced to retreat.—*Lieutenant-General James Longstreet, C.S.A., in "From Manassas to Appomattox."*

WHILE Hood was turning back from Atlanta in the great northward movement, which, in the hopes of the Confederacy, would bring the Army of Tennessee to the banks of the Ohio, there was gathering at and around Nashville a force to dispute the progress of Hood. General Thomas was sent by Sherman "to take care of Tennessee," and he was preparing to weld many fragmentary bodies of troops into a fighting army.

After a month of bold maneuvering, the advance of Hood's army appeared, on the 26th of October, at Decatur, on the south side of the Tennessee. It had been a time of perplexity to the Federal authorities and of intense alarm throughout the North. Hood had twice thrown his army between Sherman and the latter's base; had captured four garrisons, and destroyed thirty miles of railroad. His movements had been bold and brilliantly executed.

At Decatur, Hood found himself too far east to join with Forrest, whose cooperation was absolutely necessary to him. So he moved westward to Florence where the first division of his army, with but little opposition from Croxton's cavalry, crossed the Tennessee on the 31st. Forrest had gone down the river to intercept the Federal line of supplies. At John-

CHATTANOOGA FORTIFIED IN 1864

When Hood made his audacious movement upon Sherman's communications, by invading Tennessee — without however tempting the Northern commander from his grim course—Chattanooga was the only point in Thomas' Department, south of Nashville, which was heavily garrisoned. This town became the supply center for all the Federal posts maintained in eastern Tennessee. Therefore it had been well fortified, so strongly in fact that Thomas, who had just begun his great concentration movement, was able by December 1st to draw Steedman away to the Elk River and thence to Nashville. It was from a point on the hill a little to the right of the scene shown in the lower photograph on this page that the picture of Chattanooga fortified was taken.

CHATTANOOGA AND THE MILITARY BRIDGE

sonville he disabled the gunboats to such an extent that they were burned to prevent their falling into his hands. The fire spread to the Federal stores on the levee and $1,500,-000 of Government property thereby was destroyed. The garrison held firm. Forrest withdrew his troops and crossed the river above the town. He had received orders to join Hood as quickly as possible and reached Florence on November 14th. General Hood was now free to invade Tennessee. Sherman had sent the Fourth Corps, under Stanley, and the Twenty-third, under Schofield, the latter in command of both, back to Thomas, and this force was now at Pulaski to oppose Hood.

On the morning of November 19th, the army of Hood was put in motion. The day was disagreeable. It snowed and rained, and there was sleet and ice for the men to face. Over the slippery roads the army trudged, led by the cavalry of the daring Forrest. The wary Hood did not choose to be " checked at Pulaski," but passed adroitly by on the other side, urging his ranks forward toward Columbia on the Duck River.

At midnight of the 23d, General Schofield learned of the movements of Hood. He knew that if the latter reached Columbia he could easily capture the garrison at that place and then be free to cross the river and cut him off from Thomas. The sleeping troops were quickly aroused and in an hour were making their way through the night to Columbia, twenty-one miles distant. Another column, led by General Cox, starting somewhat later, was pushing rapidly over another road to the same point. It was a race between the armies of Hood and Schofield for the crossing at Columbia. The weary, footsore Federals barely won. Cox, by taking a cross-road, came to the rescue only a few miles south of Columbia, as Forrest was driving the Federal cavalry back, and the little army was saved.

The Union army entrenched itself for battle. Works were thrown up while the wagon trains were retreating beyond the river. But it was found impracticable to hold the position. All during the night of the 27th, there was a steady stream of

THE "BUSINESS OF WAR" AT AN ALABAMA RAILROAD STATION—FEDERALS CON-
CENTRATING AT STEVENSON BEFORE THE NASHVILLE BATTLE

Early in the winter of 1864, this station in the little Alabama town fairly hummed with the movement of
men and horses and supplies. Schofield's division of Thomas' army was being concentrated there for the
campaign which culminated, in the middle of December, at the bloody battle of Nashville. A business-
like crowd is shown in this picture, of soldiers and citizens, with more than one commanding figure in the
foreground. The railroad played a part most important and most vulnerable in the Western campaigns.

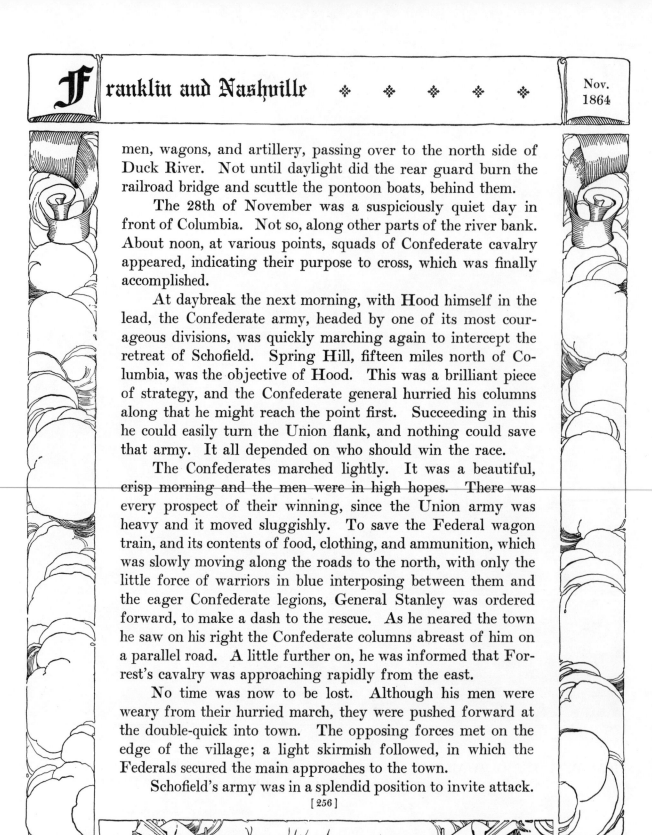

men, wagons, and artillery, passing over to the north side of Duck River. Not until daylight did the rear guard burn the railroad bridge and scuttle the pontoon boats, behind them.

The 28th of November was a suspiciously quiet day in front of Columbia. Not so, along other parts of the river bank. About noon, at various points, squads of Confederate cavalry appeared, indicating their purpose to cross, which was finally accomplished.

At daybreak the next morning, with Hood himself in the lead, the Confederate army, headed by one of its most courageous divisions, was quickly marching again to intercept the retreat of Schofield. Spring Hill, fifteen miles north of Columbia, was the objective of Hood. This was a brilliant piece of strategy, and the Confederate general hurried his columns along that he might reach the point first. Succeeding in this he could easily turn the Union flank, and nothing could save that army. It all depended on who should win the race.

The Confederates marched lightly. It was a beautiful, crisp morning and the men were in high hopes. There was every prospect of their winning, since the Union army was heavy and it moved sluggishly. To save the Federal wagon train, and its contents of food, clothing, and ammunition, which was slowly moving along the roads to the north, with only the little force of warriors in blue interposing between them and the eager Confederate legions, General Stanley was ordered forward, to make a dash to the rescue. As he neared the town he saw on his right the Confederate columns abreast of him on a parallel road. A little further on, he was informed that Forrest's cavalry was approaching rapidly from the east.

No time was now to be lost. Although his men were weary from their hurried march, they were pushed forward at the double-quick into town. The opposing forces met on the edge of the village; a light skirmish followed, in which the Federals secured the main approaches to the town.

Schofield's army was in a splendid position to invite attack.

RUSHING A FEDERAL BATTERY OUT OF JOHNSONVILLE

When Thomas began to draw together his forces to meet Hood at Nashville, he ordered the garrison at Johnsonville, on the Tennessee, eighty miles due west of Nashville, to leave that place and hasten north. It was the garrison at this same Johnsonville that, a month earlier, had been frightened into panic and flight when the bold Confederate raider, Forrest, appeared on the west bank of the river and began a noisy cannonade. New troops had been sent to the post. They appear well coated and equipped. The day after the photograph was taken (November 23d) the encampment in the picture was broken.

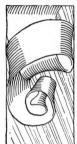

The forces were widely scattered, and the situation was indeed critical. The afternoon of November 29th records a series of lost opportunities to the Confederates. From noon until seven o'clock in the evening the little force of Stanley was completely isolated from the main army. Hood had sufficient troops literally to crush him, to cut off the retreat of Schofield, and thereby to defeat that wing of the Federal army. During the afternoon and evening there were various attempts made on the Union lines, which were stoutly resisted. The vigor of the repulse, the lack of concentration in the attack and, perhaps, the coming of evening saved the day for the Federals.

The Confederates bivouacked for the night near the pike. Brightly their camp-fires gleamed, as the Federal wagon trains and the columns of Northern soldiers trudged along through a moonless night, within a few rods of the resting Confederates. The Southern troops were plainly visible to the Federals, as they were seen moving about the camp. There was constant apprehension lest the Southern army should fall upon the passing army, but the officer who was ordered to block the Federal march made but a feeble and partial attack. Hood realized that he had lost the best opportunity for crushing Schofield that the campaign had offered, and deplored the failure most bitterly.

Schofield reached Spring Hill about seven in the evening. At the same hour the last company of his troops was leaving Columbia, about eleven miles away. All through the night the procession continued. The intrepid Stanley stood guard at a narrow bridge, as the long train wended its way in the darkness over the hills in the direction of Nashville. At daybreak, as the rear wagons safely passed, and the skirmishers were called in, the advance columns, under Cox, were reaching the outskirts of Franklin.

This village, situated on a bend of the Harpeth River, was admirably located for a great battle. On the north and west, it was protected by the river. Beyond the stream, to the

FORT NEGLEY, LOOKING TOWARD THE CONFEDERATE CENTER AND LEFT, AS HOOD'S VETERANS THREATENED THE CITY

It was Hood's hope that, when he had advanced his line to the left of the position shown in this photograph, he might catch a weak spot in Thomas' forces. But Thomas had no weak spots. From the casemate, armored with railroad iron, shown here, the hills might be easily seen on which the Confederate center and left were posted at the opening of the great battle of Nashville.

THE PRIZE OF THE NASHVILLE CAMPAIGN—THE STATE CAPITOL

[c]

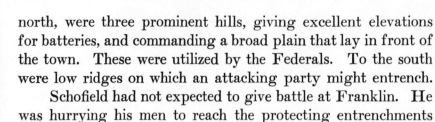

north, were three prominent hills, giving excellent elevations for batteries, and commanding a broad plain that lay in front of the town. These were utilized by the Federals. To the south were low ridges on which an attacking party might entrench.

Schofield had not expected to give battle at Franklin. He was hurrying his men to reach the protecting entrenchments of Nashville. But he would not be taken unawares. Though his men had marched and fought by turns for a week, by day and night, until they were on the point of exhaustion, yet the tired and hungry troops, before they had prepared their morning meal, laid down the musket and took up the spade. Soon entrenchments stretched along on two sides of the town. Batteries of artillery were placed at the front and in the rear, guarding the lines of probable attack. To this protecting haven, the weary regiments, one by one, filed, until, by noon, the last one had safely found its way to the entrenched walls of Franklin. The wagon trains passed over the Harpeth and the troops would soon follow after. But this was not to be. Even then, the Confederate vanguard was close at hand.

It was a glorious Indian summer afternoon. For two hours the Federal troops had been looking through the hazy atmosphere to the eastward hills. The day was already beginning to wane, when from the wooded ridge there emerged the stately columns of the army of Hood. On a rise in front of the Union lines stood Wagner's two brigades, in uniforms of blue. They were stationed, unsupported, directly in front of the Confederate approach. It was evident that "some one had blundered." But there they stood, waiting for the impact of the line in gray. A concentrated roar of musketry burst forth and they were engulfed in the on-sweeping torrent.

The Confederate ranks plunged on, carrying the helpless brigades along. With tremendous momentum they rushed toward the works. The guns along the Federal line were silent. They dare not fire on their own routed men. The weight of the oncoming mass of humanity broke through the first line of

A STATE HOUSE STOCKADED

Shortly after the occupation of Nashville by the Union forces in February, 1862, General Morton, of the U. S. Corps of Engineers, began work on its fortifications. Around the capitol were built earth parapets and stockades, and enough room was provided to mount fifteen guns. The strong, massive structure, plentifully supplied with water, could easily accommodate a regiment of infantry—enough in

THE STOCKADE AND THE PARAPET

such a citadel to hold an entire army at bay. This, however, was but a part of the entire line of defenses he planned. He was intending to fortify Morton and Houston Hills, and a third on which Fort Negley was actually constructed. The pictures show the city which the works were built to defend, but which Morton was prepared to leave to the enemy if forced to retreat within his lines.

THE NASHVILLE CAPITOL FORTIFIED

Federal infantry. The center of the Union front had been pierced. Like a wedge the Southern troops thrust themselves through the opening. Two captured batteries began an enfilading fire upon the broken Union lines, and from the right and the left the pitiless fire poured upon their flanks. The shattered regiments were past re-forming for the emergency. The teams from the captured batteries galloped to the rear. The day was nearly lost to the Union army.

Colonel Opdycke of Wagner's division had brought his brigade within the lines and was ready for the emergency. Turning toward his men to give the order to charge, he found they had already fixed their bayonets for the desperate encounter. Behind these men stood the Twelfth and Sixteenth Kentucky regiments in the same attitude. "First Brigade, forward to the works," came the ringing words of the colonel. His men scarcely needed the order. Following their gallant leader, they saw him ride forward, empty his revolver, then use it as a club in a hand-to-hand fight, and finally dismount and grasp a musket. The men fought like demons, in their desperate endeavor to stem the tide of gray.

Stanley, at his headquarters beyond the river, hád seen the impending disaster to the troops. Galloping to the scene of battle, he was about to order Opdycke to the attack. He was too late to give the command but not too late to enter the conflict. Cheering his men, he rode into the death-dealing contest in which he was presently severely wounded. The bayonet and the clubbed musket were freely used. The breach was closed, and the day was all but won by the Federals.

The recaptured guns now poured their charges of death into the shattered ranks in gray. But the courageous Southerners were not to be thus outdone. The cloud of smoke had hardly cleared from the field when they again took up the gage of battle. In sheer desperation and with an appalling recklessness of life, they thrust themselves upon the Union lines again and again, only to recoil, battered and bleeding.

THOMAS—THE "ROCK OF CHICKAMAUGA" WHO BECAME THE "SLEDGE OF NASHVILLE"

Major-General George Henry Thomas, Virginia-born soldier loyal to the Union; commended for gallantry in the Seminole War, and for service in Mexico; won the battle of Mill Spring, January 19, 1862; commanded the right wing of the Army of the Tennessee against Corinth and at Perryville, and the center at Stone's River. Only his stability averted overwhelming defeat for the Federals at Chickamauga. At Lookout Mountain and Missionary Ridge he was a host in himself. After Sherman had taken Atlanta he sent Thomas back to Tennessee to grapple with Hood. How he crushed Hood by his sledge-hammer blows is told in the accompanying text. Thomas, sitting down in Nashville, bearing the brunt of Grant's impatience, and ignoring completely the proddings from Washington to advance before he was ready, while he waited grimly for the psychological moment to strike the oncoming Confederate host under Hood, is one of the really big dramatic figures of the entire war. It has been well said of Thomas that every promotion he received was a reward of merit; and that during his long and varied career as a soldier no crisis ever arose too great for his ability.

Evening fell upon the battling hosts, and long into the night there was heard the sharp volleys of musketry. Thus closed one of the fiercest of the minor struggles of the Civil War. At midnight, Schofield withdrew from the trenches of Franklin and fell back to Thomas at Nashville.

Many gallant Southern leaders fell on the battlefield of Franklin, whose loss to the Confederacy was irreparable. Five generals and a long list of field-officers were among the killed. General Patrick Cleburne, a native of Ireland and a veteran of the British army, and General John Adams, both fell in the desperate charges at the breach in the Federal lines when Wagner's brigades were swept headlong from the front of the battle-line.

Hood appeared before the army of Thomas, on December 2d. Preparations at once began in both camps for the decisive contest. Hood was furnishing his army with supplies and with shoes, and throwing up entrenchments parallel to those of the Union army. Thomas was remounting his cavalry and increasing the strength of his works. The city was well fortified. On the surrounding hills the forts bristled with cannon. But the Federal commander was not ready for battle.

Thomas was not a born military strategist. But he was a remarkable tactician. No battle of the war was better planned and none was so nearly carried out to the letter of the plan as the battle of Nashville. It has been said that this plan of Thomas is the only one of the entire war that is now studied as a model in European military schools.

But Thomas was not acting quickly enough to satisfy Grant and the Washington authorities. Day after day, telegrams and messages poured in on him, giving advice and urging immediate action. Thomas stood firm. Finally an order for his removal was issued but never delivered. In a telegram to Halleck, Thomas stated that if it was desirable to relieve him of his command he would submit without a murmur.

Finally, preparations were completed. But, just then a

THIRTY–TWO OHIO REGIMENTS FOUGHT AT NASHVILLE—A TYPICAL GROUP OF VETERANS, FROM THE
ONE–HUNDRED–AND–TWENTY–FIFTH—"OPDYCKE'S TIGERS"

Ohio's part in 1861–65 was a large one, promptly and bravely played.   Thirty-two regiments, besides cavalry companies and artillery
batteries from that State, were in service in the operations around Nashville.   Colonel Emerson Opdycke, afterwards brevetted major-
general, commanded the One-Hundred-and-Twenty-fifth Ohio as part of the rear-guard at Spring Hill.   Some of these troops are
shown above   The lads in the lower picture made up the band of the One-Hundred-and-Twenty-fifth.

THE "TIGER BAND" OF THE ONE–HUNDRED–AND–TWENTY–FIFTH OHIO BEFORE NASHVILLE

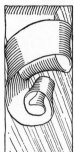

severe storm of freezing rain poured down upon the waiting armies and held the country in its frigid grasp. The ground was covered with a glare of ice. Horses and men slid and sprawled on the slippery surface. It was impossible to move an army under such conditions. Still the bombardment of messages from the East continued.

On December 14th, the ice began to melt. That night Thomas called a council of his corps commanders and laid before them his well-matured plans for the morrow's battle. Then he telegraphed to Grant that the ice had melted and the attack would be made in the morning. Had the storm continued, the attack must have been postponed and Thomas probably would not have been the hero of Nashville. Even as it was, Logan was hurrying from the East toward that city to take command of the army. When he reached Louisville, in Kentucky, on the 17th, he heard that the battle was over and he came no farther.

At four on the morning of December 15th, reveille sounded through the Union camp of fifty-five thousand soldiers. Two hours later, the men were standing in array of battle. The air was soft and even balmy. A heavy river-fog hung over the lowlands and across the city. In the dense pall, regiments of soldiers, like phantom warriors, moved across the country.

By nine o'clock the sun had pierced the mist and to the observers on the hilltops it was a brilliant spectacle. The battle-lines were rapidly forming. With the precision of a well-oiled machine, the battalions were moving to their places. Squadrons of cavalry were passing along the lowlands to take their position in the battle-line. Great guns glinted through embrasures ready to vomit forth their missiles of destruction.

The plan of the battle of Nashville as formed by Thomas was simple—a feint attack on the opposing army's right, the striking of a sudden and irresistible blow on his left, followed by successive attacks until the Southern army was battered into

THOMAS ADVANCING HIS OUTER LINE AT NASHVILLE, DECEMBER 16TH

Camp-fires were still smouldering along the side of the abatis where the lens caught the field of Nashville, while Thomas' concentric forward movement was in progress. Note the abatis to the right of the picture, the wagons moving and ready to move in the background, and the artillery on the left. White tents gleam from the distant hills. A few straggling soldiers remain. The Federals are closing with Hood's army a couple of miles to the right of the scene in the picture.

GUARDING THE LINE DURING THE ADVANCE

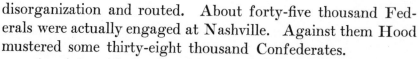

disorganization and routed. About forty-five thousand Federals were actually engaged at Nashville. Against them Hood mustered some thirty-eight thousand Confederates.

At eight o'clock, Steedman sent Colonels Morgan and Grosvenor to demonstrate on the Confederate right. This was gallantly done, in the face of a severe fire, and so closely did it resemble a genuine attack that Hood was completely deceived. At once, he drew troops from his center to strengthen the endangered flank. Then on the Union right, infantry and dismounted cavalry moved out against the weakened Confederate left.

The cooperation of these two arms of the service was almost perfect. Soon, the battle was raging along the entire front. The Federal forces were gradually converging. The Confederate lines were being crowded from their first position. Montgomery Hill, the salient point of the Confederate defense, was a strong position commanding a view of the surrounding country. It was here that one of the most daring assaults of the day was made. At one o'clock, Colonel Post's brigade dashed up the hill, direct at the works on the summit. The color-bearers forged rapidly ahead. At the top, without a moment's hesitation, the troops plunged across the works, capturing guns and men.

Still, the flail of war kept pounding at the Confederate center. Hour after hour, the Union lines, compact and unyielding, battered the ranks of the Southern troops. As the sun set on the evening of that day, the army of Hood found itself more than two miles from the place it occupied in the morning.

The new day found the Confederate general still undaunted. During the night he had formed a new line of battle. It was shorter, stronger, and more compact than that of the preceding day. Works had been thrown up in front, while behind rose a range of hills. These were strongly fortified. The second position was stronger than the first.

NASHVILLE WATCHING THE FIGHT TO A FINISH BETWEEN HOOD AND THOMAS

When Hood attacked Nashville, early in December, 1864, the Union army, under Thomas, was entrenched in a semi-circle on the wooded hills about the city, both flanks resting on the Cumberland River. Hundreds of spectators watched the fighting from the other hills. The picture at the top of this page was taken on the heights to the east, on December 15th. The view at the bottom was looking northwest. The spectators caught by the alert photographer might not have realized the tremendous significance of the struggle going on before them, but they could all witness the mathematical precision of Thomas' tactics. The checking of Hood at Nashville made Sherman's position secure in the heart of the Confederacy.

THE BATTLEFIELD FROM THE MILITARY COLLEGE

It was past noon before Thomas was ready to repeat the tactics of the preceding day. On the Confederate right was Overton's Hill, a strongly fortified position. Colonel Post was designated to lead the Federal attack. Supported by a brigade of negro troops, the assaulting columns moved up the steep ascent. With precision the lines marched toward the crest of the hill. All was well until the final dash was to be made, when a withering fire drove them back to the foot of the hill.

The extreme Confederate left also rested upon a hill. To Colonel McMillen was given the task of wresting it from the possession of the Southern troops. Forming his regiments,— the One hundred and fourteenth Illinois, the Ninety-third Indiana, the Tenth Minnesota, the Seventy-second Ohio and the Ninety-fifth Ohio—into two lines, he rapidly moved forward. The approaching lines of attack were received with a hail of musketry, and grape and canister from the Confederate artillery. But unwaveringly the cheering ranks carried the position.

The success of this charge on the right inspired the left, and again the attempt to carry Overton's Hill was made, this time successfully. These successes of the Union lines became contagious. A general forward movement was made along the entire front. It was irresistible. No troops could withstand such an impact. Hood's splendid and courageous army was routed. From thirty-eight thousand men who entered the fight it was reduced to a remnant. Flinging aside muskets and everything that would impede progress, the army that was to revivify the hopes of the failing Confederacy was fleeing in utter confusion along the Franklin pike through Brentwood Pass. This Confederate Army of Tennessee had had a glorious history. It had fought with honor from Donelson and Shiloh to Atlanta and Nashville. It had been at Murfreesboro, Chickamauga, Lookout Mountain, and Missionary Ridge. Now, shattered and demoralized, it was relentlessly pursued beyond the Tennessee River, never again to emerge as a fighting army in the Southwest.

PART IV

FROM WAR TO PEACE

———

THE SIEGE AND FALL
OF PETERSBURG

———

UNION PICKET NEAR FORT MAHONE,
THE CONFEDERATE STRONGHOLD

THE FINISHED PRODUCT

It is winter-time before Petersburg. Grant's army, after the assault of October 27th, has settled down to the waiting game that can have but one result. Look at the veterans in this picture of '64—not a haggard or hungry face in all this group of a hundred or more. Warmly clad, well-fed, in the prime of manly vigor, smiling in confidence that the end is almost now in sight, these are the men who hold the thirty-odd miles of Federal trenches that hem in Lee's ragged army. Outdoor life and constant "roughing it" affects men variously. There was many a young clerk from the city, slender of limb, lacking in muscle, a man only in the embryo, who finished his three or five years' term of service with a constitution of iron and sinews like whip-cords. Strange to say, it was the regiments from up-country and the backwoods, lumbermen and farmers, who after a short time in camp began to show most the effect of hardship

UNION VETERANS OF TRENCH AND FIELD BEFORE PETERSBURG—1864

and sickness.   They had been used to regular hours, meals at certain times, and always the same kind of food—their habits had been formed, their sleep had not been interfered with; their stomachs, by which they could tell the time of day, rebelled at being obliged to go empty, their systems had to learn new tricks.   But the city recruit, if possessed of no physical ailment or chronic trouble, seemed to thrive and expand in the open air—he was a healthy exotic that, when transplanted, adapted itself to the new soil with surprising vigor—being cheated of his sleep, and forced to put up with the irregularities of camp life was not such a shock for him as for the "to bed with the chickens and up with the lark" countryman.   This is no assuming of facts—it is the result of experience and record.   But here are men of city, farm, and backwoods who have become case-hardened to the rugged life.

PETERSBURG THE BESIEGED CITY

THE RUINED MILL

Thus we see Petersburg as, with a powerful glass, it might have been seen from the north bank of the Appomattox, looking south over the ruined town in April, 1865. As the railroad center south of Richmond, it was, at the outbreak of the war, one of the largest cities of Virginia. It was Grant who first utilized its importance in leading up to the capture of the capital. Although all missiles apparently evince a selective intelligence, at times in any bombardment there are naturally objects which give range to the gunners and become targets for their aim. Chimneys and smokestacks, and, alas! in some cases, steeples, were picked out between the sights before the lanyard was pulled. In Petersburg the churches suffered least, but buildings such as the mill and the gas-house, with its 80-foot stack, were crumbled into ruins.

WHERE THE LIGHT FAILED—GAS WORKS AT PETERSBURG

BOLINGBROKE STREET—HISTORIC HOUSES BOMBARDED

In the houses down this quiet street, liable at any moment to be pierced by shot, as some of these have been, the women of Petersburg, with all the courage the daughters of the South invariably have shown, went bravely about their self-imposed tasks, denying themselves all luxuries and frequently almost the necessities of life, to help feed and take care of the men in the trenches that faced the Federal lines. During the siege, from June, 1864, to April, 1865, led by the wives of some of the officers high in command, the Petersburg citizens, and the women especially, exhibited high heroism in nursing the wounded and aiding the army. This street was named after a distinguished Revolutionary family, whose mansion during the Revolution had been seized and made the headquarters of Benedict Arnold. Arnold, after his defection from the Continental cause, had been sent into Virginia to destroy the property of prominent Revolutionists.

[c]

A BATTERED RELIC OF COLONIAL DAYS IN PETERSBURG

This beautiful old mansion on Bo-lingbroke Street could look back to the days of buckles and small clothes; it wears an aggrieved and surprised look, as if wondering why it should have received such buffet-ings as its pierced walls, its shattered windows and doorway show. Yet it was more fortunate than some of its near-by neighbors, which were never again after the visitation of the falling shells fit habitations for mankind. Many of these handsome residences were utterly destroyed, their fixtures shattered beyond re-pair; their wainscoting, built when the Commonwealth of Virginia was

THE SHATTERED DOORWAY

ruled over by the representative of King George, was torn from the walls and, bursting into flames, made a funeral pyre of past comforts and magnificence. The havoc wrought upon the dwellings of the town was heavy; certain localities suffered more than others, and those resi-dents who seemed to dwell in the safest zones had been ever ready to open their houses to the sick and wounded of Lee's army. As Grant's troops marched in, many pale faces gazed out at them from the win-dows, and at the doorsteps stood men whose wounds exempted them from ever bearing arms again.

THE DEMOLISHED DINING–ROOM
OF A
HANDSOME MANSION

HAVOC OF BOMBARDMENT
IN A
PETERSBURG HOME

COPYRIGHT, 1911, PATRIOT PUB. CO.

In this room, nearly a hundred years before, the red-coated officers of His Britannic Majesty's troops had gathered at the long mahogany table, which, with the glittering sideboards and the old portraits, had furnished the apartment. They were unbidden guests and were invaders. It was with enforced courtesy that the lady of the house, whose husband and two sons were wearing the blue and buff of the Continental Army, received them. And now, in 1865, this lady's descendents, the heirs to the old mansion, have been forced to move by another invasion that brought home to them the stern decrees of war. The two maiden ladies of proud lineage had been forced in the early stages of the siege to move their belongings to a safer place. The house had been stripped of furnishings; against the noble old walls the Federal guns had knocked for admittance, presenting no billet of lodgment with a sweeping bow, but rudely bursting in. After the war was over, its occupants came back; but still, if you should visit them, they could point out to you the traces of the siege.

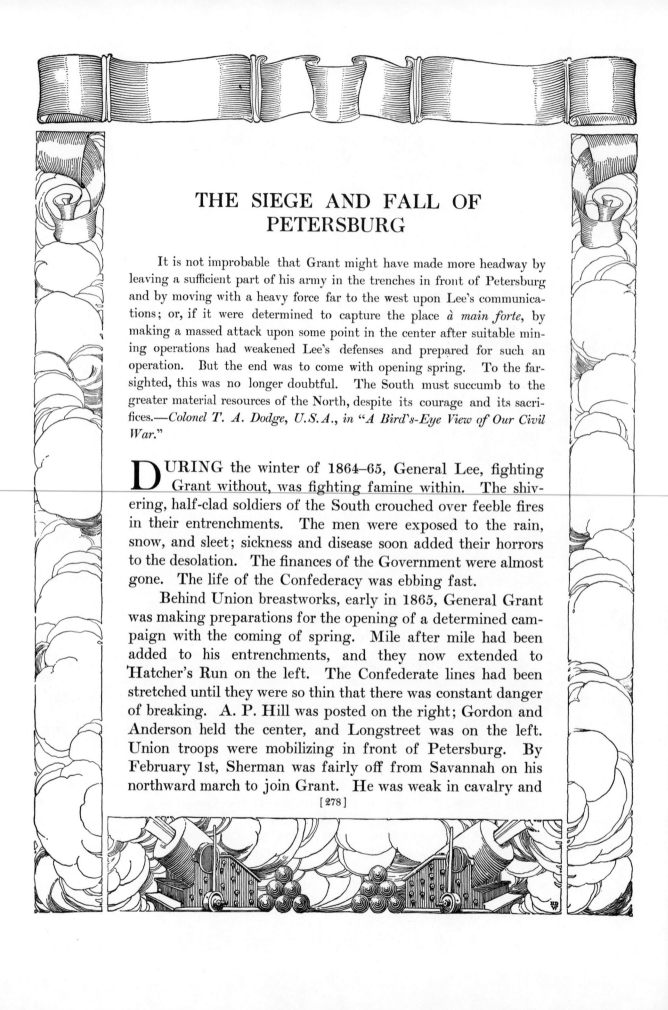

THE SIEGE AND FALL OF PETERSBURG

It is not improbable that Grant might have made more headway by leaving a sufficient part of his army in the trenches in front of Petersburg and by moving with a heavy force far to the west upon Lee's communications; or, if it were determined to capture the place *à main forte*, by making a massed attack upon some point in the center after suitable mining operations had weakened Lee's defenses and prepared for such an operation. But the end was to come with opening spring. To the far-sighted, this was no longer doubtful. The South must succumb to the greater material resources of the North, despite its courage and its sacrifices.—*Colonel T. A. Dodge, U.S.A., in "A Bird's-Eye View of Our Civil War."*

DURING the winter of 1864–65, General Lee, fighting Grant without, was fighting famine within. The shivering, half-clad soldiers of the South crouched over feeble fires in their entrenchments. The men were exposed to the rain, snow, and sleet; sickness and disease soon added their horrors to the desolation. The finances of the Government were almost gone. The life of the Confederacy was ebbing fast.

Behind Union breastworks, early in 1865, General Grant was making preparations for the opening of a determined campaign with the coming of spring. Mile after mile had been added to his entrenchments, and they now extended to 'Hatcher's Run on the left. The Confederate lines had been stretched until they were so thin that there was constant danger of breaking. A. P. Hill was posted on the right; Gordon and Anderson held the center, and Longstreet was on the left. Union troops were mobilizing in front of Petersburg. By February 1st, Sherman was fairly off from Savannah on his northward march to join Grant. He was weak in cavalry and

APPROACHING THE POST OF DANGER—PETERSBURG, 1865

A FEW STEPS NEARER THE PICKET LINE

IN BEHIND THE SHELTER

For nine months of '64–'65 the musket-balls sang past these Federal picket posts, in advance of Federal Fort Sedgwick, called by the Confederates "Fort Hell." Directly opposite was the Confederate Fort Mahone, which the Federals, returning the compliment, had dubbed "Fort Damnation." Between the two lines, separated by only fifty yards, sallies and counter-sallies were continual occurrences after dark. In stealthy sorties one side or the other frequently captured the opposing pickets before alarm could be given. No night was without its special hazard. During the day the pastime here was sharp-shooting with muskets and rifled cannon.

Grant determined to bring Sheridan from the Shenandoah, whence the bulk of Early's forces had been withdrawn, and send him to assist Sherman. Sheridan left Winchester February 27th, wreaking much destruction as he advanced, but circumstances compelled him to seek a new base at White House. On March 27th he formed a junction with the armies of the Potomac and the James. Such were the happenings that prompted Lee to prepare for the evacuation of Petersburg. And he might be able, in his rapid marches, to outdistance Grant, join his forces with those of Johnston, fall on Sherman, destroy one wing of the Union army and arouse the hopes of his soldiers, and prolong the life of his Government.

General Grant knew the condition of Lee's army and, with the unerring instinct of a military leader, surmised what the plan of the Southern general must be. He decided to move on the left, destroy both the Danville and South Side railroads, and put his army in better condition to pursue. The move was ordered for March 29th.

General Lee, in order to get Grant to look another way for a while, decided to attack Grant's line on the right, and gain some of the works. This would compel Grant to draw some of his force from his left and secure a way of escape to the west. This bold plan was left for execution to the gallant Georgian, General John B. Gordon, who had successfully led the reverse attack at Cedar Creek, in the Shenandoah, in October, 1864. Near the crater stood Fort Stedman. Between it and the Confederate front, a distance of about one hundred and fifty yards, was a strip of firm earth, in full view of both picket lines. Across this space some deserters had passed to the Union entrenchments. General Gordon took advantage of this fact and accordingly selected his men, who, at the sound of the signal gun, should disarm the Federal pickets, while fifty more men were to cross the open space quickly with axes and cut away the abatis, and three hundred others were to rush through the opening, and capture the fort and guns.

SECURITY FROM SURPRISE

THE MOLE–HILL RAMPARTS, NEAR THE CRATER

These well-made protections of sharpened spikes, as formidable as the pointed spears of a Roman legion, are *chevaux-de-frise* of the Confederates before their main works at Petersburg. They were built after European models, the same as employed in the Napoleonic wars, and were used by both besiegers and besieged along the lines south of the Appomattox. Those shown in this picture were in front of the entrenchments near Elliott's salient and show how effectually it was protected from any attempt to storm the works by rushing tactics on the part of the Federal infantry. Not far from here lies the excavation of the Crater.

At four o'clock on the morning of March 25, 1865, Gordon had everything in readiness. His chosen band wore white strips of cloth across the breast, that they might distinguish each other in the hand-to-hand fight that would doubtless ensue. Behind these men half of Lee's army was massed to support the attack. In the silence of the early morning, a gunshot rang out from the Confederate works. Not a Federal picket-shot was heard. The axemen rushed across the open and soon the thuds of their axes told of the cutting away of the abatis. The three hundred surged through the entrance, overpowered the gunners, captured batteries to the right and to the left, and were in control of the situation. Gordon's corps of about five thousand was on hand to sustain the attack but the remaining reserves, through failure of the guides, did not come, and the general found himself cut off with a rapidly increasing army surrounding him.

Fort Haskell, on the left, began to throw its shells. Under its cover, heavy columns of Federals sent by General Parke, now commanding the Ninth Corps, pressed forward. The Confederates resisted the charge, and from the captured Fort Stedman and the adjoining batteries poured volley after volley on Willcox's advancing lines of blue. The Northerners fell back, only to re-form and renew the attack. This time they secured a footing, and for twenty minutes the fighting was terrific. Again they were repulsed. Then across the brow of the hill swept the command of Hartranft. The blue masses literally poured onto the field. The furious musketry, and artillery directed by General Tidball, shrivelled up the ranks of Gordon until they fled from the fort and its neighboring batteries in the midst of withering fire, and those who did not were captured. This was the last aggressive effort of the expiring Confederacy in front of Petersburg, and it cost three thousand men. The Federal loss was not half that number.

The affair at Fort Stedman did not turn Grant from his plans against the Confederate right. With the railroads here

PRAYERS FOR RELIEF AND PRAYERS FOR VICTORY

This church at Petersburg stood near the to-bacco warehouses shown in the lower picture, and here the Federal prisoners confined in the old brick building were praying for victory as they listened to the boom of cannon and the rattle of musketry through the terrible winter of '64 and '65. But every Sunday, in this church, prayers to the God of Battles for relief from the invader were raised in fervent zeal of spirit. In all the camps, and in all the cities of the North and South, throughout the war, each side, believing firmly in the justice of its cause, had regularly and earnestly thus appealed to the Almighty for the triumph of its arms.

In the Southern army in particular, religious fervor was high. During the previous winter, while Lee's troops were encamped on the Rapidan, revivals had swept nearly every soldier into the church. General Gordon says that "not only on the Sabbath day, but during the week, night after night, for long periods these services continued, increasing in attendance and interest until they brought under religious influence the

WHERE PRAYER ROSE FOR THE WANING CAUSE

WHERE PRISONERS PRAYED FOR LIBERTY

great body of the army. Along the mountain-sides and in the forest, where the Southern camps were pitched, the rocks and woods rang with appeals for holiness and consecration, with praises for past mercies and earnest prayers for future protection and deliverance. Thousands of these brave followers of Southern banners became consistent and devoted soldiers of the Cross." And the same officer recalls that during the siege of Petersburg, especially after the attack on Fort Stedman, religious devotion was uncooled. "From the commander-in-chief to the privates in the ranks, there was a deep and sincere religious feeling in Lee's army. Whenever it was convenient or practicable, these hungry but unyielding men were holding prayer-meetings. Their supplications were fervent and often inspiring."

On the memorable 2d of April, in the Richmond church in which he had been baptized and confirmed scarcely three years before, President Jefferson Davis received the ominous tidings sent by Lee to the capital of the Confederacy that both Petersburg and Richmond would have to be evacuated before the morning of April 4th. There followed a night of terror.

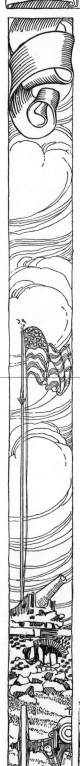

destroyed, Richmond would be completely cut off. On the morning of the 29th, as previously arranged, the movement began. Sheridan swept to the south with his cavalry, as if he were to fall upon the railroads. General Warren, with fifteen thousand men, was working his way through the tangled woods and low swamps in the direction of Lee's right. At the same time, Lee stripped his entrenchments at Petersburg as much as he dared and hurried General Anderson, with infantry, and Fitzhugh Lee, with cavalry, forward to hold the roads over which he hoped to escape. On Friday morning, March 31st, the opposing forces, the Confederates much reenforced, found themselves at Dinwiddie Court House. The woods and swamps prevented the formation of a regular line of battle. Lee made his accustomed flank movement, with heavy loss to the Federals as they tried to move in the swampy forests. The Northerners finally were ready to advance when it was found that Lee had fallen back. During the day and night, reenforcements were coming in from all sides. The Confederates had taken their position at Five Forks.

Early the next afternoon, the 1st of April, Sheridan, re-enforced by Warren, was arranging his troops for battle. The day was nearly spent when all was in readiness. The sun was not more than two hours high when the Northern army moved toward that of the South, defended by a breastwork behind a dense undergrowth of pines. Through this mass of timber the Federals crept with bayonets fixed. They charged upon the Confederates, but, at the same time, a galling fire poured into them from the left, spreading dismay and destruction in their midst. The intrepid Sheridan urged his black battle-charger, the famous Rienzi, now known as Winchester, up and down the lines, cheering his men on in the fight. He seemed to be everywhere at once. The Confederate left was streaming down the White Oak Road. But General Crawford had reached a cross-road, by taking a circuitous route, and the Southern army was thus shut off from retreat. The Federal

[284]

[Concluded on page 294]

To this gallant young Georgia officer, just turned thirty-three at the time, Lee entrusted the last desperate effort to break through the tightening Federal lines, March 25, 1865. Lee was confronted by the dilemma of either being starved out of Petersburg and Richmond, or of getting out himself and uniting his army to that of Johnston in North Carolina, to crush Sherman before Grant could reach him. Gordon was to begin this latter, almost impossible, task by an attack on Fort Stedman, which the Confederates believed to be the weakest point in the Federal fortifications. The position had been captured from them in the beginning, and they knew that the nature of the ground and its nearness to their own lines had made it difficult to strengthen it very much. It was planned to surprise the fort before daylight. Below are seen the rabbit-like burrows of Gracie's Salient, past which Gordon led his famished men. When the order came to go forward, they did not flinch, but hurled themselves bravely against fortifications far stronger than their own. Three columns of a hundred picked men each moved down the slope shown on the left and advanced in the darkness against

GENERAL JOHN B. GORDON,
C. S. A.

Stedman. They were to be followed by a division. Through the gap which the storming parties were expected to open in the Federal lines, Gordon's columns would rush in both directions and a cavalry force was to sweep on and destroy the pontoon bridges across the Appomattox and to raid City Point, breaking up the Federal base. It was no light task, for although Fort Stedman itself was weak, it was flanked by Battery No. 10 on the right and by Battery No. 11 on the left. An attacking party on the right would be exposed to an enfilading fire in crossing the plain; while on the left the approach was difficult because of ravines, one of which the Confederate engineers had turned into a pond by damming a creek. All night long General Gordon's wife, with the brave women of Petersburg, sat up tearing strips of white cloth, to be tied on the arms of the men in the storming parties so that they could tell friend from foe in the darkness and confusion of the assault. Before the sleep-dazed Federals could offer effective resistance, Gordon's men had possession of the fort and the batteries. Only after one of the severest engagements of the siege were the Confederates driven back.

GRACIE'S SALIENT—AFTER GORDON'S FORLORN HOPE HAD CHARGED

PRISONERS TO PHIL SHERIDAN

This group of the five thousand Confederate prisoners captured March 31st is eloquent of the tragedy in progress. Dire was the extremity of the Confederate cause in March, 1865. The words of the gallant leader in the last desperate and forlorn hope that charged Fort Stedman, General Gordon, give a pen-picture of the condition of the Southern fighting men: "Starvation, literal starvation, was doing its deadly work. So depleted and poisoned was the blood of many of Lee's men from insufficient and unsound food that a slight wound, which would probably not have been reported at the beginning of the war, would often cause blood-poison, gangrene and death, yet the spirits of these brave men seemed to rise as their condition grew more desperate." But not only was it physical ailments and consequent inability to fight their best which brought about the downfall, it was numbers, the overwhelming numbers that were opposed against them. In an interview with General Gordon, Lee laid before him his reports, which showed how completely he understood the situation. Of his own fifty thousand men but thirty-five thousand were fit for duty. Lee's estimate

FULL RATIONS AT LAST

of the forces of Grant was between one hundred and forty thousand and one hundred and fifty thousand. Coming up from Knoxville was Schofield with an estimated force of thirty thousand superb troops. From the valley Grant was bringing up nearly twenty thousand more, against whom, as Lee expressed it, he "could oppose scarcely a vidette." Sherman was approaching from North Carolina, and his force when united with Scofield's would reach eighty thousand. It was impossible, and yet it was after this, that Gordon made his charge. South of Hatcher's Run, at the very westernmost part of the Confederate entrenchments, Sheridan fell upon the Confederate flank. It was a complete victory. With General Merritt and General Griffin sweeping in, the cavalry charged the works and five thousand Confederates were taken prisoners, besides those killed and wounded. The Federal loss was less than seven hundred. This was the last day of March. Lined up here we see some of these captured thousands about to receive their first square meal in many months.

APRIL SECOND—WHERE LEE WATCHED

From this mound General Lee watched the final Federal attack begin near Hatcher's Run on the morning of April 2, 1865. It was a serious party of officers that gathered in this battery on the inner line of Confederate fortifications before Petersburg. On the preceding days at Hatcher's Run, and again at Five Forks, Lee had attempted to break through the besiegers, but the efforts were futile, and no sooner had they ceased than the Federal army began to gather itself for the last grapple. All night of April 1st, till four in the morning, the Federal artillery had kept up a terrific bombardment along the whole line, and at daybreak Lee saw the Sixth Corps advancing to the assault. As they broke through the Confederate lines and wheeled to attack Fort Gregg, Lee called his staff about him, telling them to witness a most gallant defense. A moment later they saw the Stars and Stripes unfurled over the parapet. The depleted and worn-out Confederates had spent themselves to the last gasp. Not even Lee's veterans could fight starvation and overwhelming numbers at once. "This is a sad business!" were Lee's words as he turned to his staff. Couriers were bringing in reports of disasters all along his lines, and he gave the orders necessary for the holding of such of the interior defenses as would enable the Army of Northern Virginia to abandon Petersburg and Richmond.

APRIL SECOND—"THIS IS A SAD BUSINESS"

As his general watched, this boy fought to stem the Federal rush—but fell, his breast pierced by a bayonet, in the trenches of Fort Mahone. It is heart-rending to look at a picture such as this; it is sad to think of it and to write about it. Here is a boy of only fourteen years, his face innocent of a razor, his feet unshod and stockingless in the bitter April weather. It is to be hoped that the man who slew him has forgotten it, for this face would haunt him surely. Many who fought in the blue ranks were young, but in the South there were whole companies made up of such boys as this. At the battle of Newmarket the scholars of the Virgina Military Institute, the eldest seventeen and the youngest twelve, marched from the classrooms under arms, joined the forces of General Breckinridge, and aided by their historic charge to gain a brilliant victory over the Federal General Sigel. The never-give-in spirit was implanted in the youth of the Confederacy, as well as in the hearts of the grizzled veterans. Lee had inspired them, but in addition to this inspiration, as General Gordon writes, "every man of them was supported by their extraordinary consecration, resulting from the conviction that he was fighting in the defense of home and the rights of his State. Hence their unfaltering faith in the justice of the cause, their fortitude in the extremest privations, their readiness to stand shoeless and shivering in the trenches at night and to face any danger at their leader's call."

AT FORT MAHONE—THE FIRST TO MEET THE ONSLAUGHT

The tall young Southerner stretched here was outside the walls of Fort Mahone, and with scores of comrades met the first shock when the onsweep of the massed lines in blue came roaring down like a torrent upon the outer works. His musket, with the ramrod out, lies beside him, showing that he has even stayed to load; the ground is strewn with cartridges frantically torn open; his hands are grasped tightly over the gaping wound through his body; he will be laid away to rest on the very spot he has so splendidly defended.

"YOU WILL SEE
A BRAVE
DEFENSE"

THREE SOLDIERS
WHO BORE OUT
LEE'S PROPHECY

bayonet and clubbed musket did bloody work here; men rolled and grappled with each other in the half darkness of the early dawn, rising to their knees to fight again. It was relentless, terrible, and from the romantic point of view magnificent. Yet as we look at these poor heaps of clay, the magnificence has vanished; horror and sorrow are the sensations that are aroused. Dead "Reb" or fallen "Yank," these men who fell, though their voices are stilled, cry from their gory beds that such things may come to pass no more—their faces and forms, twisted as they fell, speak more eloquently than any words could, for peace.

When Lee, looking toward Fort Gregg as the Federals attacked on April 2d, said, "You will see a brave defense," he spoke from intimate knowledge of his men. But even if they had been twice the number, they could not have done more than they did. If they had had three lives apiece they might have laid them down no more bravely nor uselessly. God was on the side of the bigger army. But in the outflanking trenches filled with mud, in the corners of the abatis, in the angles of the walls, and in the very last ditch, groups of men in gray fought with the desperation almost of wild animals with retreat cut off. The

[c]

FRESH AMMUNITION IN THE PATH OF THE CHARGE

A veritable battle-photograph, in the fresh path of the charge within the Confederate works that had so long held the Federals back. This picture was taken very shortly after the rattle of their muskets had rung the knell of Petersburg. Beyond the parapet are the Federal lines and the intervening plain over which the men came at the double-quick that morning. Some regiment has halted here to replenish its ammunition. Boxes of cartridges have been hurried up and impatiently broken open. There was no time for the eager men to fill pouches and belts. Grabbing handfuls of the cartridges, they have thrust them into their pockets or the breasts of their jackets. Then, leaving many of the boxes but half emptied, they pressed on, loading as they ran. The picture is an eloquent bit of still life; even the belts and cartridge-pouches cast away in impatience tell of the hurry and heat of battle.

It was the grand old Sixth Corps that crowned its splendid record on April 2d.in the last great charge of the war upon an entrenched position. Silently the troops had been brought out on the night of the 1st and placed in position just in the rear of their own picket line. The darkness hid the intended movement even from the watchful eyes of the Confederate pickets. Orders for the strictest silence had been imposed upon each man. But suddenly the pickets broke out firing, and it was only with great exertions that the officers quieted the Federal outposts. The men in the columns had maintained their positions without a sound—not a shot fired, not a word uttered. At half-past four in the early morning a signal gun from Fort Fisher boomed and flashed through the early light. Rushing forward, breaking the Confederate line of outposts, down streamed the blue masses upon the main line of the defenses. Into their faces the men in gray poured deadly volleys from behind the earthworks and lines of spiked abatis. The latter were rolled aside, carried by main force and tossed into the ditches. General Wright, in command of this

ABATIS AND DEFENDER IN THE DITCH

AFTER THE LAST GREAT CHARGE

body of men, knew from the shouts even before he saw the flag upon the breastworks that the wedge had been driven home. Leaving behind their own dead and wounded lying mingled with the bodies of the brave defenders, without waiting for orders, men from each division of the Sixth Corps pressed ahead, broke up the South Side Railroad and cut the telegraph wires. When the officers had at length calmed the ardor of their troops and re-formed the lines, a large part of the corps wheeled to the left and dashed along the Confederate entrenchments, soon overcame all resistance and swept victoriously forward as far as Hatcher's Run, capturing artillery and a large number of prisoners. There they were again re-formed, marched back to the original point of attack, and thence pushed forward in conjunction with the Twenty-fourth Corps to complete the investment of Petersburg. In this advance some Confederate batteries, very dashingly handled, inflicted considerable loss until they were driven behind the inner lines of entrenchment, when the Union troops were halted with their left resting on the Appomattox. Petersburg had fallen. The end was only a week away.

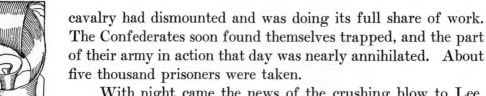
cavalry had dismounted and was doing its full share of work. The Confederates soon found themselves trapped, and the part of their army in action that day was nearly annihilated. About five thousand prisoners were taken.

With night came the news of the crushing blow to Lee. General Grant was seated by his camp-fire surrounded by his staff, when a courier dashed into his presence with the message of victory. Soon from every great gun along the Union line belched forth the sheets of flame. The earth shook with the awful cannonade. Mortar shells made huge parabolas through the air. The Union batteries crept closer and closer to the Confederate lines and the balls crashed into the streets of the doomed city. The bombardment of Petersburg was on.

At dawn of the 2nd of April the grand assault began. The Federal troops sprang forward with a rush. Despite the storms of grape and canister, the Sixth Corps plunged through the battery smoke, and across the walls, pushing the brave defenders to the inner works. The whole corps penetrated the lines and swept everything before it toward Hatcher's Run. Some of the troops even reached the South Side Railroad, where the brave General A. P. Hill fell mortally wounded.

Everywhere, the blue masses poured into the works. General Ord, on the right of the Sixth Corps, helped to shut the Confederate right into the city. General Parke, with the Ninth Corps, carried the main line. The thin gray line could no longer stem the tide that was engulfing it. The Confederate troops south of Hatcher's Run fled to the west, and fought General Miles until General Sheridan and a division from Meade appeared on the scene. By noon the Federals held the line of the outer works from Fort Gregg to the Appomattox. The last stronghold carried was Fort Gregg, at which the men of Gibbon's corps had one of the most desperate struggles of the war. The Confederates now fell back to the inner fortifications and the siege of Petersburg came to an end.

PART IV
FROM WAR TO PEACE

———

APPOMATTOX

———

IN THE WAKE OF LEE'S RETREAT

THE RUINS OF RAILROAD

BRIDGE AT PETERSBURG

APRIL, 1865

The scene that met the eyes of the Union cavalry on April 3d. The ashes of a bridge, locomotive, train and all, as they had fallen the day before on the gravelly shore of the Appotomax. When the lines southeast and west of the city were captured on April 2d, Lee had seen that retreat was the only resource left. His haggard but undaunted veterans began this final movement at eight o'clock in the evening, passing to the north side of the Appomattox by the pontoon, Pocahontas and "railroad" bridges. These were given to the flames immediately after crossing, in order to hinder the pursuit. Though there were in the fields of Mississippi and Alabama supplies enough to feed Lee's army for a whole year, the means of transportation was so poor that all through the winter they had suffered from hunger. Now the only avenue of supply that had remained in their control was seized by the Union armies. The possibility of joining with Johnston's forces, or of making a last stand where the pursuer should put himself at a disadvantage, was the hope which sustained the famished heroes in gray as they left behind them the burning bridge.

THE CAPITAL OF THE CONFEDERACY FALLEN

The ruins of the armory in the foreground, the pillars of the Petersburg and Richmond Railroad bridge across the James, a few houses in Manchester beyond the stream—this picture of desolation revives the scenes of wild commotion in Richmond on the 2d and 3d of April, 1865. On the 2d, a quiet Sunday, Jefferson Davis, at morning service in St. Paul's Church, received a despatch from General Lee, announcing the imminent fall of Petersburg and the necessity of retreating that night. Mr. Davis left his seat calmly; but by half-past eleven a strange agitation began to appear in the streets, and by noon the worst was known. A hubbub of excitement, the rumbling of trains and rattling of wagons filled the afternoon. By sunset bands of ruffians made their appearance on the prin-

THE DESERT AND THE WASTE PLACES IN RICHMOND, APRIL, 1865

cipal streets.   That night was full of the pandemonium of flight.   Orders for the burning of the arsenals and all public buildings were issued before the officers of government left the city.   To prevent drunkenness the alcoholic liquor was emptied into the gutters.   The explosion of the magazines threw high into the air burning fragments which fell upon the adjacent buildings in Richmond and even across the river in Manchester.   The hundreds of blazing piles lighted up the river with the brightness of day as it rushed sparkling beneath the high-arched bridges past the flaming cities.   At early dawn, amid the roar of the explosions and of the falling buildings, the clatter of Union cavalry was heard in the streets.   The capital of the Confederacy had fallen.

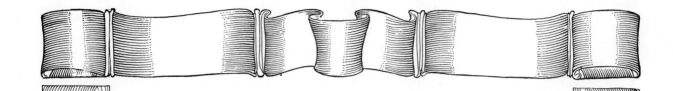

APPOMATTOX

I now come to what I have always regarded—shall ever regard—as the most creditable episode in all American history—an episode without a blemish, imposing, dignified, simple, heroic. I refer to Appomattox. Two men met that day, representative of American civilization, the whole world looking on. The two were Grant and Lee—types each. Both rose, and rose unconsciously, to the full height of the occasion—and than that occasion there has been none greater. About it, and them, there was no theatrical display, no self-consciousness, no effort at effect. A great crisis was to be met; and they met that crisis as great countrymen should. Consider the possibilities; think for a moment of what that day might have been; you will then see cause to thank God for much.—*General Charles Francis Adams, U.S.V., in Phi Beta Kappa Address delivered at the University of Chicago, June 17, 1902.*

WE are now to witness the closing scene of one of the greatest tragedies ever enacted on the world's stage. Many and varied had been the scenes during the war; the actors and their parts had been real. The wounds of the South were bleeding; the North was awaiting the decisive blow. Thousands of homes were ruined. Fortunes, great and small, had melted away by the hundreds of millions. In Richmond, the citadel of the waning Confederacy, the people were starving. The Southern army, half clad and without food, was but a shadow of its once proud self. Bravely and long the men in gray had followed their adored leader. Now the limit of endurance had been reached.

It was the second day of April, 1865. Lee realized that after Petersburg his beloved Richmond must fall. The order was given for the movement to begin at eight o'clock that night. The darkness of the early morning of the 3d was suddenly transformed into a lurid light overcasting the heavens

TWELVE HOURS AFTER, AT THE PETERSBURG COURTHOUSE

The night of April 2d was a tense one for the Federal troops in the trenches. The brigade of Colonel Ralph Ely was to charge at four o'clock in the morning, but at half-past two he learned that only the Confederate picket-lines remained. His command was formed for attack and advanced quickly across the opposing works. It then re-formed and pushed into the town, arriving at the courthouse shortly after four o'clock. At 4.28 A.M. the flag of the First Michigan Sharpshooters was floating from the staff. Major Lounsberry, in command of the detachment, was met in front of the courthouse by three citizens with a flag of truce, who surrendered the town in the name of the mayor and common council. The committee were assured of the safety of private property, and, according to the report of the mayor, so long as the brigade was in the city "the conduct of both officers and men was such as to reflect [honor] on our cause and cast a luster of glory over the profession of arms." This is one of the series of photographs taken April 3d by the enterprising artist with the Federal army; and the clock-face in the courthouse tower shows that the picture was made at ten minutes of four that afternoon.

for miles around the famous city whose name had become a household word over the civilized world. Richmond was in flames! The capital of the Confederacy, the pride of the South, toward which the Army of the Potomac had fought its way, leaving a trail of blood for four weary years, had at last succumbed to the overwhelming power of Grant's indomitable armies.

President Davis had received a despatch while attending services at St. Paul's church, Sunday morning, the 2d, advising him that the city must be evacuated that night, and, leaving the church at once, he hastened the preparations for flight with his personal papers and the archives of the Confederate Government. During that Sabbath day and night Richmond was in a state of riot. There had been an unwarranted feeling of security in the city, and the unwelcome news, spreading like an electric flash, was paralyzing and disastrous in its effect. Prisoners were released from their toils, a lawless mob overran the thoroughfares, and civic government was nullified. One explosion after another, on the morning of the 3d, rent the air with deafening roar, as the magazines took fire. The scene was one of terror and grandeur.

The flames spread to the city from the ships, bridges, and arsenal, which had been set on fire, and hundreds of buildings, including the best residential section of the capital of the Confederacy, were destroyed.

When the Union army entered the city in the morning, thousands of the inhabitants, men, women, and children, were gathered at street corners and in the parks, in wildest confusion. The commissary depot had been broken open by the starving mob, and rifled of its contents, until the place was reached by the spreading flames. The Federal soldiers stacked arms, and heroically battled with the fire, drafting into the work all able-bodied men found in the city. The invaders extinguished the flames, and soon restored the city to a state of order and safety. The invalid wife of General Lee, who was

IN PETERSBURG—AFTER NINE MONTHS OF BATTERING

This fine mansion on Bolingbroke Street, the residential section of Petersburg, has now, on the 3d of April, fallen into the hands of straggling Union soldiers. Its windows have long since been shattered by shells from distant Federal mortars; one has even burst through the wall. But it was not till the night of April 2d, when the retreat of the Confederate forces started, that the citizens began to leave their homes. At 9 o'clock in the morning General Grant, surrounded by his staff, rode quietly into the city. The streets were deserted. At length they arrived at a comfortable home standing back in a yard. There he dismounted and sat for a while on the piazza. Soon a group of curious citizens gathered on the sidewalk to gaze at the commander of the Yankee armies. But the Union troops did not remain long in the deserted homes. Sheridan was already in pursuit south of the Appomattox, and Grant, after a short conference with Lincoln, rode to the west in the rear of the hastily marching troops. Bolingbroke Street and Petersburg soon returned to the ordinary occupations of peace in an effort to repair the ravages of the historic nine months' siege.

exposed to danger, was furnished with an ambulance and corporal's guard until the danger was past.

President Lincoln, who had visited Grant at Petersburg, entered Richmond on the 4th of April. He visited President Davis' house, and Libby Prison, then deserted, and held a conference with prominent citizens and army officers of the Confederacy. The President seemed deeply concerned and weighted down with the realization of the great responsibilities that would fall upon him after the war. Only ten days later the nation was shaken from ocean to ocean by the tragic news of his assassination.

General Lee had started on his last march by eight o'clock on the night of the 2d. By midnight the evacuation of both Petersburg and Richmond was completed. For nine months the invincible forces of Lee had kept a foe of more than twice their numerical strength from invading their stronghold, and only after a long and harassing siege were they forced to retreat. They saw the burning city as their line of march was illuminated by the conflagration, and emotions too deep for words overcame them. The woods and fields, in their fresh, bright colors of spring, were in sharp contrast to the travel-worn, weather-beaten, ragged veterans passing over the verdant plain. Lee hastened the march of his troops to Amelia Court House, where he had ordered supplies, but by mistake the train of supplies had been sent on to Richmond. This was a crushing blow to the hungry men, who had been stimulated on their tiresome march by the anticipation of much-needed food. The fatality of war was now hovering over them like a huge black specter.

General Grant did not proceed to Richmond, but leaving General Weitzel to invest the city, he hastened in pursuit of Lee to intercept the retreating army. This pursuit was started early on the 3d. On the evening of that date there was some firing between the pursuing army and Lee's rear guard. It was Lee's design to concentrate his force at Amelia Court

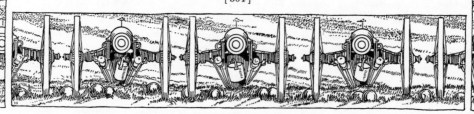

SUPPORTING THE PURSUIT OF LEE'S ARMY

A Federal wagon-train moves out of Petersburg to feed the troops pursuing Lee, in those early April days of '65. The Army of Northern Virginia has taken no supply trains on its hurried departure from Petersburg and Richmond. It depends on forage. Within the next week Grant's troops are to be brought almost to a like pass. If the surrender had not come when it did, the pursuit would have been brought to a stop for the time being by lack of subsistence. The South Side Railroad, which crossed Indian Town Creek on the trestle shown in the smaller picture, was the only railroad line in the possession of the Confederates at the end of the siege of Petersburg. It was their only avenue of supplies, but Sheridan's victory at Five Forks made it possible to cut the line. Lee was thus compelled to evacuate both Richmond and Petersburg. The bridge is to the west of Petersburg on the main line of the railroad.

THE LAST RAILROAD INTO PETERSBURG

House, but this was not to be accomplished by the night of the 4th. Not until the 5th was the whole army up, and then it was discovered that no adequate supplies were within less than fifty miles. Subsistence could be obtained only by foraging parties. No word of complaint from the suffering men reached their commander, and on the evening of that disappointing day they patiently and silently began the sad march anew. Their course was through unfavorable territory and necessarily slow. The Federals were gaining upon their retreating columns. Sheridan's cavalry had reached their flank, and on the 6th there was heavy skirmishing. In the afternoon the Federals had arrived in force sufficient to bring on an engagement with Ewell's corps in the rear, at Sailor's Creek, a tributary of the Appomattox River. Ewell was surrounded by the Federals and the entire corps captured. General Anderson, commanding the divisions of Pickett and Johnson, was attacked and fought bravely, losing many men. In all about six thousand Confederate soldiers were left in the hands of the pursuing army.

On the night of the 6th, the remainder of the Confederate army continued the retreat and arrived at Farmville, where the men received two days' rations, the first food except raw or parched corn that had been given them for two days. Again the tedious journey was resumed, in the hope of breaking through the rapidly-enmeshing net and forming a junction with Johnston at Danville, or of gaining the protected region of the mountains near Lynchburg. But the progress of the weak and weary marchers was slow and the Federal cavalry had swept around to Lee's front, and a halt was necessary to check the pursuing Federals. On the evening of the 8th, Lee reached Appomattox Court House. Here ended the last march of the Army of Northern Virginia.

General Lee and his officers held a council of war on the night of the 8th and it was decided to make an effort to cut their way through the Union lines on the morning of the next day. On the 7th while at Farmville, on the south side of the

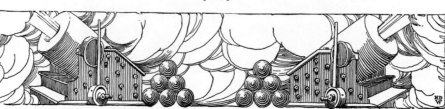

WAITING TO PRESS THE ADVANTAGE

This is a scene near the railroad station on April 3, 1865. Muskets of the Federal troops are stacked in the foreground. Evidences of the long bombardment appear in the picture. The foot-bridge shown in the smaller picture is at the point where the old river road crossed the run west of Old Town Creek. In the distance can be seen the trestle of the South Side Railroad. This bridge shook under the hurrying feet of Meade's heavy advancing column, as the pursuit of Lee was pressed.

ON THE LINE OF PURSUIT

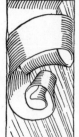

Appomattox River, Grant sent to Lee a courteous request for the surrender of the Army of Northern Virginia, based on the hopelessness of further resistance on the part of that army. In reply, Lee expressed sympathy with Grant's desire to avoid useless effusion of blood and asked the terms of surrender.

The next morning General Grant replied to Lee, urging that a meeting be designated by Lee, and specifying the terms of surrender, to which Lee replied promptly, rejecting those terms, which were, that the Confederates lay down their arms, and the men and officers be disqualified for taking up arms against the Government of the United States until properly exchanged. When Grant read Lee's letter he shook his head in disappointment and said, "It looks as if Lee still means to fight; I will reply in the morning."

On the 9th Grant addressed another communication to Lee, repeating the terms of surrender, and closed by saying, "The terms upon which peace can be had are well understood. By the South laying down their arms they will hasten that most desirable event, save thousands of human lives, and hundreds of millions of property not yet destroyed. Sincerely hoping that all our difficulties may be settled without the loss of another life, I subscribe myself, etc."

There remained for Lee the bare possibility, by desperate fighting, of breaking through the Federal lines in his rear. To Gordon's corps was assigned the task of advancing on Sheridan's strongly supported front. Since Pickett's charge at Gettysburg there had been no more hopeless movement in the annals of the war. It was not merely that Gordon was overwhelmingly outnumbered by the opposing forces, but his hunger-enfeebled soldiers, even if successful in the first onslaught, could count on no effective support, for Longstreet's corps was in even worse condition than his own. Nevertheless, on the morning of Sunday, the 9th, the attempt was made. Gordon was fighting his corps, as he said, "to a frazzle," when Lee came at last to a realizing sense of the futility of it all and

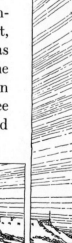

THE FRESHET THAT DELAYED GRANT'S PURSUIT

The roads leading west from Petersburg crossed and recrossed the Appomattox and its tributaries. The spring floods impeded, though they did not actually check, Grant's impetuous pursuit of Lee. By the time Lee had reached Amelia Court House (April 5th), Grant's van was at Jetersville. Lee halted to bring up provisions; as he said in his official report, the ensuing delay proved fatal to his plans. The provisions that he expected to find at Amelia Court House were captured by the Federals.

THE FLOODED APPOMATTOX

ordered a truce. A meeting with Grant was soon arranged on the basis of the letters already exchanged. The conference of the two world-famous commanders took place at Appomattox, a small settlement with only one street, but to be made historic by this meeting. Lee was awaiting Grant's arrival at the house of Wilmer McLean. It was here, surrounded by staff-officers, that the terms were written by Grant for the final surrender of the Army of Northern Virginia. The terms, and their acceptance, were embodied in the following letters, written and signed in the famous " brick house " on that memorable Sunday:

> APPOMATTOX COURT HOUSE, VIRGINIA,
> APRIL 9, 1865.

GENERAL: In accordance with the substance of my letter to you of the 8th instant, I propose to receive the surrender of the Army of Northern Virginia on the following terms, to wit: Rolls of all the officers and men to be made in duplicate, one copy to be given to an officer to be designated by me, the other to be retained by such officer or officers as you may designate. The officers to give their individual paroles not to take up arms against the Government of the United States until properly exchanged; and each company or regimental commander to sign a like parole for the men of their commands. The arms, artillery, and public property to be parked and stacked, and turned over to the officers appointed by me to receive them. This will not embrace the side-arms of the officers, nor their private horses or baggage. This done, each officer and man will be allowed to return to his home, not to be disturbed by the United States authority so long as they observe their paroles and the laws in force where they may reside.

> U. S. GRANT, *Lieutenant-General.*

General R. E. Lee.

> HEADQUARTERS ARMY OF NORTHERN VIRGINIA,
> APRIL 9, 1865.

GENERAL: I have received your letter of this date containing the terms of the surrender of the Army of Northern Virginia as proposed by you. As they are substantially the same as those expressed in your

THE LANDMARK OF THE CONFEDERATES' LAST STAND

The Union army, after the fall of Petersburg, followed the streaming Confederates, retreating westward, and came upon a part of Gordon's troops near High Bridge over the Appomattox, where the South Side Railroad crosses the river on piers 60 feet high. Hancock's (Second) Corps arrived on the south bank just after the Confederates had blown up the redoubt that formed the bridge head, and set fire to the bridge itself. The bridge was saved with the loss of four spans at the north end, by Colonel Livermore, whose party put out the fire while Confederate skirmishers were fighting under their feet. A wagon bridge beside it was saved by the men of Barlow's division. Mahone's division of the Confederate army was drawn up on a hill, north of the river behind redoubts, but when Union troops appeared in force the Confederates again retreated westward along the river.

HIGH BRIDGE

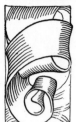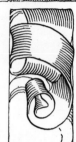

letter of the 8th instant, they are accepted. I will proceed to designate the proper officers to carry the stipulation into effect.

R. E. LEE, *General.*

Lieutenant-General U. S. Grant.

When Federal officers were seen galloping toward the Union lines from Appomattox Court House it was quickly surmised that Lee had surrendered. Cheer after cheer was sent up by the long lines throughout their entire length; caps and tattered colors were waved in the air. Officers and men alike joined in the enthusiastic outburst. It was glad tidings, indeed, to these men, who had fought and hoped and suffered through the long bloody years.

When Grant returned to his headquarters and heard salutes being fired he ordered it stopped at once, saying, " The war is over; the rebels are our countrymen again; and the best sign of rejoicing after the victory will be to abstain from all demonstration in the field."

Details of the surrender were arranged on the next day by staff-officers of the respective armies. The parole officers were instructed by General Grant to permit the Confederate soldiers to retain their own horses—a concession that was most welcome to many of the men, who had with them animals brought from the home farm early in the war.

There were only twenty-eight thousand men to be paroled, and of these fewer than one-third were actually bearing arms on the day of the surrender. The Confederate losses of the last ten days of fighting probably exceeded ten thousand.

The Confederate supplies had been captured by Sheridan, and Lee's army was almost at the point of starvation. An order from Grant caused the rations of the Federal soldiers to be shared with the " Johnnies," and the victorious " Yanks " were only too glad to tender such hospitality as was within their power. These acts of kindness were slight in themselves, but they helped immeasurably to restore good feeling and to

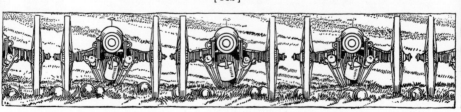

APPOMATTOX STATION—LEE'S LAST ATTEMPT TO PROVISION HIS RETREATING ARMY

At this railroad point, three miles from the Court House, a Confederate provision train arrived on the morning of April 8th. The supplies were being loaded into wagons and ambulances by a detail of about four thousand men, many of them unarmed, when suddenly a body of Federal cavalry charged upon them, having reached the spot by a by-road leading from the Red House. After a few shots the Confederates fled in confusion. The cavalry drove them on in the direction of Appomattox Court House, capturing many prisoners, twenty-five pieces of artillery, a hospital train, and a large park of wagons. This was Lee's last effort to obtain food for his army.

FEDERAL SOLDIERS WHO PERFORMED ONE OF THE LAST DUTIES AT APPOMATTOX

A detail of the Twenty-sixth Michigan handed out paroles to the surrendered Confederates.

McLEAN'S RESIDENCE AT THE BEGINNING OF THE WAR—BEAUREGARD'S HEADQUARTERS AT BULL RUN

THE HOMES

OF

WILMER McLEAN

By an extraordinary coincidence the two historic houses on this and the facing page belonged to the same man. In 1861, Wilmer McLean lived near Manassas Station, and his house was chosen by General Beauregard as headquarters. In the engagement of July 18th, preceding the great battle, a Federal cannon-ball landed in the fireplace and spoiled the general's dinner. During the famous battle of the following Sunday the household was subject to the constant alarms of a long-fought field. To avoid the scene of active military operations McLean removed to the village of Appomattox and spent nearly four years tranquilly enough. But he found himself once more the center of warlike activity. Only half a mile west of the town Grant's messenger had found Lee resting under an apple-tree. After read-

ing Grant's letter, he started with his military secretary for Appomattox Court House. In the village they met Wilmer McLean, who, after stopping for a moment at the first house they came to, conducted the party to his own home. It was Sunday, three years and nine months since that Sunday of Bull Run. At half-past one, April 9th, the negotiations took place to the left of the central doorway; during them General Lee sat by a small oval table near the window, half hidden by the pillar at the top of the step. For the table General Sheridan paid Mr. McLean twenty dollars in gold. The rest of the furniture used on that historic occasion was largely seized by others of those present. The house itself remained no longer in obscurity, but became one of the most famous land-marks in American history.

associate for all time with Appomattox the memory of reunion rather than of strife. The things that were done there can never be the cause of shame to any American. The noble and dignified bearing of the commanders was an example to their armies and to the world that quickly had its effect in the genuine reconciliation that followed.

The scene between Lee and his devoted army was profoundly touching. General Long in his " Memoirs of Lee " says: " It is impossible to describe the anguish of the troops when it was known that the surrender of the army was inevitable. Of all their trials, this was the greatest and hardest to endure." As Lee rode along the lines of the tried and faithful men who had been with him at the Wilderness, at Spotsylvania, and at Cold Harbor, it was not strange that those ragged, weather-beaten heroes were moved by deep emotion and that tears streamed down their bronzed and scarred faces. Their general in broken accents admonished them to go to their homes and be as brave citizens as they had been soldiers.

Thus ended the greatest civil war in history, for soon after the fall of the Confederate capital and the surrender of Lee's army, there followed in quick succession the surrender of all the remaining Southern forces.

While these stirring events were taking place in Virginia, Sherman, who had swept up through the Carolinas with the same dramatic brilliancy that marked his march to the sea, accomplishing most effective work against Johnston, was at Goldsboro. When Johnston learned of the fall of Richmond and Lee's surrender he knew the end had come and he soon arranged for the surrender of his army on the terms agreed upon at Appomattox. In the first week of May General " Dick " Taylor surrendered his command near Mobile, and on the 10th of the same month, President Jefferson Davis, who had been for nearly six weeks a fugitive, was overtaken and made a prisoner near Irwinsville, Georgia. The Southern Confederacy was a thing of the past.

PART V

ENGAGEMENTS OF
THE CIVIL WAR

MAY 1864—MAY 1865

THE END
RUINS OF THE RICHMOND ARSENAL,
APRIL 1865

ENGAGEMENTS OF THE CIVIL WAR

WITH LOSSES ON BOTH SIDES

MAY, 1864—JUNE, 1865

CHRONOLOGICAL summary and record of historical events, and of important engagements between the Union and the Confederate armies, in the Civil War in the United States, showing troops participating, losses and casualties, collated and compiled by George L. Kilmer from the official records of the Union and Confederate armies filed in the United States War Department. Minor engagements are omitted; also some concerning which statistics, especially Confederate, are not available.

MAY, 1864.

1 to 8.—Hudnot's Plantation, and near Alexandria, La. *Union*, Lee's Cav. Division of Gen. Banks' army; *Confed.*, Troops of Gen. Richard Taylor's command. Losses: *Union*, 33 killed, 87 wounded; *Confed.*, 25 killed, 100 wounded.

4 to 21.—Yazoo City expedition, including Benton and Vaughan, Miss. *Union*, 11th, 72d, and 76th Ill., 5th Ill. Cav., 3d U. S. Colored Cav., 7th Ohio Battery; *Confed.*, Troops of Gen. Jos. E. Johnston's command. Losses: *Union*, 5 killed, 20 wounded.

5 to 17.—Kautz's Cavalry Raid from Suffolk to City Point, Va. *Union*, 5th and 11th Pa. Cav., 3d N. Y. Cav., 1st D. C. Cav., 1 section 4th Wis. Battery; *Confed.*, Holcombe Legion, detachment 59th Va. and Home Guards. Losses: *Union*, 14 killed, 60 wounded, 27 missing; *Confed.*, 180 (about) wounded and captured.

5.—Roanoke River, N. C. *Union*, gunboats, *Ceres*, *Commodore Hull*, *Mattabesett*, *Sassacus*, *Seymour*, *Wyalusing*, *Miama*, and *Whitehead*; *Confed.*, iron-clad ram *Albemarle*. Losses: *Union*, 5 killed, 26 wounded; *Confed.*, 57 captured.

—Dunn's Bayou, Red River, La. *Union*, 56th Ohio, gunboats *Signal*, *Covington*, and transport *Warner*; *Confed.*, Gen. Richard Taylor's command on shore.

Losses: *Union*, 35 killed, 65 wounded, 150 missing; *Confed.**

5 to 7.—Wilderness, Va. *Union*, Forces commanded by Gen. U. S. Grant; Army of the Potomac, Maj.-Gen. George G. Meade; Second Corps, Maj.-Gen. Hancock; Fifth Corps, Maj.-Gen. Warren; Sixth Corps, Maj.-Gen. Sedgwick; Cavalry Corps, Maj.-Gen. Sheridan; and Ninth Corps, Maj.-Gen. Burnside. *Confed.*, Army of Northern Virginia, Gen. R. E. Lee; First Corps, Lieut.-Gen. Longstreet; Second Corps, Lieut.-Gen. Ewell; Third Corps, Lieut.-Gen. A. P. Hill; Cavalry Corps, Maj.-Gen. Stuart. Losses: *Union*, 2246 killed, 12,137 wounded, 3383 missing; *Confed.* (estimate) 2000 killed, 6000 wounded, 3400 missing; *Union*, Brig.-Gens. Wadsworth and Hays killed; *Confed.* Gens. Jones and Jenkins killed, and Stafford, Longstreet, and Pegram wounded.

5 to 9.—Rocky Face Ridge, Ga., including Tunnel Hill, Mill Creek Gap, and Buzzard's Roost. *Union*, Military Division of the Mississippi, commanded by Gen. W. T. Sherman: Army of the Cumberland, Maj.-Gen. Thomas; Army of the Tennessee, Maj.-Gen. McPherson; Army of the Ohio, Maj.-Gen. John M. Schofield, Elliott's and Stoneman's Cavalry; *Confed.*, Army of Tennessee, Gen. J. E. Johnston, commanding; Hardee's Corps, Hood's Corps, Wheeler's Cavalry.

* No record found.

FORT MORGAN FALLEN AFTER A STUBBORN DEFENSE

Among the decisive events of 1864 was the Union victory of Mobile Bay, August 23d. These smoke-blackened walls of the citadel, Fort Morgan, its shattered face, are silent witnesses to the stubborn nature of the defense, and the folds of the American flag in the distance proclaim the success of Farragut's attack. Gradually the Confederacy was being hemmed in and its resources exhausted. The bay fight itself took place on the morning of August 5th. The success of Admiral Farragut at New Orleans in the previous year had made him eager to close the remaining great gulf port to the blockade runners. After several months of effort he secured the necessary coöperation of a land force, and of four monitors to deal with the powerful Confederate ram *Tennessee*. The naval operations were entirely successful, but Fort Morgan had received hardly a scratch, and the commander sturdily refused to surrender. A constant bombardment of two weeks was necessary to reduce it, during which the woodwork caught fire and threatened to set off the great powder magazines. It was only when defense was obviously futile that General Page raised the white flag of surrender.

Losses: *Union,* 200 killed, 637 wounded; *Confed.,* 600 killed and wounded.

6.—James River, near City Point, Va. *Union,* gunboat *Commodore Jones; Confed.,* Torpedo operators on shore. Losses: *Union,* 23 killed, 48 wounded and gunboat destroyed.

6 and 7.—Richmond and Petersburg Railroad, near Chester Station, Va. *Union,* Portion of Tenth and Eighteenth Corps; *Confed.,* Hagood's Brigade. Losses: *Union,* 48 killed, 256 wounded; *Confed.,* 50 killed, 200 wounded.

7.—Bayou La Mourie, La. *Union,* Portion of Sixteenth Corps; *Confed.,* Gen. Taylor's command. Losses: *Union,* 10 killed, 31 wounded.

8.—Todd's Tavern, Va. *Union,* Sheridan's Cav.; *Confed.,* Stuart's Cav. Losses: *Union,* 40 killed, 150 wounded; *Confed.,* 30 killed, 150 wounded.

8 to 18.—Spotsylvania, Fredericksburg Road, Laurel Hill, and Ny. River, Va. *Union,* Army of the Potomac, Maj.-Gen. Meade; *Confed.,* Army of Northern Virginia, Gen. R. E. Lee. Losses: *Union,* 2725 killed, 13,416 wounded, 2258 missing; *Confed.,* 1000 killed, 5000 wounded, 3000 missing; *Union,* Maj.-Gen. Sedgwick and Brig.-Gens. Rice and Stevenson killed; *Confed.* Gens. Daniel and Perrin killed; Maj.-Gen. Ed. Johnson and Brig.-Gen. Steuart captured.

9.—Varnell's Station, Ga. *Union,* First Div. McCook's Cav.; *Confed.,* Wheeler's Cav. Losses: *Union,* 4 killed, 25 wounded, 100 captured.

9 and 10.—Swift Creek or Arrowfield Church, Va. *Union,* Tenth and Eighteenth Corps, Army of the James; *Confed.,* Gen. Beauregard's command. Losses: *Union,* 90 killed, 400 wounded; *Confed.,* 500 killed, wounded, and missing.

—Cloyd's Mountain and New River Bridge, Va. *Union,* 12th, 23d, 34th, and 36th Ohio, 9th, 11th, 14th, and 15th W. Va., 3d and 4th Pa. Reserves; *Confed.,* Gen. A. G. Jenkins' command. Losses: Union, 108 killed, 508 wounded; *Confed.,* 600 killed and wounded, 300 missing.

9 to 25.—Sheridan's Cavalry Raid in Virginia, including engagements at Beaver Dam Station, South Anna Bridge, Ashland, and Yellow Tavern. *Union,* Sheridan's Cav.; *Confed.,* Stuart's Cav.

Losses: *Union,* 50 killed, 174 wounded, 200 missing; *Confed.,* killed and wounded not recorded, 100 captured; *Confed.,* Maj.-Gen. J. E. B. Stuart and Brig.-Gen. Jas. B. Gordon killed.

12 to 16.—Fort Darling, Drewry's Bluff, Va. *Union,* Army of the James, Gen. B. F. Butler, commanding; Tenth Corps; Eighteenth Corps; *Confed.,* Gen. Beauregard's command. Losses: *Union,* 390 killed, 2380 wounded, 1390 missing; *Confed.,* 400 killed, 2000 wounded, 100 missing.

12 to 17.—Kautz's Raid on Petersburg and Lynchburg Railroad, Va. *Union,* 6 killed, 28 wounded.

13 to 16.—Resaca, Ga. *Union,* Fourth, Fourteenth, Twentieth, and Cavalry Corps, Army of the Cumberland, Maj.-Gen. Thomas; Fifteenth and Sixteenth Corps, Army of the Tennessee, Maj.-Gen. McPherson, and Twenty-third Corps, Army of the Ohio, Maj.-Gen. Schofield; *Confed.,* Army of Tennessee, Gen. J. E. Johnston, commanding; Army of Mississippi, Lieut.-Gen. Leonidas Polk. Losses: *Union,* 600 killed, 2147 wounded; *Confed.,* 300 killed, 1500 wounded, 1000 missing.

15.—New Market, Va. *Union,* Maj.-Gen. Sigel's command; *Confed.,* Gen. J. C. Breckinridge's command. Losses: *Union,* 93 killed, 482 wounded, 256 missing; *Confed.,* 42 killed, 522 wounded.

18.—Rome and Kingston, Ga. *Union,* Second Division of Fourteenth Corps and Cavalry, Army of the Cumberland. *Confed.,* Gen. Johnston's command. Losses: *Union,* 16 killed, 59 wounded.

—Bayou De Glaize or Calhoun Station, La. *Union,* Portions of Sixteenth, Seventeenth Corps, and Cavalry of Nineteenth Corps; *Confed.,* Gen. Taylor's command. Losses: *Union,* 60 killed, 300 wounded; *Confed.,* 500 killed and wounded.

19 to 22.—Cassville, Ga. *Union,* Twentieth Corps, Maj.-Gen. Hooker; *Confed.,* Gen. Johnston's command. Losses: *Union,* 10 killed, 46 wounded.

20.—Bermuda Hundred, Va. *Union,* Tenth and Eighteenth Corps, Army of the James; *Confed.,* Gen. Beauregard's command. Losses: *Union,* 702 killed and wounded. *Confed.,* (estimate) 700 killed, wounded, and missing.

While the navy was perfecting the blockade along the coast, General Grant at Petersburg was trying to get across Lee's entrenchments. In the fall a partially successful attempt was made on the lines between Petersburg and Richmond. On the night of September 28th–29th, the Tenth Army Corps under General D. B. Birney, and the Eighteenth Army Corps under General Ord, crossed the James near this place, drove back the Confederate skirmishers, and by half-past seven in the morning advanced three miles north through the dense woods to Fort Harrison. Stannard's division then came upon open ground before a strong line of earthworks mounting

heavy guns, and protected by a battery on the crest of a hill. The troops charged fourteen hundred yards across a deeply plowed field in the face of a galling fire of artillery and musketry. After a pause at the foot of a hill, the head of the column carried the parapet of the fort and planted the flag on one of its massive traverses. In an attempt to drive the Confederates entirely from the position General Ord was severely wounded. On September 30th the Confederate General R. H. Anderson, commanding Longstreet's Corps, attacked the captured fort, making three separate charges, but was repulsed with a loss of some two thousand men.

WHERE ORD CROSSED THE JAMES

PALISADES AND PARAPET AT FORT HARRISON

Engagements of the Civil War

23 to 28.—North Anna River, Jericho Ford or Taylor's Bridge, and Totopotomoy Creek, Va. *Union*, Second, Fifth, and Ninth Corps, Army of the Potomac, Maj.-Gen. Meade; *Confed.*, Army of Northern Virginia, Gen. R. E. Lee. Losses: *Union*, 186 killed, 942 wounded, 165 missing; *Confed.*, 2000 killed and wounded.

24.—Wilson's Wharf, Va. *Union*, 10th U. S. Colored, 1st D. C. Cav., Battery B U. S. Colored Artil.; *Confed.*, Fitzhugh Lee's Cav. Losses: *Union*, 2 killed, 24 wounded; *Confed.*, 20 killed, 100 wounded.

25 to June 4.—Dallas, Ga., also called New Hope Church and Allatoona Hills. *Union*, Fourth, Fourteenth, Twentieth, and Cavalry Corps, Army of the Cumberland, Maj.-Gen. Thomas; Twenty-third Corps, Maj.-Gen. Schofield; Fifteenth, Sixteenth, and Seventeenth Corps, Army of the Tennessee, Maj.-Gen. McPherson—Division of the Mississippi, Maj.-Gen. Sherman; *Confed.*, Army of Tennessee, Gen. J. E. Johnston, commanding. Losses: *Union*, 2400 killed, wounded, and missing; *Confed.*, 369 killed, 1921 wounded.

26 to 29.—Decatur and Moulton, Ala. *Union*, 1st, 3d, and 4th Ohio Cav., Second Cavalry Division; *Confed.*, Roddey's Cav. Losses: *Union*, 48 killed and wounded; *Confed.*, 60 killed and wounded.

27 and 28.—Hanovertown, Hawes' Shop, and Salem Church, Va. First and Second Divisions, Cavalry Corps, Maj.-Gen. Sheridan; *Confed.*, detachments of Lee's Army. Losses: *Union*, 25 killed, 119 wounded, 200 missing; *Confed.*, 475 killed, wounded, and missing.

30.—Hanover and Ashland, Va. *Union*, Wilson's Cavalry; *Confed.*, Young's Cav. Losses: *Union*, 26 killed, 130 wounded. —Old Church, Va. *Union*, Torbert's Cavalry; *Confed.*, Cavalry of the Army of Northern Virginia. Losses: *Union*, 16 killed, 74 wounded.

JUNE, 1864.

1 to 12.—Cold Harbor, Va., including Gaines' Mill, Salem Church, and Hawes' Shop. *Union*, Second, Fifth, Sixth, Ninth, and Eighteenth Corps and Sheridan's Cavalry; *Confed.*, Army of Northern Virginia, reinforced by the fresh divisions of Breckinridge, Pickett, and Hoke. Losses: *Union*, 1844 killed, 9077 wounded, 1816 missing; *Confed.*, 1200 killed and wounded, 500 missing.

2.—Bermuda Hundred, Va. *Union*, Tenth Corps; *Confed.*, Gen. Beauregard's command. Losses: *Union*, 25 killed, 100 wounded; *Confed.*, 100 killed and wounded.

4.—Panther Gap, W. Va. *Union*, Hayes's Brigade of Second Division, Army of West Virginia; *Confed.*, Gen. Breckinridge's command. Losses: *Union*, 25 killed and wounded; *Confed.*, 25 killed and wounded.

5.—Piedmont, W. Va. *Union*, portion of Army of West Virginia, commanded by Maj.-Gen. Hunter; *Confed.*, Gen. Vaughn's Cav. Losses: *Union*, 130 killed, 650 wounded; *Confed.*, 460 killed, 1450 wounded, 1060 missing. *Confed.* Gen. W. E. Jones killed.

6.—Old River Lake or Lake Chicot, Ark. *Union*, Sixteenth Corps; *Confed.*, Marmaduke's Cav. Losses: *Union*, 40 killed, 70 wounded; *Confed.*, 100 killed and wounded.

9.—Mt. Sterling, Ky. *Union*, Burbridge's Cav; *Confed.*, Morgan's Cav. Losses: *Union*, 35 killed, 150 wounded; *Confed.*, 50 killed, 200 wounded, 250 captured.

9 to 30.—Kenesaw Mountain, Marietta or Big Shanty, Ga., including general assault on the 27th, Pine Mt., Golgotha, Culp's House, and Powder Springs. *Union*, Fourth, Fourteenth, and Twentieth Corps, Army of the Cumberland, Maj.-Gen. Thomas; Fifteenth, Sixteenth, and Seventeenth Corps, Army of the Tennessee, Maj. Gen. McPherson; Twenty-third Corps, Maj.-Gen. Schofield. Division of the Mississippi, Maj.-Gen. W. T. Sherman; *Confed.*, Army of Tennessee—Gen. J. E. Johnston, commanding. Losses: *Union*, 1370 killed, 6500 wounded, 800 missing; *Confed.*, 468 killed, 3480 wounded, missing not recorded. *Union*, Brig.-Gen. Harker killed and Col. D. McCook mortally wounded; *Confed.*, Lieut.-Gen. Polk killed.

10.—Petersburg, Va. *Union*, portion of Tenth Corps and Kautz's Cav.; *Confed.*, Gen. R. E. Colston's command. Losses: *Union*, 20 killed, 67 wounded.

THE OPPOSING

LINES

NEAR RICHMOND

This picture represents the main bomb-proof at Fort Brady. After the capture of Fort Harrison the Union authorities strengthened that position by constructing a line of fortifications southward to the James. Fort Brady was at the southern end, commanding the river. The bomb-proof was built of heavy cross timbers, covered with fifteen feet of solid earth, and its entrances were at such an angle as to be safe from any cross-fire. The lower

picture shows similar precautions of the Confederates. Though Fort Harrison was lost, Fort Gilmer, a little farther north, was held, and a line of entrenchments was strengthened from the rear of Harrison to the James. This particular picture shows a ditch twenty-seven feet deep dug to prevent the running of mines from the adjacent Federal lines. The man in shirt-sleeves standing in the ditch is General Peter S. Michie, acting Chief Engineer for the Union armies about Petersburg. He had directed the construction of Fort Brady, and is now, in April, 1865, investigating the Confederate engineering operations.

A WELL-PROTECTED MAGAZINE, FORT BRADY

THE 27-FOOT DITCH AT FORT GILMER, GUARD AGAINST FEDERAL MINES

[c]

Engagements of the Civil War

—Brice's Cross Roads, near Guntown, Miss. *Union*, 81st, 95th, 108th, 113th, 114th, and 120th Ill., 72d and 95th Ohio, 9th Minn., 93d Ind., 55th and 59th U. S. Colored, Brig.-Gen. Grierson's Cavalry, the 4th Mo., 2d N. J., 19th Pa., 7th and 9th Ill., 7th Ind., 3d and 4th Iowa, and 10th Kan. Cav., 1st Ill. and 6th Ind. Batteries, Battery F 2d U. S. Colored Artil; *Confed.*, Forrest's Cav. Losses: *Union*, 223 killed, 394 wounded, 1623 missing; *Confed.*, 96 killed, 396 wounded.

—Cynthiana and Kellar's Bridge, Ky. *Union*, 168th and 171st Ohio; *Confed.*, Morgan's Cav. Losses: *Union*, 21 killed, 71 wounded, 980 captured; *Confed.**

10 and 11.—Lexington, W. Va. *Union*, Second Division Army of West Virginia; *Confed.*, McCausland's Cav. Losses: *Union*, 6 killed, 18 wounded.

11 and 12.—Cynthiana, Ky. *Union*, Burbridge's Cav.; *Confed.*, Morgan's Cav. Losses: *Union*, 150 killed and wounded; *Confed.*, 300 killed and wounded, 400 captured.

—Trevilian Station, Va. *Union*, Sheridan's Cav.; *Confed.*, Gen. Wade Hampton's Cav. Losses: *Union*, 102 killed, 470 wounded, 435 missing; *Confed.* (incomplete) 59 killed, 258 wounded, 295 missing.

13.—White Oak Swamp Bridge, Va. *Union*, Wilson's and Crawford's Cav.; *Confed.*, detachments of the Army of Northern Virginia. Losses: *Union*, 50 killed, 250 wounded.

14.—Lexington, Mo. *Union*, Detachment 1st Mo. Cav. Losses: *Union*, 8 killed, 1 wounded.

15.—Samaria Church, Malvern Hill, Va. *Union*, Wilson's Cav.; *Confed.*, Hampton's Cav. Losses: *Union*, 25 killed, 3 wounded; *Confed.*, 100 killed and wounded.

15 to 19.—Petersburg, Va., commencement of the siege that continued to its fall (April 2, 1865). *Union*, Tenth and Eighteenth Corps, Army of the James, Maj.-Gen. B. F. Butler; Second, Fifth, Sixth, and Ninth Corps, Army of the Potomac, Maj.-Gen. Geo. G. Meade; *Confed.*, Gen. Beauregard's command, reenforced by two divisions of Lee's army on June 18th. Losses: *Union*, 1688 killed, 8513 wounded, 1185 missing; *Confed.* (estimate), 5000 killed, wounded, and missing.

16.—Otter Creek, near Liberty, Va. *Union*, Hunter's command in advance of the Army of West Virginia; *Confed.*, McCausland's Cav. Losses: *Union*, 3 killed, 15 wounded.

17 and 18.—Lynchburg, Va. *Union*, Sullivan's and Crook's divisions and Averell's and Duffié's Cav., Army of West Virginia; *Confed.*, Gen. Jubal Early's command. Losses: *Union*, 100 killed, 500 wounded, 100 missing; *Confed.*, 200 killed and wounded.

19.—Destruction of the *Confed.* cruiser *Alabama*, off Cherbourg, France, by U. S. cruiser *Kearsarge*. Losses: *Union*, 3 wounded; *Confed.*, 9 killed, 21 wounded, 10 drowned, and 70 captured.

21.—Salem, Va. *Union*, Averell's Cav.; *Confed.*, Gen. McCausland's Cav. Losses: *Union*, 6 killed, 10 wounded; *Confed.*, 10 killed and wounded.

22 and 23.—Weldon Railroad, Williams' Farm or Jerusalem Plank Road, Va. *Union*, Second and Sixth Corps and First Division of Fifth Corps, Army of the Potomac; *Confed.*, Gen. A. P. Hill's Corps. Losses: *Union*, 142 killed, 654 wounded, 2166 missing; *Confed.**

22 to 30.—In front of Petersburg, Va. *Union*, Fifth, Ninth, Tenth, and Eighteenth Corps; *Confed.*, Army of Northern Virginia. Losses: *Union*, 112 killed, 506 wounded, 800 missing.

—Wilson's Raid on the Weldon Railroad, Va. *Union*, Kautz's and Wilson's Cav.; *Confed.*, Gen. W. H. F. Lee's Cav. Losses: *Union*, 71 killed, 262 wounded, 1119 missing; *Confed.*, 365 killed and wounded.

23 and 24.—Jones's Bridge and Samaria Church, Va. *Union*, Torbert's and Gregg's Cavalry Divisions; *Confed.*, Hampton's Cav. Losses: *Union*, 54 killed, 235 wounded, 300 missing; *Confed.*, 250 killed and wounded.

25 to 29.—Clarendon, St. Charles River, Ark. *Union*, 126th Ill. and 11th Mo., 9th Iowa and 3d Mich. Cav., Battery D 2d Mo. Artil.; *Confed.*, Gen. Price's command. Losses: *Union*, 1 killed, 16 wounded; *Confed.*, 30 killed and wounded.

* No record found.

THE LAST PORT CLOSED

Fort Fisher, captured January 15, 1865. With the capture of Fort Fisher, Wilmington, the great importing depot of the South, on which General Lee said the subsistence of his army depended, was finally closed to all blockade runners. The Federal navy concentrated against the fortifications of this port the most powerful naval force ever assembled up to that time—fifty-five ships of war, including five ironclads, altogether carrying six hundred guns. The upper picture shows the nature of the palisade, nine feet high, over which some two thousand marines attempted to pass; the lower shows interior of the works after the destructive bombardment.

INSIDE FORT FISHER—WORK OF THE UNION FLEET

Engagements of the Civil War

JULY, 1864.

1 to 31.—In front of Petersburg, including Deep Bottom, New Market, and Malvern Hill, on the 27th, and Federal mine explosion on the 30th under a Confederate fort. *Union,* Second, Fifth, Ninth, Tenth, and Eighteenth Corps; *Confed.,* Army of Northern Virginia. Losses: *Union,* 853 killed, 3468 wounded, 1558 missing; *Confed.**

2 to 5.—Nickajack Creek or Smyrna, Ga. *Union,* troops under command of Maj.-Gen. Sherman; *Confed.,* Gen. Johnston's command. Losses: *Union,* 60 killed, 310 wounded; *Confed.,* 100 killed and wounded.

2 to 10.—Expedition from Vicksburg to Jackson, Miss. *Union,* First Division, Seventeenth Corps; *Confed.,* Gen. Wirt Adam's command. Losses: *Union,* 220 killed, wounded, and missing; *Confed.**

3.—Fort Johnson, James Island, S. C. *Union,* Troops of Department of the South; *Confed.,* Gen. W. B. Taliaferro's command. Losses: *Union,* 19 killed, 97 wounded, 135 missing; *Confed.**

4 to 7.—Bolivar and Maryland Heights, Va. *Union,* Maj.-Gen. Sigel's Reserve Division; *Confed.,* Gen. Jubal Early's command. Losses: *Union,* 20 killed, 80 wounded.

5 to 7.—John's Island, S. C. *Union,* Maj.-Gen. Foster's troops; *Confed.,* Gen. W. B. Taliaferro's command. Losses: *Union,* 16 killed, 82 wounded; *Confed.,* 33 killed, 92 wounded.

5 to 18.—Smith's Expedition, La Grange, Tenn., to Tupelo, Miss. *Union,* First and Third Divisions Sixteenth Corps, one brigade U. S. Colored Troops and Grierson's Cav.; *Confed.,* Forrest's Cav. Losses: *Union,* 85 killed, 567 wounded; *Confed.,* 210 killed, 1049 wounded, 149 missing.

6 to 10.—Chattahoochee River, Ga. *Union,* Army of the Ohio, Maj.-Gen. Schofield; Army of the Tennessee, Maj.-Gen. McPherson; Army of the Cumberland, Maj.-Gen. Thomas—Division of the Mississippi, Maj.-Gen. W. T. Sherman; *Confed.,* Gen. J. E. Johnston's command. Losses: *Union,* 80 killed, 450 wounded, 200 missing.

7.—Solomon's Gap and Middletown, Md. *Union,* 8th Ill. Cav., Potomac Home Brigade, and Alexander's Baltimore Battery; *Confed.,* Gen. Early's command. Losses: *Union,* 5 killed, 20 wounded.

9.—Monocacy, Md. *Union,* First and Second Brigades of Third Division, Sixth Corps, and detachment of Eighth Corps; *Confed.,* Gordon's, Breckinridge's and Rodes' divisions under Gen. Jubal Early. Losses: *Union,* 98 killed, 594 wounded, 1188 missing; *Confed.**

11 to 22.—Rousseau's raid in Alabama and Georgia, including Ten Islands and Stone's Ferry, Ala., and Auburn and Chewa Station, Ga. *Union,* 8th Ind., 5th Iowa, 9th Ohio, 2d Ky., and 4th Tenn. Cav., Battery E 1st Mich. Artil.; *Confed.,* Troops of Gen. J. E. Johnston's command. Losses: *Union,* 3 killed, 30 wounded; *Confed.,* 95 killed and wounded.

12.—Fort Stevens, Washington, D.C. *Union,* Part of Nineteenth Corps, First and Second Divisions Sixth Corps, Marines, Home Guards, citizens, and convalescents; *Confed.,* Gen. Early's command. Losses: *Union,* 280 killed and 319 wounded; *Confed.**

17 and 18.—Snicker's Gap and Island Ford, Va. *Union,* Army of West Virginia, Maj.-Gen. Crook and portion of Sixth Corps; *Confed.,* Gen. Early's command. Losses: *Union,* 30 killed, 181 wounded, 100 missing.

18.—Ashby's Gap, Va. *Union,* Duffié's Cav.; *Confed.** Losses: *Union,* 124 killed and wounded.

19 and 20.—Darksville, Stevenson's Depot, and Winchester, Va. *Union,* Averell's Cav.; *Confed.,* Cavalry of Gen. Early's command. Losses: *Union,* 38 killed, 175 wounded, 300 captured; *Confed.,* 300 killed and wounded, 300 captured.

20.—Peach Tree Creek, Ga. *Union,* Fourth, Fourteenth, and Twentieth Corps, Maj.-Gen. Geo. H. Thomas; *Confed.,* Gen. J. B. Hood's army. Losses (estimates): Union, 300 killed, 1410 wounded; *Confed.,* 1113 killed, 2500 wounded, 1183 missing.

22.—Atlanta, Ga. (Hood's first sortie.) *Union,* Fifteenth, Sixteenth, and Seventeenth Corps, Maj.-Gen. McPherson;

* No record found.

THE REFUGE OF THE DEFENDERS

When the wounded leaders (Lamb and Whiting) in command of Fort Fisher saw it was impossible to hold out much longer, they were removed on stretchers along the sea-coast to Battery Buchanan, pictured at the bottom of the page. The spent musket-balls from the stubborn battle still raging in the fort fell like hailstones around the party. The garrison itself soon retreated to Buchanan, where two miles of level sand separated them from the Federal troops, now in full possession of the fort. But they were defenseless, for the guns in Buchanan had been spiked, and no means of escape was at hand. Consequently, when the Federal General J. C. Abbot arrived in the night with two regiments, Colonel Lamb surrendered to him and his superior, General A. H. Terry, the works, with the force of a thousand men and some sixty officers. Though the Federal army captured Fort Fisher, the coöperation of the fleet was necessary to success. During the two days of almost ceaseless bombardment a thousand tons of shot and shell were poured upon the defenses, wrecking nearly every gun and wounding or killing those of the garrison who dared to man the pieces.

Engagements of the Civil War

Confed., Gen. J. B. Hood's command. Losses: *Union*, 500 killed, 2141 wounded, 1000 missing; *Confed.*, 2482 killed, 4000 wounded, 2017 missing. *Union*, Gen. McPherson killed.

23 and 24.—Kernstown and Winchester, Va. *Union*, Portion of Army of West Virginia; *Confed.*, Gen. Early's command. Losses: *Union*, 1200 killed and wounded; *Confed.*, 600 killed and wounded.

26.—Wallace's Ferry, Ark. *Union*, 15th Ill. Cav., 60th and 56th U. S. Colored Troops, Co. E 2d U. S. Colored Artil.; *Confed.*, Gen. Price's command. Losses: *Union*, 16 killed, 32 wounded; *Confed.*, 150 wounded.

26 to 31.—Stoneman's raid to Macon, Ga. *Union*, Stoneman's and Garrard's Cav.; *Confed.*, Cavalry of Gen. Hood's army, local garrisons and Home Guards. Losses: *Union*, 100 killed and wounded, 900 missing; *Confed.**

—McCook's raid to Lovejoy's Station, Ga. *Union*, 1st Wis., 5th and 8th Iowa, 2d and 8th Ind., 1st and 4th Tenn., and 4th Ky. Cav.; *Confed.*, detachments of Gen. Hood's command. Losses: *Union*, 100 killed and wounded, 500 missing.

27.—Mazzard Prairie, Fort Smith, Ark. *Union*, 6th Kan. Cav.; *Confed.*, Gen. Price's command. Losses: *Union*, 12 killed, 17 wounded, 152 captured; *Confed.*, 12 killed, 20 wounded.

28.—Atlanta, Ga. (Second sortie; at Ezra Church.) *Union*, Fifteenth, Sixteenth, and Seventeenth Corps, Maj.-Gen. Howard; *Confed.*, Gen. Hood's command. Losses: *Union*, 100 killed, 600 wounded; *Confed.*, 642 killed, 3000 wounded, 1000 missing.

28 to Sept. 2.—Siege of Atlanta, Ga. *Union*, Army of the Military Division of the Mississippi, Maj.-Gen. W. T. Sherman; *Confed.*, Army of Tennessee, Gen. J. B. Hood, commanding. Losses: Careful estimates place the casualties at 40,000 on each side.

AUGUST, 1864.

1 to 31.—In front of Petersburg, Va. *Union*, Second, Fifth, Ninth, and Eighteenth Corps; *Confed.*, Army of Northern Virginia. Losses: *Union*, 158 killed, 623 wounded, 296 missing; *Confed.**

2.—Green Springs, W. Va. *Union*, 153d Ohio; *Confed.*, troops of Gen. J. H. Morgan's command. Losses: *Union*, 1 killed, 5 wounded, 90 missing; *Confed.*, 5 killed, 22 wounded.

5 to 23.—Forts Gaines and Morgan, Mobile Bay, Ala. *Union*, Thirteenth Corps and Admiral Farragut's fleet of war vessels; *Confed.*, fleet commanded by Admiral Buchanan and land forces under Gen. D. H. Maury. Losses: *Union*, 145 killed, 170 wounded; *Confed.*, 12 killed, 20 wounded, 280 captured.

7.—Moorefield, Va. *Union*, 14th Penna., 8th Ohio, 1st and 3d W. Va., and 1st N. Y. Cav.; *Confed.*, McCausland's and Bradley T. Johnson's Cav. Losses: *Union*, 9 killed, 22 wounded; *Confed.*, 100 killed and wounded, 400 missing.

9.—Explosion of ammunition at City Point, Va. Losses: *Union*, 70 killed, 130 wounded.

10 and 11.—Berryville Pike, Sulphur Springs Bridge and White Post, Va. *Union*, Torbert's Cav.; *Confed.*, Gen. Early's command. Losses: *Union*, 30 killed, 70 wounded, 200 missing.

13.—Near Snicker's Gap, Va. *Union*, 144th and 149th Ohio; *Confed.*, Gen. R. H. Anderson's command. Losses: *Union*, 4 killed, 10 wounded, 200 missing; *Confed.*, 2 killed, 3 wounded.

14 to 18.—Strawberry Plains, Va. *Union*, Second and Tenth Corps and Gregg's Cav.; *Confed.*, detachments from Gen. Lee's army at Petersburg. Losses: *Union*, 327 killed, 1855 wounded, 1400 missing; *Confed.* (estimate), 1000 killed, wounded, and missing.

15.—Fisher's Hill, near Strasburg, Va. *Union*, Sixth and Eighth Corps and 1st Cav. Division Army of the Potomac; *Confed.*, Gen. Early's command. Losses: *Union*, 30 wounded.

16.—Crooked Run, Front Royal, Va. *Union*, Merritt's Cav.; *Confed.*, Kershaw's division and Fitzhugh Lee's Cav. Losses: *Union*, 13 killed, 58 wounded; *Confed.*, 30 killed, 150 wounded, 300 captured.

17.—Gainesville, Fla. *Union*, 75th Ohio Mounted Inf. Losses: *Union*, 16 killed, 30 wounded, 102 missing.

* No record found.

RUINS OF CHARLESTON—EVACUATED FEBRUARY 18, 1865

A center of Southern civilization lies in ashes. The Circular Church has been reduced to bare blackened walls and topless tower. The famous Mills House, to the right, has been swept by the flames. The private mansions in the foreground are completely destroyed, nothing but the steps remaining of the one in front. But the photograph, taken only two months later, shows also a mighty power of recuperation. The scaffolding is already up for the repair of the steeple of the church. The evacuation of Charleston had not been the result of any Federal attack, but of Sherman's advance through the heart of South Carolina. On February 17th the city was reluctantly evacuated.

Engagements of the Civil War

—Winchester, Va. *Union,* New Jersey Brigade of Sixth Corps and Wilson's Cav.; *Confed.,* Gen. Early's command. Losses: *Union,* 50 wounded, 250 missing.

18, 19, and 20.—Six-mile House, Weldon Railroad, Va. *Union,* Fifth and Ninth Corps and Kautz's and Gregg's Cav.; *Confed.,* Gen. A. P. Hill's corps, Bushrod Johnson's division, Dearing's brigade and Hampton's Cav. Losses: *Union,* 251 killed, 1155 wounded, 2879 missing; *Confed.**

18 to 22.—Raid on the Atlanta and West Point Railroad. *Union,* Kilpatrick's Cav.; *Confed.,* W. H. Johnson's Cav. Losses: *Union,* 400 wounded.

21.—Summit Point, Berryville, and Flowing Springs, Va. *Union,* Sixth Corps, and Merritt's and Wilson's Cav.; *Confed.,* Rodes' and Ramseur's divisions. Losses: *Union,* 600 killed and wounded; *Confed.,* 400 killed and wounded.

—Memphis, Tenn. *Union,* detachments of 8th Iowa and 113th Ill., 39th, 40th, and 41st Wis., 61st U. S. Colored, 3d and 4th Iowa Cav., Battery G 1st Mo. Lt. Artil.; *Confed.,* Forrest's Cav. Losses: *Union,* 30 killed, 100 wounded; *Confed.,* 100 killed and wounded.

21 and 22.—Oxford, Miss. *Union,* 4th Iowa, 11th and 21st Mo., 3d Iowa Cav., 12th Mo. Cav.; *Confed.,* Forrest's Cav. Losses: *Confed.**

23.—Abbeville, Miss. *Union,* 10th Mo., 14th Iowa, 5th and 7th Minn., 8th Wis.; *Confed.,* Forrest's Cavalry. Losses: *Union,* 20 wounded; *Confed.,* 34 killed, wounded, and missing.

24.—Jones' Hay Station and Ashley Station, Ark. *Union,* 9th Iowa and 8th and 11th Mo. Cav.; *Confed.,* Troops of Gen. Price's command. Losses: *Union,* 5 killed, 41 wounded; *Confed.,* 60 wounded.

24 and 25.—Bermuda Hundred, Va. *Union,* Tenth Corps; *Confed.,* troops of Gen. Lee's command. Losses: *Union,* 31 wounded; *Confed.,* 61 missing.

24 to 27.—Halltown, Va. *Union,* portion of Eighth Corps; *Confed.,* Gen. Early's command. Losses: *Union,* 30 killed, 141 wounded; *Confed.,* 130 killed and wounded.

25.—Smithfield and Shepherdstown or Kearneysville, Va. *Union,* Merritt's and Wilson's Cav.; *Confed.,* Gen. Early's command. Losses: *Union,* 10 killed, 90 wounded, 100 missing; *Confed.,* 300 killed and wounded.

—Ream's Station, Va. *Union,* Second Corps and Gregg's Cav.; *Confed.,* Gen. A. P. Hill's command. Losses: *Union,* 140 killed, 529 wounded, 2073 missing; *Confed.,* 720 killed and wounded.

29.—Smithfield, Va. *Union,* Third Division Sixth Corps and Torbert's Cav.; *Confed.,* Gen. Early's command. Losses: *Union,* 10 killed, 90 wounded; *Confed.,* 200 killed and wounded.

31 and Sept. 1.—Jonesboro, Ga. *Union,* Fourteenth, Fifteenth, Sixteenth, Seventeenth Corps and Cavalry Corps; *Confed.,* Gen Hardee's Corps, Gen. S. D. Lee's Corps, Army of Tennessee, Gen. J. B. Hood, commanding. Losses: *Union,* 1149 killed and wounded; *Confed.,* 1400 killed, wounded, and missing.

SEPTEMBER, 1864.

1 to 8.—Rousseau's pursuit of Wheeler in Tenn. *Union,* Rousseau's Cav., 1st and 4th Tenn., 2d Mich., 1st Wis., 8th Iowa, 2d and 8th Ind., and 6th Ky.; *Confed.,* Wheeler's Cav. Losses: *Union,* 10 killed, 30 wounded; *Confed.,* 300 killed, wounded, and captured.

1 to Oct. 30.—In front of Petersburg. *Union,* Army of the Potomac; *Confed.,* Army of Northern Virginia. Losses: *Union,* 170 killed, 822 wounded, 812 missing; *Confed.**

2.—Federal occupation of Atlanta, Ga. (Evacuation by Hood's rear-guard during the night of the 1st.) *Union,* Twentieth Corps. Losses: *Confed.,* 200 captured.

3 and 4.—Berryville, Va. *Union,* Eighth and Nineteenth Corps and Torbert's Cav.; *Confed.,* Anderson's command. Losses: *Union,* 30 killed, 182 wounded, 100 missing; *Confed.,* 25 killed, 100 wounded, 70 missing.

4.—Greenville, Tenn. *Union,* 9th and 13th Tenn., and 10th Mich. Cav.; *Confed.,* Morgan's Cav. Losses: *Union,* 6 wounded; *Confed.,* 10 killed, 60 wounded, 75 missing; *Confed.,* Gen. John H. Morgan killed.

* No record found.

THE FORT

THAT NEVER

SURRENDERED

SUMTER FROM

THE SAND–BAR,

APRIL, 1865

COPYRIGHT, 1911, PATRIOT PUB. CO.

THE UNION PHOTOGRAPHER IN SUMTER AT LAST

The shapeless ruins of Sumter, demolished by eighteen months of almost constant fire from Federal batteries, appear in the top picture, of April 14, 1865, the anniversary of Major Anderson's evacuation in 1861. Next comes the Federal fleet dressed with flags for the celebration; and below, a group at the foot of the pole listening to Henry Ward Beecher. In the foreground stand the soldiers and sailors who had taken part in the ceremonies of raising on the shining white staff the very flag that had been lowered exactly four years earlier.

RAISING THE FLAG, APRIL 14TH

On the night of this gala occasion President Lincoln was shot in Washington. Sumter had in a sense become a symbol of the Confederacy. Repeated efforts had been made to conquer its garrisons. But with a tenacity of purpose typical of the South, its shattered walls were transformed into an earthwork impregnable to assault and lending the aid of its six heavy guns to the defenses of Charleston Harbor. It was evacuated only on the night of February 17th, when South Carolina needed every man that could possibly be summoned to oppose Sherman.

10.—Capture of Fort Hell, Va. *Union,* 99th Pa., 20th Ind., 2d U. S. Sharpshooters. Losses: *Union,* 20 wounded; *Confed.,* 90 prisoners.

13.—Lock's Ford, Va. *Union,* Torbert's Cav.; *Confed.,* Gen. Early's command. Losses: *Union,* 2 killed, 18 wounded; *Confed.,* 181 captured.

16.—Sycamore Church, Va. *Union,* 1st D. C. and 13th Pa. Cav. Losses: *Union,* 400 killed, wounded, and captured; *Confed.,* 50 killed and wounded.

16 and 18.—Fort Gibson, Ind. Ter. *Union,* 79th U. S. Colored and 2d Kan. Cav. Losses: *Union,* 38 killed, 48 missing.

19 to 22.—Winchester and Fisher's Hill, Va. *Union,* Sixth, Eighth, and 1st and 2d Divisions of the Nineteenth Corps, Averell's and Torbert's Cav., Maj.-Gen. Phil. Sheridan; *Confed.,* Gen. Jubal Early's command. Losses: *Union,* 749 killed, 4440 wounded, 357 missing; *Confed.,* 250 killed, 1777 wounded, 2813 captured; *Union,* Brig.-Gens. Russell and Mulligan killed; *Confed.,* Maj.-Gen. Rodes and Brig.-Gen. Godwin killed.

23.—Athens, Ala. *Union,* 106th, 110th, and 114th U. S. Colored, 3d Tenn. Cav., reenforced by 18th Mich. and 102d Ohio; *Confed.,* Forrest's Cav. Losses: *Union,* 950 missing; *Confed.,* 5 killed, 25 wounded.

26 and 27.—Pilot Knob or Ironton, Mo. *Union,* 47th and 50th Mo., 14th Iowa, 2d and 3d Mo. Cav., Battery H 2d Mo. Lt. Artil.; *Confed.,* Gen. Sterling Price's command. Losses: *Union,* 28 killed, 56 wounded, 100 missing; *Confed.,* 1500 killed and wounded.

27.—Centralia, Mo. *Union,* three cos. 39th Mo.; *Confed.,* Price's forces. Losses: *Union,* 122 killed, 2 wounded.
—Marianna, Fla. *Union,* 7th Vt., 82d U. S. Colored and 2d Maine Cav.; *Confed.,* Troops of Col. A. B. Montgomery's command, including Anderson's militia. Losses: *Union,* 32 wounded; *Confed.,* 81 missing.

28 and 30.—New Market Heights or Laurel Hill, Va. *Union,* Tenth and Eighteenth Corps and Kautz's Cav.; *Confed.,* Gen. R. S. Ewell's command, supported by Longstreet's Corps under R. H. Anderson. Losses: *Union,* 400 killed, 2029

wounded; *Confed.,* 2000 killed and wounded.

30 and Oct. 1.—Poplar Springs Church, Va. *Union,* First Division Fifth Corps and Second Division Ninth Corps; *Confed.,* Gen. A. P. Hill's Corps. Losses: *Union,* 187 killed, 900 wounded, 1802 missing; *Confed.* (estimate), 800 killed and wounded, 100 missing.
—Arthur's Swamp, Va. *Union,* Gregg's Cav.; *Confed.,* Hampton's Cav. Losses: *Union,* 60 wounded, 100 missing; *Confed.**

OCTOBER, 1864.

2.—Waynesboro, Va. *Union,* portion of Custer's and Merritt's Cav.; *Confed.,* Gen. Early's command. Losses: *Union,* 50 killed and wounded.
—Saltville, Va. *Union,* 11th and 13th Ky. Cav., 12th Ohio, 11th Mich., 5th and 6th U. S. Colored Cav., 26th, 30th, 35th, 37th, 39th, 40th, and 45th Ky. Mounted Inf.; *Confed.,* Gen. Breckinridge's Infantry, Col. Giltner's Cav., 13th Va. Reserves (Home Guards). Losses: *Union,* 54 killed, 190 wounded, 104 missing; *Confed.,* 18 killed, 71 wounded, 21 missing.

5.—Allatoona Pass, Ga. *Union,* 7th, 12th, 50th, 57th, and 93d Ill., 39th Iowa, 4th Minn., 18th Wis., and 12th Wis. Battery; *Confed.,* Gen. French's command. Losses: *Union,* 142 killed, 352 wounded, 212 missing; *Confed.,* 127 killed, 456 wounded, 290 missing.

7 and 13.—Darbytown Road Va. *Union,* Tenth Corps and Kautz's Cav.; *Confed.,* troops of Gen. R. E. Lee's command. Losses: *Union,* 105 killed, 502 wounded, 206 missing; *Confed.**

9.—Tom's Brook, Fisher's Hill or Strasburg, Va. *Union,* Merritt's, Custer's and Torbert's Cav.; *Confed.,* Rosser's and Lomax's Cav. Losses: *Union,* 9 killed, 67 wounded; *Confed.,* 100 killed and wounded, 180 missing.

13.—Reconnaissance to Strasburg, Va. *Union,* Maj.-Gens. Emory's and Crook's troops; *Confed.,* Gen. Early's command. Losses: *Union,* 30 killed, 144 wounded, 40 missing.
—Dalton, Ga. *Union,* troops under Col. Johnson, 44th U. S. Colored; *Confed.,*

* No record found.

The calm sunlight of April, 1865, is falling on the northern face of the fort which had withstood a severer bombardment than any other fortification attacked during the Civil War. This wall was across the fort from the one upon which the heavy Union batteries on Morris Island concentrated their fire. But many a shot passing over the southern wall struck this rampart from the inside, making breaches that had to be patched with gabions. Patched in this way it continued to the end of the war, frowning across the waters of the bay upon the blockading fleet and the Union batteries. Thus it looked when, on February 18, 1865, Colonel Bennet, in command of the United States forces at Charleston, was rowed across from Cummins Point toward Fort Moultrie. Forty yards east of Sumter he met a boat filled with musicians who had been left behind by the Confederates. He directed one of his subordinates to proceed to Sumter and raise the American flag above the ramparts—for the first time in four years.

SUMTER ONCE MORE IN PEACE

THE DESERTED DEFENSES

Sumter, inside the face of which the outside is shown above. The skill with which gabions were employed to strengthen the ramparts is apparent. A description of the relinquishment of the position follows in the words of Major John Johnson: "On the night of the 17th of February, 1865, the commander, Captain Thomas A. Huguenin, silently and without interruption effected the complete evacuation. He has often told me of the particulars, and I have involuntarily accompanied him in thought and feeling as, for the last time, he went the rounds of the deserted fort. The ordered casements with their massive guns were there, but in the stillness of that hour his own footfall alone gave an echo from the arches overhead. The labyrinthine galleries, as he traversed them, were lighted for a moment by his lantern; he passed out from the shadows to step aboard the little boat awaiting him at the wharf, and the four years' defense of Fort Sumter was at an end."

WITHIN THE DEADLY ZONE AT PETERSBURG

The officers' quarters of Fort Sedgwick, a bomb-proof structure, was a post of honor in the Federal line, as it invariably drew the hottest fire.   It stands immediately behind the salient at which the guns were served. On the right is the "Blessed Well" of Fort Damnation.   The commands garrisoning this fort were changed more frequently than any other.   Regiments were continually moved from one part of the line to the camps near City Point to recuperate, while fresh troops were brought up from that base to take their places. General John Grubb Park commanded the Ninth Corps, and it was this body of Federal troops that advanced from behind Fort Sedgwick and, supported by its guns, seized the Confederate entrenchments opposite in an assault made on April 2, 1865.

A WINTER DUG-OUT

CAVE DWELLERS

A CONFEDERATE MILL IN '65—WHERE THE SOUND OF THE GRINDING WAS LOW

The wonder is that Lee's starving army was able to hold out as long as it did. This well-built flour-mill was one of many which in times of peace carried on an important industry in the town. But long before the siege closed, all the mills were empty of grain and grist. Could Lee have kept the flour-mills of Petersburg and Richmond running during the last winter of the war, disaster would not have come to his famished forces so early in 1865. At the beginning of the year but one railroad, a canal, and a turnpike remained by which supplies could be gotten into Petersburg from Wilmington, N. C., and Charleston, S. C. These were the last two ports that the blockade-runners still dared venture into with supplies for the Confederacy. Not only was food scarce, but the de- serters from Lee's army, averaging about a hundred daily, re- vealed plainly the fact that the Confederate troops with their threadbare, insufficient clothing, were in a most pitiable condi- tion. Not only was food lacking, but ammunition was running low. During 1864 the supply of per- cussion-caps for the Confederate army had been kept up only by melting the copper stills throughout the South. Now even these were exhausted, and there were no more supplies of cop- per in sight. Hundreds of heartrend- ing letters were intercepted and sent to Lee's headquarters. "Mothers, wives, and sisters wrote of their inability to respond to the appeals of hungry children for bread or to provide proper care and remedies for the sick, and in the name of all that was dear appealed to the men to come home.

COPYRIGHT, 1911, PATRIOT PUB. CO.

THE FINAL CAPTURE—FORT MAHONE

It is April 3, 1865. On the parapet in the middle of the line of officers stands Lieutenant J. B. Krepps, of the Second Pennsylvania Heavy Artillery. The regiment was attached to the Ninth Corps, of which Potter's division had captured the fort on the previous afternoon. "Fort Damnation," as it was called by the Federal soldiers, was the last to fall in the general assault. Potter's men gained possession of it only after the most desperate fighting from traverse to traverse. Even then, after a breathing space, the Confederates, in a brave assault, recaptured a portion of the works and held on until driven back by a brilliant charge of Griffin's men.

CHEERING THE VICTORS OF PETERSBURG, APRIL 3D

Here, on the gabioned parapet of "Fort Hell" (Sedgwick), the garrison left behind, with shouts and waving of hats and firing of muskets, are signalling their enthusiasm at the success of their comrades, who now hold the works of the old antagonist, "Fort Damnation," across the way. Such scenes were enacted all along the lines on the 3d, when the victory became assured. The long siege of nearly a year was over and the men knew that its consequences were momentous. If there were to be more fighting it would be against a retreating army, without any of the weary waiting in cramped fortifications. The army was soon to be on the move; Lee was already evacuating Petersburg.

Gen. Hood's advance troops. Losses: *Union,* 400 missing.

15.—Glasgow, Mo. *Union,* 43d Mo., and detachments of 17th Ill., 9th Mo. Militia, 13th Mo. Cav., 62d U. S. Colored; *Confed.,* Gen. Sterling Price's command. Losses: *Union,* 400 wounded and missing; *Confed.,* 50 killed and wounded.

19.—Cedar Creek, Va. (Sheridan's Ride.) *Union,* Sixth Corps, Eighth Corps, and First and Second Divisions Nineteenth Corps, Merritt's, Custer's, and Torbert's Cav.; *Confed.,* Gen. Jubal Early's army. Losses: *Union,* 644 killed, 3430 wounded, 1591 captured or missing; *Confed.,* 320 killed, 1540 wounded, 1050 missing; *Union,* Brig.-Gen. Bidwell and Col. Thoburn killed; *Confed.,* Maj.-Gen. Ramseur killed.

26 to 29.—Decatur, Ala. *Union,* 18th Mich., 102d Ohio, 68th Ind., and 14th U. S. Colored; *Confed.,* Gen. J. B. Hood's army. Losses: *Union,* 10 killed, 45 wounded, 100 missing; *Confed.,* 100 killed, 300 wounded.

27.—Hatcher's Run, Va. *Union,* Gregg's Cav., Second and Third Divisions Second Corps, Fifth and Ninth Corps; *Confed.,* Gen. Hill's Corps, Fitzhugh Lee's and M. C. Butler's Cav. Losses: *Union,* 166 killed, 1047 wounded, 699 missing; *Confed.,* 200 killed, 600 wounded, 200 missing (Federal estimate).

—Destruction at Plymouth, N. C., of the *Confed.* ram *Albemarle,* by Lieut. W. B. Cushing, U. S. N., and 14 officers and men. Losses: *Union,* 2 drowned, 11 captured. *Confed.**

—Morristown, Tenn. *Union,* Gen. Gillem's Cav.; *Confed.,* Forrest's Cav. Losses: *Union,* 8 killed, 42 wounded; *Confed.,* 240 missing.

27 and 28.—Fair Oaks, Va. *Union,* Tenth and Eighteenth Corps and Kautz's Cav.; *Confed.,* Gen. Longstreet's command. Losses: *Union,* 120 killed, 783 wounded, 400 missing; *Confed.,* 60 killed, 311 wounded, 80 missing.

28 and 30.—Newtonia, Mo. *Union,* Col. Blunt's Cav.; *Confed.,* Gen. Price's command. Losses: *Confed.,* 250 killed and wounded.

29.—Beverly, W. Va. *Union,* 8th Ohio Cav.; *Confed.,* troops of Gen. Breckinridge's command. Losses: *Union,* 8 killed, 25 wounded, 13 missing; *Confed.,* 17 killed, 27 wounded, 92 missing.

NOVEMBER, 1864.

5.—Fort Sedgwick or Fort Hell, Va. *Union,* Second Corps; *Confed.,* troops of Gen. Lee's Army of Northern Virginia. Losses: *Union,* 5 killed, 10 wounded; *Confed.,* 15 killed, 35 wounded.

12.—Newtown and Cedar Springs, Va. *Union,* Merritt's, Custer's, and Powell's Cav.; *Confed.,* troops of Gen. Early's command. Losses: *Union,* 84 wounded, 100 missing; *Confed.,* 150 killed, wounded, and missing.

13.—Bull's Gap., Tenn. *Union,* 8th, 9th, and 13th Tenn. Cav.; *Confed.,* advance of Gen. Hood's army. Losses: *Union,* 5 killed, 36 wounded, 200 missing; *Confed.**

17.—Bermuda Hundred, Va. *Union,* 209th Pa.; *Confed.,* troops of Gen. Lee's army. Losses: *Union,* 10 wounded, 120 missing; *Confed.,* 10 wounded.

21.—Griswoldville, Ga. *Union,* Walcutt's Brigade First Division, Fifteenth Corps, and First Brigade Third Division Cav.; *Confed.,* Gen. Gustavus W. Smith's Georgia Militia. Losses: *Union,* 13 killed, 69 wounded; *Confed.,* 5 killed, 472 wounded, 2 missing.

22.—Rood's Hill, Va. *Union,* Torbert's Cav.; *Confed.,* Gen. Early's command. Losses: *Union,* 18 killed, 52 wounded; *Confed.**

24.—Lawrenceburg, Campbellville, and Lynnville, Tenn. *Union,* Hatch's Cav.; *Confed.,* Cavalry of Hood's army. Losses: *Union,* 75 killed and wounded; *Confed.,* 50 killed and wounded.

26.—Sandersville, Ga. *Union,* Third Brigade First Division, Twentieth Corps; *Confed.,* Wheeler's Cav. Losses: *Union,* 100 missing; *Confed.,* 100 missing.

26 to 29.—Sylvan Grove, Waynesboro', Browne's Cross Roads, Ga. *Union,* Kilpatrick's Cav.; *Confed.,* Wheeler's Cav. Losses: *Union,* 46 wounded; *Confed.**

29 and 30.—Spring Hill and Franklin, Tenn. *Union,* Fourth and Twenty-third Corps and Cav.; *Confed.,* Gen. J. B. Hood's army. Losses: *Union,* 189 killed, 1033 wounded, 1104 missing; *Confed.,* 1750 killed, 3800 wounded, 702 missing.

* No record found.

HAVOC UNCONFINED—THE RICHMOND ARSENAL

As the camera clicks in April, 1865, the long-defended citadel of the Confederacy is at last deserted; its munitions of war no longer ready for service against an enemy; its armies at a distance, retreating as rapidly as their exhausted condition permits. These fire-blasted and crumbling walls are a fit symbol of the condition of the South at the close of the war. The scene at this arsenal on the night of April 2d was one of the most brilliant and splendid of the whole conflict. The arsenal was near the Richmond & Petersburg Railroad at the James River. The high-arched bridges ablaze across the stream, the deafening reports of exploding magazines, the columns of white smoke rising high into the sky lurid from thousands of shells bursting in the arsenal, the falling of the broken fragments among the already panic stricken fugitives—all these features created a scene such as the world has seldom witnessed. Early in the morning of April 3d the clatter of Federal cavalry was heard in the streets. The Stars and Stripes waved. Richmond was the capital of the Confederacy no longer.

Union, Maj.-Gens. Stanley and Bradley wounded; *Confed.,* Maj.-Gen. Cleburne, Brig.-Gens. Adams, Strahl, Gist, and Granbury killed, Maj.-Gen. Brown and Brig.-Gens. Carter, Manigault, Quarles, Cockrell, and Scott wounded.

30.—Honey Hill or Grahamsville, S. C. *Union,* 25th Ohio, 56th and 155th N. Y., 26th, 32d, 35th, and 102d U. S. Colored, 54th and 55th Mass. Colored; *Confed.,* Georgia Militia under Gen. G. W. Smith, S. C. Battery. Losses: *Union,* 91 killed, 631 wounded; *Confed.,* 8 killed, 42 wounded.

DECEMBER, 1864.

1.—Stony Creek Station, Weldon Railroad, Va. *Union,* Gregg's Cav.; *Confed.,* Capt. Waldhauer's command and Gen. Fitzhugh Lee's Cav. Losses: *Union,* 40 wounded; *Confed.,* 175 captured.

1 to 14.—In front of Nashville, Tenn. *Union,* Fourth, Twenty-third Corps; First and Third divisions of Sixteenth Corps; Wilson's Cav.; *Confed.,* Gen. Hood's army. Losses: *Union,* 16 killed, 100 wounded; *Confed.**

1 to 31.—In front of Petersburg. *Union,* Army of the Potomac; *Confed.,* troops of Lee's army. Losses: *Union,* 40 killed, 329 wounded; *Confed.**

4.—Block-house No. 7, Tenn. *Union,* Gen. Milroy's troops; *Confed.,* Gen. Bate's division of Hood's army. Losses: *Union,* 100 killed, wounded, and missing; *Confed.,* 87 killed, wounded and missing.

5 to 8.—Murfreesboro', Tenn. *Union,* Gen. Rousseau's troops; *Confed.,* Gen. Bate's command. Losses: *Union,* 30 killed, 175 wounded; *Confed.,* 197 missing.

6 to 9.—Deveaux's Neck, S. C. *Union,* 56th, 127th, 144th, 155th, and 157th N. Y., 25th Ohio, 26th, 32d, 33d, 34th, and 102d U. S. Colored, 54th and 55th Mass. Colored, 3d R. I. Artil., Naval brigade Bat. F, 3d N. Y. Lt. Art., and gunboats; *Confed.,* troops of Gen. Samuel Jones' command. Losses: *Union,* 39 killed, 390 wounded, 200 missing; *Confed.,* 400 killed and wounded.

7 to 11.—Weldon Railroad Expedition. *Union,* Fifth Corps, Third Division of Second Corps, and Second Division Cavalry Corps, Army of the Potomac; *Confed.,* Gen. A. P. Hill's command. Losses: *Union,* 100 killed and wounded; *Confed.**

8 and 9.—Hatcher's Run, Va. *Union,* First Division, Second Corps, 3d and 13th Pa. Cav., 6th Ohio Cav.; *Confed.,* Gen. Hill's command. Losses: *Union,* 125 killed and wounded; *Confed.**

8 to 28.—Raid to Gordonsville, Va. *Union,* Merritt's and Custer's Cav.; *Confed.,* Cavalry of Gen. Early's army. Losses: *Union,* 43 killed and wounded. *Confed.**

10 to 21.—Siege of Savannah, Ga. *Union,* Fourteenth, Fifteenth, Seventeenth, and Twentieth Corps of Sherman's army; *Confed.,* Gen. W. J. Hardee's command. Losses: *Union,* 200 killed and wounded; *Confed.* (estimate), 800 killed, wounded, and missing.

12 to 21.—Federal raid from Bean's Station, Tenn., to Saltville, Va., including Abingdon, Glade Springs, and Marion. *Union,* Stoneman's Cav.; *Confed.,* Gen. J. C. Breckinridge's command. Losses: *Union,* 20 killed, 123 wounded; *Confed.,* 126 wounded, 500 missing.

13.—Fort McAllister, Ga. *Union,* Second Division of Fifteenth Corps; *Confed.,* Garrison commanded by Maj. W. G. Anderson. Losses: *Union,* 24 killed, 110 wounded; *Confed.,* 48 killed and wounded, 200 missing.

15 and 16.—Nashville, Tenn. *Union,* Fourth Corps; First and Third Divisions Thirteenth Corps; Twenty-third Corps; Wilson's Cav., and detachments colored troops, convalescents; *Confed.,* Gen. J. B. Hood's army. Losses: *Union,* 387 killed, 2558 wounded; *Confed.,* 4462 killed, wounded, and missing.

17.—Franklin, Tenn. *Union,* Wilson's Cav.; *Confed.,* Forrest's Cav. Losses: *Confed.,* 1800 wounded and sick captured. (Incident of Hood's retreat from Nashville.)

25.—Fort Fisher, N. C. *Union,* Tenth Corps and North Atlantic Squadron, commanded by Rear-Admiral D. D. Porter; Flag-Ship, *Malvern;* Iron-Clads: *Canonicus, Mahopac, Monadnock, New Ironsides, Saugus;* Screw-Frigates: *Colorado, Minnesota, Wabash;* Side-Wheel Steamers (first class): *Powhatan, Susque-*

* No record found.

EMPTY VAULTS—THE EXCHANGE BANK, RICHMOND, 1865

The sad significance of these photographs is all too apparent. Not only the bank buildings were in ruins, but the financial system of the entire South. All available capital had been consumed by the demands of the war, and a system of paper currency had destroyed credit completely. Worse still was the demoralization of all industry. Through large areas of the South all mills and factories were reduced to ashes, and everywhere the industrial system was turned topsy-turvy. Truly the problem that confronted the South was stupendous.

WRECK OF THE GALLEGO FLOUR MILLS

Engagements of the Civil War

hanna; Screw Sloops: *Brooklyn, Juniata, Mohican, Shenandoah, Ticonderoga, Tuscarora;* Screw Gun-Vessels: *Kansas, Maumee, Nyack, Pequot, Yantic;* Screw Gun-Boats: *Chippewa, Huron, Seneca, Unadilla;* Double-Enders: *Iosco, Mackinaw, Maratanza, Osceola, Pawtuxet, Pontoosuc, Sassacus, Tacony;* Miscellaneous Vessels: *Fort Jackson, Monticello, Nereus, Quaker City, Rhode Island, Santiago de Cuba, Vanderbilt;* Powder Vessel: *Louisiana;* Reserve: *A. D. Vance, Alabama, Britannia, Cherokee, Emma, Gettysburg, Governor Buckingham, Howquah, Keystone State, Lilian, Little Ada, Moccasin, Nansemond, Tristram Shandy, Wilderness; Confed.,* North Carolina troops in garrison, commanded by Col. William Lamb, Gen. Hoke's Division outside. Losses: *Union,* 8 killed, 38 wounded; *Confed.,* 3 killed, 55 wounded, 280 prisoners.

28.—Egypt Station, Miss. *Union,* 4th and 11th Ill. Cav., 7th Ind., 4th and 10th Mo., 2d Wis., 2d N. J., 1st Miss. and 3d U. S. Colored Cav.; *Confed.,* troops of Gen. Gardner's army under Gen. Gholson. Losses: *Union,* 23 killed, 88 wounded; *Confed.,* 500 captured; *Confed.,* Brig.-Gen. Gholson killed.

JANUARY, 1865.

11.—Beverly, W. Va. *Union,* 34th Ohio and 8th Ohio Cav.; *Confed.,* Gen. Breckinridge's command. Losses: *Union,* 5 killed, 20 wounded, 583 missing; *Confed.**

12 to 15.—Fort Fisher, N. C. *Union,* Portions of Twenty-fourth and Twenty-fifth Corps and Admiral Porter's fleet; Same ships as Dec. 25th above, with the exception that the *Nyack, Keystone State,* and *Quaker City* were not present and the *Montgomery, Cuyler, Aries, Eolus, Fort Donelson,* and *Republic* had been added to the fleet; *Confed.,* Same as Dec. 25th above. Losses: *Union,* 184 killed, 749 wounded; *Confed.,* 400 killed and wounded, 2083 captured.

25 to Feb. 9.—Combahee River and River's Bridge, Salkahatchie, S. C. *Union,* Fifteenth and Seventeenth Corps; *Confed.,* Wade Hampton's Cav. Losses: *Union,* 138 killed and wounded; *Confed.**

FEBRUARY, 1865.

5 to 7.—Dabney's Mills, Hatcher's Run, Va. *Union,* Fifth Corps and First Division Sixth Corps and Gregg's Cav.; *Confed.,* troops of Gen. A. P. Hill's and Gen. J. B. Gordon's Corps. Losses: *Union,* 171 killed, 1181 wounded, 186 missing; *Confed.,* 1200 killed and wounded; *Confed.,* Gen. Pegram killed.

8 to 14.—Williston, Blackville, and Aiken, S. C. *Union,* Kilpatrick's Cav.; *Confed.,* Wheeler's Cav. Losses: *Union *; Confed.,* 240 killed and wounded, 100 missing.

10.—James Island, S. C. *Union,* Maj.-Gen. Gillmore's command; *Confed.,* troops of Gen. Hardee's command. Losses: *Union,* 20 killed, 76 wounded; *Confed.,* 20 killed, and 70 wounded.

11.—Sugar Loaf Battery, Federal Point, N. C. *Union,* Portions of Twenty-fourth and Twenty-fifth Corps; *Confed.,* Gen. Hoke's command. Losses: *Union,* 14 killed, 114 wounded. *Confed.**

16 and 17.—Columbia, S. C. *Union,* Fifteenth Corps, Army of the Tennessee, commanded by Major-General John A. Logan; *Confed.,* troops of Gen. Beauregard's command. Losses: *Union,* 20 killed and wounded; *Confed.**

18 to 22.—Fort Anderson, Town Creek, and Wilmington, N. C. *Union,* Twenty-third and Twenty-fourth Corps, and Porter's gunboats; *Confed.,* Gen. Hoke's command. Losses: *Union,* 40 killed, 204 wounded; *Confed.,* 70 killed, 400 wounded, 375 missing.

22.—Douglas Landing, Pine Bluff, Ark. *Union,* 13th Ill. Cav.; *Confed.,* troops of Gen. Kirby Smith's command. Losses: *Union,* 40 killed and wounded; *Confed.,* 26 killed and wounded.

27 to March 25.—Cavalry raid in Virginia. *Union,* First and Third divisions of Sheridan's Cav.; *Confed.,* Gen. Jubal Early's command. Losses: *Union,* 35 killed and wounded; *Confed.,* 1667 prisoners.

MARCH, 1865.

2.—Waynesboro, Va. *Union,* Sheridan's Cavalry Corps. *Confed.,* Maj.-Gen. Jubal Early's command, Rosser's Cav.

* No record found.

SIGNS OF PEACE—CONFEDERATE ARTILLERY CAPTURED AT RICHMOND AND WAITING SHIPMENT

Never again to be used by brother against brother, these Confederate guns captured in the defenses about Richmond are parked near the wharves on the James River ready for shipment to the national arsenal at Washington, once more the capital of a united country. The reflection of these instruments of destruction on the peaceful surface of the canal is not more clear than was the purpose of the South to accept the issues of the war and to restore as far as in them lay the bases for an enduring prosperity. The same devotion which manned these guns so bravely and prolonged the contest as long as it was possible for human powers to endure, was now directed to the new problems which the cessation of hostilities had provided. The restored Union came with the years to possess for the South a significance to be measured only by the thankfulness that the outcome had been what it was and by the pride in the common traditions and common blood of the whole American people. These captured guns are a memory therefore, not of regret, but of recognition, gratitude, that the highest earthly tribunal settled all strife in 1865.

COEHORNS, MORTARS, LIGHT AND HEAVY GUNS

Losses: *Union*; Confed.*, killed and wounded not recorded, 1603 captured.

8 to 10.—Wilcox's Bridge, N. C. *Union*, Palmer's, Carter's, and Ruger's Divisions, of Gen. Schofield's command; *Confed.*, forces under Gen. Bragg from Hood's Army of Tennessee, and Hoke's North Carolina division. Losses: *Union*, 65 killed, 379 wounded, 953 missing; *Confed.*, 1500 killed, wounded, and missing.

16.—Averysboro', N. C. *Union*, Twentieth Corps and Kilpatrick's Cav.; *Confed.*, Gen. Hardee's command. Losses: *Union*, 93 killed, 531 wounded; *Confed.*, 108 killed, 540 wounded, 217 missing.

19 to 21.—Bentonville, N. C. *Union*, Fourteenth, Fifteenth, Seventeenth, and Twentieth Corps, and Kilpatrick's Cav.; *Confed.*, Gen. J. E. Johnston's army and Wade Hampton's Cav. Losses: *Union*, 191 killed, 1168 wounded, 287 missing; *Confed.*, 239 killed, 1694 wounded, 673 missing.

20 to April 6.—Stoneman's raid into Southwestern Va. and North Carolina. *Union*, Palmer's, Brown's, and Miller's Cavalry Brigades; *Confed.** Losses.*

22 to April 24.—Wilson's Raid, Chickasaw, Ala., to Macon, Ga. *Union*, Gen. James H. Wilson's Cav.; *Confed.*, Forrest's Cav., local garrison and State Militia. Losses: *Union*, 63 killed, 345 wounded, 63 missing; *Confed.*, 22 killed, 38 wounded, 6766 prisoners.

25.—Fort Stedman, in front of Petersburg, Va. *Union*, First and Third Divisions Ninth Corps; *Confed.*, Gen. John B. Gordon's Corps, supported by Lee's artillery in the forts. Losses: *Union*, 70 killed, 424 wounded, 523 captured; *Confed.*, 800 killed and wounded, 1881 missing (Federal estimate).

—Petersburg Trenches. Second and Sixth Corps; *Confed.*, Gen. R. E. Lee's command. Losses: *Union*, 103 killed, 864 wounded, 209 missing; *Confed.*, killed and wounded not recorded, 834 captured.

26 to April 9.—Siege of Mobile, Ala., including Spanish Fort and Fort Blakely. *Union*, Thirteenth and Sixteenth Corps and Acting Rear-Admiral Thatcher's fleet; *Confed.*, Gen. D. H. Maury's land forces, five gunboats under Commodore Farrand. Losses: *Union*, 213 killed, 1211 wounded; *Confed.*, 500 killed and wounded, 3000 to 4000 captured.

29.—Quaker Road, Va. *Union*, Warren's Fifth Corps and Griffin's First Division, Army of the Potomac; *Confed.*, Part of Gen. R. E. Lee's Army. Losses: *Union*, 55 killed, 306 wounded; *Confed.*, 135 killed, 400 wounded, 100 missing.

31.—Boydton and White Oak Roads, Va. *Union*, Second and Fifth Corps; *Confed.*, part of Gen. R. E. Lee's command. Losses: *Union*, 177 killed, 1134 wounded, 556 missing; *Confed.*, 1000 killed, 235 missing.

—Dinwiddie C. H., Va. *Union*, First, Second, and Third Divisions Cavalry of the Army of the Potomac; *Confed.*, Cav. under Gen. Fitzhugh Lee and Gen. W. H. F. Lee. Losses: *Union*, 67 killed, 354 wounded; *Confed.*, 400 killed and wounded.

APRIL, 1865.

1.—Five Forks, Va. *Union*, First, Second, and Third Cav. Divisions and Fifth Corps; *Confed.*, Gen. Geo. E. Pickett's command, Gen. Fitzhugh Lee's Cav., including Rosser's and Munford's Divisions. Losses: *Union*, 124 killed, 706 wounded; *Confed.**

2.—Selma, Ala. *Union*, Second Division Cav., Military Division of the Mississippi; Forrest's Cav. Losses: *Union*, 42 killed, 270 wounded, 7 missing; *Confed.*, killed and wounded,* 2700 captured.

—Fall of Petersburg, Va. *Union*, Second, Sixth, Ninth, and Twenty-fourth Corps; *Confed.*, Part of Gen. A. P. Hill's and Gen. J. B. Gordon's Corps. Losses: *Union*, 296 killed, 2565 wounded, 500 missing; *Confed.*, killed and wounded not recorded, 3000 prisoners (estimate).

3.—Fall of Richmond, Va. *Union*, Gen. Weitzel's command; *Confed.*, Local Brigade and other forces under command of Gen. R. S. Ewell. Losses: *Confed.*, 6000 prisoners, of whom 500 were sick and wounded.

5.—Amelia Springs, Va. *Union*, Crook's Cav.; *Confed.*, Gary's Cav. Losses: *Union*, 20 killed, 96 wounded; *Confed.**

* No record found.

One of the proudest days of the nation—May 24, 1865—here lives again. The true greatness of the American people was not displayed till the close of the war. The citizen from the walks of humble life had during the contest become a veteran soldier, equal in courage and fighting capacity to the best drilled infantry of Marlborough, Frederick the Great, or Napoleon. But it remained to be seen whether he would return peacefully to the occupations of peace. European nations made dark predictions. "Would nearly a million men," they asked, "one of the mightiest military organizations ever trained in war, quietly lay aside this resistless power and disappear into the unnoted walks of civil life?" Europe with its standing armies thought not. Europe was mistaken. The disbanded veterans lent the effectiveness of military order and discipline to the industrial and commercial development of the land they had come to love with an increased devotion. The pictures are of Sherman's troops marching

THE RETURN OF THE SOLDIERS—THE GRAND REVIEW

THE SAME SCENE, A FEW SECONDS LATER

down Pennsylvania Avenue. The horsemen in the lead are General Francis P. Blair and his staff, and the infantry in flashing new uniforms are part of the Seventeenth Corps in the Army of Tennessee. Little over a year before, they had started with Sherman on his series of battles and flanking marches in the struggle for Atlanta. They had taken a conspicuous and important part in the battle of July 22d east of Atlanta, receiving and finally repulsing attacks in both front and rear. They had marched with Sherman to the sea and participated in the capture of Savannah. They had joined in the campaign through the Carolinas, part of the time leading the advance and tearing up many miles of railway track, and operating on the extreme right after the battle of Bentonville. After the negotiations for Johnston's surrender were completed in April, they set out on the march for the last time with flying colors and martial music, to enter the memorable review at Washington in May, here preserved.

Engagements of the Civil War

6.—Sailor's Creek, Va. *Union,* Second and Sixth Corps and Sheridan's Cav.; *Confed.,* Gen. R. S. Ewell's command, and part of Gen. R. H. Anderson's. Losses: *Union,* 166 killed, 1014 wounded; *Confed.,* 6000 killed, wounded, and captured. (Federal estimate.)

7.—High Bridge and Farmville, Appomattox River, Va. *Union,* Second Corps and portion of Twenty-fourth Corps; *Confed.,* rearguard of Gordon's and Longstreet's Corps and Fitzhugh Lee's Cav. Losses: *Union,* 571 killed, 71 wounded, and missing; *Confed.**

8 and 9.—Appomattox C. H., Va. *Union,* Twenty-fourth Corps, one division of the Twenty-fifth Corps and Sheridan's Cav.; *Confed.,* Gen. Fitzhugh Lee's Cav. Losses: *Union,* 200 killed and wounded; *Confed.,* 500 killed and wounded.

9.—Gen. R. E. Lee surrendered the Army of Northern Virginia to the Army of the Potomac and the Army of the James; Lieut.-Gen. U. S. Grant. *Confed.,* surrendered and paroled, 27,805.

12 and 13.—Montgomery, Ala. *Union,* Second Brigade, First Division Cav.; *Confed.,* Gen. D. W. Adams' command. Losses: not recorded.

16.—West Point, Ga. *Union,* 2d and 4th Ind. Cav., 18th Indpt. Bat. Ind. Light Artil.; *Confed.,* Brig.-Gen. R. C. Tyler with 300 men. Losses: *Union,* 7 killed, 29 wounded; *Confed.,* 19 killed, 28 wounded, 218 missing. Brig.-Gen. R. C. Tyler killed. Last organized Confederate resistance East of the Mississippi. —Columbus, Ga. *Union,* Fourth Division Cav.; *Confed.,* Gen. D. W. Adams' command. Losses: *Union,* 6 killed, 24 missing; *Confed.,* killed and wounded not recorded, 1200 captured.

26.—Gen. Jos. E. Johnston surrendered the Army of Tennessee and other commands to the Army of the Tennessee, the Army of Georgia and the Army of Ohio; Maj.-Gen. W. T. Sherman. *Confed.,* surrendered and paroled, 31,243.

MAY, 1865.

4.—Gen. Richard Taylor surrendered with Army of the Department of Alabama to Maj.-Gen. E. R. S. Canby. *Confed.,* surrendered, 42,293.

10.—Capture of Jefferson Davis, President of the Confederate States of America, at Irwinsville, Ga., by the 1st Wis. and 4th Mich. Cav. Losses: *Union,* 2 killed, 4 wounded, caused by the pursuing parties firing into each other. —Tallahassee, Fla. Surrender of Gen. Samuel Jones' command to detachment of Wilson's U. S. Cav. under Maj.-Gen. McCook. *Confed.,* surrendered, 8000.

11.—Chalk Bluff, Ark. Surrender of Gen. Jeff. Thompson's command to forces under Gen. M. Grenville Dodge; *Confed.,* surrendered, 7454.

12 and 13.—Palmetto Ranch, near Brownsville, Tex. *Union,* 34th Ind., 62d U. S. Colored and 2d Tex. Cav. under command Col. F. H. Barrett; *Confed.,* troops commanded by Brig.-Gen. Jas. H. Slaughter. Losses: *Union,* 115 killed and wounded; *Confed.**

23 and 24.—Grand Review of the Federal armies on Pennsylvania Avenue, Washington. Lieut.-Gen. U. S. Grant, Maj.-Gen. George G. Meade and Maj.-Gen. W. T. Sherman occupied the reviewing stand.

26.—Surrender of Gen. E. Kirby Smith (Army of the Trans-Mississippi Department) to Maj.-Gen. E. R. S. Canby. *Confed.,* surrendered, 17,686. —In addition to the surrenders noted above, there were paroled at Cumberland, Maryland, and other stations, 9337; in the Department of Washington, 3390; in Virginia, Tennessee, Alabama, Louisiana, and Texas, 13,922; at Nashville and Chattanooga, Tenn., 5029. Miscellaneous paroles in the Department of Virginia amounted to 9072. Total number paroled, according to the statistics of the War Department, was 174,223.

* No record found.

Review of Twentieth Army Corps, May 24, 1865. To the strains of popular airs the Grand Army of the Republic marched from the shadow of the Capitol to the front of the Executive Mansion. But amid the bayonets flashing in the sunlight each soldier was saddened by the thought of companions in arms who were not by his side and who would never return to waiting mother or sweetheart. In the Union armies alone three hundred and fifty-nine thousand men had lain down their lives in the Civil War, and the losses in the Southern armies raised the total to over seven hundred thousand. Most of these were young fellows, their years of vigorous activity yet unlived. If by a sudden catastrophe Cleveland or Pittsburgh were utterly destroyed, the loss to the nation would not be so great. Behind the glamor of military achievement lies the cruel cost to be compensated for only by the necessity for deciding the questions that had threatened the foundations of the American nation.

"WHEN THIS CRUEL WAR IS OVER"

READY TO TILL THE FIELDS OF PEACE

The record of the Twentieth Corps was distinguished. It was engaged in the constant battling and skirmishing of the Atlanta Campaign. In the final operations these troops were the first to enter the city on the morning of September 2, 1864, and it was to General Slocum, their commander, that the mayor surrendered. For two months they held Atlanta and its approaches from the North while the rest of Sherman's army was engaged in attacking Hood's retreating columns. In the march to the sea the corps was commanded by General A. S. Williams. At Savannah the troops again had the honor of being the first to enter an evacuated city, the second division marching in on the morning of December 21, 1864. In the march through the Carolinas the corps was in the thick of the fight at Bentonville, repulsing successive attacks with the aid of its artillery. Another change in the commanding officer was made on April 2d, when General J. A. Mower succeeded General A. S. Williams

A NATION'S JOY AND GRIEF—"WELCOME BRAVE SOLDIERS" BELOW CRAPE AND THE FLAG AT HALF-MAST FOR LINCOLN

THE MARCH OF THE GRAND ARMY

This vivid photograph has been identified, by one who witnessed the procession, as a view on F Street, Washington. The jaunty bearing of the men in front is as striking to the reader now as it was to that eye-witness nearly half a century ago. The view on the page facing shows the signs of joy and grief mingled on the same day. The flag at half mast, the windows draped in crape, express silently the grief that filled the heart of both North and South at the news of Lincoln's assassination. The vision of his majestic figure now rose calmly and grandly above the animosities of the stormy conflict as one to whom every section of the land he saved could point with pride, and say, "Here is an American." All sections could join, too, in applauding the banner, "Welcome Brave Soldiers." For in the war all were Americans, and all can join in pride over the courage of the American soldier from North and South. The soldiers who led in the battle line, Blue and Gray alike, led also in reëchoing the words of Webster: "Union now and forever, one and inseparable."

THE FINAL ACT OF THE DRAMA

This is the finale, the last tableau of the Great Drama of the Civil War—a drama that for four years had held the stage of half a continent with all civilization for an audience. In late April of '65 a photographer visited Point Lookout Prison, Maryland, and was present when the last Confederate prisoners took the oath of allegiance to the flag under whose shadow they stand as their hands touch simultaneously the Bibles—one held by each group of four. At the desk, administering the oath, sits the Commander of the Department of St. Mary's, General James Barnes, who since recovering from his wounds at Gettysburg had been in charge of more captured Confederates than there were in Lee's last army. It is a moving

THE LAST CONFEDERATE PRISONERS TAKE THE OATH AT POINT LOOKOUT

sight; it stirs the emotions, to look at the faces of these men, now returning from exile to their war-ridden country and desolated homes. Theirs is the hardest task in all the world—to conquer defeat and begin anew, under changed surroundings and conditions, the struggle for existence. Bravely the Southerners faced it, as bravely as they had faced the line of blue-clad men who are their enemies no longer. Long before fifty years had passed, when again the war cloud had risen and the country called for men, during the Spanish War, in the great camps at Chickamauga—"the sons of those sires, at the same camp-fires, cheered one flag where their fathers fought."

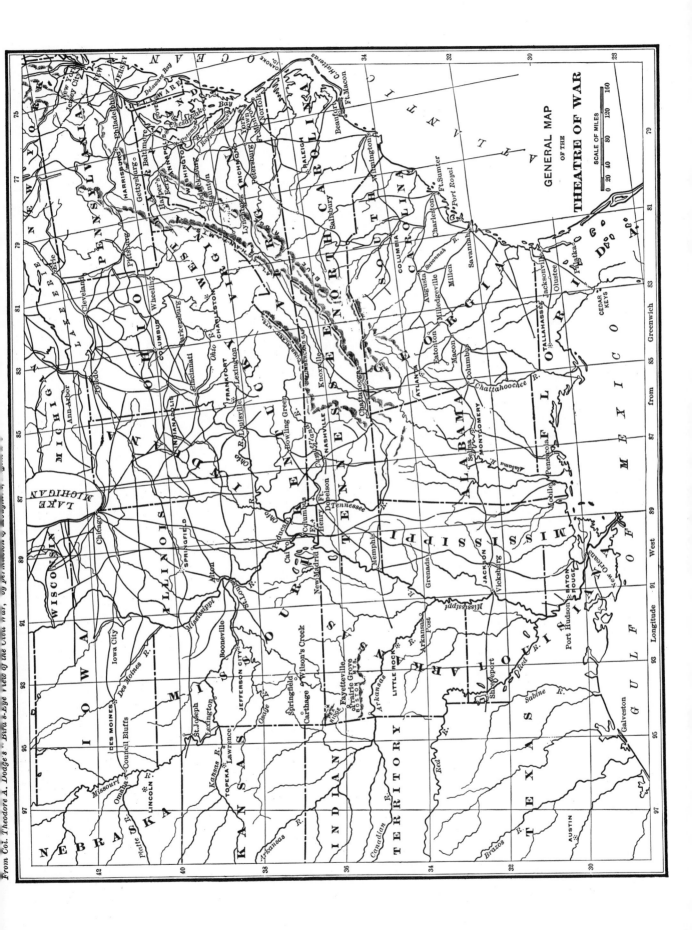

From Col. Theodore A. Dodge's "Bird's-Eye View of the Civil War," by permission of Houghton, Mifflin & Co.

GENERAL MAP
OF THE
THEATRE OF WAR

SCALE OF MILES

0 20 40 80 120 160

The Photographic History
of The Civil War

TWO VOLUMES IN ONE.
The Cavalry

"SIR—THE GUARD IS FORMED!"

This picture of guard-mounting is one of the earliest Civil War cavalry photographs. It was taken in 1861 at the Cavalry School of Practice and Recruiting Depot, at Carlisle barracks, Pennsylvania. The guard wears full-dress uniform. The adjutant is presenting it to the new Officer of the Day, on the right.

"STAND TO HORSE!"—AN AMERICAN VOLUNTEER CAVALRYMAN, OCTOBER, 1862

"He's not a regular—but he's 'smart.'" This tribute to the soldierly bearing of the trooper above was bestowed, forty-nine years after the taking of the picture, by an officer of the U. S. cavalry, himself a Civil War veteran. The recipient of such high praise is seen as he "stood to horse" a month after the battle of Antietam. The war was only in its second year, but his drill is quite according to army regulations— hand to bridle, six inches from the bit. His steady glance as he peers from beneath his hat into the sunlight tells its own story. Days and nights in the saddle without food or sleep, sometimes riding along the 60-mile picket-line in front of the Army of the Potomac, sometimes faced by sudden encounters with the Southern raiders, have all taught him the needed confidence in himself, his horse, and his equipment.

The Photographic History
of The Civil War

Complete and Unabridged

TWO VOLUMES IN ONE.

Volume 2
The Decisive Battles
*The Cavalry

EDITOR

THEO. F. RODENBOUGH
Brigadier-General United States Army (Retired)

Contributors

THEO. F. RODENBOUGH
Brigadier-General United States Army
(Retired)

CHARLES D. RHODES
Captain, General Staff, United States
Army

HOLMES CONRAD
Major Cavalry Corps, Army of Northern
Virginia

JOHN A. WYETH, M.D., LL.D.
Captain Quirk's Scouts, Confederate
States Army

THE BLUE & GREY PRESS

CONTENTS

Photograph Descriptions throughout Volume IV
 Roy Mason

PREFACE

TO the public at large, the volume prepared by General Rodenbough and his associates will be not only instructive but decidedly novel in its view-point. In the popular conception the cavalryman figures as the most dashing and care-free among soldiers. He is associated primarily with charges at a gallop to the sound of clashing sabers and bugle calls, and with thrilling rescues on the field.

Adventurous, indeed, are the exploits of "Jeb" Stuart, Custer, and others recounted in the pages that follow, together with the typical reminiscences from Dr. Wyeth.

The characteristic that stands dominant, however, throughout this volume shows that the soldiers in the cavalry branch were peculiarly responsible. Not only must they maintain a highly trained militant organization, ready to fight with equal efficiency either mounted or on foot, but to them fell the care of valuable, and frequently scarce, animals, the protection of the armies' supplies, the transmission of important messages, and dozens more special duties which must usually be performed on the cavalryman's own initiative. On such detached duty there was lacking the shoulder to shoulder comradeship that large masses of troops enjoy. Confronted by darkness, distance, and danger, the trooper must carry out his orders with few companions, or alone.

The discussion of organization and equipment is most important to an understanding of the cavalryman as he actually worked. The Federal methods, described at length in this volume, naturally involved a larger system and a more elaborate growth than those of the South with its waning resources. In other respects, however, the Confederate organization differed from that of the Union. The feeling for locality in the South manifested itself at the beginning of the war through the formation of companies and regiments on a geographical basis, and the election of officers by the men of the companies themselves. Thus, in spite of the want of military arms and ordnance stores, and the later disastrous scarcity of horses, the Confederates "hung together" in a manner that recalls the English yeomen archers who fought so sturdily, county by county.

Altogether it was a gallant and devoted part that the American cavalryman, Federal or Confederate, played on his hard-riding raids and his outpost duty, as well as his better-known battles and charges, from 1861 to 1865.

THE PUBLISHERS.

THE EVOLUTION
OF THE
AMERICAN CAVALRYMAN

THE FIRST EXPERIMENT

The men on dress parade here, in 1862, are much smarter, with their band and white gloves, their immaculate uniforms and horses all of one color, than the troopers in the field a year later. It was not known at that time how important a part the cavalry was to play in the great war. The organization of this three months' regiment was reluctantly authorized by the War Department in Washington. These are the Seventh New York Cavalry, the "Black Horse," organized at Troy, mustered in November 6, 1861, and mustered out

SEVENTH NEW YORK CAVALRY, 1862

March 31, 1862. They were designated by the State authorities Second Regiment Cavalry on November 18, 1861, but the designation was changed by the War Department to the Seventh New York Cavalry. The seven companies left for Washington, D. C., November 23, 1861, and remained on duty there till the following March. The regiment was honorably discharged, and many of its members saw real service later. General I. N. Palmer, appears in the foreground with his staff, third from the left.

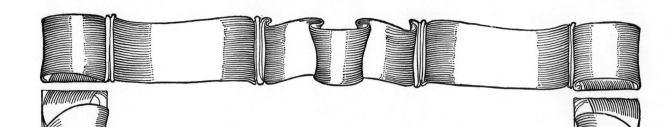

CAVALRY OF THE CIVIL WAR
ITS EVOLUTION AND INFLUENCE

By Theo. F. Rodenbough
Brigadier-General, United States Army (Retired)

IT may surprise non-military readers to learn that the United States, unprepared as it is for war, and unmilitary as are its people, has yet become a model for the most powerful armies of Europe, at least in one respect. The leading generals and teachers in the art and science of war now admit that our grand struggle of 1861–65 was rich in examples of the varied use of mounted troops in the field, which are worthy of imitation.

Lieutenant-General von Pelet-Narbonne, in a lecture before the Royal United Service Institution of Great Britain, emphatically maintains that " in any case one must remember that, from the days of Napoleon until the present time, in no single campaign has cavalry exercised so vast an influence over the operations as they did in this war, wherein, of a truth, the personality of the leaders has been very striking; such men as, in the South, the God-inspired Stuart, and later the redoubtable Fitzhugh Lee, and on the Northern side, Sheridan and Pleasonton."

For a long time after our Civil War, except as to its political or commercial bearing, that conflict attracted but little attention abroad. A great German strategist was reported to have said that " the war between the States was largely an affair of armed mobs "—a report, by the way, unverified, but which doubtless had its effect upon military students. In the meantime other wars came to pass in succession—Austro-Prussian (1866), Franco-German (1870), Russo-Turkish (1877), and later the Boer War and that between Russia and Japan.

[16]

THE AMERICAN CAVALRYMAN—1864

The type of American cavalryman developed by the conditions during the war fought equally well on foot and on horseback. In fact, he found during the latter part of the war that his horse was chiefly useful in carrying him expeditiously from one part of the battlefield to the other. Except when a mounted charge was ordered, the horses were far too valuable to be exposed to the enemy's fire, be he Confederate or Federal. It was only when cavalry was fighting cavalry that the trooper kept continually mounted. The Federal sabers issued at the beginning of the war were of long, straight Prussian pattern, but these were afterward replaced by a light cavalry saber with curved blade. A carbine and revolver completed the Federal trooper's equipment.

In none of these campaigns were the cavalry operations conspicuous for originality or importance as auxiliary to the main forces engaged.

Meanwhile, the literature of the American war—official and personal—began to be studied, and its campaigns were made subjects for text-books and monographs by British authors, which found ready publishers. Nevertheless, the American cavalry method has not gained ground abroad without a struggle. On the one hand, the failure of cavalry in recent European wars to achieve success has been made use of by one class of critics, who hold that " the cavalry has had its day "; that " the improved rifle has made cavalry charges impracticable "; that it has degenerated into mere mounted infantry, and that its value as an arm of service has been greatly impaired.

On the other hand it is held by the principal cavalry leaders who have seen service in the field—Field-Marshal Lord Roberts, Generals French, Hamilton, and Baden-Powell (of Boer War fame), De Negrier and Langlois of France, and Von Bernhardi of Germany, and others, (1) that while the method of using modern cavalry has changed, the arm itself is more important in war than ever; (2) that its scope is broadened; (3) that its duties require a higher order of intelligence and training of its personnel—officers and men, and (4), above all, that it is quite possible to turn out a modern horse-soldier, armed with saber and rifle, who will be equally efficient, mounted or dismounted.

Still the battle of the pens goes merrily on—the champions of the *arme blanche* or of the rifle alone, on the one side, and the defenders of the combination of those weapons on the other. The next great war will demonstrate, beyond peradventure, the practical value of " the American idea," as it is sometimes called.

A glance at the conditions affecting the use of mounted troops in this country prior to our Civil War may be instructive;

THE *ARME BLANCHE* OR THE RIFLE

The eternal question that has confronted cavalry experts ever since long-range firearms became effective, is whether the modern cavalry-man should use the saber—the *arme blanche*—or the rifle, or both the arms together. The failure of cavalry to achieve success in recent European wars has been used by one class of critics to prove that "the cavalry has had its day" and that "the improved rifle had made cavalry charges impracticable." On the other hand, many of the experienced cavalry leaders of the present day hold that it is quite possible to turn out a modern horse-soldier, armed with saber and rifle, who will be equally efficient, mounted or dismounted. In 1911 an American board of officers recommended, however, that the United States troopers should give up their revolvers on the principle that two arms suffice—the carbine for long distance, the saber for hand-to-hand fighting.

it will show that eighty-five years of great and small wars, Indian fighting, and frontier service, proved to be a training school in which the methods followed by Sheridan, Stuart, Forrest, and others of their time had been really initiated by their famous predecessors—Marion, the " Swamp Fox," and " Light Horse Harry " Lee of the War for Independence, Charlie May and Phil Kearny of the Mexican War, and those old-time dragoons and Indian fighters, Harney and Cooke.

Before the Revolution of 1776, the colonists were generally armed with, and proficient in the use of, the rifle—of long barrel and generous bore—and familiarity with the broken and wooded surface of the country made them formidable opponents of the British from the start, who both in tactical methods and armament were very inferior to the American patriots. Fortescue, an English writer, records the fact that " at the time of the Lexington fight there was not a rifle in the whole of the British army, whereas there were plenty in the hands of the Americans, who understood perfectly how to use them."

In the mountains of Kentucky and Tennessee, bodies of horsemen, similarly armed, were readily formed, who, if ignorant of cavalry maneuvers, yet with little preparation became the finest mounted infantry the world has ever seen; distinguishing themselves in numerous affairs, notably at King's Mountain, South Carolina, September 25, 1780, where two thousand sturdy " Mountain Men," hastily assembled under Colonels Sevier, Shelby, and Campbell, surrounded and almost annihilated a force of twelve hundred men (one hundred and twenty being regulars) under Major Ferguson, of the British army. Marion, the partisan, led a small brigade of mounted infantry, who generally fought on foot, although at times charging and firing from the saddle. There were also small bodies of cavalry proper, using the saber and pistol, with effect, against the British cavalry in many dashing combats.

The War of 1812 was not conspicuous for mounted operations, but the irregular warfare which preceded and followed

[20]

GRADUATES OF "THE ROUGH SCHOOL OF WAR"

The photograph reproduced above through the courtesy of Captain Noble D. Preston, who served with the Tenth New York Cavalry here represented, shows to what stage the troopers had progressed in the rough school of war by the winter of 1862-3. The Tenth New York was organized at Elmira, N. Y., September 27, 1861, and moved to Gettysburg, Penn., December 24th, where it remained till March, 1862. It took part in the battle of Fredericksburg in December, 1862, and participated in the famous "mud march," January, 1863, about the time this photograph was taken. The men had ample time for schooling and training in the Middle Department, in Maryland and the vicinity of Washington. They proved their efficiency in Stoneman's raid in April, 1863, and at Brandy Station and Warrenton. Later they accompanied Sheridan on his Richmond raid in May, 1864, in the course of which Stuart met his death, and they were still "on duty" with Grant at Appomattox.

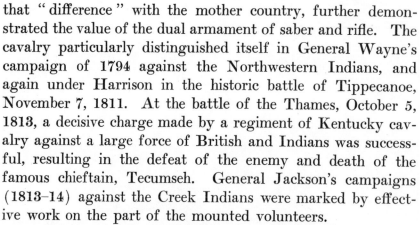

that "difference" with the mother country, further demonstrated the value of the dual armament of saber and rifle. The cavalry particularly distinguished itself in General Wayne's campaign of 1794 against the Northwestern Indians, and again under Harrison in the historic battle of Tippecanoe, November 7, 1811. At the battle of the Thames, October 5, 1813, a decisive charge made by a regiment of Kentucky cavalry against a large force of British and Indians was successful, resulting in the defeat of the enemy and death of the famous chieftain, Tecumseh. General Jackson's campaigns (1813–14) against the Creek Indians were marked by effective work on the part of the mounted volunteers.

In 1833, Congress reorganized the regular cavalry by creating one regiment, followed in 1836 by another, called respectively, the First and Second United States Dragoons. The First Dragoons were sent to the Southwest to watch the Pawnees and Comanches. On this expedition, it was accompanied by Catlin, the artist, who made many of his Indian sketches then. These regiments have been in continuous service ever since.

The first service of the Second Dragoons was against the Seminole Indians, in Florida, and for seven years the regiment illustrated the adaptability of the American soldier to service in the field under the most trying circumstances. "There was at one time to be seen in the Everglades, the dragoon (dismounted) in water from three to four feet deep; the sailor and marine wading in the mud in the midst of cypress stumps; and the infantry and artillery alternately on the land, in the water, or in boats." Here again, the combined mounted and dismounted action of cavalry was tested in many sharp encounters with the Indians.

It was but a step from the close of the Florida war to the war with Mexico, 1846–47. The available American cavalry comprised the two regiments of dragoons and seven new regiments of volunteers. The regular regiments were in splendid

THE FIRST UNITED STATES REGULAR CAVALRY

The sturdy self-reliance of these *sabreurs*, standing at ease though without a trace of slouchiness, stamps them as the direct successors of Marion, the "Swamp Fox," and of "Light-Horse Harry" Lee of the War for Independence. The regiment has been in continuous service from 1833 to the present day. Organized as the First Dragoons and sent to the southwest to watch the Pawnees and Comanches at the time it began its existence, the regiment had its name changed to the First United States Regular Cavalry on July 27, 1861, when McClellan assumed command of the Eastern army. This photograph was taken at Brandy Station in February, 1864. The regiment at this time was attached to the Reserve Brigade under General Wesley Merritt. The troopers took part in the first battle of Bull Run, were at the siege of Yorktown, fought at Gaines' Mill and Beverly Ford, served under Merritt on the right at Gettysburg, and did their duty at Yellow Tavern, Trevilian Station, and in the Shenandoah Valley under Sheridan; and they were present at Appomattox.

condition. The most brilliant exploit was the charge made by May's squadron of the Second Dragoons upon a Mexican light battery at Resaca de la Palma, May 9, 1846, which resulted in the capture of the battery and of General La Vega, of the Mexican artillery. This dashing affair was afterward to be repeated many times in the great struggle between the North and South.

The sphere of action, however, which had the most direct bearing upon the cavalry operations of the war was that known as "the Plains." The experience gained in the twelve years from 1848 to 1860, in frequent encounters with the restless Indian tribes of the Southwest, the long marches over arid wastes, the handling of supply trains, the construction of military roads, the exercise of command, the treatment of cavalry horses and draught animals, and the numerous other duties falling to officers at frontier posts, far distant from railroad or telegraph, all tended to temper and sharpen the blades that were to point the "path of glory" to thousands destined to ride under the war-guidons of Sheridan, Stuart, Buford, Pleasonton, Fitzhugh Lee, Stanley, Wilson, Merritt, Gregg, and others—all graduates of the service school of "the Plains."

At the outbreak of the Civil War, the military conditions in the two sections were very unequal. The South began the struggle under a commander-in-chief who was a graduate of West Point, had seen service in the regular army, had been a Secretary of War (possessing much inside information as to the disposition of the United States forces) and who, in the beginning at least, was supreme in the selection of his military lieutenants and in all matters relating to the organization and equipment of the Confederate troops.

On the other hand the North lacked similar advantages. Its new President was without military training, embarrassed rather than aided by a cabinet of lawyers and politicians as military advisers, captains of the pen rather than of the sword, and "blind leading the blind." Mr. Lincoln found himself

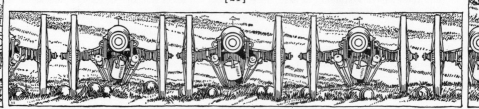

AMERICAN LANCERS—THE·SIXTH PENNSYLVANIA

Few people have heard that there was an American regiment of lancers in '61–'63.   Colonel Richard Rush's regiment, the Sixth Penn-sylvania, attempted to fight in this European fashion during the great conflict in which so much was discovered about the art of war. The Pennsylvanians carried the lance from December, 1861, until May, 1863, when it was discarded for the carbine, as being unsuited to the wooded country of Virginia through which the command operated.   The regiment was organized in Philadelphia by Colonel Richard H. Rush, August to October, 1861, and was composed of the best blood in that aristocratic city.   The usual armament of Federal volunteer cavalry regiments at the outset of the war consisted of a saber and a revolver.   At least two squadrons, consisting of four troops of from eighty-two to a hundred men, were armed with rifles and carbines.   Later, all cavalry regiments were supplied with single-shot carbines, the decreased length and weight of the shorter arm being a decided advantage to a soldier on horseback.

surrounded by office-seekers—especially those claiming high military command as a reward for political services. It is true that the Federal Government possessed a small, well-trained army, with a large proportion of the officers and nearly all of the enlisted men loyal to their colors, which, together with a few thousand organized militia, would have formed a valuable nucleus for war had it been properly utilized at the start. From its ranks some were selected who achieved distinction as leaders when not hampered by association with incompetent "generals." For at least one year, the inexhaustible resources of the North were wasted for want of competent military direction and training.

If these field conditions marked the genesis of the Civil War in all arms of service, they were especially true of the mounted troops. In 1860, the "athletic wave" had not made its appearance in the United States, and out-of-door amusements had not become popular above the Mason and Dixon line. In the more thickly settled North, the young men of cities and towns took rather to commercial and indoor pursuits; in the South, the sports of a country life appealed to young and middle-aged alike, and the rifle and the saddle furnished particular attractions to a large majority. So it happened that the Confederates (their President an erstwhile dragoon) had only to mobilize the cavalry companies of the militia scattered through the seceding States, and muster, arm, and equip the thousands of young horsemen, each bringing his own horse and eager to serve the Confederacy.

The trials of many of the newly recruited organizations, until the beginning of the third year of the war, are illustrated in the following extract from a typical regimental history:* Captain Vanderbilt describes in graphic terms his first experience in escort duty (December 10, 1862) :

Please remember that my company had been mustered into the service only about six weeks before, and had received horses less than a

* "History of the Tenth New York Cavalry." (Preston, N. Y.)

[26]

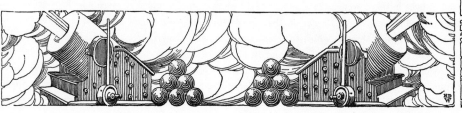

VOLUNTEERS AT DRILL—A NEW YORK REGIMENT

It was New York State that furnished the first volunteer cavalry regiment to the Union—Autumn, 1861. The fleet horsemen of the Confederacy soon taught the North the need of improving that arm of the service. But it requires time to train an efficient trooper, and the Union cavalrymen were helpless at first when opposed to the natural horsemen of the South. After a purgatory of training they were hurried into the field, often to fall victims to some roving body of Confederates who welcomed the opportunity to appropriate superior arms and equipment. The regiment in this photograph is the Thirteenth New York Cavalry at Prospect Hill, Virginia. They are no longer raw troopers but have become the "eyes" of Washington and its chief protection against the swift-riding Mosby and his men. The troopers were drilled on foot as well as mounted.

month prior to this march; and in the issue we drew everything on the list—watering-bridles, lariat ropes, and pins—in fact, there was nothing on the printed list of supplies that we did not get. Many men had extra blankets, nice large quilts presented by some fond mother or maiden aunt (dear souls), sabers and belts, together with the straps that pass over the shoulders, carbines and slings, pockets full of cartridges, nose bags and extra little bags for carrying oats, haversacks, canteens, and spurs—some of them of the Mexican pattern as large as small wind-mills, and more in the way than the spurs of a young rooster, catching in the grass when they walked, carrying up briers, vines, and weeds, and catching their pants, and in the way generally—curry-combs, brushes, ponchos, button tents, overcoats, frying-pans, cups, coffee-pots, etc. Now the old companies had become used to these things and had got down to light-marching condition gradually, had learned how to wear the uniform, saber, carbine, etc.; but my company had hardly time to get into proper shape when " the general " was sounded, " boots and saddles " blown.

Such a rattling, jingling, jerking, scrabbling, cursing, I never heard before. Green horses—some of them had never been ridden— turned round and round, backed against each other, jumped up or stood up like trained circus-horses. Some of the boys had a pile in front on their saddles, and one in the rear, so high and heavy it took two men to saddle one horse and two men to help the fellow into his place. The horses sheered out, going sidewise, pushing the well-disposed animals out of position, etc. Some of the boys had never ridden anything since they galloped on a hobby horse, and they clasped their legs close to-gether, thus unconsciously sticking the spurs into their horses' sides.

Well, this was the crowd I commanded to mount on the morning I was ordered by General Smith to follow him. We got in line near headquarters, and when we got ready to start we started all over. He left no doubt about his starting! He went like greased lightning! In less than ten minutes Tenth New York cavalrymen might have been seen on every hill for two miles rearward. Poor fellows! I wanted to help them, but the general was " On to Richmond "; and I hardly dared look back for fear of losing him. I didn't have the remotest idea where he was going, and didn't know but he was going to keep it up all day. It was my first Virginia ride as a warrior in the field. My uneasi-

A CAVALRY LEADER AT GETTYSBURG—GENERAL DAVID McM. GREGG AND STAFF

The Federal army at Gettysburg owed much to the cavalry. As Gettysburg was the turning-point in the fortunes of the Union army, it also marked an epoch in the development of the cavalry, trained in methods which were evolved from no foreign text-books, but from stern experience on the battlefields of America. The Second Cavalry Division under Gregg patrolled the right flank of the Federal army, with occasional skirmishing, until Stuart's arrival July 3d with the Confederate horse. Gregg's division and Custer's brigade were then on the right of the line. The ensuing cavalry battle was one of the fiercest of the war. W. H. F. Lee's brigade made the first charge for Stuart, as did the First Michigan Cavalry for Gregg. Countercharge followed upon charge. In a dash for a Confederate battleflag, Captain Newhall was received by its bearer upon the point of the spear-head and hurled to the ground. Finally the Confederate brigades withdrew behind their artillery, and the danger that Stuart would strike the rear of the Union army simultaneously with Pickett's charge was passed. This photograph shows Gregg with the officers of his staff.

ness may be imagined. I was wondering what in the mischief I should say to the general when we halted and none of the company there but me. He was the first real live general I had seen who was going out to fight. Talk about the Flying Dutchman! Blankets slipped from under saddles and hung from one corner; saddles slipped back until they were on the rumps of horses; others turned and were on the under side of the animals; horses running and kicking; tin pans, mess-kettles, patent sheet-iron stoves the boys had seen advertised in the illustrated papers and sold by the sutlers of Alexandria—about as useful as a piano or folding bed—flying through the air; and all I could do was to give a hasty glance to the rear and sing out at the top of my voice, " C-l-o-s-e u-p! " But they couldn't " close." Poor boys! Their eyes stuck out like those of maniacs. We went only a few miles, but the boys didn't all get up till noon.

It was not until May, 1861, that the War Department at Washington reluctantly authorized the organization of a regiment of volunteer cavalry from New York with the proviso that the men furnish the horses, an allowance being made for use and maintenance. This system applied in the South, but was soon abandoned in the North. The door once open, other regiments were speedily formed, containing at least the crude elements of efficient cavalry. As a rule, the men regarded the horses with mingled curiosity and respect, and passed through a purgatory of training—" breaking in," it was sometimes called—before they had acquired the requisite confidence in themselves, plus horses and arms. All too soon they were " pitchforked " into the field, often to fall victims to some roving body of Confederates who were eager to appropriate the superior arms and equipment of the Federals.

Within a year in the rough school of war, these same helpless recruits became fairly efficient cavalry, at home in the saddle, able to deliver telling blows with the saber, and to ride boot-to-boot in battle charges. During the first two years of the war the Confederate cavalry exercised a tremendous moral effect. Beginning with the cry of " The Black Horse

THIRTEENTH NEW YORK CAVALRY—RESERVES AT GETTSYBURG

These were some of the few men who would have stood between Lee and the Northern Capital if the tide of battle which hung in the balance three days at Gettsyburg had rolled with the line in gray. The organization of the Thirteenth New York Cavalry was not completed till June 20, 1863, ten days before Gettysburg. Six companies left New York State for Washington on June 23d, and took their part in patrolling the rear of the Army of the Potomac during the three fateful days. They were more than raw recruits; the regiment had been made up by the consolidation of several incomplete organizations. Had the troopers arrived a few days earlier they probably would have been brigaded with Pleasonton's cavalry. A week after Gettysburg they were back in New York quelling the draft riots. Thereafter they spent their time guarding Washington, when this photograph was taken, and scouting near the armies in the Virginia hills.

Cavalry," at the First Bull Run, so terrible to the panic-stricken Federal troops in their race to Washington and safety; Mosby's frequent dashes at poorly guarded Union trains and careless outposts; and Stuart's picturesque and gallant promenade around McClellan's unguarded encampment on the Chickahominy, in 1862, the war record of the Southern horse notwithstanding its subsequent decline and the final disasters of 1864–65 will always illumine one of the brightest pages of cavalry history.

The Gettysburg campaign, June 1 to July 4, 1863, was exceptionally full of examples of the effective use of mounted troops. They began with the great combat of Beverly Ford, Virginia, June 9th, in which for twelve hours, eighteen thousand of the flower of the horsemen of the armies of the Potomac and Northern Virginia, in nearly equal proportions, struggled for supremacy, with many casualties,* parting by mutual consent at the close of the day. This was followed by a series of daily skirmishes during the remainder of the month, in efforts to penetrate the cavalry screen which protected each army in its northward progress, culminating on the first day of July at Gettysburg in the masterly handling of two small brigades of cavalry.

It was here that General Buford delayed the advance of a division of Confederate infantry for more than two hours, winning for himself, in the opinion of a foreign military critic,† the honor of having "with the inspiration of a cavalry officer and a true soldier selected the battlefield where the two armies were about to measure their strength." The important actions on the third day comprised that in which Gregg prevented Stuart from penetrating the right rear of the Union line (largely a mounted combat with saber and pistol), and the affair on the Emmittsburg Road on the same day where

*The Second U. S. Cavalry alone losing 57 per cent. killed and wounded of its officers engaged.

†The Comte de Paris in "The Civil War in America."

STABLES FOR SIX THOUSAND HORSES

GIESBORO—ONE OF THE BUSIEST SPOTS OF THE WAR

The cavalry depot at Giesboro, D. C., established in July, 1863, was the place where remounts were furnished to the cavalry and artillery of the Army of the Potomac during the last two years of the war.   The tents in the lower photograph are those of the officers in charge of that immense establishment, where they received and issued thousands of horses.   Convalescents who had lost their mounts, with men to be remounted, were drawn upon to help take care of the horses, until their departure for the front.   This photograph was taken in May, 1864, when Grant and Lee were grappling in the Wilderness and at Spottsylvania, only seventy miles distant.   The inspection of horses for remounting was made by experienced cavalry officers, while the purchasing was under the Quartermaster's Department.

Merritt and Farnsworth menaced the Confederate left and, according to General Law,* neutralized the action of Hood's infantry division of Longstreet's corps by bold use of mounted and dismounted men, contributing in no small degree to the Federal success.

In the West, during the same period, the cavalry conditions were not unlike those in the East, except that the field of operations extended over five States instead of two and that numerous bands of independent cavalry or mounted riflemen under enterprising leaders like Forrest, Morgan, Wharton, Chalmers, and Wheeler of the Confederate army, for two years had their own way. The Union generals, Lyon, Sigel, Pope, Rosecrans, and others, loudly called for more cavalry, or in lieu thereof, for horses to mount infantry. Otherwise, they agreed, " it was difficult to oppose the frequent raids of the enemy on communications and supply trains."

Ultimately, Generals Grant and Rosecrans initiated a system of cavalry concentration under Granger and Stanley, and greater efficiency became manifest. About the time of the battle of Stone's River, or Murfreesboro, the Federal horse began to show confidence in itself, and in numerous encounters with the Confederates—mounted and dismounted—acquitted itself with credit, fairly dividing the honors of the campaign. The names of Grierson, Streight, Wilder, and Minty became famous not only as raiders but as important factors in great battles, as at Chickamauga, where the " obstinate stand of two brigades of [Rosecrans'] cavalry against the Confederate infantry gave time for the formation of the Union lines."

The most conspicuous cavalry operations of the war were those of 1864–65: Sheridan's Richmond raid, in which the South lost the brilliant and resourceful Stuart, and the harassing flank attacks on Lee's army in advance of Grant's infantry, which, ending in the campaign at Appomattox, simultaneously with Wilson's successful Selma raid, marked

* " Battles and Leaders of the Civil War."

THE CAVALRY DEPOT IN THE DISTRICT OF COLUMBIA

This photograph of the cavalry depot at Giesboro is peaceful and orderly enough with the Stars and Stripes drooping lazily in the wind, but it does not betray the hectic activity "behind the scenes." Not long after the depot was established the entire Second United States Cavalry was sent there to be remounted, recruited, and refitted. This operation took about a month, and they were ordered to rejoin the army in October, 1863. Every company had a special color of horse at the outset, but this effect was speedily lost in the field, except for the grays. "These were easily recruited," said an old cavalryman, "because nobody wanted grays. They were too conspicuous. No, I don't mean that they attracted the enemy's fire, but a gray horse that lies down in muddy places is very apt to get dirty. If you were coming in from a night of picket duty, would you rather take a rest, or spend your time getting your horse ready for inspection? The dark-coated animals did not show the dirt so much."

[G]

EVER–BUSY TROOPERS AT DRILL

The swiftly moving Confederate troopers, under dashing leaders like Stuart and Wheeler, allowed the heads of the Union cavalry not a moment of peace. When infantry went into winter quarters they could live in comparative comfort and freedom from actual campaigning until the roads became passable again for their heavy wagon-trains in the spring. But Confederate raiders knew neither times nor seasons, and there were many points when the damage they might do would be incalculable. So the Federal cavalry's winter task

UNION CAVALRY IN WINTER QUARTERS

was to discover, if possible, the Confederates' next move, and to forestall it. This photograph shows three troops drilling on the plain beside their winter quarters. The stark trees and absence of grass indicate clearly the time of the year, and the long shadows show as truly as a watch that the time of day was late afternoon. A swift night-march may be in store for the troopers on the plain, or they may return to the shelter of their wooden huts. It is probable, however, that they cannot enjoy their comfort for more than a week or two.

the collapse of the war. Under most discouraging conditions the Confederate cavalry disputed every inch of territory and won the sincere admiration of their opponents.

Major McClelland, of Stuart's staff, thus impartially summarizes the situation: *

"During the last two years no branch of the Army of the Potomac contributed so much to the overthrow of Lee's army as the cavalry, both that which operated in the Valley of Virginia and that which remained at Petersburg. But for the efficiency of this force it is safe to say that the war would have been indefinitely prolonged. From the time that the cavalry was concentrated into a corps until the close of the war, a steady progress was made in discipline. Nothing was spared to render this arm complete. Breech-loading arms of the most approved pattern were provided; horses and accouterments were never wanting, and during the last year of the war Sheridan commanded as fine a body of troops as ever drew sabers.

"On the other hand, two causes contributed steadily to diminish the numbers and efficiency of the Confederate cavalry. The Government committed the fatal error of allowing the men to own their horses, paying them a *per diem* for their use, and the muster valuation in cases where they were killed in action; but giving no compensation for horses lost by any other casualties of a campaign. . . . Toward the close of the war many were unable to remount themselves, and hundreds of such dismounted men were collected in a useless crowd, which was dubbed 'Company Q.' The second cause was the failure or inability of the Government to supply good arms and accouterments. Our breech-loading arms were nearly all captured from the enemy and the same may be said of the best of our saddles and bridles. From these causes, which were beyond the power of any commander to remedy, there was a steady decline in the numbers of the Confederate cavalry and, as compared with the Federal cavalry, a decline in efficiency."

* "Life and Campaigns of Major-General J. E. B. Stuart."

CHAPTER
TWO

THE FEDERAL CAVALRY
ITS ORGANIZATION
AND EQUIPMENT

"BOOTS AND SADDLES"—THIRD DIVISION, CAVALRY
CORPS, ARMY OF THE POTOMAC, 1864

A SPREADING SECTION OF THE FEDERAL CAVALRY ORGANIZATION IN 1864

At Belle Plain Landing on the Potomac lay a chief base of supplies for Grant's armies in the spring of 1864. On April 4th Sheridan had been given charge of all the cavalry. He had found the corps much run down and the horses in poor condition. In a month he had effected a decided change for the better in the condition and *morale* of his ten thousand men, and was begging to be allowed to use them as an independent corps to fight the Confederate cavalry. Though they had been relieved of much of the arduous picket duty that they formerly performed, they were still considered as auxiliaries, to protect the flanks and front of the infantry. On May 7th Grant's army advanced with a view to taking Spotsylvania Court House.

CAVALRY IN CLOVER AT THE BELLE PLAIN LANDING

Thus was precipitated the cavalry battle at Todd's Tavern, and in part at least Sheridan's earnest desire became fulfilled. The battle was between Hampton's and Fitzhugh Lee's commands of Stuart's cavalry and Gregg's division, assisted by two brigades of Torbert's division under the command of General Merritt. After a severe engagement the Confederate cavalry broke and were pursued almost to Spotsylvania Court House. This photograph shows some of the Federal horses recuperating at Belle Plain Landing before this cavalry engagement on a large scale. The cavalry were in clover here near the tents and ships that meant a good supply of forage. There was no such loafing for horses and men a little later in that decisive year.

THE BELLE PLAIN CAVALRY

A CLOSER VIEW

This photograph brings the eye a little nearer to the cavalry at Belle Plain landing than the picture preceding. One can see the horses grazing by the side of the beautiful river. A group of cavalrymen have ridden their mounts into the water. The test of the efficient trooper was his skill in caring for his horse. Under ordinary circumstances, in a quiet camp like the above, it might be safe to turn horses out to graze and let them drink their fill at the river. But when on the march a staggering animal with parched throat and fast-glazing eyes whinnied eagerly at the smell of water, it was the trooper who had to judge its proper allowance. One swallow too many for a heated horse on a long march, multiplied by the number of troopers still ignorant of horsemanship, meant millions of dollars loss to the Union Government in the early stages of the war. Comparatively few horses were destroyed by wounds on the battlefield as compared with those lost through the ignorance of the troopers as to the proper methods of resting a horse, and as to the science of how, when, and what to feed him, and when to allow him to drink his fill. The Southern horsemen, as a rule more experienced, needed no such training, and their superior knowledge enabled the Confederate cavalry, with little "organization" in the strict sense of the word, to prove nevertheless a mighty weapon for their cause.

NEARER STILL

AT THE RIVER'S BRINK

This view brings us to the very edge of the water, where Sheridan's troopers were getting their mounts into shape for the arduous duties of the summer and fall. They are sitting at ease on the barebacked horses which have walked out into the cool river to slake their thirst. The wagon with the four-mule team bears the insignia of the Sixth Army Corps, commanded by Sedgwick. The canvas top is somewhat wrinkled, so it is impossible to see the entire device, which was in the shape of a Greek cross. It was during the campaign which followed these preparations that Sheridan had his famous interview with Meade, in which the former told his senior that he could whip Stuart if allowed to do so. General Grant determined to give Sheridan the opportunity that he sought, and on the very day of the interview Meade directed that the cavalry be immediately concentrated and that Sheridan proceed against the Confederate cavalry. On May 9th the expedition started with a column thirteen miles long. Stuart, however, was nothing loth to try conclusions with the Federal cavalry once more. He finally overtook it on May 11th at Yellow Tavern. The Confederate horse, depleted in numbers and equipment alike, was no longer its former brilliant self, and in this engagement the Confederacy lost James B. Gordon and Stuart, the leader without a peer.

WITH THE FARRIERS

OF THE

FEDERAL CAVALRY

These photographs were made at the headquarters of the Army of the Potomac in August, 1863, the month following the battle of Gettysburg, where the cavalry had fully demonstrated its value as an essential and efficient branch of the service. Every company of cavalry had its own farrier, enlisted as such. These men not only had to know all about the shoeing of horses, but also had to be skilled veterinary surgeons, such as each regiment has at the present day, coming next in pay to a second lieutenant. Plainly visible are the small portable anvil on an overturned bucket and the business-like leather aprons of the men. An army "marches upon its stomach," but cavalry marches upon its horses' feet, which must be cared for. In the larger photograph the men have evidently just become aware that their pictures are being taken. In the smaller exposure in the corner, the man holding the horse on the right has faced about to show off his horse to the best advantage; the horse holder on the left is facing the camera, arms akimbo, and a cavalryman in the rear has led up his white-faced mount to insure his inclusion in the picture.

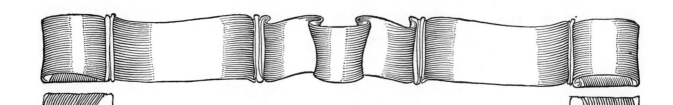

THE FEDERAL CAVALRY
ITS ORGANIZATION AND EQUIPMENT

By Charles D. Rhodes

Captain, General Staff, United States Army

A T the outbreak of the great Civil War in America, the regular cavalry at the disposal of the Federal Government consisted of the First and Second Regiments of Dragoons, one regiment of Mounted Rifles, and the First and Second Regiments of Cavalry. Early in the year 1861, the Third Cavalry was added to the others, and soon after, all six regiments were designated as cavalry and numbered serially from one to six.

The old regiments had been composed of ten troops, subdivided into five squadrons of two troops each, but the organization of the Sixth Cavalry Regiment called for twelve troops. In July, 1861, this organization was extended to all regular regiments, and in September of the same year the volunteer regiments, which had started out with ten troops each, were organized in a like manner. As the war progressed, the squadron organization was abandoned. When a regiment was subdivided for detached service, it was usually into battalions of four troops each.

The early war organization of cavalry troops called for one hundred enlisted men to a troop, officered by a captain, a first lieutenant, a second lieutenant, and a supernumerary second lieutenant. But in 1863, troops were given an elastic strength, varying between eighty-two and one hundred enlisted men, and the supernumerary lieutenant was dropped. Each regiment, commanded by a colonel, had a lieutenant-colonel and three majors, with a regimental commissioned and

[46]

THE FIRST EXTENSIVE FEDERAL CAVALRY CAMP—1862

This photograph shows the cavalry camp at Cumberland Landing just before McClellan advanced up the Peninsula. The entire strength of the cavalry the previous autumn had aggregated 8,125 men, of which but 4,753 are reported as "present for duty, equipped." It was constantly drilled during the fall and winter of 1861, with enough scouting and outpost duty in the Virginia hills to give the cavalry regiments a foretaste of actual service. In the lower photograph we get a bird's-eye view of Cumberland Landing where McClellan's forces were concentrated after the siege of Yorktown and the affair at Williamsburgh, preparatory to moving on Richmond. The cavalry reserve with the Peninsular army under that veteran horseman Philip St. George Cooke, was organized as two brigades under General Emry and Colonel Blake, and consisted of six regiments. Emry's brigade comprised the Fifth United States Cavalry, Sixth United States Cavalry, and Rush's Lancers—the Sixth Pennsylvania Cavalry. Blake's brigade consisted of the First United States Cavalry, the Eighth Pennsylvania Cavalry, and Barker's squadron of Illinois Cavalry.

AT CUMBERLAND LANDING

non-commissioned staff, which included two regimental surgeons, an adjutant, quartermaster, commissary, and their subordinates.

Owing, however, to losses by reason of casualities in action, sickness, and detached service, and through the lack of an efficient system of recruiting, whereby losses could be promptly and automatically made good with trained men, the cavalry strength, in common with that of other arms, always showed an absurd and oftentimes alarming discrepancy between the troopers actually in ranks and the theoretical organization provided by the existing law. Again, the losses in horse-flesh were so tremendous in the first years of the war, and the channels for replacing those losses were so inadequate and unsystematized, that regiments oftentimes represented a mixed force of mounted and unmounted men. Although the value of the dismounted action of cavalry was one of the greatest developments of the war, its most valuable asset, mobility, was wholly lacking when its horses were dead or disabled.

Cavalry is a most difficult force to organize, arm, equip, and instruct at the outbreak of war. Not only must men be found who have some knowledge of the use and handling of horses, but the horses themselves must be selected, inspected, purchased, and assembled. Then, after all the delays usually attending the organizing, arming, and equipping of a mounted force, many months of patient training, dismounted and mounted, are necessary before cavalry is qualified to take the field as an efficient arm. It is an invariable rule in militant Europe to keep cavalry at all times at war strength, for it is the first force needed to invade or to repel invasion, and, except perhaps the light artillery, the slowest to "lick into shape" after war has begun. In the regular cavalry service, it was a common statement that a cavalryman was of little real value until he had had two years of service.

It is, therefore, small wonder that during the first two years of the great struggle, the Federal cavalry made only a

[48]

COPYRIGHT, 1911, REVIEW OF REVIEWS CO.

BEEF FOR THE CAVALRY AT COMMISSARY HEADQUARTERS

So seldom did the cavalry get a chance to enjoy the luxuries to be had at commissary headquarters that they took advantage of every opportunity. It is February, 1864, and the cavalry officer in the picture can look forward to a month or two more of fresh beef for his men. Then he will find his troop pounding by the desolate farmhouses and war-ridden fields, as the army advances on Richmond under Grant. While the infantry lay snug in winter-quarters, the troopers were busy scouring the Virginia hills for signs of the Confederates, or raiding their lines of communication and destroying their supplies. It took a large part of the time of the Northern and Southern infantry to repair the damage done by the cavalry. The cavalry often had to live by foraging, or go without food. Miles of railroad destroyed, bridges burned, telegraph wires cut, a sudden cessation of the source of supplies caused hundreds of miles of marching and counter-marching, beside the actual work of repairing by the engineering corps. It was Van Dorn's capture of Holly Springs that forced Grant to abandon his overland march against Vicksburg and return to Memphis in December, 1862.

poor showing. The regular cavalry was but a handful, and when President Lincoln issued his call for volunteers, little or no cavalry was accepted. Even when need for it was forced on the North, it took the Federal War Department a long time to realize that an efficient cavalry ready for field service could not be extemporized in a day.

Strange as it may now seem, the Federal authorities intended, in the beginning, to limit the cavalry force of the Union army to the six regular regiments; and even such a veteran soldier as General Scott gave it as his opinion that, owing to the broken and wooded character of the field of operations between the North and South, and the improvements in rifled cannon, the duties of cavalry would be unimportant and secondary.

Only seven troops of regular cavalry were available for the first battle of Bull Run, in 1861, but the firm front which they displayed in covering the confused and precipitate retreat of the Federal army, probably saved a large part of the main body from capture; but they never received the recognition that was deserved. However, the importance of cavalry was not altogether unappreciated, for we find, at Gettysburg, the Union cavalry of the Army of the Potomac aggregating nearly thirteen thousand officers and men. The close of the war saw Sheridan at Appomattox with fifteen thousand cavalrymen, while Wilson, in the South, was sweeping Mississippi and Alabama with an army of horsemen. But the evolution of this vast host from insignificant beginnings was a slow process, fraught with tremendous labor.

In the South, lack of good highways forced the Southerner to ride from boyhood, while contemporaneously the Northerner, with his improved roads, employed wheeled vehicles as a means of transportation. But aside from this positive advantage to Southern organization, the Confederate leaders seemed, from the very beginning of the Civil War, to appraise cavalry and its uses at its true valuation; while the Northern

AT THE BUSY OFFICE OF A CAVALRY QUARTERMASTER

This photograph was taken at Brandy Station in the spring of 1864. The sign on the wooden door of the little tent tells where "A. Q. M." held forth. The cavalrymen are evidently at ease. They have not yet met Stuart in the Wilderness. The quartermaster of a cavalry corps was the nearest approach to perpetual motion discovered during the war. His wagon-train could receive only the most general directions. He could never be certain where the men he was to supply with food could be found at any given time. He had to go exploring for his own regiments, and watch vigilantly that he did not incidentally feed the Confederates. He had to give precedence to ammunition-trains; dark often found his wagons struggling and floundering in the wake of their vanished friends. The quartermaster was responsible for their movements and arrivals. Besides carrying a map of the country in his head, he assumed immense responsibilities.

[G]

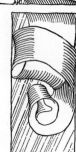

cavalry, even when finally mounted and equipped, was so mis-used and mishandled by those in control of military operations, that it was almost always at a disadvantage.

One of the first efforts of the War Department looking to the organization of Federal cavalry, is seen in the following circular letter, addressed by the Secretary of War to the Governors of the States:

War Department, Washington,
May 1, 1861.

To the Governors of the Several States,

And All Whom it may Concern:

I have authorized Colonel Carl Schurz to raise and organize a vol-unteer regiment of cavalry. For the purpose of rendering it as efficient as possible, he is instructed to enlist principally such men as have served in the same arm before. The Government will provide the regiment with arms, but cannot provide the horses and equipments. For these neces-saries we rely upon the patriotism of the States and the citizens, and for this purpose I take the liberty of requesting you to afford Colonel Schurz your aid in the execution of this plan.

(Signed) Simon Cameron,
Secretary of War.

Yet, in his report of preliminary operations in the first year of the war, General McClellan says:

Cavalry was absolutely refused, but the governors of the States com-plied with my request and organized a few companies, which were finally mustered into the United States service and proved very useful.

The armament of the volunteer cavalry regiments, organ-ized with some show of interest after the battle of Bull Run, was along the same general lines as that of the regular regi-ments. Though suffering from a general deficiency in the number which could be purchased from private manufacturers —there being no reserve stock on hand—each trooper was armed with a saber and a revolver as soon as circumstances per-mitted. At least two squadrons (four troops) in each regi-

[52]

A WELL-EQUIPPED HORSE OF THE FIRST MASSACHUSETTS CAVALRY—1864

The saddle-bags and hooded stirrup of Captain E. A. Flint's horse shown in this photograph are "regulation," but the outfit of a regular cavalry horse did not call for a breast-strap. It was more apt to be used among the volunteers. The regulars as a rule preferred a single rein, curb bit, and no breast-strap or martingale. No breast-straps were issued, but they were found useful when cavalry was pounding up a slope, leaping fences, walls, and ditches, and otherwise putting unusual strain on the belly-band. The hooded stirrup was useful both to keep out rain and to keep the foot warm in winter. The saddle and blanket equipment in the photograph also conform to regulations. This is one of the horses and men that charged Stuart's cavalry so fiercely on the night of the third day at Gettysburg. The First Massachusetts was in the second division, under General David McM. Gregg. The photograph was taken in November, 1864, at the headquarters of the Army of the Potomac, then thoroughly in touch with its ample "supply trains."

JUST BEFORE SHERIDAN CAME, 1864

This photograph shows the Eighteenth Pennsylvania in winter-quarters near Brandy Station in March, 1864, a month before the most important event in the history of the Federal cavalry—the unifying of the cavalry branch under the aggressive Sheridan. After Kilpatrick's raid on Richmond, ending the 2d of March, these troopers rested in camp until Sheridan left for his Richmond raid on May 9th. A month in camp is a long time for cavalry, and here one has a good opportunity to see with what rapidity and ease a trooper had learned to make himself comfortable. Barrels have been placed upon the chimneys in order to

THE EIGHTEENTH PENNSYLVANIA CAVALRY

increase their draft. Light enclosures of poles have been thrown up for the horses, and fodder has been stacked up on the hill. With stumps and cross-pieces the McClellan saddles are kept out of the wet and mud. The saddles were covered with rawhide instead of leather, and were more uncomfortable when they split than an ill-fitting shoe. The troopers themselves look fairly contented, and some of them are not so lean and angular as in the days of scouting and hard riding. There is plenty of work ahead of them, however, nearer Richmond, which will quickly enable them to rid themselves of any superfluous flesh.

ment were armed with rifles or carbines. Later, all cavalry regiments were supplied with single-shot carbines, the decreased length and weight of the shorter arm being a decided advantage to a soldier on horseback. One volunteer regiment, the Sixth Pennsylvania Cavalry (Rush's Lancers), was armed with the lance in addition to the pistol, twelve carbines being afterwards added to the equipment of each troop for picket and scouting duty. But in May, 1863, all the lances were discarded for carbines as being unsuited for the heavily wooded battle-grounds of Virginia.

The carbines issued were of various pattern—the Sharp's carbine being succeeded by the Spencer, which fired seven rounds with more or less rapidity but which was difficult to reload quickly. In the later years of the war, certain regiments were armed with the Henry rifle, an improved weapon firing sixteen shots with great accuracy. A Colt's rifle, firing six rounds, and a light, simple carbine called the Howard, were also in evidence among cavalry regiments at the close of the war. Previous to, and during the first year of the war, the Burnside was favorably thought of by the Federal officers. This carbine was the invention of General Ambrose E. Burnside, and was manufactured in Bristol, Rhode Island. Its chief value lay in its strength and the waterproof cartridges used. But its chief objection also lay in the high cost and the difficulty in obtaining this cartridge, which was manufactured of sheet brass, an expensive metal at that time. Another arm, similar to Burnside's and made with a tapering steel barrel, was the Maynard, which was manufactured by the Maynard's Arms Company, Washington, District of Columbia.

At the beginning, the sabers issued were of the long, straight, Prussian pattern, but these were afterwards replaced by a light cavalry saber with curved blade. Many of these were fitted with attachments so as to be fastened to the end of the carbines in the form of a bayonet. There also was an ordinary saber handle which allowed of their being carried at the

CAVALRY STABLES AT GRANT'S HEADQUARTERS, CITY POINT, IN 1864

City Point was Grant's base of supplies during the operations about Petersburg, in 1864. Sheridan at last was handling his cavalry as a separate command, and was soon to go to the Shenandoah. Brigadier-General David McM. Gregg was in command of the cavalry which remained with Grant. The First Massachusetts, First New Jersey, Tenth New York, Sixth Ohio, and Twenty-first Pennsylvania formed the First Brigade, and the First Maine, Second Pennsylvania, Fourth Pennsylvania, Eighth Pennsylvania, Thirteenth Pennsylvania, and Sixteenth Pennsylvania were the Second Brigade. Some of these men had been on Sheridan's Richmond and Trevilian raids. This shows the comparative comfort of City Point. To the left is a grindstone, where sabers might be made keen.

hip, as a side-arm, for which purpose it was well adapted, having a curved edge with a sharp point.

The standard pistol was the Colt's revolver, army or navy pattern, loaded with powder and ball and fired with percussion caps. Within its limitations, it was a very efficient weapon.

The saddle was the McClellan, so-called because adopted through recommendations made by General McClellan after his official European tour, in 1860, although it was in reality a modification of the Mexican or Texan tree. It was an excellent saddle, and in an improved pattern is, after fifty years of trial, still the standard saddle of the United States regular cavalry. In its original form it was covered with rawhide instead of leather, and when this covering split, the seat became very uncomfortable for the rider.

Although the original recruiting regulations required cavalry troopers to furnish their own horses and equipments, this requirement was later modified, and the Government furnished everything to the recruit, in volunteer as well as in regular regiments. Many troopers sold their private horses to the Government and then rode them in ranks. It was argued by some cavalry officers of that period that this system was eminently successful in securing men for the cavalry who could ride and who would care for horses.

As is usual in a country weak in trained cavalry and utterly unprepared for war, vexatious delays occurred in receiving the equipment of newly organized cavalry regiments. Long after the Western regiments were organized, they were kept inactive from lack of equipment, for which the Federal Government had made no provision in the way of reserve supplies. In some instances months elapsed before saddles were received, and in several cases arms were even longer in putting in an appearance. The interim was employed by the commanders in teaching their men to ride and drill, to use their arms, and to care for their horses. In the absence of saddles,

THE FAR-REACHING FEDERAL CAVALRY ORGANIZATION—WATER-TANK AT THE LOUISIANA DEPOT

Water—that word alone spells half the miseries and difficulties of the cavalry, especially in the parched Southern country. Although an infantry column could camp beside a little spring, cavalry horses had to plod wearily on till they reached a river, a stream, or at least a fair-sized pool. Even then, some officer grown wise in war might pronounce the water unfit for drinking, and the troopers must rein up their thirsty, impatient steeds, wild to plunge their noses in the cool morass, and ride patiently on again till good water was found. The place is Green-ville in Louisiana, where one of the six great Union cavalry depots was located. The site of the camp was selected by General Richard Arnold, Chief of Cavalry, Department of the Gulf. On June 8, 1864, from New Orleans, he requested permission to move his camping ground. "Present camping-ground of the First and Fifth Brigades of my command near Banks is entirely unsuitable, and I ask permission to move to this side of the river, at or near Greenville. I can find no more suitable place on either side of the river within twenty miles of the city." Permission to move was granted June 14, 1864.

various makeshifts were used on the horses' backs, and the troopers were even drilled bareback.

This probationary period was a wearisome one for the cavalry recruit. A trooper must perforce learn much of what his comrade of the infantry knows, and in addition must be taught all that pertains to horses and horsemanship. Those who had been fascinated by the glamour and dash of the cavalry life doubtless wished many times, during those laborious days, that they had the more frequent hours of recreation granted their neighbors of the infantry. The reward of the Federal cavalry came in those later days when, after painstaking and unremitting instruction covering many months and enlightening experiences in the field, they gained that confidence in themselves and their leaders, which resulted in the ultimate destruction of the opposing cavalry, and the decisive triumph of the Federal arms.

But good cavalry cannot be made in a month, or even in a year. The first year of the war saw the Confederate cavalry plainly superior in every way, and there were humiliating instances of the capture by the *corps d'élite* of the South, of whole squadrons of Northern horsemen. The second year of the tremendous struggle passed with much improvement in the Federal cavalry, but with a still marked lack of confidence in itself. It was not until the third year of its organization and training that the Union cavalry really found itself, and was able to vindicate its reputation in the eyes of those who in the preceding period were wont to sneeringly remark that " no one ever sees a dead cavalryman!

The drill regulations of the period, called tactics in those days, were the " '41 Tactics " or " Poinsett Tactics," authorized for dragoon regiments in the year 1841, by the Honorable J. R. Poinsett, Secretary of War. These drill regulations were in the main a translation from the French, and although occasional attempts were made to improve them, they continued in use by the Eastern cavalry of the Union armies throughout the

WELL-GROOMED OFFICERS OF THE THIRTEENTH NEW YORK CAVALRY

Many of the Federal cavalry officers were extremely precise in the matter of dress, paying equal attention to their horses' equipment, in order to set a good example to their men. Custer was a notable example. This photograph shows full dress, fatigue dress, a properly equipped charger, an orderly, sentry, cavalry sabres and the short cavalry carbine. Except for the absence of revolvers, it is an epitome of the dress and equipment which the Federal Government supplied lavishly to its troopers during the latter half of the war. At the outset, the volunteer cavalrymen were required to supply their own horses, a proper allowance being made for food and maintenance. In 1861, the Confederate cavalry had no Colt's revolvers, no Chicopee sabers, and no carbines that were worth carrying. Their arms were of the homeliest type and of infinite variety. This photograph was taken in July, 1865, when Washington no longer needed watching.

war. The Western cavalry used the "'41 Tactics" until late in the year 1864, and thereafter a system of drill formulated by General Philip St. George Cooke, which was published in 1862 by the War Department and prescribed a single-rank formation for the cavalry.

After all the months of drill, how different were those days of actual service in the field—weary marches in mud, rain, and even snow; short rations for men and for horses when the trains were delayed or when there were no trains; bivouacs on the soggy ground with saddles for pillows; gruesome night rides when troopers threw reins on the necks of horses and slept in their saddles; nerve-racking picket duty in contact with the foe's lines, where the whinny of a horse meant the wicked "ping" of a hostile bullet.

Like all soldiers new to the rigors of actual service in war, the Union volunteer cavalry, in those early days, loaded themselves and their horses with an amount of superfluous baggage which provoked sarcasm from the seasoned soldier and which later experience taught them wholly to discard. Some articles were absolutely necessary; much was entirely useless and oftentimes unauthorized.

In addition to his arms, which weighed not a little, the volunteer cavalryman carried a huge box of cartridges and another of percussion caps; from his shoulder depended a haversack filled with rations, and to which was often attached not only a tin cup but a coffee-pot. A canteen of water, a nose-bag of corn, a shelter tent, a lariat and picket pin, extra horseshoes and nails, a curry-comb and brush, a set of gun-tools and cleaning materials, and saddle-bags filled with extra clothing brought the weight of the trooper and his kit to a figure which was burdensome to an animal in even the best of condition. When to these articles of equipment were added an overcoat, extra blankets, additional boots, and the odds and ends of luxuries, which the recruit is wont to stow away surreptitiously, the result was a lame and broken-down horse, hundreds of troopers

BREAD AND COFFEE FOR THE CAVALRYMAN

The mess-house for cavalry ordered to Washington.—In the field the cavalrymen were glad when they could get the regular rations—bacon and hard bread. During the winter, in permanent camp, they occasionally enjoyed the luxury of soft bread. But they were kept so constantly employed, reconnoitering the enemy's position, watching the fords of the Rappahannock, and engaged in almost constant skirmishing, even in severe winter weather while the infantry was being made comfortable in winter-quarters, that this mess-house was regarded as a sort of Mecca by the troopers sent to Washington to be organized and remounted. Soft bread was not the only luxury here, and when they rejoined their commands their comrades would listen with bated breath to their thrilling stories of soup and eggs and other Lucullan delicacies. There was an army saying that it takes a good trooper to appreciate a good meal.

afoot, and the whole cavalry service rendered inefficient and almost useless.

As an evidence of the lack of discipline and of the ignorance of things military, which marked those early days of the cavalry service, it may be mentioned that many credulous troopers purchased so-called invulnerable vests, formed of thin steel plates and warranted by the makers to ward off a saber stroke or stop a leaden bullet. Dents in the armor were pointed out as evidence of this remarkable quality. Of course the vests were sooner or later discarded, but while retained they added about ten pounds to the burden of the already overloaded horse.

It is stated that the first time the Confederate cavalrymen, who rode light, met some of these remarkably equipped troopers, they wondered with amazement whether the Union horsemen were lifted into the saddle after the latter was packed, or whether the riders mounted first, and then had the numberless odds and ends of their equipment packed around them.

An anecdote is related of a humane Irish recruit, who, when he found his horse was unable to carry the heavy load allotted him, decided as an act of mercy to share the load with his charger. So, unloading nearly a hundred pounds from the horse, he strapped the mass to his own broad shoulders; and remounting his steed, rode off, quite jubilant over his act of unselfishness.

But it did not take long for cavalrymen in the field to learn with how little equipment the soldier may live and fight efficiently, and with how much greater zest the horses can withstand the long marches when the load is cut down to the limit of actual needs. There was danger then of the opposite extreme, and that absolutely necessary articles would be conveniently dropped and reported as " lost in action " or as " stolen." The net result, however, was that after one or two campaigns, the Federal cavalrymen learned to travel light, and, better than anything else, learned that quality of discipline

THE HAY BUSINESS OF THE GOVERNMENT

The matter of proper feed for cavalry horses was a constant perplexity to the Federal Government until the men had learned how to care for their mounts. During the first two years of the war two hundred and eighty-four thousand horses were furnished to the cavalry, although the maximum number of cavalrymen in the field at any time during this period did not exceed sixty thousand. The enormous number of casualties among the horses was due to many causes, among which were poor horsemanship on the part of the raw troopers mustered in at the beginning of the war, and the ignorance and gross inefficiency on the part of many officers and men as to the condition of the horses' backs and feet, care as to food and cleanliness, and the proper treatment of the many diseases to which horses on active service are subject. In such a tremendous machine as the quartermaster's department of the Army of the Potomac, containing at the beginning of the war many officers with absolutely no experience as quartermasters, there were necessarily many vexatious delays in purchasing and forwarding supplies, and many disappointments in the quality of supplies, furnished too often by scheming contractors. By the time the photograph above reproduced was taken, 1864, the business of transporting hay to the army in the field had been thoroughly systematized, as the swarming laborers in the picture attest.

AT THE HAY WHARF, ALEXANDRIA

GOVERNMENT HAY–WHARF AT ALEXANDRIA, VIRGINIA

The army which McClellan took to the Peninsula had to be created from the very foundation. The regular army was too small to furnish more than a portion of the general officers and a very small portion of the staff, so that the staff departments and staff officers had to be fashioned out of perfectly raw material. Artillery, small-arms, and ammunition were to be manufactured, or purchased from abroad; wagons, ambulances, bridge-trains, camp equipage, hospital stores, and all the vast impedimenta and material indispensable for an army in the field were to be manufactured. The tardiness with which cavalry remounts were forwarded to the regiments was a frequent subject of complaint. General McClellan complained that many of the horses furnished were "totally unfitted for the service and should never have been re-

SENTRY GUARDING FEED FOR FEDERAL HORSES, 1864

ceived." General Pope had in fact reported that "our cavalry numbered on paper about four thousand men, but their horses were completely broken down, and there were not five hundred men, all told, capable of doing such service as should be expected of cavalry." The demand for horses was so great that in many cases they were sent on active service before recovering sufficiently from the fatigue incident to a long railway journey. One case was reported of horses left on the cars fifty hours without food or water, and then being taken out, issued, and used for immediate service. Aside, too, from the ordinary diseases to which horses are subject, the Virginia soil seemed to be particularly productive of diseases of the feet. That known as "scratches" disabled thousands of horses during the Peninsula campaign and the march of Pope.

[G]

MEN WHO SHOD A MILLION HORSES

This photograph presents another aspect of the gigantic system whereby the Union cavalry became organized and equipped so as to prove irresistible after 1863. In the fiscal year 1864 the Union Government bought and captured nearly 210,000 horses. The army in the field required about 500 new horses every day. Sheridan's force alone required 150 new horses a day during the Shenandoah campaign. At Giesboro, the big remount depot near Washington, they handled 170,622 horses in 1864, and in June, 1866, they had

PART OF THE GIGANTIC ORGANIZATION OF THE FEDERAL CAVALRY

only 32 left. This was exclusive of 12,000 or 13,000 artillery horses handled at the same depot. All these animals had to be shod. This photograph shows some of the men who did it, with the implements of their trade. The army in the field kept this army at home busy supplying its manifold needs. The Southerners' only array of men was at the front. At home, they had only an army of women, knitting, weaving, and sewing for the ragged soldiers in the field. The men wholesale had left their businesses and enlisted.

which subordinates the comfort and pleasure of the individual to the greatest good of the greatest number.

The trouble was that upon the organization of so many regiments of volunteer cavalry, both officers and men were naturally uninstructed and therefore inefficient. Horses were overloaded, marches were prolonged beyond endurance and without proper halts for rest, forage was not always regularly provided, and troopers were not held down to those many little things which, whether in the saddle or in camp, make for the endurance of the horse and for the mobility of mounted troops.

Tactically, both officers and men of the newly made cavalry had everything to learn. In spite of the splendid natural material which was attracted to the mounted service, and the lavish expenditures of the Federal Government in its behalf, the first period of the war only emphasized the fact that, given unlimited resources in the way of men, horses, and equipment, efficient cavalry cannot be developed inside of two years or more.

To be fully prepared at the outbreak of war, regular cavalry should be kept during peace at its war strength; while if reserves of militia cavalry cannot be conveniently maintained during peace, ample reserve supplies of arms and equipment should be laid by, and such encouragement given to the breeding and rearing of saddle-horses as will enable the Government to place cavalry in the field without all the vexatious and humiliating delays which attended the fitting out of the Federal cavalry force in 1861 and 1862.

CHAPTER
THREE

THE CONFEDERATE CAVALRY
IN THE EAST

GENERAL "JEB" STUART
LEADER OF
THE VIRGINIA CAVALRY

BRIGADIER–GENERAL

BEVERLY H. ROBERTSON

C.S.A.

SUCCESSOR TO ASHBY

AS COMMANDER OF

THE "VALLEY" CAVALRY

IN 1862

MAJOR–GENERAL

W. H. F. LEE,

C.S.A.

IN 1862 COLONEL OF

THE NINTH VIRGINIA CAVALRY

IN "FITZ" LEE'S BRIGADE

UNDER STUART

**CONFEDERATE
CAVALRY
LEADERS**

MAJOR–GENERAL
THOMAS L. ROSSER,
C.S.A.

IN 1862 COLONEL OF THE
FIFTH VIRGINIA CAVALRY
IN "FITZ" LEE'S BRIGADE
UNDER STUART

BRIGADIER–GENERAL
WILLIAM E. JONES,
C.S.A.

IN 1862 COLONEL OF
THE SEVENTH VIRGINIA
CAVALRY IN THE ARMY
OF THE VALLEY

ACTIVE IN THE
EARLY VIRGINIA
CAMPAIGNS

ONE OF THE REGIMENTS THAT STUART ELUDED

A glance at the gallant and hardy bearing of Rush's Lancers as they looked in 1862, and at their curious weapons, suggestive more of Continental than of American warfare, brings sufficient testimony to the high quality of the men who endeavored to curb the Confederate leader, Stuart, and the resources behind them. The usual armament of the Union volunteer cavalry regiments consisted of a saber, a revolver, and a single-shot carbine. The Sixth Pennsylvania was provided with lances in addition to the pistol, twelve carbines being afterwards added to the equipment of each troop for picket and scouting duty. A clean cut, smart-looking lot they are by the streaming pennants—the privates, recruited from the fashionable athletic set of the day in Philadelphia, no less than the officer, so intent upon the coffee that his orderly is pouring out. But it was vainly that in North or South, in Pennsylvania or in Virginia, in Federal territory or along the banks of the Chickahominy, the men of this crack Pennsylvania regiment tried to catch Stuart and his

LANCERS IN THE FEDERAL CAVALRY

fleet command. At Tunstall's Station, Virginia, they were two hours late; at Emmittsburg, Maryland, an hour early. On the occasion of Stuart's famous raid on Chambersburg, in October, 1862, General Pleasonton, irritated by the audacity of the daring Southerner, had made every disposition to head off the raiders before they reached the Potomac. General Pleasonton himself, with eight hundred men; Colonel Richard H. Rush, with his unique lancers, and General Stoneman, with his command, were all scouring the country in search of Stuart, who was encumbered with many captured horses, but was moving steadily toward the Potomac. A march of thirty-two miles from Chambersburg brought the wily Stuart to Emmittsburg about seven o'clock on the evening of the 11th. One hour before their arrival six companies of the Lancers, at that time attached to the Third Brigade, had passed through the town on their way to Gettysburg. But until the day of his death, Stuart often managed so that the Union cavalry came too early or too late.

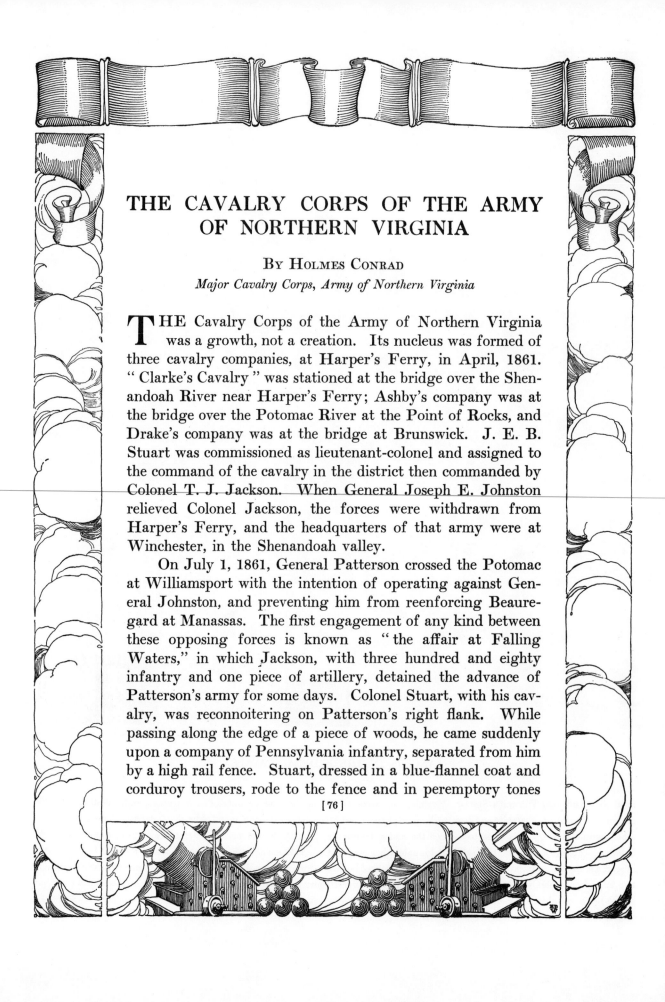

THE CAVALRY CORPS OF THE ARMY OF NORTHERN VIRGINIA

By Holmes Conrad

Major Cavalry Corps, Army of Northern Virginia

THE Cavalry Corps of the Army of Northern Virginia was a growth, not a creation. Its nucleus was formed of three cavalry companies, at Harper's Ferry, in April, 1861. "Clarke's Cavalry" was stationed at the bridge over the Shenandoah River near Harper's Ferry; Ashby's company was at the bridge over the Potomac River at the Point of Rocks, and Drake's company was at the bridge at Brunswick. J. E. B. Stuart was commissioned as lieutenant-colonel and assigned to the command of the cavalry in the district then commanded by Colonel T. J. Jackson. When General Joseph E. Johnston relieved Colonel Jackson, the forces were withdrawn from Harper's Ferry, and the headquarters of that army were at Winchester, in the Shenandoah valley.

On July 1, 1861, General Patterson crossed the Potomac at Williamsport with the intention of operating against General Johnston, and preventing him from reenforcing Beauregard at Manassas. The first engagement of any kind between these opposing forces is known as "the affair at Falling Waters," in which Jackson, with three hundred and eighty infantry and one piece of artillery, detained the advance of Patterson's army for some days. Colonel Stuart, with his cavalry, was reconnoitering on Patterson's right flank. While passing along the edge of a piece of woods, he came suddenly upon a company of Pennsylvania infantry, separated from him by a high rail fence. Stuart, dressed in a blue-flannel coat and corduroy trousers, rode to the fence and in peremptory tones

ONE OF THE EARLIEST CONFEDERATE CAVALRY EXPLOITS

A month before the first battle of Bull Run, the bridge at Berlin, Md., six miles below Harper's Ferry, was thoroughly destroyed in one of the first exploits of the Confederate cavalry. It was not yet organized. A few detached bands here and there—the Clarke company at the bridge over the Shenandoah River near Harper's Ferry, Ashby's company at the bridge over the Potomac River at the Point of Rocks, and Drake's company at the bridge at Brunswick—were operating along the first Confederate line of defense. But they had already begun to demonstrate their daring and effectiveness. This was the prelude to the bold rides of Stuart and Forrest, to the swift raids of Morgan and the terror-inspiring Mosby. It was acts like this that hampered the Union leaders, and detained an army between Washington and the Confederates. Not until the Union cavalry had learned to retaliate, and to meet and fight the exhausted Confederate horsemen on their own ground and in their own way, did the Union generals get complete possession of their infantry.

ordered the Federals to pull down the fence at once, which they did. The cavalry rode into their midst, and without the firing of a pistol took the entire company of thirty or forty men.

On the 18th of July, Johnston withdrew his army from Winchester, and moved toward Manassas. Stuart's entire command consisted of twenty-one officers and three hundred and thirteen men. All were well mounted and at home on horseback. Yet for arms they could muster but few sabers of regulation make and still fewer revolvers, although double-barreled shotguns and rifles were prevalent.

This command reached Manassas on the evening of the 20th of July, and went into camp. The next morning, at early dawn, it was aroused by the firing of a signal gun by the Federals. In the afternoon, General T. J. Jackson's brigade, while fully occupied in front, was threatened by the advance of a heavy attacking column on its left. Stuart was sent to its relief, and moving in column on Jackson's left, he soon came in view of a formidable line of Zouaves moving upon Jackson. The appearance of the head of Stuart's column arrested the movement of the opponents, attracted their fire, and finally caused their withdrawal, for which Jackson, in his report, made grateful acknowledgment.

During the summer and fall, the cavalry occupied and held Mason's and Munson's hills and picketed as far as Falls Church and at points along the Potomac. With the exception of an affair at Lewinsville, in September, the period was uneventful and free from striking incidents. In September, 1861, Stuart was commissioned brigadier-general, and in December occurred the battle of Dranesville, in which he commanded the Confederate forces, but the result of the engagement afforded him no ground for congratulation.

In March, 1862, the Confederates evacuated Manassas, and moved below Richmond. The advance of McClellan up the Peninsula toward Williamsburg, afforded but little opportunity for cavalry operations other than protecting the flanks

FALLS CHURCH, ON THE CONFEDERATE PICKET LINE IN '61—NEARLY THREE MILES FROM WASHINGTON

This typical cross-roads Virginia church, less than three miles from Washington, lay on the end of the line patroled by the Confederate cavalry pickets in the summer and fall of '61. Strange-looking soldiers were those riders in Colonel J. E. B. Stuart's command, without uniforms, armed with rifles and double-barreled shot-guns, with hardly a saber or a revolver. While McClellan was drilling his army in Washington and metamorphosing it from an "armed mob" into an efficient fighting machine, the Confederate horsemen occupied and held Mason's and Munson's Hill and picketed at points along the Potomac. With the exception of an affair at Lewinsville in September there was little actual fighting. In that month Stuart was commissioned brigadier-general, and in December occurred the battle of Dranesville, in which he commanded the Confederate forces, but failed to carry the day. Soon, however, he leaped into fame.

and rear of the army as it withdrew within the lines around Richmond. Toward the middle of June was effected that brilliant movement which so distinctly illustrates the daring and skill of Stuart and the unfailing endurance of his men. He passed around the entire Federal army, obtaining the information he sought and returning to camp with the substantial rewards of his prowess.

During the Seven Days' battles around Richmond, but little opportunity was afforded for cavalry operations beyond the ordinary work of obtaining information on the front and flanks, but in the latter part of June, Stuart reached White House, where a Federal gunboat had been seen on the Pamunkey. Seventy-five dismounted cavalrymen, armed with carbines and deployed as skirmishers, approached the vessel, whereupon a body of sharpshooters was landed from the gunboat and advanced to meet them. A single howitzer of the Stuart horse artillery opened on the war-ship from a position on which her guns could not be brought to bear. The shells from the howitzer greatly distressed her, and withdrawing her sharpshooters, she disappeared down the river.

On no occasion was the audacity of Stuart and the temper of his men more severely tested than in October, when there was carried through the movement to Chambersburg, Pennsylvania, which was reached on the 10th. The advance was bold and perilous enough, but it was tame in comparison with the return. The Union forces had been thoroughly aroused, and dispositions had been ordered, intended and calculated to head off the invaders before they could recross the Potomac. Leaving Chambersburg, a march of nearly thirty-two miles brought Stuart and his men to Emmittsburg at about seven o'clock on the evening of the 11th. One hour before their arrival, four companies of the Sixth Pennsylvania Cavalry had passed through the town on their way to Gettysburg. General Pleasonton with eight hundred men, Colonel Rush with his regiment, and General Stoneman with his command were scouring

[80]

A CONFEDERATE HORSE AT AN HISTORIC VIRGINIA SPOT, IN MAY, 1862

When '61 came, the young men in the North were to be found rather at commercial and indoor pursuits, as compared to those in the South. There the sports of country life appealed in preference, and the rifle and saddle were more familiar than the counting-house. Thus the Confederate cavalrymen saw nothing wrong in the proposition that they should furnish their own mounts throughout the war. The name of the beautiful horse in this photograph was "Secesh." Its upraised ears and alert expression of interest in the man who is waving his hat in the foreground, to make it look at the camera, proves it a "well-bred" animal. "Secesh" was captured by the Federals in 1862 at Yorktown, and the spot where the photograph was taken is historic. It is the cave excavated in the marl bluff by Cornwallis in 1781, for secret councils.

the country in search of Stuart, who was encumbered with
many captured horses in his march toward the Potomac. Pleasonton had so interpreted Stuart's movements as to make it clear
to his mind that Stuart must cross the river at the mouth of
the Monocacy, but, as a matter of fact, White's Ferry was the
point at which the Confederate purposed to get over. Colonel
W. H. F. Lee commanded the advance, and as he approached
the ferry, he found it guarded by a force of Federal infantry.

Lee had arranged his plan of attack upon these troops
when it occurred to him to try a milder method. He sent a
flag of truce to the Union commander and demanded the un-
conditional surrender of his men within fifteen minutes. To
this there was no response, and Colonel Lee then opened with
one gun, which fire was not returned. In a few moments the
Union infantry quit their impregnable position and withdrew
down the river. Stuart and his returning legions, with all their
plunder, then crossed the Potomac in safety.

Several companies in the Virginia cavalry regiments were
mounted on thoroughbred racers, sired by horses whose names
are as household words in racing annals. One experience, in
the summer of 1861, demonstrated their unfitness for cavalry
service. After General Patterson had crossed the Potomac at
Williamsport and occupied Martinsburg, the First Virginia
Cavalry was in camp in an apple orchard, about two miles
south of that town. A section of a Federal battery of two
rifled guns advanced and took position a few hundred yards
from the orchard, and threw some percussion shells over the
cavalrymen. The missiles struck soft earth beyond and did not
explode, but their screams, as they passed over the camp, were
appalling. One of the companies, mounted on thoroughbreds,
had no more control over their steeds than they had over the
shells that frightened them. The commander of the company
sought to divert attention from the noise by keeping the horses
in motion, but no sooner were they brought into line than they
broke and ran. A hundred yards distant was a fence, eight

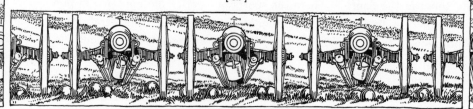

A SOUTHERN ROADSTER IN 1862, AT THE SPOT WHERE STUART ON HIS FAMOUS
RAID ESCAPED FROM DANGER

The spring, the rangy endurance of this Virginia riding-horse, halted on the highway near Charles City
Court House, illustrates one factor in the dismay the Confederate cavalrymen were able to implant in the
hearts of their Northern opponents during the first two years of the war. This horse, by the way, is tread-
ing the very road where Stuart, two years before, had escaped across the Chickahominy from the vengeful
army riding in his wake after he had ridden completely around its rear. Such raids, until the North had
created an efficient cavalry force, destroyed millions of dollars' worth of Federal property and exercised a
tremendous moral effect. The cry of "The Black Horse Cavalry" terrified still further the panic-stricken
Federal troops at Bull Run; Mosby's brilliant dashes at poorly guarded Union wagon trains and careless
outposts taught the Northern leaders many a lesson, and Stuart's two raids around McClellan's army, on
the Peninsula and in Maryland, resulted in the systematic upbuilding of a Federal cavalry. In the
latter years of the war, when the South was exhausted of such horses, their cavalry became less efficient,
but nothing can dim the luster of their performances in those first two hopeful and momentous years.

[G]

rails high. They cleared this like deer, and moved to the north-west. The rifled guns returned to Martinsburg, and the regiment remained in the orchard, but it was two days before all those race-horses found their way back to the regiment. Blooded horses proved unfit for the service; they fretted and exhausted themselves on a quiet march, and proved to be unmanageable in field engagements.

June, 1863, witnessed the most spectacular tournament in which the cavalry of the opposing armies in Virginia ever engaged. The Army of Northern Virginia was entering upon the campaign that was to culminate in the three days' battle of Gettysburg, and the entire cavalry force had been assembled for review, at Brandy Station. General Pleasonton, commander of the Union Cavalry Corps, wished to cross the Rappahannock to ascertain the disposition of General Lee's army. Two fords led across the river in that vicinity, Beverly and Kelly's, and these were promptly approached by the inquisitive Northerners. The second and third divisions of cavalry and a brigade of infantry were ordered to cross at Kelly's Ford; the first cavalry division, with another brigade of infantry, was ordered to cross at Beverly Ford. Several batteries of artillery accompanied each column, and never were batteries more gallantly served or skilfully commanded. On the morning of the 9th of June, the Eighth New York Cavalry crossed at Beverly Ford. One company of the Sixth Virginia, under Captain Gibson, formed the picket at this point. Stuart's headquarters had been on Fleetwood Hill from which, however, he had, luckily, removed his baggage at an early hour.

General Buford's force of Federal cavalry which crossed at Beverly Ford was, in the opinion of all of us, quite enough to satisfy the wishes of reasonable men, and Stuart had not reckoned on a further assault on his rear. But General Gregg, with another division of Federal cavalry, crossed at Kelly's Ford, and thus had Fleetwood Hill, which was the key to the situation between the two hostile forces. A disabled

THE BANKS OF THE CHICKAHOMINY IN '62—WHEN STUART CROSSED IT IN THE FIRST GREAT RAID OF THE WAR

This small but quick-rising little stream came nearer than the entire Union army to stopping Stuart in his famous "ride around McClellan" on the Peninsula, June 13–15, 1862. This was the first of the great Confederate raids that served to startle the Union into a recognition of the maladministration of its cavalry. After a brush with a squadron the Fifth United States Cavalry, commanded by Captain W. B. Royall, and a short halt at Old Church, he marched with only twelve hundred cavalrymen, by night, down through New Kent to Sycamore Ford on the Chickahominy, thence straight back to Richmond along the James River road. His entire loss was one man killed and a few wounded; yet he brought prisoners and plunder from under McClellan's very nose. Of most importance, he discovered the exact location of the Federal right wing, so that Jackson attacked it a few days later successfully. The cavalry gained confidence in itself, and the Confederacy rang with praises of its daring. The one really dangerous moment to the adventurous party came when the Chickahominy was reached on the homeward journey and was found to be swollen suddenly, and impassable even by swimming. Only Stuart's promptness in tearing down a mill and building a bridge with its timbers got his men across before the Federals hove in sight.

6-pounder howitzer had been left on Fleetwood Hill, under charge of Lieutenant Carter, and with this disabled gun and a very limited amount of ammunition, General Gregg was held in check until aid from General W. E. Jones' brigade could be sent. Gregg very naturally supposed that so important a position would not have been left unprotected, and that a stronger protection than one howitzer would have been afforded it. One dash by him with but a single regiment would have taken the position, and placed Stuart in a very uncomfortable situation.

From early morn till the stars arose did the battle of Brandy Station rage. The full cavalry forces of both armies were engaged, and neither could claim the advantage in gallantry or skill. The greater credit is due, perhaps, to the Federals, because they were the attacking party, and their assault had to be made by crossing a swollen river in the face of a cavalry corps that had the advantage of being on its own ground, and had the means of concentrating at each of the fords, which were the only ways the Federals had of getting access to the field. In no engagement between these two cavalry corps were sabers used so freely, or charges by regiments in line made so frequently and furiously.

General Lee was then advancing toward Pennsylvania; Stuart was screening this movement by keeping to the east of the Blue Ridge, and marching northward. The country was checkered with stone fences, strongly built and in good condition. Along the turnpike from Washington to Winchester, passing through Aldie, Middleburg, Upperville, and Paris there was continuous and severe fighting in which the cavalry alone participated. A Federal force, formed of the second cavalry division under General Gregg, with Kilpatrick's brigade and a battery of artillery, moved swiftly and with determination. Captain Reuben Boston had been placed with his Confederate squadron on the right of the road, with instructions to hold it. It appeared later that this little band had been

BRIGADIER–GENERAL THOMAS T. MUNFORD, C.S.A.

From the Peninsula to the last stand of the Confederate cavalry at Sailor's Creek, General Munford did his duty both gallantly and well. As colonel of the Second Virginia Cavalry he masked the placing of a battery of thirty-one field pieces upon the bluff at White Oak swamp, June 30, 1862. When the screen of cavalry was removed, the gunners opened up and drove a Union battery of artillery and a brigade of McClellan's infantry rear-guard from a large field just across the White Oak stream. His was the regiment which picketed the roads leading in the direction of the Federal forces upon the occasion of Jackson's famous raid around Pope's army to Manassas Junction. At Antietam he commanded a brigade of dismounted cavalry, comprising the Second and Twelfth Virginia regiments and eight guns, and he was with Longstreet and Hill at South Mountain. General Munford and General Rosser were two brigadiers of Fitzhugh Lee when the latter assumed command of all the cavalry of the Army of Northern Virginia in March, 1865. Munford's diminished brigade was swept before the Federal infantry fighting bravely at Five Forks, but with undiminished courage it drove back Crook on the north side of the Appomattox River only two days before Lee's surrender to Grant.

stationed too far to the front to receive aid from the rest of
the regiment, and hence, after receiving and repulsing several
attacks, Boston fell, with a remnant of his squadron, into the
hands of the Sixth Ohio Cavalry.

Peremptory orders were frequently given without due
consideration, and they were as frequently obeyed, even when
the person so ordered knew that they were destructive. In
this same campaign, Colonel Duffié, of the First Rhode Island
Cavalry, was ordered to encamp at Middleburg on the night
of June 17th, and his line of march was prescribed. He followed that line and it disclosed to him the presence of the
Confederates at many points along its course. He reached
Middleburg, and despatched an officer to General Kilpatrick,
at Aldie, to advise him of the situation, but Kilpatrick's troops
were too exhausted to go to Duffié's relief, and the latter's
regiment was attacked in the morning by Robertson's Confederate brigade, and two hundred of his men fell into Robertson's hands.

Many brilliant incidents of the Gettysburg campaign tes-
tify to the efficiency of the cavalry on both sides. While Stuart
was off on the left of the Confederate army, Robertson's brigade was on the right. General W. E. Jones was sent, with
three regiments, to protect the wagon train near Fairfield.
Near that place, the Sixth United States Cavalry, under Major
Starr, met the Seventh Virginia, and decidedly worsted that
gallant regiment; but the Sixth Virginia, under Major Flour-
noy, took its place, and the tide was turned. The Sixth United
States was routed, its brave commander was wounded and
captured, with one hundred and eighty-four of his command.

As Lee fell back from Gettysburg, the Potomac River
was much swollen. From the 8th to the 11th of July, Stuart
was engaged in guarding the front of the Confederate army,
waiting for the waters to fall. Cavalry engagements, of more
or less severity, with the divisions of Buford and Kilpatrick,
took place at Boonesboro, Beaver Creek, Funkstown, and in

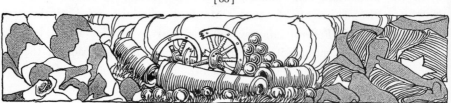

A RESTFUL SCENE AT GENERAL McDOWELL'S HEADQUARTERS—TAKEN WHILE
STUART'S CAVALRY WAS EXTREMELY BUSY

The Federals were camping in peaceful and luxurious fashion, August, 1862, quite unconscious that Jackson with Stuart's cavalry, was cutting in between them and Washington. It would have seemed madness to the Union generals in command of one hundred thousand men, with potential reinforcements of fifty thousand more, that the Confederate leaders should split their army of only fifty-five thousand and separate the parts by two days' march. It turned out that the Confederate generals were "mad," but that there was brilliant method in their madness. Twice they had attempted to turn the Federal right, when Pope lay across the Rappahannock waiting for McClellan's return from the Peninsula, and twice the watchful Pope had foiled the attempt. It was not until Jackson left Early's brigade in an exposed position across the hastily repaired bridge at Rappahannock Station that he managed to delude the Union general into accepting this point as his real objective. Leaving Early quite as mystified as his opponent, Jackson dispatched Stuart with all the cavalry to Catlett's Station, on the Orange & Alexandria Railroad, where Pope's supply trains were parked. The night of August 23d was pitchy black, and the rain was descending in torrents, when the Confederate horsemen burst into Pope's camp. A few hours later they rode away with the Federal general's uniform and horses, his treasure-chest and personal effects, a member of his staff, and some three hundred prisoners, leaving the blazing camp behind them. The retreat of the cavalry was the final indication that there would be no more efforts to turn his right. Two days later Jackson, with twenty thousand men, marched around the Union right and, joined by Stuart's cavalry, captured the immense supply-department depot at Manassas Junction.

REPAIRING AFTER STUART'S RAID

In a single night Stuart's cavalry, falling upon the Orange & Alexandria Railroad at Catlett's Station, thirty-five miles from Washington, had done damage to Pope's railroad connection which it took days to repair. This was on August 22d, and only the heavy rainstorm prevented the burning of a large quantity of army stores at Catlett's. Stuart's troopers got away with two hundred and twenty horses from the wagon trains and all the personal baggage of General Pope and his staff. The superior railroad facilities of the Federals were in this instance turned into a means of danger and delay, necessitating the detachment of a large repair force and enabling Lee's army to seize advantage elsewhere.

COPYRIGHT, 1911, REVIEW OF REVIEWS CO.

A MILITARY TRAIN UPSET BY CONFEDERATES

This is part of the result of General Pope's too rapid advance to head off Lee's army south of the Rappahannock River. Although overtaking the advance of the Confederates at Cedar Mountain, Pope had arrived too late to close the river passes against them. Meanwhile he had left the Orange & Alexandria Railroad uncovered, and Jackson pushed a large force under General Ewell forward across the Bull Run Mountains. On the night of August 26, 1863, Ewell's forces captured Manassas Junction, while four miles above the Confederate cavalry fell upon an empty railroad train returning from the transfer of Federal troops. The train was destroyed. Here we see how well the work was done.

front of Sharpsburg. Thus was the advance of Meade's army delayed until the Confederates had recrossed the river.

In September, 1863, the Cavalry Corps of the Army of Northern Virginia was reorganized, and Stuart's headquarters were at Culpeper Court House. On the 18th, Kilpatrick's division crossed the Rappahannock, and pressing its way with celerity and vigor toward Culpeper, captured three guns of the Confederate horse artillery. On the 22d, Buford encountered Stuart at Jack's shop, in Madison County, and a fierce engagement occupied the divisions of both Buford and Kilpatrick, with the result that Stuart withdrew across the Rapidan.

In October, General Lee entered upon what is known as the Bristoe campaign, which aimed at turning the right flank of the Federal army in Culpeper County. To cover this movement, Stuart distributed his command over a wide extent of country and along the Rapidan. On the 10th, Stuart was ordered to make a reconnaissance toward Catlett's Station. He sent Lomax forward, who moved to Auburn, and there learned that the Federals were in force at Warrenton Junction. He further discovered that the entire Federal wagon train was parked in a position easy of access. It was most desirable that its commissary supplies should be so applied as to appease the hunger of his half-starved cavalrymen. Stuart consequently moved in that direction, and on reaching a piece of woods there was plainly seen, about half a mile beyond, the vast park of wagons. Stuart gazed long and ardently at this coveted prize, but as he gazed, the hopeful expression on his countenance faded away and was succeeded by one of vexation and disappointment. Beyond the park of wagons, his practised eye discerned a moving cloud of dust, which appeared to be passing on the left of the wagons. It was growing dusk; tidings from his rear seemed to disconcert him, and he appeared to those who were near to be anxiously awaiting something. He rearranged his column; some pieces of artillery were put in front, and behind these a medical transport wagon, and then

THE TRAIN "STONEWALL" JACKSON AND STUART STOPPED AT BRISTOE

By a move of unparalleled boldness, "Stonewall" Jackson, with twenty thousand men, captured the immense Union supplies at Manassas Junction, August 26, 1862. His was a perilous position. Washington lay one day's march to the north; Warrenton, Pope's headquarters, but twelve miles distant to the southwest; and along the Rappahannock, between "Stonewall" Jackson and Lee, stood the tents of another host which outnumbered the whole Confederate army. "Stonewall" Jackson had seized Bristoe Station in order to break down the railway bridge over Broad Run, and to proceed at his leisure with the destruction of the stores. A train returning empty from Warrenton Junction to Alexandria darted through the station under heavy fire. The line was promptly torn up. Two trains which followed in the same direction as the first went crashing down a high embankment. The report received at Alexandria from the train which escaped ran as fol-

lows: "No. 6 train, engine Secretary, was fired into at Bristoe by a party of cavalry some five hundred strong. They had piled ties on the track, but the engine threw them off. Secretary is completely riddled by bullets." It was a full day before the Federals realized that "Stonewall" Jackson was really there with a large force. Here, in abundance, was all that had been absent for some time; besides commissary stores of all sorts, there were two trains loaded with new clothing, to say nothing of sutler's stores, replete with "extras" not enumerated in the regulations, and also the camp of a cavalry regiment which had vacated in favor of Jackson's men. It was an interesting sight to see the hungry, travel-worn men attacking this profusion and rewarding themselves for all their fatigues and deprivations of the preceding few days, and their enjoyment of it and of the day's rest allowed them. There was a great deal of difficulty for a time in finding what each man needed most, but this was overcome through a crude barter of belongings as the day wore on.

the cavalry. Thus formed, he moved to the front, leaving wagons and moving dust far to our right.

At some distance ahead, there rose from the plain a wooded ridge, extending northeast and southwest. Toward the end nearest to us we headed, and began its ascent, in the order in which we were formed. The front of the column reached the top and moved on to the further end, from which the ridge fell with more precipitousness than the end which we had ascended. When the last file of the rear regiment was well up on the ridge and protected by the trees, no room remained for more. We were dismounted and lay down, holding the bridle-reins in our hands.

In less than an hour a heavy column of infantry approached the ridge from the direction in which we had come. It passed to the left and moved along very close to the ridge and toward its further end. Almost at once, another column, like unto the first and moving by its side, passed to the right of the ridge, and at about the same distance from it, in a parallel line toward the same end of the ridge. So near were these moving columns, and so still were we, that all night long we could hear the conversation carried on among our foemen on either side of us.

The hours seemed interminable, but those marching columns seemed even longer. Daylight came, but still they marched. Should sunrise find us still so beleaguered, our chances of escape would be small. As the earliest rays of the sun routed the mists, the long-hoped-for rear of these columns went by, and halted but a few rods beyond the further end of our ridge. During the night, Stuart had sent messengers to General Lee, telling him of our situation and asking for relief. That relief was sent, but it miscarried. As the sun rose higher, Stuart opened on the rear of these two columns, which had halted for breakfast, had made their fires, and were boiling their coffee. The four guns did some execution, and the Federals, startled by this " bolt from the blue," ran—not, as we hoped,

MANASSAS JUNCTION, WHERE THE FEDERAL WAR DEPARTMENT ENTERTAINED
UNEXPECTED GUESTS

"Stonewall" Jackson and twenty thousand men were the unexpected guests of the North at Manassas Junction on August 26, 1862. The ragged and famished Confederates, who had marched over fifty miles in the last two days, had such a feast as they never knew before. The North had been lavish in its expenditures for the army. No effort had been spared to feed, clothe, and equip them, and for the comfort of the individual soldier the purse-strings of the nation were freely loosed. Streets of warehouses, crammed to the doors, a line of freight cars two miles in length, thousands of barrels of flour, pork, and biscuit, ambulances, field-wagons, and pyramids of shot and shell, met the wondering gaze of the Confederate soldiery. The sutlers' stores contained a wealth of plunder. "Here," says General George H. Gordon, describing the scene that followed, "a long, yellow-haired, barefooted son of the South claimed as prizes a tooth-brush, a box of candies, and a barrel of coffee, while another, whose butternut homespun hung round him in tatters, crammed himself with lobster salad, sardines, potted game, and sweetmeats, and washed them down with Rhenish wine. Nor was the outer man neglected. From piles of new clothing, the Southerners arrayed themselves in the blue uniforms of the Federals. The naked were clad, the barefooted were shod, and the sick provided with luxuries to which they had long been strangers." All unportable stores were destroyed.

from the danger that presented itself, but ran, and with intrepid force, toward us. They charged the steep ascent, struck down the commander of a North Carolina regiment, and only desisted when the fire from our guns repelled them. Stuart withdrew from the ridge. He had extricated himself in safety, and what would have been stigmatized as his folly, had we been routed, became a proof of his genius and heroic courage.

The object of the Bristoe campaign was accomplished as far as such objects are generally accomplished, but, on the 18th of October, Stuart was at Buckland, with Kilpatrick in front of him. A device suggested by Fitzhugh Lee proved successful. Stuart withdrew and Kilpatrick followed him hopefully, but Fitzhugh Lee had taken a position which threw him in Kilpatrick's rear. Upon an agreed signal, Stuart turned on Kilpatrick in front and Lee struck his rear, and a rout ensued in which Davies' brigade bore the brunt. It ran, and the race extended over five miles. Custer, however, saved his artillery and crossed Broad Run in safety.

On the 28th of February following, Custer made a brilliant, and in the main successful, foray from Madison Court House into Charlottesville, with about fifteen hundred cavalry. Near Charlottesville were four battalions of artillery, resting in fond security in winter quarters. The guns were all saved but horses were taken, and some of the quarters were burned, with the loss of clothing and blankets.

Kilpatrick was moving on Richmond with about thirty-five hundred cavalry. Colonel Ulric Dahlgren and about four hundred and fifty men were pushed rapidly toward the Virginia Central Railroad, which they struck at Frederick's Hall, where they captured eight officers who were sitting on a court martial, and moved toward the James River. Thence they moved down on the north side of the James to Richmond, where they attacked the outer entrenchments. Hampton attacked Kilpatrick's camp and drove him from it, compelling his return to Fredericksburg. Colonel Dahlgren made a wide

OUT OF REACH

OF THE

CONFEDERATE CAVALRY

U. S. MILITARY

ENGINES STORED

IN ALEXANDRIA, 1863

By the middle of 1863 the Federal generals had learned the wisdom of storing in a safe place, under a heavy guard, anything they wanted to keep. Of especial value was the rolling stock of the military railroads, which when not in use was ordered out of the danger zone. General J. E. B. Stuart with his tireless troopers had proved himself so ignorant of the meaning of the words "danger" or "distance" that the Federals had lost their confidence of the previous year, when they believed that the mere interposition of an army of a hundred thousand men was sufficient to protect a base of supplies. This photograph was taken about the time the battle of Gettysburg was raging, and Stuart was causing a diversion by throwing shells near Washington. It was not until the Army of the Potomac returned to Virginia, with headquarters established at Brandy Station, that any great number of these iron horses were allowed out of their stables. By that time the Union cavalry had received the experience and equipment to meet the Confederate troopers in their own way, and threatened the railroads running into Richmond. Organization and numbers had begun to tell.

circuit, crossing the Pamunkey and the Mattapony, but at length he fell into an ambuscade near King and Queen Court House where he lost his life, as did many of his command.

We have reached now, in the order of time, the Wilderness campaign which opened May 4, 1864. General Grant's object was to interpose his army between Lee and Richmond. Sheridan, with about ten thousand cavalry and several batteries, had moved to Hamilton's Crossing and thence toward Richmond, on the Telegraph road. General Wickham, with his brigade, followed in pursuit. Near Mitchell's shop he was joined by Fitzhugh Lee, with about five thousand cavalry. Stuart, now in command, moved toward Yellow Tavern, which he reached before the appearance of Sheridan's troopers. They did appear, however, and attempted to drive Stuart from the Telegraph road. A severe fight ensued, in which Stuart lost heavily in officers, but maintained his position.

About four o'clock in the afternoon, a brigade of Federal cavalry attacked Stuart's extreme left, and he, after his fashion, hurried to the point of danger. One company of the First Virginia Cavalry was bearing the entire burden. Stuart joined himself to this little band and attacked the flank of the Union cavalry. The First Virginia drove the Federals back. Many of the latter, having lost their horses in the fight, were keeping up on foot. One of these dismounted men turned, as he ran, and firing at the general with his pistol, inflicted the wound from which he shortly afterward died.

Now, to turn back, when General Johnston, on the 18th of July, 1861, moved from the Shenandoah valley to Manassas, he left a body of cavalry, under Colonel McDonald, scattered throughout the country between the Shenandoah River and the North Mountains. In this body was a company from Fauquier County, commanded by Turner Ashby. Later on, this company was organized into a huge regiment of which McDonald was colonel; Turner Ashby, lieutenant-colonel, and Oliver Funsten, major. The duty assigned to this regiment

[98]

COVERING LEE'S RETREAT FROM PENNSYLVANIA

This photograph is an excellent illustration of the cavalry's method of destroying the railroads between the two capitals. The light rails were placed across piles of ties. The ties were lighted and the rails heated until of their own weight they bent out of shape. Mile upon mile of railroad could thus be destroyed in a day. New rails had to be brought before it was possible to rebuild the line. Note the tangle of telegraph wires. The telegraph lines were also destroyed wherever the Confederate position was known and it was therefore impossible to tap them and read the Union leaders' messages. The Army of Northern Virginia and the Army of the Potomac spent the month of October, 1863, when this photograph was taken, maneuvering for position along the Rappahannock. On October 20th the Army of the Potomac was occupying Warrenton and Lee had retired to the north bank of the Rappahannock, having destroyed the Orange and Alexandria Railroad from Bristoe Station to the river, and by the 22d, both armies were again in camp.

[G—7]

THE PRIZE THAT IMPERILLED STUART ON HIS DARING RAID INTO THE
FEDERAL LINES

In this striking photograph of 1863 appears the prize at which General J. E. B. Stuart gazed
long and ardently during his reconnaissance to Warrenton Station on the 10th of October,
1863, after Lee's Bristoe campaign. His half-starved cavalrymen urgently needed just such
a wagon-train as that. But, as they peered from their ambush, the hopeful expressions
faded away. Beyond the park of wagons Stuart's practiced eye had discerned a moving
cloud of dust. That night he was confined to a little ridge, with the Union columns moving
to the right and left of his isolated force. By dawn the rear of the passing columns were
cooking their breakfasts at the foot of the ridge. By the bold device of firing into them and

PART OF THE "VAST PARK OF WAGONS" ON WHICH THE CONFEDERATES GAZED
FROM AMBUSH, OCTOBER 10, 1863

repelling their first attack, Stuart disconcerted the pursuit and made good his escape. This view of the wagons "in park," or gathered in one large body in an open field, represents a train of the Sixth Corps, Army of the Potomac, near Brandy Station, during the autumn days of 1863, after the Gettysburg campaign. The wagons in the foreground are ambulances, while immediately in their rear stand the large army wagons used for subsistence and quartermaster's stores. The horses are harnessed to the vehicles preparatory to the forward movement. It took this train across the Rappahannock River toward Culpeper and the Rapidan, where history indicates that they formed part of those upon which Stuart gazed so covetously.

was the guarding of the Potomac River on a line nearly one hundred and twenty-five miles in length. No more striking and picturesque figure than Ashby ever won the confidence and affections of his followers. Since his boyhood he had been famed as a horseman, even in that land of centaurs. Throughout all those marvelous campaigns in the Valley, which have made Jackson immortal, Turner Ashby, as brigadier-general, commanded the cavalry that formed an impenetrable screen between Jackson and the Federal armies in his front.

In May and June, 1862, Jackson moved up the Shenandoah valley, Generals Banks and Saxton following with fourteen thousand troops. General Fremont, with his army, was approaching Strasburg from the direction of Moorefield, while General Shields, who had crossed the Blue Ridge from the east, was moving up Luray Valley on Jackson's left flank, with still another division. Jackson waited at Strasburg nearly twenty-four hours for one of his regiments, which he had left below him, to rejoin his command. Meanwhile Fremont approached within ten miles, was met by General Richard Taylor, and held in check until Jackson, starting his wagon trains off before him, had followed in a leisurely manner, while Ashby, with his cavalry, kept back Fremont, who was pressing Jackson's rear. Shields was moving rapidly in the hope of intercepting Jackson before he could cross the Blue Ridge, which Shields supposed he was striving to do. A few miles south of Harrisonburg, Jackson turned toward Port Republic, encountered Fremont's cavalry, under Colonel Percy Wyndham, which Ashby quickly routed, capturing Colonel Wyndham and a large part of his command. Fremont sent forward General Bayard and his command, which met the Fifty-eighth Virginia, near Cross Keys. General Ashby dismounted, and placing himself at the head of this infantry regiment, received the bullet which ended his career.

His former regiment, with certain additions, was organized into a brigade consisting of the Second, Sixth, Seventh,

A SAD SIGHT FOR THE CAVALRYMAN

This pitiful scene after the battle of Gettysburg illustrates the losses of mounts after each engagement, which told heaviest on the Southern cavalry. Up to the next winter, 1863–4, it was well organized and had proved its efficiency on many fields. But from that period its weakness increased rapidly. The sources of supplies of both men and horses had been exhausted simultaneously; many of the best and bravest of men and officers had fallen in battle. From then onward it was a struggle for bare existence, until at Appomattox the large-hearted Lee pointed out to Grant that the only mounts left to the Confederacy were those that his men were actually riding. Be it recorded to the Northern general's credit that he gave im-. mediate instructions that every Confederate who owned his horse should be allowed to take it home for plowing and putting in his crop. This photograph shows staff officers' horses killed at Gettysburg.

and Twelfth Virginia regiments, and the Seventeenth Battalion which soon afterward became the Eleventh Virginia Cavalry. After Ashby's death, this brigade was, for a time, commanded by Colonel Munford. General Shields reached the village of Port Republic, where Jackson encountered him and drove him back down Luray Valley, and thus ended the Valley campaign of that year.

General Beverly Robertson was now assigned to the command of the old Ashby brigade. On the 2d of August, a sharp hand-to-hand encounter took place in the streets of Orange Court House, between the Seventh Virginia, and the Fifth New York and First Vermont, both commanded by General Crawford, in which Colonel Jones and Lieutenant-Colonel Marshall, of the Seventh Virginia, were wounded. The Sixth Virginia coming up, the Federals reluctantly gave way, and were pursued as far as Rapidan Station.

On December 29th, 1862, General W. E. Jones was assigned to the command of the Valley District, and in March, 1863, he moved to Moorefield Valley, with the view of gathering much-needed supplies of food, and also with the intention of destroying the Cheat River viaduct, on the Baltimore and Ohio Railroad. The south branch, at Petersburg in Hardy County, West Virginia, was high, and the fords were almost impassable. The artillery and the loaded wagon trains were sent back to Harrisonburg, and Jones, with his cavalry alone, undertook the invasion of West Virginia. At Greenland Gap, on the summit of the Alleghany Mountains, a body of Federal infantry held a blockhouse, strongly built and gallantly defended. This was taken only after the loss of several men, and the wounding of Colonel Dulany of the Seventh Virginia. It was repeatedly charged by the dismounted cavalry, and was finally taken by stratagem rather than assault.

The Cheat River viaduct was reached on the 26th of April, and found to be guarded by three hundred infantry entrenched in a blockhouse, too strong to be taken in a moment, and time

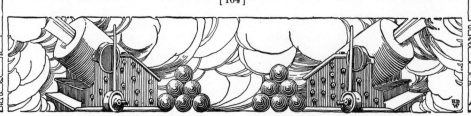

HORSES KILLED IN BATTLE—A SERIOUS LOSS

The number of horses killed in battle was, after all, but a small fraction of those destroyed by exhaustion, starvation, and disease during the Civil War. When Lee's army marched into Pennsylvania he had issued stringent orders against plundering. The orders were almost implicitly obeyed except when it came to the question of horses. The quartermasters, especially of artillery battalions, could seldom report their commands completely equipped. The Confederacy had no great cavalry depots like Giesboro, or those at St. Louis or Greenville in Louisiana. When a mount was exhausted he had to be replaced. Some of the farmers actually concealed their horses in their own houses, but a horseless trooper was a veritable sleuth in running down a horse, whether concealed in the parlor or in the attic. The Confederates offered to pay for the horses, but in Confederate currency. The owners occasionally accepted it on the principle that it was "better than nothing." The animals thus impressed in Pennsylvania were for the most part great, clumsy, flabby Percherons and Conestogas, which required more than twice the feed of the compact, hard-muscled little Virginia horses. It was pitiable to see these great brutes suffer when they were compelled to dash off at full gallop with a field-piece after pasturing on dry broom-sedge and eating a quarter of a feed of weevil-infested corn.

A CAVALRY HORSE PICKETED
AT THE EVENING BIVOUAC

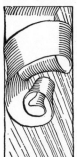

did not allow of tarrying. On April 28th, the command reached Morgantown, where it crossed on a suspension bridge to the west side of the Monongahela, and after dark moved on Fairmont. Here the Federals were found in considerable force, which, after some fighting, was dispersed, and the object of the visit to that point being the destruction of the fine iron bridge, of three spans of three hundred feet each, that work was entered upon and continued until the bridge was destroyed.

Oiltown, near Elizabeth Court House, on the Little Kanawha River, was owned mainly by Southern men who had first engaged in the oil industry. There were found thousands of gallons of oil, in barrels, tanks, and in deep flatboats then on the water. All was burned, and Dante might have gained some new impressions of the regions described by him, from the scenes that presented themselves to the destroyers. The dense, black smoke rose to the heights of hundreds of feet; the intense heat caused by the burning oil excited a breeze, and the flatboats filled with burning oil, floated down the river toward Elizabeth. After thirty days incessant marching, without supplies of food, save what was taken from the people, without artillery or wagons of any kind, the expedition returned with seven hundred prisoners, one thousand cattle and twelve hundred horses, and with a loss of ten killed and forty-two wounded.

Jones was back in the Valley the last week of May, and, by crossing the mountains, joined Stuart near Culpeper Court House. A little later he took conspicuous part in the battle of Brandy Station and the ensuing campaign. The events and incidents of that and the following campaigns to the death of General Stuart, have been already related.

General Thomas L. Rosser had been assigned to the command of the old Ashby brigade, and soon proved himself a most efficient cavalry commander. In January, 1864, then under General Early in the Valley District, he was in command of the cavalry. On January 29th, Rosser crossed the

A SECOND "ARMY" OPPOSED TO THE CONFEDERATE CAVALRY—A FEDERAL CAVALRY MESS-HOUSE

The Confederate cavalry, like the Confederacy itself, was hastened to its fall because of the exhaustion of resources. While horseflesh was growing scarcer and poorer in quality in Virginia, and proper fodder had become little but a memory since Sheridan's devastation of the Shenandoah Valley, the Union Government, with its immense resources, was able to systematize the handling of supplies for its cavalry corps, establishing half a dozen huge cavalry remount depots, and devoting the proper amount of attention to every branch of the work. This photograph shows the mess-house at the Government stables in Washington. The Confederacy barely supplied food for the troopers themselves, while the Union Government was able to build mess-houses for those who were engaged in caring for the troopers' wants.

mountains to Moorefield, in Hardy County, West Virginia, and there learning that a large wagon train of supplies was moving from New Creek to Petersburg, moved forward to take it. He found parked at Medley a train of ninety-five wagons, guarded by three hundred infantry and a small body of cavalry. He moved one regiment toward the rear of this body, placed others on the flank, and then opened with one gun on its front. The effect was to stampede the teamsters, and the infantry were unable to withstand the attack by dismounted cavalry, so that in a short time the wagons, with some prisoners, fell into Rosser's hands. On the 1st of February, moving upon the Baltimore and Ohio Railroad, at Patterson's Creek, he captured the guard there, and brought out about twelve hundred cattle and some sheep.

On the 7th of June, Sheridan was sent with two divisions to communicate with Hunter, and to break up the Virginia Central Railroad and the James River Canal. He started on this mission with eighty-nine hundred cavalry. On the morning of the 8th, Hampton, who had succeeded Stuart in the command of the Cavalry Corps of the Army of Northern Virginia, moved with two divisions and some batteries of horse artillery to look after this movement. His first step was to intercept Sheridan before he reached the railroad. On the night of the 10th, he had reached Green Spring Valley, three miles from Trevilian Station, and there encamped. At this time General Fitzhugh Lee was at Louisa Court House, and Custer, with his characteristic boldness, took an unguarded road around Hampton's right and essayed to reach Trevilian. He captured ambulances, caissons, and many led horses. Near at hand was Thompson's battery, wholly unmindful of danger, and this Custer essayed to take. But Colonel Chew, commander of the battalion of artillery to which this belonged, deployed a South Carolina regiment to hold Custer in check until he could get another battery into position. This he soon did, and Rosser, coming up with his brigade at the moment,

A WAR–TIME VIEW OF STUART'S GRAVE

"Gen'l Stuart—wounded May 11, 1864—died May 12, 1864." This simple head-slab on its wooded hill near Richmond toward the close of the war spelt a heavy blow to the Confederate cause. In that struggle against heavier and heavier odds, every man counted. And when destroying Fate chose for its victim the leader whose spirit had never fallen, whose courage had never failed, no matter how dangerous the raid, how fierce the charge and counter-charge—well might the Confederacy mourn. To the memory of this American chevalier, tributes came not only from comrades but from opponents. One of these, Theophilus F. Rodenbough—a Federal captain at the time of Stuart's death, later a cavalry historian and a contributor to other pages of this volume—wrote, twenty years after the tragedy, this fitting epitaph: "Deep in the hearts of all true cavalrymen, North and South, will ever burn a sentiment of admiration mingled with regret for this knightly soldier and generous man."

compelled Custer to relinquish his well-earned gains and betake himself to flight, while all his plunder fell into Rosser's hands.

Custer, however, remained that night near Trevilian, from which Rosser strove to drive him, but his reward was a severe wound which disabled him from further action that day. Desperately did Sheridan endeavor to drive Hampton from his path, and the fight continued through three days, but the result was the withdrawal of Sheridan's forces, and his rejoining Grant. General Grant, in his "Memoirs," states of this withdrawal that "Sheridan went back because the enemy had taken possession of a crossing by which he proposed to go west, and because he heard that Hunter was not at Charlottesville."

In September, Lee's army was sorely in need of beef. Scouts reported at Coggin's Point a large but well-guarded herd of cattle, and on the morning of the 11th, Hampton, with his cavalry, started to capture it. Notice of this movement had got abroad, and near Sycamore Church a regiment of Federal cavalry was awaiting the assault. The cattle were protected by a strong abatis, through which cavalry could not pass, and a deliberate attack was required. Accordingly the Seventh Virginia was dismounted and moved forward, while other regiments were sent around the obstruction. The herders then broke down the fence of the corral, and tried by firing pistols to stampede the cattle, and thus get them beyond Hampton's reach. But Hampton's cavalry were born cowboys, and, heading off the frightened cattle, soon rounded them up, so that the expedition returned with twenty-five hundred cattle to Lee's starving soldiers. On the 17th, General B. F. Butler informed General Grant that "three brigades of Hampton's cavalry turned our left and captured about two thousand cattle, and our telegraph construction party."

Rosser returned to the Valley with his brigade, and on November 27th started on the "New Creek raid," so called from a village on the Baltimore and Ohio Railroad, about

BRIGADIER–GEN-
ERAL JAMES B.
GORDON, C.S.A.

KILLED DURING
SHERIDAN'S RAID ON
RICHMOND,
MAY 11, 1864

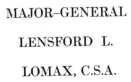

MAJOR–GENERAL
LENSFORD L.
LOMAX, C.S.A.

WITH THE
CONFEDERATE CAVALRY
IN THE
SHENANDOAH

twenty-two miles west from Cumberland. A Federal scouting party had been sent out from New Creek on the 26th, and Rosser, marching all night, arrived within six miles of New Creek at daylight on the morning of the 27th. The village was strongly fortified, with one heavy gun enfilading the road on which Rosser was moving toward it. General W. H. Payne's brigade was put in front, with about twenty men in blue overcoats. The column moved slowly toward its object, and citizens along the road, and travelers at that early hour thought it was the returning party that had gone out the night before on a scout. Less than a mile from the two, the first picket was reached. These men jocularly mocked the empty-handed returning party, but they were silently surrounded and taken along with the column. New Creek was reached and entered. On the left was a high hill, not steep, on which an infantry force of twelve hundred men was encamped. The Federal troops were engaged in drying their blankets and preparing their breakfast, when the mounted column of Confederates, suddenly breaking into line, charged the hill, and, without the loss of a single life, took eight hundred of these infantry. The Confederates then proceeded to destroy the railroad bridge, and gather as much as they could carry away of the large supplies they found stored at that point. Rosser, encumbered with many hundred cattle and sheep, and a long train of captured stores, turned his column homeward.

At Beverly, a village seventy-five miles west from Staunton, there were stored large supplies, guarded by a Federal garrison that did not exceed one thousand men. Rosser, learning of this fact, took three hundred men from the several brigades and started before daylight from Swoope's Depot, on January 10th. He spent that night, or a part of it, on a mountain-side, without fires. The snow was deep, and the weather bitterly cold. Before daylight on the morning of the 11th, he was on a hill west of Beverly, overlooking the garrison of Federal infantry in their wooden huts on the plain below. The moon

BRIGADIER–GENERAL M. CALVIN BUTLER, C. S. A.

General Butler was a leader under Wade Hampton, who played an important part in the defeat of Sheridan with eight thousand men at Trevilian Station, June 12, 1864, just one month after the death of Stuart. Between 2 P.M. and dark, Butler, in command of Hampton's division of cavalry, repulsed seven determined assaults of Sheridan's men. During the day Butler was unable to keep his batteries in exposed positions entirely manned, but between sunset and dark, when the Federal cavalrymen made their last desperate effort, the howitzers were remanned and double-shotted with canister. The Federals emerged from the woods a stone's throw from the Confederate lines, and the canister tore great holes in their lines. It was at this engagement that General Butler lost his leg.

was full and shining brilliantly on snow over a foot in depth. Dismounting a part of his command, and moving them in line in front, with the mounted men behind, Rosser moved upon the sleeping host. Had they remained in their strong huts and used their rifles, the disaster might have been averted, but as the result, five hundred and eighty prisoners, and ten thousand rations fell into the hands of the invaders.

On the morning of February 21, 1865, a portion of McNeill's command, under Lieutenant Jesse McNeill, entered the city of Cumberland, Maryland, an hour before daylight. Major-General Crook, the commander of the Department of West Virginia, and Brigadier-General Kelley, his able lieutenant, were quietly sleeping, the one at the St. Nicholas Hotel, and the other at the Revere House. Six thousand troops, of all arms, occupied the city. Sergeant Vandiver called on General Crook, while some other member of the command performed the like civility to General Kelley. These two officers were persuaded to accompany their ill-timed callers on their return to Dixie, and were entertained in Richmond at an official hostelry there. Rosser and his command were present at Appomattox, but did not participate in the surrender, but while that ceremony was in progress, this command passed on to Lynchburg, and dissolved into their individual elements.

Up to the winter of 1863–64, the Confederate cavalry was well organized and had proven its efficiency on many fields, but its weakness from that period grew rapidly. The sources of supplies of both men and horses had been exhausted, and the best and the bravest of men and officers had fallen in battle.

On the other hand, when General Sheridan took command of the Federal cavalry, a new and far more vigorous life was imparted to it. Armed with repeating carbines and fighting on foot, as well as mounted, it became the most formidable arm of the Federal service. When the war ended, it was but reasonable to aver that the cavalry of the Army of the Potomac was the most efficient body of soldiers on earth.

CHAPTER

FOUR

———

RAIDS OF THE
FEDERAL CAVALRY

———

WELL-CONDITIONED MOUNTS, EQUIPPED FOR A LONG RAID
1862

FEDERAL CAVALRY LEAVING CAMP

The well-filled bags before and behind each trooper indicate a long and hard trip in store. Both the Confederate and Federal cavalry distinguished themselves by their endurance on their arduous and brilliant raids. The amount of destruction accomplished by this arm of the service was well-nigh incalculable. Stuart, Mosby, Forrest on one side—Sheridan, Grierson, Kilpatrick on the other—each in turn upset the opponents' calculations and forced them to change their plans. It was Van Dorn's capture at Holly Springs that caused Grant's first failure against Vicksburg. It was not until after the surrender at Appomattox that Lee learned

THE ARM THAT DEALT A FINAL BLOW TO THE CONFEDERACY

the final crushing blow—that the rations destined for his men had been captured by Sheridan. Up and down the Rappahannock the cavalry rode and scouted and fought by day and by night, sometimes saddled for sixty hours, often sleeping by regiments on the slowly moving columns of horses. It was Grierson who reported, after his ride from Vicksburg to Baton Rouge, that the Confederacy was but a hollow shell—all of its men were on the battle-line. It was Stuart who twice circled McClellan's army, on the Peninsula and in Maryland, and who caused Lincoln to recall the schoolboy game: "Three times round and out."

REPAIRING CONFEDERATE DAMAGE

The busy Federal engineers are rebuilding the railroad bridge across Cedar Run, near Catlett's Station, destroyed by the Confederates on the previous day, October 13th, when they fell back before the Army of the Potomac under General Meade. The fall of 1863 was a period of small cavalry battles. On September 16th the Army of the Potomac crossed the Rappahannock and took position near Culpeper Court House. During the next few weeks the cavalry was actively engaged in reconnoitering duty. On October 10th General John Buford was sent across the Rappahannock with the First Cavalry Division (consisting of the Eighth Illinois, Twelfth Illinois, four companies Third Indiana, six companies Eighth New York, Sixth New York, Ninth New York, Seventeenth Pennsylvania, and

FEDERAL ENGINEERS AT WORK OCTOBER 14, 1863

Third West Virginia, two companies) to uncover, if possible, the upper fords of the river. Buford forced a passage over the Germanna Ford, and bivouacked that night at Morton's Ford, where he recrossed the Rapidan and engaged a body of the enemy. At daylight on October 14th, the Confederates attacked Gregg's Second Cavalry Division, but he held his position tenaciously while General Warren got the Second Corps across Cedar Run. It seldom took over a few hours to rebuild one of these bridges. Sometimes the troops tore down the nearest wooden houses to get boards and timber. This wrecking of houses was very arduous work. The trees in the foreground have been sacrificed for construction purposes.

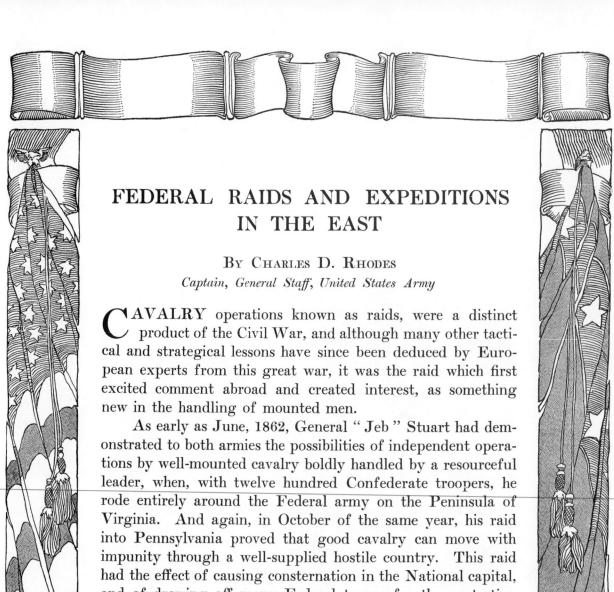

FEDERAL RAIDS AND EXPEDITIONS IN THE EAST

By Charles D. Rhodes
Captain, General Staff, United States Army

CAVALRY operations known as raids, were a distinct product of the Civil War, and although many other tactical and strategical lessons have since been deduced by European experts from this great war, it was the raid which first excited comment abroad and created interest, as something new in the handling of mounted men.

As early as June, 1862, General "Jeb" Stuart had demonstrated to both armies the possibilities of independent operations by well-mounted cavalry boldly handled by a resourceful leader, when, with twelve hundred Confederate troopers, he rode entirely around the Federal army on the Peninsula of Virginia. And again, in October of the same year, his raid into Pennsylvania proved that good cavalry can move with impunity through a well-supplied hostile country. This raid had the effect of causing consternation in the National capital, and of drawing off many Federal troops for the protection of Washington.

Stuart's successful raids caused some modification of the previous short-sighted policy of always attaching Union cavalry to infantry commands, and although until Sheridan's time, the raids made by the Federal cavalry in the East were not remarkably successful and the time for their initiation not well chosen, the Federal cavalry constantly increased in powers of mobility and independence of action.

Early in 1863, General Hooker detached Stoneman with the Cavalry Corps from the main operations of the Army of

COLONEL ULRIC DAHL-
GREN, WHO MET HIS
DEATH IN THE RAID
UPON RICHMOND

As Stuart threatened Washington, so Kilpatrick in turn
threatened the Capital of the
South. He was accompanied
by Colonel Ulric Dahlgren
who was to leave him near
Spotsylvania with five hundred picked men, to cross the
James, enter Richmond on
the south side, after liberating
the prisoners at Belle Isle,
and unite with Kilpatrick's
main force March 1, 1864.
The latter left Stevensburg
with four thousand cavalry
and a battery of horse artillery
on the night of Sunday, the
28th of February, crossed the
Rapidan at Ely's Ford, surprised and captured the
picket there, and marched
rapidly toward Richmond.
On March 1st the column was
within five miles of the
city. Failing to connect with
Dahlgren, Kilpatrick finally
withdrew, but not until he
had driven in the force
sent to oppose him to the
inner lines of the Richmond
defenses. This was the nearest that any body of Union
troops got to Richmond before its fall. Colonel Dahlgren met his death upon this
raid, and part of his command was captured, the rest
escaping to Kilpatrick, March
2d, at Tunstall's Station,
near White House.

UNION CAVALRYMEN IN RICHMOND—NOT UNTIL 1865

the Potomac, with orders to cross the Rappahannock for a raid on the communications with Richmond—turning Lee's left flank and inflicting on him every possible injury.

During Stoneman's absence the sanguinary battle of Chancellorsville was fought by the Army of the Potomac, and as the success of the raid depended in great measure upon a Federal victory at Chancellorsville, it was not, strategically at least, a success. The detachment of the Union troopers deprived General Hooker of cavalry at a time when he particularly needed a screening force to conceal his movements by the right flank; and it is probable that if Stoneman's cavalry had been present with the Army of the Potomac, it would have given ample warning of "Stonewall" Jackson's secret concentration opposite the Union right, which well nigh caused a decisive defeat for the Union army.

But Stoneman's raid destroyed millions of dollars' worth of Confederate property, and although it cut Lee's communications for a short time only, its moral effect was considerable, as shown by the Confederate correspondence since published.

The Stoneman raid was followed in February, 1864, by the famous raid of General Judson Kilpatrick, having as its objective the taking of the city of Richmond and the liberation of the Union prisoners confined therein. General Meade assisted the raid by demonstrations against Lee's left and by sending Custer on a minor raid into Albemarle County. It was supposed, at the time, that Richmond was comparatively defenseless, and that Kilpatrick's force might take the city before reenforcements from either Petersburg or Lee's army on the Rapidan could reach it.

Kilpatrick's force consisted of nearly four thousand men. Near Spotsylvania, about five hundred men under Colonel Ulric Dahlgren were detached for the purpose of crossing the James River, and, after liberating the Union prisoners at Belle Isle, attacking Richmond from the south.

Dahlgren's   little   command   destroyed   considerable

TROOPERS OF THE FIRST MASSACHUSETTS JUST AFTER THEIR ATTEMPT TO RAID RICHMOND IN 1864

A GROUP OF OFFICERS, FIRST MASSACHUSETTS CAVALRY

The officers and men of the First Massachusetts Cavalry formed part of General Judson Kilpatrick's force in his Richmond raid. The men look gaunt and hungry because they are down to "fighting weight." Starvation, fatigue, exposure, and nights in the saddle soon disposed of any superfluous flesh a trooper might carry. These men heard the laugh of the Confederate sentries inside the fortifications of the Southern Capital, and turned back only when success seemed impossible. Kilpatrick's object had been to move past the Confederate right flank, enter Richmond, and release the Union captives in its military prisons. This bold project had grown out of President Lincoln's desire to have his proclamation of amnesty circulated within the Confederate lines. The plan included also a raid upon communications and supplies. A joint expedition, under Dahlgren, met defeat, and Kilpatrick, not hearing from it, turned back.

Confederate property, but through the alleged treachery of a guide, the raiders were led out of their course. A portion of the command became separated; Dahlgren, with about one hundred and fifty troopers, was ambushed near Walkerton, and the leader killed and most of his force captured. The remainder of Dahlgren's command, under Captain Mitchell, managed to rejoin Kilpatrick, who had meanwhile threatened Richmond from the north, and who, finding the city prepared for his attack, finally withdrew across the Chickahominy and joined General Butler on the Peninsula, March 3, 1864.

The Kilpatrick raid failed in its main object, but that it might easily have succeeded seems evident from Confederate correspondence, which shows that the interception of a despatch from Dahlgren to Kilpatrick, asking what hour the latter had fixed for a simultaneous attack upon Richmond, alone made it possible for the Confederates successfully to defend the city.

When, early in 1864, General Grant gave Sheridan the long hoped for opportunity to "whip Stuart," and until the final end at Appomattox, this peerless cavalry leader never missed an opportunity to cut loose from the main army, drawing off from Grant's flanks and rear the enterprising and oftentimes dangerous Confederate cavalry, cutting Lee's communications with the South and Southwest time and again, and destroying immense quantities of the precious and carefully husbanded supplies of the Army of Northern Virginia.

Sheridan's Richmond raid, probably the most daring and sensational of these more or less independent operations, had for its object, not so much the destruction of Confederate property, as to draw Stuart and his cavalry away from the Union army's long lines of supply-trains, and then to defeat the great Confederate trooper.

In May, 1864, Sheridan's splendid body of horsemen, ten thousand in number and forming a column thirteen miles in length, moved out from the vicinity of Spotsylvania, through Chilesburg and Glen Allen Station. At Yellow Tavern the

A STILL SMOKING WRECK ON THE PATH OF THE FEDERAL RAIDERS

This photograph shows the ruins of the bridge over the North Anna, which were still smoking when the photographer arrived with the Union troops at the end of Sheridan's raid. He had ridden nearer to Richmond than any other Union leader before its fall. On the night of May 11, 1864, his column of cavalry could see the lights of the city and hear the dogs barking, and the following day an enterprising newsboy slipped through the lines and sold copies of the Richmond *Inquirer*. Sheridan declared that he could have taken Richmond, but that he couldn't hold it. The prisoners told him that every house was loopholed and the streets barricaded, and he did not think it worth the sacrifice in men. But in the death of Stuart at Yellow Tavern, Sheridan had dealt a blow severer than a raid into the Capital would have been.

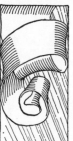

decisive conflict which Sheridan had sought with the Confederate cavalry took place. The latter were driven back upon Richmond; the gallant and knightly Stuart received his mortal wound, and the Union cavalry gained complete control of the highway leading to the Confederate capital. The casualties on both sides were severe.

Pushing on rapidly by way of the Meadow Bridge, Sheridan actually found himself and his force within the outer fortifications of the city of Richmond, and in imminent peril of annihilation. In fact, a portion of the command was in such close proximity to the city proper, that officers could plainly discern its lights and hear the dogs barking a warning to the city's defenders of the presence of an army of invaders.

But with his usual genius for overcoming difficulties, Sheridan quickly extricated his command from its hazardous and uncomfortable position, and pressing on over Bottom's Bridge and past Malvern Hill successfully reached Haxall's Landing on the James River, where the command was furnished much needed supplies. On May 17th, the raiding force began its retrograde movement to rejoin Grant, which was successfully accomplished on the 24th near Chesterfield Station, Virginia. Sheridan's casualties suffered on the raid were six hundred and twenty-five men killed, wounded, and captured, and three hundred horses.

General Grant describes the results attained in this famous raid as follows:

Sheridan, in this memorable raid, passed entirely around Lee's army, encountered his cavalry in four engagements, and defeated them in all; recaptured four hundred Union prisoners, and killed and captured many of the enemy; destroyed miles of railroad and telegraph, and freed us from annoyance by the cavalry for more than two weeks.

This brilliant success by the Cavalry Corps of the Army of the Potomac, was followed in June by one scarcely less important in its moral and material effect upon the Confederacy

THE RETURN OF SHERIDAN'S TROOPERS—MAY 25, 1864

After their ride of sixteen days to the very gates of Richmond, Sheridan and his men rejoined Grant near Chesterfield Station. The photographer caught the returning column just as they were riding over the Chesterfield bridge. On the 21st they had crossed the Pamunkey near White House on the ruins of the railroad bridge, which they took only six hours to repair. Two regiments at a time, working as pioneers, wrecked a neighboring house, and with its timbers soon had the bridge ready to bear the weight of horses and artillery. The only mishap was the fall of a pack-mule from the bridge into the water thirty feet below. It takes much, however, to disturb the equanimity of an army mule. It turned a somersault in the air, struck an abutment, disappeared under water, came up, and swam tranquilly ashore without disturbing its pack. This speaks well for the ability as saddle-packers of Sheridan's men. The total results of this important raid were the destruction of an immense quantity of supplies, damage to Confederate communications, the death of Stuart, and the saving to the Union Government of the subsistence of ten thousand horses and men for three weeks. It perfected the *morale* of the cavalry corps, with incalculable benefit to the Union cause. The casualties on the raid were six hundred and twenty-five men killed and wounded.

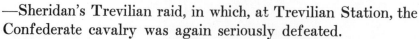

—Sheridan's Trevilian raid, in which, at Trevilian Station, the Confederate cavalry was again seriously defeated.

The purpose of the raid was to injure Lee's lines of supply, and to draw off the Southern cavalry during Grant's movement forward by the left flank, following his unsuccessful attempt to take the strong Confederate position at Cold Harbor by direct assault.

Sheridan started on June 7, 1864, with about eight thousand cavalrymen, the trains and supplies being cut down to the absolute minimum. Wilson's division remained with the Army of the Potomac. By June 11th, the command was in the vicinity of Trevilian Station, where the enemy was encountered. Here, Torbert's division, pressing back the Confederate's pickets, found the foe in force about three miles from Trevilian, posted behind heavy timber. At about the same time, Custer was sent by a wood road to destroy Trevilian Station, where he captured the Confederate wagons, caissons, and led horses.

Assured of Custer's position, Sheridan dismounted Torbert's two remaining brigades, and aided by one of Gregg's, carried the Confederate works, driving Hampton's division back on Custer, and even through his lines. Gregg's other brigade had meanwhile attacked Fitzhugh Lee, causing the entire opposing cavalry to retire on Gordonsville.

Following this victory, Sheridan continued his raid and finally reached White House on the Pamunkey, on June 20th, where he found orders directing him to break up the supply depot there and conduct the nine hundred wagons to Petersburg. This was successfully accomplished.

It is interesting to note that in this period of great activity for the Cavalry Corps (May 5th to August 1, 1864) the casualties in the corps were nearly forty-nine hundred men, and the loss in horses from all causes about fifteen hundred. The captures by the cavalry exceeded two thousand men and five hundred horses, besides many guns and colors.

CHAPTER
FIVE

FEDERAL RAIDS
IN THE WEST

A BLOCKHOUSE ON THE TENNESSEE

SIX HUNDRED MILES IN SIXTEEN DAYS

Seventeen hundred men who marched 600 miles in sixteen days, from Vicksburg to Baton Rouge.   On April 17, 1863, Grant despatched Grierson on a raid from LaGrange, Tennessee, southward as a means of diverting attention from his own movements against Vicksburg, and to disturb the Confederate line of supplies from the East.   Grierson destroyed sixty miles of tracks and telegraph, numberless stores and munitions of war, and brought his command safely through to Baton Rouge.   These two pictures by Lytle, the Confederate Secret Service agent at Baton Rouge, form one of the most remarkable feats of wet-plate photography.   The action continued as he moved his camera a trifle to the right, and the result is a veritable "moving picture."   In the photograph on the left-hand page, only the first troop is dismounted and unsaddled,   In the photo-

HOW GRIERSON'S RAIDERS LOOKED TO THE CONFEDERATE SECRET SERVICE CAMERA

graph on the right-hand page two troops are already on foot.   Note the officers in front of their troops.   The photograph was evidently a long time exposure, as is shown by the progress of the covered wagon which has driven into the picture on the left-hand page.   It was at the conclusion of this remarkable raid that Grierson reported that "the Confederacy was a hollow shell."   All of its population able to carry arms was on the line of defense.   Captain John A. Wyeth, the veteran Confederate cavalryman who contributes to other pages of this volume, wrote when he saw these photographs: "I knew General Grierson personally, and have always had the highest regard for his skill and courage as shown more particularly in this raid than in anything else that he did, although he was always doing well."

[G—9]

FEDERAL RAIDS AND EXPEDITIONS IN THE WEST

By Charles D. Rhodes
Captain, General Staff, United States Army

THE military operations of the Union armies in the South and West were not lacking in famous raids, having for their main objects the destruction of the supply centers of the Confederacy, the cutting of railroads and lines of communication between these centers and the Southern troops, and the drawing away from important strategic operations of large bodies of the foe. One of the most famous of these raids was that made by Colonel B. H. Grierson in the spring of 1863.

Starting from La Grange, Tennessee, on April 17th, with three cavalry regiments of about seventeen hundred men, Grierson made a wonderful march through the State of Mississippi, and finally reached the Union lines at Baton Rouge, Louisiana, on May 2d.

On April 21st, Grierson had detached a regiment under Colonel Hatch, Second Iowa Cavalry, to destroy the railroad bridge between Columbus and Macon, and then return to La Grange. At Palo Alto, Hatch had a sharp fight with Confederate troops under General Gholson, defeating them without the loss of a man. Much of Hatch's success during his entire raid was due to the fact that his regiment was armed with Colt's revolving rifles. Hatch then retreated along the railroad, destroying it at Okolona and Tupelo, and arriving at La Grange on April 26th, with the loss of but ten troopers. The principal object of his movement—to decoy the Confederate troops to the east, and thus give Grierson ample opportunity to get well under way, was fully attained.

GRIERSON—THE RAIDER WHO PUZZLED PEMBERTON

To the enterprise of Lytle, the Confederate Secret Service photographer, we owe this portrait of Colonel B. H. Grierson, at rest after his famous raid. He sits chin in hand among his officers, justly proud of having executed one of the most thoroughly successful feats in the entire war. It was highly important, if Grant was to carry out his maneuver of crossing the Mississippi at Grand Gulf and advance upon Vicksburg from the south, that Pemberton's attention should be distracted in other directions. The morning after Admiral Porter ran the batteries, Grierson left La Grange, Tennessee, to penetrate the heart of the Confederacy, sweeping entirely through Mississippi from north to south, and reaching Baton Rouge on May 2d. Exaggerated reports flowed in on Pemberton as to Grierson's numbers and whereabouts. The Confederate defender of Vicksburg was obliged to send out expeditions in all directions to try to intercept him. This was one of the numerous instances where a small body of cavalry interfered with the movements of a much larger force. It was Van Dorn, the Confederate cavalryman, who had upset Grant's calculations four months before.

Meanwhile Grierson had continued his raid with less than one thousand horsemen, breaking the Southern Mississippi, and the New Orleans, Jackson, and Great Northern railroads. Near Newton the raiders burned several bridges, and destroyed engines and cars loaded with commissary stores, guns, and ammunition; at Hazelhurst, cars and ammunition; and at Brookhaven, the railroad depot and cars.

Having no cavalry available to watch Grierson's movements, the Confederates were kept in a state of excitement and alarm. Rumors exaggerated his numbers, and he was reported in many different places at the same time. Several brigades of Confederate infantry were detached to intercept him, but he evaded them all.

In sixteen days, Grierson marched six hundred miles—nearly thirty-eight miles a day—destroying miles of railroad, telegraph, and other property; but most of all, he distracted the Confederates' attention from Grant's operations against Vicksburg at the critical time when the latter was preparing to cross the Mississippi River near Grand Gulf. In its entirety, the Grierson raid was probably the most successful operation of its kind during the Civil War.

The appearance of Morgan's men on the north bank of the Ohio River (July, 1863) created great consternation in Indiana and Ohio. The Governor of Indiana called out the " Home Guards " to the number of fifty thousand, and as Morgan's advance turned toward Ohio, the Governor of the " Buckeye State " called out fifty thousand " Home Guards " from his State. At Corydon, Indiana, the " Home Guards " gave the invaders a brisk little battle, and delayed their advance for a brief time.

On July 1, 1864, General A. J. Smith assembled a large force at La Grange, Tennessee, for a raid on Tupelo, Mississippi, in which a cavalry division under General Grierson took a prominent part in defeating the formidable General Forrest as he had probably never been defeated before. The raid

A FEDERAL CAVALRY CAMP AT BATON ROUGE

This photograph of an Illinois regiment's camp at Baton Rouge was taken in 1863, just before the Port Hudson campaign upon which Grierson and his men accompanied General Banks. The troopers have found fairly comfortable quarters. The smoke rising from their camp-fires lends a peaceful touch to the scene. A cavalry camp occupied more space than an infantry camp. The horses are tethered in long lines between the tents, about the width of a street-way. They are plainly visible in this photograph, tethered in this fashion, a few of them grazing about the plain. In the foreground by the officers' quarters, a charger stands saddled, ready for his master. This is an excellent illustration of a camp laid out according to Federal army regulations.

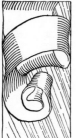

resulted in the burning of all bridges and trestles north and south of Tupelo, and the destruction of the railroad.

During the raid, a portion of the cavalry division was newly armed with seven-shot Spencer carbines, capable of firing fourteen shots per minute. The Confederates were astonished and dismayed by the tremendous amount of lead poured into their ranks, and after the Tupelo fight one of the Confederate prisoners wonderingly asked a cavalryman, "Say, do you all load those guns you all fight with on Sunday, and then fire 'em all the week?"

In the spring of the following year, 1865, General James H. Wilson, who had commanded a division in Sheridan's Army of the Shenandoah, began, under the direction of General Thomas, an important demonstration against Selma and Tuscaloosa, Alabama, in favor of General Canby's operations against Mobile and central Alabama. This great raid, which severed the main arteries supplying life-blood to the Confederacy, was destined to be the culminating blow by the Federal cavalry inflicted on the already tottering military structure of the Southern Confederacy.

Starting on March 22, 1865, and marching in three separate columns on a wide front, because of the devastated condition of the country, Wilson began his movement by keeping the Confederate leaders completely in ignorance as to whether Columbus, Selma, or Tuscaloosa, was his real objective. At Selma, April 2d, a division of Wilson's dismounted cavalry, facing odds in position, gallantly carried the Confederate semipermanent works surrounding the city, in an assault which swept all before it.

General Wilson's report says:

The fortifications assaulted and carried consisted of a bastioned line, on a radius of nearly three miles, extending from the Alabama River below to the same above the city. The part west of the city is covered by a miry, deep, and almost impassable creek; that on the east side by a swamp, extending from the river almost to the Summerfield

A DESTRUCTIVE RAID IN MISSISSIPPI

The burning of all bridges and trestles north and south of Tupelo and the destruction of the railroad was the result of General A. J. Smith's raid on that point in 1864. General Smith started from Lagrange, Tenn., on July 1st, accompanied by a cavalry division under General Grierson, who took a prominent part in defeating the formidable General Forrest as he had probably never been defeated before. The Union cavalry raids in the West were more uniformly successful than the raids of the cavalry with the Army of the Potomac. The greater part of the Confederate cavalry was busy attacking the supply-trains of the armies in the North or striking at the long lines of communication. The story of the campaigns in the West, where there were fewer photographers and communication was slower is not so well-known as that of the more immediate East, but the deeds performed there were of quite equal dash and daring and importance to the result.

GENERAL A. J. SMITH

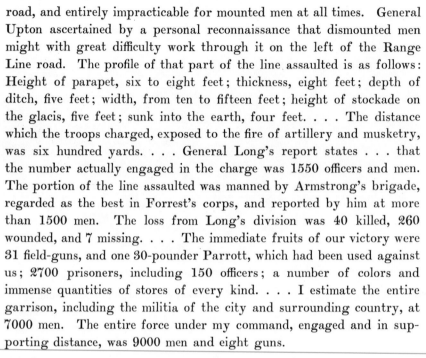

road, and entirely impracticable for mounted men at all times. General Upton ascertained by a personal reconnaissance that dismounted men might with great difficulty work through it on the left of the Range Line road. The profile of that part of the line assaulted is as follows: Height of parapet, six to eight feet; thickness, eight feet; depth of ditch, five feet; width, from ten to fifteen feet; height of stockade on the glacis, five feet; sunk into the earth, four feet. . . . The distance which the troops charged, exposed to the fire of artillery and musketry, was six hundred yards. . . . General Long's report states . . . that the number actually engaged in the charge was 1550 officers and men. The portion of the line assaulted was manned by Armstrong's brigade, regarded as the best in Forrest's corps, and reported by him at more than 1500 men. The loss from Long's division was 40 killed, 260 wounded, and 7 missing. . . . The immediate fruits of our victory were 31 field-guns, and one 30-pounder Parrott, which had been used against us; 2700 prisoners, including 150 officers; a number of colors and immense quantities of stores of every kind. . . . I estimate the entire garrison, including the militia of the city and surrounding country, at 7000 men. The entire force under my command, engaged and in supporting distance, was 9000 men and eight guns.

On April 8th and 9th, Wilson's entire cavalry corps, excepting Croxton's brigade, crossed the Alabama River, and having rendered Selma practically valueless to the Confederacy by his thorough destruction of its railroads and supplies, Wilson marched into Georgia by way of Montgomery. On April 12th, the mayor of Montgomery surrendered that city to the cavalry advance guard, and after destroying great quantities of military stores, small arms, and cotton, the cavalry corps moved, on April 14th, with General Upton in advance, and on the 16th captured the cities of Columbus and West Point.

The capture of Columbus lost to the South 1200 prisoners, fifty-two field-guns, the ram *Jackson* (six 7-inch guns), nearly ready for sea, together with such tremendously valuable aids in prolonging the war as fifteen locomotives and two hundred and fifty cars, one hundred and fifteen thousand bales of cot-

FLEET STEAMING UP THE ALABAMA RIVER IN WAR-TIME

The sight of the stern-wheelers splashing up the Alabama River into the heart of the threatened Confederacy has been preserved by a curious chance. This photograph was secured by a Scotch visitor to the States on his wedding-trip in 1865. He took it home. A generation later his son came to America, bringing his father's collection of pictures. He settled in New Orleans. An editor of the PHOTOGRAPHIC HISTORY, traveling in search of photographs to round out the collection, perceived this to be unique as a war-time scene on the river where Wilson and Forrest were making history. The Alabama River was not only one of the great arteries of the South along which it conveyed its supplies, but it was also the scene of much of its naval construction which the blockade precluded on the coast. Wilson's raid resulted in the capture at Columbus of the Confederate ram *Jackson* with six 7-inch guns, when she was nearly ready for the sea. Just a year previous, in April, 1864, the hull of the Confederate iron-clad ram *Tennessee* was constructed on the Alabama River, just above Selma. Admiral Buchanan sent James M. Johnston, C. S. N., with two steamers to tow her down to Mobile. The work was all done at high pressure for fear of just such a raid as Wilson's. The incident is somewhat similar to the saving of Admiral Porter's Red River fleet in May, 1864.

ton, four cotton factories, a navy yard, arms and ammunition factories, three paper-mills, over one hundred thousand rounds of artillery ammunition, besides immense stores of which no account was taken.

This great and decisive blow to the material resources of the Confederacy, was followed by the surrender of the cities of Macon and Tuscaloosa, and other successes, until, on April 21st, Wilson's victorious progress was ordered suspended by General Sherman, pending the result of peace negotiations between the Federal and Confederate Governments.

This great movement was made in a hostile country which had been stripped of supplies except at railroad centers, and in which no aid or assistance could be expected from the inhabitants of the country. As an evidence of some of the hardships attending the operations of separate columns composing Wilson's corps, General Croxton states in an official report that from Elyton (March 30th) through Trion and Tuscaloosa, Alabama, to Carrollton, Georgia (April 25th), his command marched six hundred and fifty-three miles through a mountainous country so destitute of supplies that the troops could only be subsisted and foraged with the greatest effort. The brigade swam four rivers and destroyed five large iron works (the last remaining in the cotton States), three factories, numerous mills, and quantities of supplies. The losses of the brigade during this important movement, were but four officers and one hundred and sixty-eight men, half of whom were made prisoners by the Confederates while straggling from the command.

CHAPTER
SIX

CONFEDERATE RAIDS
IN THE WEST

THE PRIZE OF THE CONFEDERATE RAIDER—
A FEDERAL COMMISSARY CAMP
ON THE TENNESSEE

CAMP IN THE TENNESSEE MOUNTAINS, 1863

The soldiers leaning on their sabers by the mountain path would have smiled in grim amusement at the suggestion that a life like theirs in "the merry greenwood" must be as care-free, picturesque, and delightful as the career of Robin Hood, according to old English ballads. These raiders of 1863 could have drawn sharp contrasts between the beauty of the scene in this photograph—the bright sunshine dappling the trees, the mountain wind murmuring through the leaves, the horse with his box of fodder, the troopers at ease in the shade—and the hardships that became every-day matters with the cavalry commands whose paths led them up and down the arduous western frontier. On such a pleasant summer day the Civil War photographer was able to make an exposure.

A PLEASANT INTERLUDE FOR THE WESTERN CAVALRYMAN

But the cavalryman's duty called at all hours and at all seasons; and the photographer could not portray the dreary night rides over rocks made slippery with rain, through forests hanging like a damp pall over the troopers rocking with sleep in their saddles, every moment likely to be awakened by the bark of the enemy's carbines. It is undoubtedly true that there is something more dashing about the lot of a cavalryman, but on account of his greater mobility he was ordered over more territory and ran more frequent if not greater risks than the infantryman. But this was the sort of day the cavalryman laughed and sang. Though the storm-clouds and war-clouds, the cloud of death itself, lay waiting, the trooper's popular song ran: "If you want to have a good time, jine the cavalry."

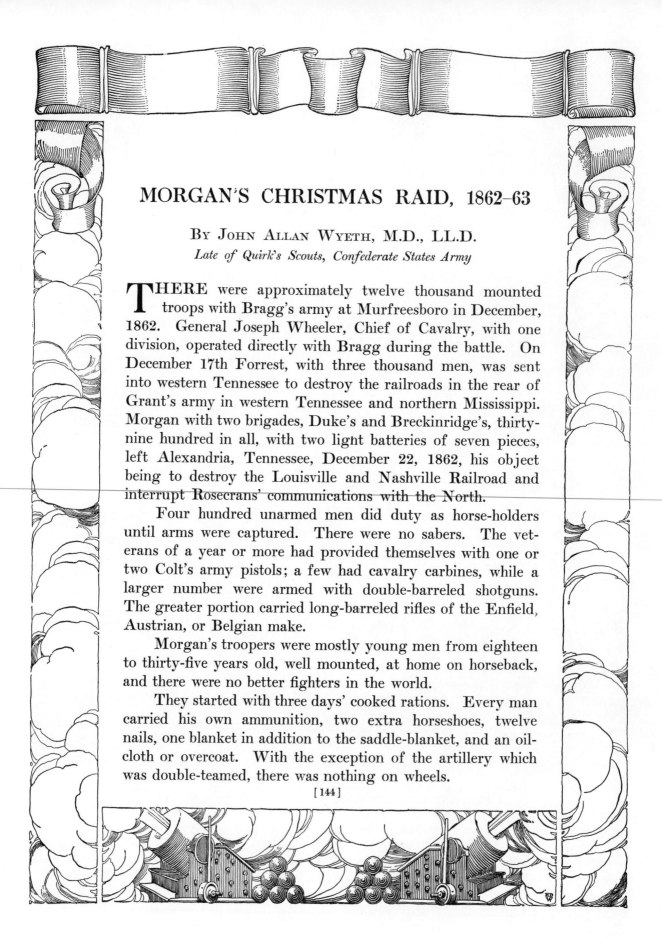

MORGAN'S CHRISTMAS RAID, 1862–63

By John Allan Wyeth, M.D., LL.D.

Late of Quirk's Scouts, Confederate States Army

THERE were approximately twelve thousand mounted troops with Bragg's army at Murfreesboro in December, 1862. General Joseph Wheeler, Chief of Cavalry, with one division, operated directly with Bragg during the battle. On December 17th Forrest, with three thousand men, was sent into western Tennessee to destroy the railroads in the rear of Grant's army in western Tennessee and northern Mississippi. Morgan with two brigades, Duke's and Breckinridge's, thirty-nine hundred in all, with two light batteries of seven pieces, left Alexandria, Tennessee, December 22, 1862, his object being to destroy the Louisville and Nashville Railroad and interrupt Rosecrans' communications with the North.

Four hundred unarmed men did duty as horse-holders until arms were captured. There were no sabers. The veterans of a year or more had provided themselves with one or two Colt's army pistols; a few had cavalry carbines, while a larger number were armed with double-barreled shotguns. The greater portion carried long-barreled rifles of the Enfield, Austrian, or Belgian make.

Morgan's troopers were mostly young men from eighteen to thirty-five years old, well mounted, at home on horseback, and there were no better fighters in the world.

They started with three days' cooked rations. Every man carried his own ammunition, two extra horseshoes, twelve nails, one blanket in addition to the saddle-blanket, and an oil-cloth or overcoat. With the exception of the artillery which was double-teamed, there was nothing on wheels.

[144]

A GROUP OF
CONFEDERATE CAVALRY
IN THE WEST

Old cavalrymen find this photograph absorbing; it brings to life again the varied equipment of the Confederate cavalrymen in the West. The only uniformity is found with respect to carbines, which are carried by all except the officers. Three of the men in the center have pistols thrust in their belts, ready for a fight at close quarters. Some have belts crossed over their chests, some a single belt, still others none at all. One of the single belts acts as a carbine sling, the other as a canteen strap. Horse holders have fallen out with the chargers visible behind the line of men. The Western photographers, Armstead & Carter, were the artists enterprising enough to secure this photograph. The territory their travels covered in Mississippi and Tennessee changed hands so frequently that fortunately for posterity an opportunity at last did come to photograph a troop of the swift-traveling and little interviewed warriors that composed the Confederate cavalry. They did important service in the West.

AN OFFICER

Under Forrest and Wheeler they helped Bragg to defeat Rosecrans at Chickamauga, and their swift raids were a constant menace to the Union supplies. This photograph was probably taken late in the war, as up to the third year the Confederate troopers could not boast equipments even so complete as shown in this photograph. In 1861 the Confederate cavalry had no Colt revolvers, no Chicopee sabers, and no carbines that were worth carrying. Their arms were of the homeliest type and of infinite variety. At the battle of Brandy Station, in 1863, every man was armed with at least one, and sometimes several, Army and Navy revolvers and excellent sabers. The civilian saddles had given place to McClellans, and that man was conspicuous who could not boast a complete outfit of saddle, bridle, blankets—woolen and rubber—and arms, all taken from the generous foe. The Confederate cavalry in the West failed to secure equally complete outfits, although they looked to the same source of supply.

In three short winter days, over little-used highways through a rough and hilly country, they rode a distance of ninety miles to Glasgow, Kentucky, arriving at dark, December 24th. The order was to start at daylight, stop from eleven to twelve to feed, unsaddle, curry, and rest, then on until night. As the advance guard reached one corner of the public square, several companies of the Second Michigan Cavalry with no idea that Morgan's men were near, rode into sight a few yards away. In the *mêlée* which ensued, one Federal was killed and two wounded, and a Confederate captain and one soldier were mortally and one lieutenant slightly wounded. Twenty prisoners were captured, among them the adjutant of the regiment, whose equipment the writer appropriated. A number of Christmas turkeys which these excellent foragers had strapped to their saddles were also taken by us.

Ten miles north of Glasgow, on December 25th, with our company of fifty men a mile in advance of the main column, the vedette reported the Federals in line of battle in our front. We were ordered to load and cap our guns, and then rode briskly forward. When about two hundred yards from the Federal lines, Captain Quirk halted us, called off horse-holders, and we advanced on foot. Reaching the top of a rise in the lane with a high worm-fence on either side, the Federals gave us a lively volley, which we returned from the fence corners. The fight had scarcely opened, when a second detachment of Federals (Company C, Fifth Indiana), which had been in ambush to our right, charged to within a few yards of the road abreast of and in the rear of our position, and fired into us at practically muzzle range. Several of our men were wounded, our captain being twice hit. The fusillade stampeded the horses and horse-holders who fled in panic to the rear, leaving us on foot in the presence of a superior force. Five members of our company were captured. The rest of us scrambled over the opposite fence and ran for a scrub-oak thicket, one or two hundred yards across a field.

FEDERAL CAVALRY GUARDING THE CHATTANOOGA STATION

General Rosecrans looked narrowly to his line of communications when he set out from Nashville to attack General Braxton Bragg in the latter part of December, 1862. The Confederate cavalry leader, General Wheeler, was abroad. At daylight on December 30th he swooped down at Jefferson on Starkweather's brigade of Rousseau's division, in an attempt to destroy his wagon-train. From Jefferson, Wheeler proceeded to La Vergne, where he succeeded in capturing the immense supply trains of McCook's Corps. Seven hundred prisoners and nearly a million dollars' worth of property was the Union Government's penalty for not heeding the requests of the commanding general for more cavalry. A train at Rock Spring and another at Nolensville shared the same fate at Wheeler's hands, and at two o'clock on the morning of the 31st Wheeler completed the entire circuit of Rosecrans' army, having ridden in forty-eight hours.

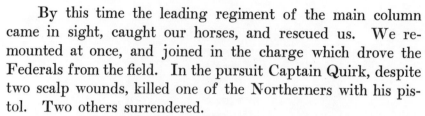

By this time the leading regiment of the main column came in sight, caught our horses, and rescued us. We remounted at once, and joined in the charge which drove the Federals from the field. In the pursuit Captain Quirk, despite two scalp wounds, killed one of the Northerners with his pistol. Two others surrendered.

On the further march to Green River and Hammondsville that day, we captured a sutler's huge outfit, the contents of which were appropriated. That night we camped in the woods between Hammondsville and Upton Station on the Louisville and Nashville Railroad. We had had a merry Christmas.

Early December 26th, we struck the road at Upton, capturing a number of Union soldiers guarding the track. Here General Morgan overtook the scouts. Attached to his staff was a telegraph operator, a quick-witted young man named Ellsworth, better known by the nickname of "Lightning." After the wire was tapped, I sat within a few feet of General Morgan and heard him dictate messages to General Boyle, in Louisville, and other Federal commanders, making inquiries as to the disposition of the Federal forces, and telling some tall stories in regard to the large size of his own command and its movements. While thus engaged, a train with artillery and other material came in sight from the north, but the wary engineer saw us in time to reverse his engine and escape. Heavy cannonading was now heard at Bacon Creek Bridge stockade, which after a stout resistance surrendered, and the bridge was destroyed. That same afternoon before dark, the stockade at Nolin was taken by Duke and another bridge burned.

We camped that night, December 26th, a few miles from Elizabethtown, which place, guarded by eight companies of an Illinois regiment, six hundred and fifty-two men and officers, we captured on the 27th. A number of brick warehouses near the railroad station had been loopholed and otherwise strengthened for defense. The town was surrounded, the artillery

LIEUTENANT–GENERAL

JOSEPH WHEELER,

C. S. A.

After his exploits in Tennessee, and the days of Chickamauga, Chattanooga, and Knoxville, where his cavalry were a constant menace to the Union lines of communication, so much so that the railroads were guarded by blockhouses at vulnerable points, Wheeler joined Johnston with the remnant of his men. Their swift movements went far to make it possible for Johnston to pursue his Fabian policy of constantly striking and retreating before Sherman's superior force, harassing it to the point of desperation. Wheeler operated on Sherman's flank later in the Carolinas, but the power of the Confederate cavalry was on the wane, and the end was soon to come.

ONE OF THE BLOCKHOUSES ON THE NASHVILLE AND CHATTANOOGA RAILROAD IN 1864

brought up, and after the raiders fired a number of shells and solid shot, which knocked great holes in the houses, the garrison surrendered.

On the 28th, the two great trestles on the Louisville and Nashville Railroad at Muldraugh's Hill were destroyed. They were each from sixty to seventy-five feet high, and nine hundred feet long, constructed entirely of wood. They were guarded by two strong stockade forts, garrisoned by an Indiana regiment of infantry. Both strongholds were assailed at the same time, the artillery doing effective work, and in less than two hours, the two garrisons of seven hundred men were prisoners. They were armed with new Enfield rifles, one of the most effective weapons of that day.

After burning the trestles, the command moved to Rolling Fork River. The greater portion crossed that night and proceeded toward Bardstown. Five hundred men under Colonel Cluke, with one piece of artillery, attacked the stockade at the bridge over Rolling Fork River, but before it could be battered down, a column three thousand strong under Colonel Harlan (later a Justice of the Supreme Court), compelled his withdrawal. A sharp engagement between our rear guard and Harlan's command took place at Rolling Fork. Colonel Basil W. Duke recrossed to take command and led Cluke's five hundred men and Quirk's scouts in such a vigorous attack that the Federal commander hesitated to press his advantage.

At this moment, Duke was wounded by a fragment of a well-aimed shrapnel which struck him on the head and stunned him. The same shell killed several horses. Captain Quirk and two of the scouts placed Duke astride the pommel of the saddle on which our captain was seated, who, with one arm around the limp body, guided his faithful horse into the swollen stream. Quirk and Duke were both small in stature, and the powerful big bay carried his double load safely across. A carriage was impressed, filled with soft bedding, and in this our wounded colonel was placed, and carried safely along with the command.

BLOCKHOUSES GARRISONED

AGAINST

WHEELER'S CAVALRY

In 1863 an attempt to supplement his lack of cavalry for the guarding of his line of communications was made by Rosecrans, through the building of blockhouses along the railroad, garrisoned by small forces of infantry. The attempt was not uniformly successful. The Confederate horsemen under Wheeler sometimes advanced on foot and succeeded in carrying the blockhouses and enforcing the surrender of its garrison. The cavalry were the real trouble-makers for the generals in the field who were attempting to victual their armies. The problem became less complex in the last two years of the war, when the Federal cavalry was trained to higher efficiency and the power of the Confederates had dwindled following the exhaustion of their supply of horses.

Colonel Harlan reported his loss as three killed and one
wounded. We did not lose a man, and with the exception of
Duke, our wounded rode out on their horses.

We reached Bardstown at dusk on the 29th. Between
daylight and sunrise, December 30th, I witnessed one of the
frequent incidents in all warfare—the pillaging of the largest
general store in this town. The men who had crowded in
through the doors they had battered down, found difficulty in
getting out with their plunder through the surging crowd,
which was pressing to get in before everything was gone. One
trooper induced the others to let him out by holding an ax in
front of him, cutting edge forward. His arm clasped a bundle
of a dozen pairs of shoes and other plunder, while on his head
was a pyramid of eight or ten soft hats, telescoped one into the
other just as they had come out of the packing-box.

About midday a chilling rain set in, which soon turned into
sleet. Reaching Springfield in the gloom of December 30th,
we were ordered on to Lebanon, nine miles further, to drive in
the pickets there and build fires in order to give the foe the
impression that we were up in force and were only awaiting
daylight to attack. We piled rails and made fires until late at
night, while Morgan was making a detour along a narrow and
little-used country road around Lebanon. Later we overtook
the command, and acted as rear guard throughout that awful
night. Between the bitter, penetrating cold, the fatigue, the
overwhelming desire to sleep, so difficult to overcome and under
the conditions we were experiencing so fatal if yielded to, the
numerous halts to get the artillery out of bad places, the impenetrable darkness, and the inevitable confusion which attends
the moving of troops and artillery along a narrow country
road, we endured a night of misery never to be forgotten.

As morning neared, it became our chief duty to keep each
other awake. All through the night the sleet pelted us unmer-
cifully, and covered our coats and oilcloths with a sheet of ice.
Time and time again we dismounted, and holding on to the

General Chalmers was the right-hand man of General Forrest. His first service was at Shiloh. During Bragg's invasion of Kentucky he attacked Munfordville, September 14, 1862, but was repulsed. He took part in a Confederate charge at Murfreesboro, December 31st of the same year, and was so severely wounded as to disqualify him for further duty on that field. He commanded two brigades on Forrest's expedition of April 12, 1864, when the latter captured Fort Pillow and was unable to restrain the massacre. He served with Forrest at Nashville and led Hood's cavalry at the battle of Franklin, delaying the Federal cavalry long enough to enable the Confederate army to make good its escape. He was with Forrest when the latter was defeated by Wilson on the famous

Wilson raid through Alabama and Georgia in the spring of 1865, and remained with the cavalry until it crumbled with the Confederacy to nothing. The lower photograph of the rails laid across the piles of ties shows how the Confederate cavalry, east and west, destroyed millions of dollars' worth of property. While Generals Lee and Bragg and Hood were wrestling with the Union armies, the Confederate cavalry were dealing blow after blow to the material resources of the North. But in vain; the magnificently equipped Union pioneer corps was able to lay rails nearly as fast as they were destroyed by the Confederates, and when the Army of Northern Virginia shot its weight in men from the ranks of Grant's army in the fearful campaign of 1864, the ranks were as constantly replenished.

BRIGADIER–GENERAL JAMES R. CHALMERS

IN THE WAKE OF THE RAIDERS

stirrup leather, trudged on through the slush and ice to keep from freezing.

Daylight found us several miles south of Lebanon and the strong Federal command concentrated there to catch us, but we kept on without halting, for another heavy column was reported moving out from Mumfordville and Glasgow to intercept us at Columbia or Burkesville, before we could recross the Cumberland River.

About ten o'clock on the morning of December 31st, as the rear guard was crossing Rolling Fork some five or six miles south of Lebanon, there occurred an incident of more than ordinary interest. Captain Alexander Tribble, Lieutenant George B. Eastin, and a private soldier were sent on a detour to New Market, four or five miles from the line of march, to secure a supply of shoes which were reported stored at that point. As they were returning to overtake the command, they were pursued by a squad of Federal cavalry. Being well mounted, the three kept a safe distance ahead of their pursuers. Glancing backward over a long, straight stretch of road, they observed, as the chase proceeded, that all but three of their pursuers had checked up, and they determined at the first favorable place to ride to one side and await the approach of their pursuers and attack them. The place selected was the ford at the river. At this point Eastin checked his horse and turned sharply to the right, concealing himself under the bank. Tribble continued into the middle of the stream, which here was about fifty yards wide, and stopped his horse where the water was about two feet deep. For reasons satisfactory to himself, the private soldier kept on, leaving the two officers to confront the three Federals, who now were in sight, coming at full speed toward the river and from fifty to one hundred yards apart. The leading Federal was Colonel Dennis J. Halisy of the Sixth Kentucky Cavalry. As he came near Eastin, the latter fired at him with his six-shooter, which fire Halisy returned. Both missed, and as Eastin now had the drop on his adversary,

[154]

"By all means," telegraphed Grant to Thomas, "avoid a foot-race to see which, you or Hood, can beat to the Ohio." This was the voicing of the Union general's fear in December, 1864, that Hood would cross the Cumberland River in the vicinity of Nashville and repeat Bragg's march to the Ohio. A cavalry corps was stationed near the Louisville and Nashville Railroad fortified bridge, and a regiment of pickets kept guard along the banks of the stream, while on the water, gunboats, ironclads, and "tinclads" kept up a constant patrol. The year before the Confederate raider, John H. Morgan, had evaded the Union guards of the Cumberland and reached the border of Pennsylvania, before he was forced to surrender. On December 8th a widespread report had the Confederates across the Cumberland, but it proved that only a small detachment had been sent out to reconnoiter—sufficient, however, to occasion Grant's telegram. Note the huge gates at the end of the bridge ready to be rushed shut in a moment.

THE VALLEY OF THE CUMBERLAND, FROM THE TOP OF THE NASHVILLE MILITARY ACADEMY

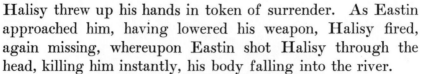

Halisy threw up his hands in token of surrender. As Eastin approached him, having lowered his weapon, Halisy fired, again missing, whereupon Eastin shot Halisy through the head, killing him instantly, his body falling into the river.

While this combat was taking place, the next in order of the Federals had closed with Captain Tribble. These two opened fire without effect when Tribble spurred his horse toward his adversary, threw his arm around him, and dragged him with himself from the saddle into the river. Tribble fell on top, and strangled his foe into surrendering. At this moment, the third Union trooper came on the scene, only to throw up his hands and deliver himself to the two Confederates.

Midday, December 31st, we rested an hour, and then on to Campbellsville where we arrived at dark, having been thirty-six hours in the saddle. That night we slept eight hours, and New Year's Day, 1863, left for Columbia, and thence on throughout the whole bitter cold night without stopping, passing through Burkesville on the morning of January 2d, where we recrossed the Cumberland.

This was Morgan's most successful expedition. The Louisville and Nashville Railroad was a wreck from Bacon Creek to Shepherdsville, a distance of sixty miles. We had captured about nineteen hundred prisoners, destroyed a vast amount of Government property, with a loss of only two men killed, twenty-four wounded, and sixty-four missing. The command returned well armed and better mounted than when it set out. The country had been stripped of horses. Every man in my company led out an extra mount.

During our absence the battle of Murfreesboro had been fought. The Confederates had captured twenty-eight pieces of artillery, and lost four—and although Bragg retreated, he had hammered his opponent so hard, that it was nearly six months before he was ready to advance. Morgan's destruction of the Louisville and Nashville Railroad was an important factor in this enforced delay.

RUINS OF SALTPETRE WORKS

IN TENNESSEE

1863

Saltpetre being one of the necessary ingredients of powder, it was inevitable that when cotton-mills, iron-works, and every useful industry were suffering destruction by the Union cavalry in Tennessee, the saltpetre factory should share the same fate. The works were foredoomed, whether by the Union cavalry or by the Confederate cavalry, in order to prevent them from falling into Union hands. The enterprising photographer seized a moment when the cavalry was at hand. A dejected charger is hanging his head by the side of the ruined mill. Two men are standing at the left of the house, of which nothing remains but the framework and chimney. The importance of destroying these works could hardly have been over-estimated. It was the case half a century later, as stated by Hudson Maxim and other military authorities, that collision between America and a foreign country with a powerful navy would bring, as that country's first move, the cutting off of our saltpetre supply from South America and thus the crippling of our ability to manufacture powder.

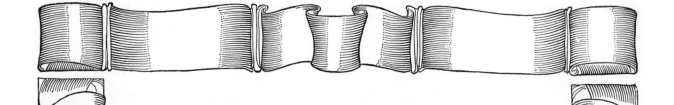

THE DESTRUCTION OF ROSECRANS' GREAT WAGON TRAIN

By John Allan Wyeth, M.D., LL.D.
(Late of Quirk's Scouts, Confederate States Army)

THE Confederate cavalry was an important factor in Bragg's defeat of Rosecrans' army at Chickamauga. Forrest was in full command on the right, while Wheeler, six miles away, covered the Confederate left wing.

Bragg had placed them thus wide apart for the reason that Forrest had flatly refused to serve under his chief of cavalry. After Wheeler's disastrous assault on Fort Donelson, February 3, 1863, where Forrest had two horses shot under him, and his command lost heavily, he bluntly told his superior in rank he would never serve under him again, and he never did.

The records of these two days of slaughter at Chickamauga—for twenty-six per cent. of all engaged were either killed or wounded—show how these great soldiers acquitted themselves. Forrest's guns fired the first and last shots on this bloody field. It was Wheeler's vigilance and courage which checked every move and defeated every advance on the Federal right, and finally in his last great charge on Sunday, pursued the scattered legions of McCook and Crittenden through the cedar brakes and blackjack thickets in their wild flight toward Chattanooga. And it was this alert soldier who on Monday, September 21st, in the Chattanooga valley, five miles from the field of battle, made an additional capture of a train of ninety wagons and some four hundred prisoners. The success of his operations at Chickamauga may be judged from his official report:

THE PRECARIOUS MILITARY RAIL-
ROAD IN 1864

A close look down the line will convince the beholder that this is no modern railroad with rock-ballasted road-bed and heavy rails, but a precarious construction of the Civil War, with light, easily bent iron which hundreds of lives were sacrificed to keep approximately straight. In order to supply an army it is absolutely necessary to keep open the lines of communication. An extract from General Rosecrans' letter to General Halleck, written October 16, 1863, brings out this necessity most vividly: "Evidence increases that the enemy intend a desperate effort to destroy this army. They are bringing up troops to our front. They have prepared pontoons, and will probably operate on our left flank, either to cross the river and force us to quit this place and fight them, or lose our communication. They will thus separate us from Burnside. We cannot feed Hooker's troops on our left, nor can we spare them from our right depots and communications, nor has he transportation. . . . Had we the railroad from here to Bridgeport, the whole of Sherman's and Hooker's troops brought up, we should not probably outnumber the enemy. This army, with its back to the barren mountains, roads narrow and difficult, while the enemy has the railroad and the corn in his rear, is at much disadvantage." The railway repairs of Sherman's army in the Atlanta campaign were under the management of Colonel Wright, a civil engineer, with a corps of two thousand men. They often had to work under a galling fire until the Confederates had been driven away, but their efficiency and skill was beyond praise. The ordinary wooden railway bridges were reconstructed with a standard pattern of truss, of which the parts were interchangeable, safely in the rear.

" During the battle, with the available force (which never exceeded 2000 men) not on other duty (such as guarding the flanks), we fought the enemy vigorously and successfully, capturing 2000 prisoners, 100 wagons and teams, a large amount of other property, and 18 stands of colors, all of which were turned over to the proper authorities."

After Rosecrans' army had sheltered itself behind the fortifications of Chattanooga, Forrest was ordered in the direction of Loudon and Knoxville to watch Burnside, whose corps occupied the latter place, while Wheeler remained in command of the cavalry with Bragg in front of Chattanooga.

When Bragg consulted Wheeler in regard to an expedition north of the Tennessee to break Rosecrans' lines of communications, Wheeler informed him that few of the horses were able to stand the strain of such an expedition. He was, however, ordered to do the best he could, and a few days after the battle all the best mounts were assembled for the raid.

We reached the Tennessee River on September 30th, at or near Cottonport, about forty miles east of Chattanooga, and although our crossing was opposed by some squadrons of the Fourth Ohio Cavalry, posted in the timber which lined the north bank, under cover of two 6-pounder Parrott guns, we succeeded in fording the river, which here was not more than two or three feet deep at this dry season of the year. From this point, without meeting with any material opposition, we made our way rapidly across Walden's Ridge and descending into the Sequatchie valley at Anderson's Cross Roads, early on the morning of October 2d, encountered the advance guard of an infantry escort to an enormous wagon train loaded with supplies for the army in Chattanooga. Parts of two regiments under Colonel John T. Morgan were ordered to charge the escort of the train, which they did, but were repulsed, and came back in disorder. I was standing near Colonel A. A. Russell who commanded the Fourth Alabama Cavalry, when General Wheeler rode up and ordered him to lead his regiment in. As soon as our line could be formed, we rode forward at

THE INADEQUATE REDOUBT

AT

JOHNSONVILLE

When, most unexpectedly, the Confederate General Nathan B. Forrest appeared on the bank opposite Johnsonville, Tennessee, November 4, 1864, and began firing across the Tennessee River, a distance of about four hundred yards, the fortifications of the post were quite inadequate. They consisted only of a redoubt for six guns on the spur of the hill overlooking the town and depot (seen clearly in the distance above), and two advanced batteries and rifle-pits. Three gunboats were in the river. Their commander, afraid of falling into the hands of the enemy, ordered his gunboats set afire and abandoned. The ranking officer of the troops ashore followed his example and ordered all transports and barges destroyed in the same way. A terrible conflagration which consumed between one and two million dollars' worth of Federal property ensued. On the 30th of November the few remaining stores not burned or captured by Forrest having been removed by railroad to Nashville, the post was evacuated.

full speed, and receiving a volley at close quarters, were successful in riding over and capturing the entire escort within a few minutes. We found ourselves in possession of an enormous wagon train, and such a scene of panic and confusion I had never witnessed. Our appearance directly in the rear of Rosecrans' army, which was not more than twenty miles away, was wholly unexpected. As a matter of precaution, the Federal general had directed Colonel E. M. McCook with a division of cavalry, then near Bridgeport, to move up the Sequatchie valley, and be within supporting distance of this train, but he failed to be in position at the critical moment.

When the fighting with the escort began, the teamsters had turned about in the hope of escape in the direction of Bridgeport. As we came nearer, they became panic-stricken and took to their heels for safety, leaving their uncontrolled teams to run wild. Some of the wagons were overturned, blocking the road in places with anywhere from ten to fifty teams, some of the mules still standing, some fallen and tangled in the harness, and all in inextricable confusion. For six or eight miles we followed this line of wagons, with every half-mile or so a repetition of this scene. As we proceeded, men were detailed to set fire to the wagons and to kill the mules, since it was impossible to escape with the livestock. After a run of six or seven miles, I ventured to stop for a few minutes to help myself to a tempting piece of cheese and some crackers which I saw in one of the wagons. Filling my haversack, I was on the point of remounting, when General Wheeler rode up and ordered me to " get out of that wagon and go on after the enemy," which order I obeyed, and had the honor of riding side by side with my commander for some distance further among the captured wagons. As he turned back, he ordered the small squadron that was in advance, to go on until the last wagon had been destroyed, which order was fully executed.

By this time the smoke of the burning train was visible for many miles, and soon the explosions of fixed ammunition, with

THE EVACUATION OF JOHNSONVILLE AFTER FORREST'S SUCCESSFUL RAID

When General Forrest swooped down on Johnsonville the landings and banks, several acres in extent, were piled high with freight for Sherman's army. There were several boats and barges yet unloaded for want of room. Forrest captured *U. S. Gunboat 55* and three transports and barges. Owing to a misunderstanding of Forrest's orders to a prize-crew, two Union gunboats recaptured the transport *Venus,* loaded with stores which Forrest had transferred from the steamer *Mazeppa,* captured at Fort Heiman, and also some of Forrest's 20-pounder Parrott guns, which his exhausted horses could no longer draw. Colonel R. D. Mussey U. S. A., reports that the Thirteenth U. S. Colored Infantry and a section of Meig's battery stood their ground well. This was one of Forrest's swift raids which imperiled the stores of the Union armies.

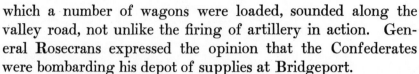

which a number of wagons were loaded, sounded along the valley road, not unlike the firing of artillery in action. General Rosecrans expressed the opinion that the Confederates were bombarding his depot of supplies at Bridgeport.

General Rosecrans, in his official report, admitted the loss of five hundred wagons, so that there must have been from one to two thousand mules destroyed. While the wagons were still burning, and before those of us who had gone to the extreme limit of the train could return to the main column, Colonel McCook, in command of the Federal cavalry, arrived on the scene and formed his line of battle between us and our main column.

The capture and destruction of this immense train was one of the greatest achievements of General Wheeler's cavalry, and I was proud of the fact that the Fourth Alabama, unaided, did the fighting which took it. Its loss was keenly felt by the Federals, for it added to the precarious situation of the army in Chattanooga, and reduced rations to a cracker a day per man for several days in succession. General Wheeler reported:

"The number of wagons was variously estimated from eight hundred to fifteen hundred. . . . The quartermaster in charge of the train stated that there were eight hundred six-mule wagons, besides a great number of sutler's wagons. The train was guarded by a brigade of cavalry in front and a brigade of cavalry in rear, and on the flank, where we attacked, were stationed two regiments of infantry." General Rosecrans in a despatch to General Burnside dated October 5, 1863, said, "Your failure to close your troops down to our left has cost five hundred wagons loaded with essentials, the post of McMinnville, and heaven only knows where the mischief will end." From my own observation, I believe that five hundred would not be very far from correct. We missed about thirty wagons which had turned off in a narrow and little-used roadway, and were already partly toward Walden's Ridge.

CHAPTER

SEVEN

PARTISAN RANGERS
OF THE CONFEDERACY

AFTER A VISIT BY THE CONFEDERATE RAIDERS—ON THE FEDERAL
LINE OF COMMUNICATION IN VIRGINIA, 1862

COLONEL JOHN S. MOSBY AND SOME OF HIS MEN

Speaking likenesses of Colonel John S. Mosby, the famous Confederate independent leader and his followers—chiefly sons of gentlemen attracted to his standard by the daring nature of his operations. His almost uniform success, with the spirit of romance which surrounded his exploits, drew thousands of recruits to his leadership. Usually his detachments were small—twenty to eighty men. The names and locations in the group are as follows: Top row, left to right: Lee Herverson, Ben Palmer, John Puryear, Tom Booker, Norman Randolph, Frank Raham; second row: Parrott, John Troop, John W. Munson, Colonel John S. Mosby, Newell, Neely, Quarles; third row: Walter Gosden, Harry T. Sinnott, Butler, Gentry.

FAIRFAX COURT HOUSE, AFTER MOSBY'S CAPTURE OF STOUGHTON

If you had said "Mosby" to the Federal cavalrymen that this picture shows loitering before Fairfax Court House in June, 1863, they might have gnashed their teeth in mortification; for only a couple of months before, the daring Confederate partisan had entered the nearby headquarters of General Edwin H. Stoughton, and had "captured" him from the very midst of the army. When Lee retired behind the Blue Ridge and began to advance up the Shenandoah in the summer of 1863, Hooker's line was spread out from Fairfax Court House on the north to Culpeper on the south. Hooker followed up Lee closely on the other side of the Blue Ridge, leaving three corps, the Second, Fifth, and Twelfth, held in reserve at Fairfax Court House within twenty miles of Washington, for the protection of the Capital. The Federal cavalry sought and scouted in vain to locate the elusive partisan. It was at this time that Mosby performed one of the most audacious feats of his career. On March 8, 1863, with a small band of carefully picked men, he rode safely through the Union picket lines, where the sentries mistook him for their own scouts returning from one of their vain searches for himself. Upon reaching the vicinity of Fairfax Court House, Mosby entered the house used as headquarters by General Stoughton, woke the general and demanded his person. Believing that the town had surrendered, Stoughton made no resistance.

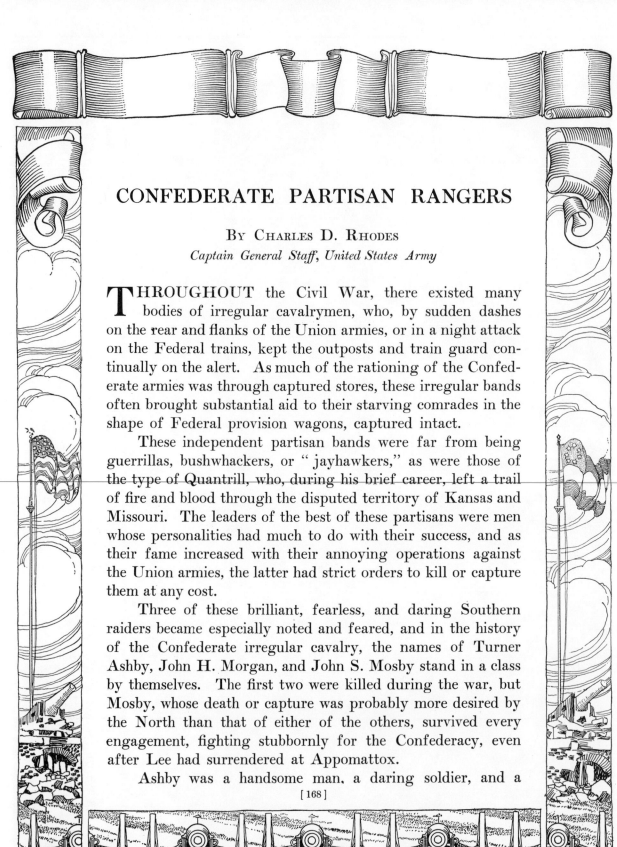

CONFEDERATE PARTISAN RANGERS

By Charles D. Rhodes
Captain General Staff, United States Army

THROUGHOUT the Civil War, there existed many bodies of irregular cavalrymen, who, by sudden dashes on the rear and flanks of the Union armies, or in a night attack on the Federal trains, kept the outposts and train guard continually on the alert. As much of the rationing of the Confederate armies was through captured stores, these irregular bands often brought substantial aid to their starving comrades in the shape of Federal provision wagons, captured intact.

These independent partisan bands were far from being guerrillas, bushwhackers, or " jayhawkers," as were those of the type of Quantrill, who, during his brief career, left a trail of fire and blood through the disputed territory of Kansas and Missouri. The leaders of the best of these partisans were men whose personalities had much to do with their success, and as their fame increased with their annoying operations against the Union armies, the latter had strict orders to kill or capture them at any cost.

Three of these brilliant, fearless, and daring Southern raiders became especially noted and feared, and in the history of the Confederate irregular cavalry, the names of Turner Ashby, John H. Morgan, and John S. Mosby stand in a class by themselves. The first two were killed during the war, but Mosby, whose death or capture was probably more desired by the North than that of either of the others, survived every engagement, fighting stubbornly for the Confederacy, even after Lee had surrendered at Appomattox.

Ashby was a handsome man, a daring soldier, and a

[168]

THE WORK OF THE RANGER—RAILROAD IRON ON THE FIRE

A pile of bent and twisted railroad iron across a heap of smouldering ties was often the only indication found by the Union soldiers that Mosby had paid them another visit. The daring Confederate ranger himself seemed to have a charmed life. Even after he became well-established as a partisan, his men were never organized as a tactical fighting body, and had no established camp. His expeditions often led him far within the Union lines, and when the command was nearly surrounded and the situation apparently hopeless, Mosby would give the word and the detachment would suddenly disintegrate, so that there was no longer any "Mosby and his band"—until the next time.

superb horseman. At the outbreak of the war, he received a commission as captain of a band of picked rangers, working in conjunction with the main operations of the Confederate armies, but unhampered by specific instructions from a superior. He was rapidly promoted. As colonel of a partisan band he was a continual menace to the Federal trains, and moved with such rapidity as oftentimes to create the impression that several bodies of mounted troops were in the field instead of but one. Falling upon an isolated column of army wagons at dawn, he would strike a Federal camp thirty miles away by twilight of the same day. His men were picked by their leader with great care, and although there is reason to believe that Southern writers surrounded these troopers with a halo of romance, there is no disputing that they were brave, daring, and self-sacrificing.

Ashby himself was looked upon by many officers and men in the Union armies as a purely mythical character. It was said that no such man existed, and that the feats accredited to Ashby's rangers were in reality the work of several separate forces. Much of the mystery surrounding this officer was due to his beautiful white horse, strong, swift, and a splendid jumper. He and his horse, standing alone on a hill or ridge, would draw the Union troops on. When the latter had reached a point where capture seemed assured, Ashby would slowly mount and canter leisurely out of sight. When his pursuers reached the spot where he had last been seen, Ashby and his white charger would again be observed on the crest of a still more distant hill.

Only once during his spectacular career in the Confederate army was Ashby outwitted and captured, but even then he made his escape before being taken a mile by his captors—a detachment of the First Michigan Cavalry.

The Confederate leader was surrounded before he was aware of the presence of the Union troops, and the latter were within fifty rods of him when he saw several of them pushing

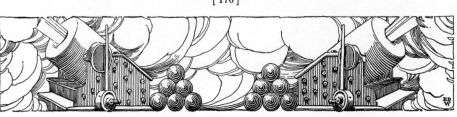

COLONEL JOHN SINGLETON MOSBY

It is hard to reconcile Mosby's peaceful profession of a lawyer at Bristol, Washington County, Louisiana, before the war with the series of exploits that subsequently made him one of the most famous of the partisan leaders in the war. After serving under General Joseph E. Johnston in the Shenandoah in 1861–62, he was appointed by General E. B. Stuart as an independent scout. His independent operations were chiefly in Virginia and Maryland. His most brilliant exploit was the capture in March, 1863, of Brigadier-General Stoughton at Fairfax Courthouse, far inside the Federal lines. He followed Lee's army into Pennsylvania in June, 1863, and worried the flanks of the Federal army as it moved southward after Gettysburg. In January, 1864, he was repulsed in a night attack on Harper's Ferry; in May he harassed the rear of Grant's army as it advanced on Fredericksburg; a little later he made a long raid into Maryland, and in August he surprised and captured Sheridan's entire supply-train near Berryville. In September he was wounded at Falls Church, but the following month he captured two Federal paymasters with $168,000, tore up the Baltimore & Ohio Railroad tracks, destroyed rolling-stock, and made a prisoner of Brigadier-General Alfred Duffié. In December, 1864, he was promoted to be a colonel, and at the close of the war was paroled by the intercession of no less a person than Grant himself.

along a cross-road which afforded the only avenue of escape. Nevertheless, Ashby made a dash for freedom. Vaulting into the saddle, the daring rider raced to beat the foremost Union trooper to the open road. Sergeant Pierson, who was in command of the little body of flankers, rode the only horse which could equal the speed of Ashby's fleet charger, and he and the Southerner reached the road crossing together—Pierson far in advance of his comrades. As Pierson neared Ashby, the latter fired at him with his revolver, but the Union trooper did not attempt to return the fire and Ashby himself replaced his weapon in the holster.

As the two men, magnificently mounted, came together, Ashby drew a large knife and raised it to strike. Pierson was a bigger and stronger man than Ashby, and reaching over, he seized Ashby's wrist with one hand while with the other he grasped the partisan leader's long black beard. Then, throwing himself from his horse, Pierson dragged the Confederate officer to the ground, and held him until the remaining Union troopers reached the scene of the struggle and disarmed Ashby.

The white horse had instantly stopped when Ashby was pulled from his back, and the captive was allowed to ride him back to the Union lines, slightly in advance of his captors, Sergeant Pierson at his side. The detachment had gone but a short distance when the mysterious white horse wheeled suddenly to one side, bounded over the high plantation fence which lined the roadside, and dashed away across the fields. Before the Union troops could recover from their surprise, Ashby was again free, and it was not long before he was once more reported by the Federal scouts as standing on a distant hill, engaged in caressing his faithful horse.

Only a few weeks later, this famous horse, which had become so familiar to the Union troops, was shot and killed by a sharpshooter belonging to the Fifth Michigan, who was attempting to bring down Ashby. Not long after, while leading his men in a cavalry skirmish, at Harrisonburg, during

MEN WHO TRIED TO CATCH MOSBY

GUARDING THE CAPITAL—CAMP OF THE THIRTEENTH NEW YORK CAVALRY

The Thirteenth New York horsemen were constantly held in the vicinity of Washington endeavoring to cross swords with the elusive Mosby, when he came too near, and scouting in the Virginia hills. This shows their camp at Prospect Hill at the close of the war. During most of their service they were attached to the Twenty-second Army Corps. The Administration policy of always keeping a large army between the Confederates and Washington resulted in the turning of the National Capital into a vast military camp. Prospect Hill became the chief center of cavalry camps during the latter part of the war.

"Stonewall" Jackson's famous Valley campaign, Ashby met his own death, on June 6, 1862. As he fell, his last words to his troopers were: "Charge men! For God's sake, charge!"

Next to the gallant Ashby there was no partisan leader whose death created a greater loss to the South than John Hunt Morgan. He was a slightly older man than Ashby and had seen service in the Mexican War. When the call to arms sounded, he was one of the first to organize a company of cavalry and pledge his support to the Southern cause. He was fearless and tireless, a hard rider, and a man of no mean ability as a tactician and strategist. Morgan's men were picked for their daring and their horsemanship, and until the day of his death, he was a thorn in the flesh of the Union commanders.

Starting before daybreak, Morgan and his troopers would rush along through the day, scarcely halting to rest their weary and jaded horses. When, worn to the very limit of endurance, the exhausted animals refused to go farther, the cavalrymen would quickly tear off saddle and bridle, and leaving the horse to live or die, would hurry along to the nearest farm or plantation and secure a fresh mount.

At night, far from their starting-point, the dust-covered troopers threw themselves, yelling and cheering, on the Union outposts, riding them down and creating consternation in the camp or bivouac. Then, with prisoners or perhaps captured wagon trains, the rangers rode, ghostlike, back through the night, while calls for reenforcements were being passed through the Federal lines. By dawn, Morgan and his weary horsemen would have safely regained their own lines, while oftentimes the Union troops were still waiting an attack at the spot where the unexpected night raid had been made. Morgan's famous raid through the State of Ohio exerted a moral and political influence which was felt throughout the entire North.

On their raids, Morgan's men were usually accompanied by an expert telegraph operator. They would charge an isolated telegraph office on the railroad communications of the

GENERAL JOHN H. MORGAN, C.S.A.

Morgan was a partisan leader who differed in method from Mosby. His command remained on a permanent basis. In the summer of 1863 Bragg decided, on account of his exposed condition and the condition of his army, weakened by detachments sent to the defense of Vicksburg, to fall back from Tullahoma to Chattanooga. To cover the retreat he ordered Morgan to ride into Kentucky with a picked force, breaking up the railroad, attacking Rosecrans' detachments, and threatening Louisville. Morgan left Burkesville July 2d, with 2,640 men and four guns. Ten thousand soldiers were watching the Cumberland but Morgan, exceeding his instructions, effected a crossing and rode northward. After a disastrous encounter with the Twenty-fifth Michigan at a bridge over the Green River, he drew off and marched to Brandenburg, capturing Lebanon on the way. By this time Indiana and Ohio were alive with the aroused militia, and Morgan fled eastward, burned bridges and impressed horses, marched by night unmolested through the suburbs of Cincinnati, and was finally forced to surrender near New Lisbon, Ohio, on July 26th. He escaped from the State Penitentiary at Columbus, Ohio, by tunneling on November 27, 1863, and took the field again.

Union army, and, capturing the operator, would place their own man at the telegraph key. In this way they gained much valuable and entirely authentic information, which, as soon as known, was rushed away to the headquarters of the army.

At other times, Morgan's operator would "cut in" on the Federal telegraph lines at some distant point, and seated on the ground by his instrument, would read the Union messages for many hours at a time. This service to the Confederate leaders was of inestimable value, and created a feeling among the Union signal-men that even cipher messages were not entirely safe from Morgan's men.

As Morgan was promoted from grade to grade, and the size of his command increased accordingly, he became more and more of an annoyance and even a terror to the North. His troopers were no longer mere rangers, but developed into more or less trained cavalry. Yet even then, his command showed a partiality for sudden and highly successful attacks upon Union outposts and wagon trains. The death of Morgan occurred near Greeneville, Tennessee, on September 4, 1864, when, being surrounded, he was shot down in a dash for life.

Colonel John S. Mosby, with his raiding detachments of varying size, was probably the best known and the most anxiously sought by the Union forces of any of the partisan leaders. Mosby's absolute fearlessness, his ingenious methods of operating, as well as his innate love of danger and excitement, all combined to make his sudden descents upon the Federal lines of communication spectacular in the extreme.

His almost uniform success and the spirit of romance which surrounded his exploits, drew thousands of recruits to his leadership, and had he desired, he could have commanded a hundred men for every one who usually accompanied him on his forays. But he continued throughout the war using small detachments of from twenty to eighty men, and much of his success was probably due to this fact, which permitted sudden appearances and disappearances. From beginning to end

BRIGADIER–GENERAL TURNER ASHBY, C. S. A.

Such a will-o'-the-wisp was Turner Ashby, the audacious Confederate cavalryman, that he was looked upon by many officers and men in the Union armies as a purely mythological character. It was widely declared that no such man existed, and that the feats accredited to Ashby's rangers were in reality the work of many different partisan bands. His habit of striking at different and widely divergent points in rapid succession went far toward substantiating this rumor. He would fall upon an isolated wagon-train at dawn, and by twilight of the same day would strike a Federal camp thirty miles or more away. But Ashby was a real character, a daring soldier, a superb horseman, and the right-hand man of "Stonewall" Jackson. Careless of the additional danger, he customarily rode a beautiful white horse. After he was captured by the First Michigan cavalry, it was due to the courage and splendid jumping ability of this animal that he was able to make good his escape. Ashby met his death in a "Valley" cavalry skirmish at Harrisonburg on June 6, 1862, crying to his troopers in his last words: "Charge, men! For God's sake, charge!"

of the war, Mosby's raiders were a constant menace to the Union troops, and the most constant vigilance was necessary to meet successfully his skilfully planned stratagems.

On March 8, 1863, Mosby performed one of the most daring and effective feats of his career. In this case, as well as in others, it was the supreme boldness of the act which alone made it possible. Even with their knowledge of Mosby's methods, the Union officers could hardly conceive of such an apparently rash and unheard-of exploit being successful.

With a small band of carefully picked men, Mosby rode safely through the Union picket-lines, where the sentries believed the party to be Federal scouts returning from a raid. Upon reaching the vicinity of Fairfax Court House, Mosby entered the house used as headquarters by General Edwin H. Stoughton, woke the general, and demanded his surrender. Believing that the town had surrendered, the Union leader made no resistance. Meanwhile, each trooper in Mosby's little command had quietly secured several prisoners. Stoughton was forced to mount a horse, and with their prisoners Mosby and his cavalcade galloped safely back to their lines.

It was with similar strokes, original in conception and daring in execution, that Mosby kept thousands of Federal cavalry and infantry away from much-needed service at the front. After he became well established as a partisan ranger, his men were never organized as a tactical fighting body, and never had, as with other troops, an established camp. Through his trusty lieutenants, the call would be sent out for a designated number of men " for Mosby." This was the most definite information as to their mission that these volunteers ever received. In fact, they always moved out with sealed orders, but at the appointed time and place the rangers would assemble without fail. That Mosby wanted them was sufficient.

Many of these men were members of regular cavalry regiments home on furlough, others were farmers who had been duly enlisted in the rangers, and were always subject to call,

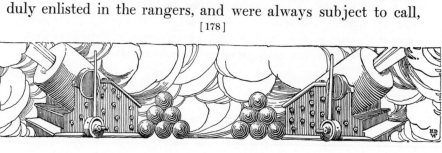

PROTECTION AGAINST THE "JAYHAWKERS" OF LOUISIANA

The lookout tower in the midst of this Federal cavalry camp in the northwest part of Baton Rouge, Louisiana, is a compliment to the "jayhawkers"—soldiers not affiliated with any command—and nondescript guerilla bands which infested this region along the banks of the Mississippi. Here the land is so level that lookout towers were built wherever a command stopped for more than a few hours. The soldiers found it safer also to clear away the brush and obstructing trees for several hundred yards on all sides of their camps, in order to prevent the roving Confederate sharpshooters from creeping up and picking off a sentry, or having a shot at an officer. The guerilla bands along the Mississippi even had some pieces of ordnance, and used to amuse themselves by dropping shells on the Union "tin-clad" gunboats from lofty and distant bluffs.

still others were troopers whose mounts were worn out, and whose principal object was to secure Northern horses. The Union cavalry always claimed that among Mosby's men were a number who performed acts for which they were given short shrift when caught. Of course, the nature of the service performed by these rangers was subversive of discipline, and it is quite possible that many deeds were committed which the leader himself had absolutely nothing to do with and would not have sanctioned. But this is true with all warfare.

Mosby's expeditions often led him far within the Union lines, and the command was often nearly surrounded. On such occasions Mosby would give the word and the detachment would suddenly disintegrate, each trooper making his way back to his own lines through forests and over mountains as best he could. Frequently his men were captured. But Mosby seemed to bear a charmed life, and in spite of rewards for his capture and all manner of plans to entrap him, he continued his operations as a valuable ally to the main Confederate army.

Of course much of his success was due to the fact that he was ever operating in a friendly country. He could always be assured of authentic information, and wherever he went was certain of food, fresh horses, and means of concealment.

In 1864, Mosby was shot during one of his forays, and was left, apparently dying, by the Union troops, who failed to recognize him, in the house where he had been surprised. Learning soon after that the wounded Confederate was the famous leader of Mosby's rangers, the troops hastily returned to capture him or secure his dead body. But in the meantime, Mosby's men had spirited him away, and within a short time he and his men were again raiding Federal trains and outposts.

Until the very end of the war he kept up his indefatigable border warfare, and it was not until after the surrender at Appomattox, that Mosby gathered his men about him for the last time, and telling them that the war was over, pronounced his command disbanded for all time.

CHAPTER FOUR

CAVALRY
PICKETS, SCOUTS
AND COURIERS

A VETERAN SCOUT
OF THE
THIRTEENTH NEW YORK CAVALRY

WHY FEDERAL
CAVALRY HISTORY
BEGAN LATE

These four Federal troopers holding their horses, side by side with an equal number of infantry, are typical of the small detachments that split up the cavalry into units of little value during the first two years of the war. The cavalry also furnished guides, orderlies, and grooms for staff officers. The authorities divided it up so minutely among corps, division, and brigade commanders as completely to subvert its true value. It was assigned to accompany the slow-moving wagon-trains, which could have been equally well guarded by an infantry detail, and was practically never used as a coherent whole. "Detachments

CAVALRY WITH INFANTRY

ON

PROVOST-GUARD DUTY

from its strength were constantly increased, and it was hampered by instructions which crippled it for all useful purposes." This photograph was taken in February, 1865, after the cavalry had proved itself. The companies attached at that time to the provost-guard were Company K of the First Indiana Cavalry, Companies C and D of the First Massachusetts Cavalry, and the Third Pennsylvania Cavalry. The officer is inspecting the arms of the Zouaves at the right, and the troopers with their white gauntlets are much more spick and span than if they were assigned to the long rides and open air life of active campaigning.

CAVALRY GUARDING THE ORANGE & ALEXANDRIA RAILROAD, 1864

Here it is apparent why the Northern generals found it necessary to detach large portions of their armies along their lines of communication, to guard against the impending raids of the Confederate cavalry. The destruction of the bridge in this photograph, part of Grant's line of communication in the Wilderness campaign, would have delayed his movements for days and have compelled him to detach a strong body to recapture the railroad, and another to rebuild the bridge. Hence this strong force detailed as a guard. Cavalry boots

READY TO FORESTALL A CONFEDERATE RAID

and sabers are visible in the photograph, with the revolver, distinctive of that branch of the service. The photographer evidently posed his men. Note the hands thrust into the breasts of their jackets, or clasped in front of them, the folded arms, and the jaunty attitudes. The two boys at the left of the picture seem hardly old enough to be real soldiers. The tangle of underbrush along the banks suggest the mazes of the Wilderness where Grant was baffled in his overland campaign.

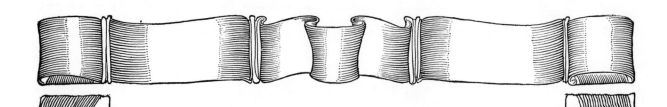

OUTPOSTS, SCOUTS AND COURIERS

By Charles D. Rhodes
Captain, General Staff, United States Army

AN army on the march is protected from surprise and annoyance by advance, rear, and flank guards, or by independent cavalry scouting far to the front until contact with the enemy is established. When it halts, its security is maintained through outposts, instructed to observe the front and flanks while it sleeps, and to act as a barrier to the entrance of patrols and spies, or to resist strenuously any sudden and unexpected advance of a hostile force.

Outpost duty, therefore, is most important, not alone as a protective measure, but because deductions from many campaigns have shown that troops which suffer continuously from many night alarms either lose nerve or become indifferent, so that, in either case, discipline and efficiency suffer.

In the Federal armies, outpost or picket duty in the presence of their enterprising adversaries was ever fatiguing, nerve-racking, and dangerous. Organizations went on picket for twenty-four continuous hours, and, in the cavalry, horses at the advanced posts remained saddled and bridled for hours at a time, ready for instant use. Except by the supports and reserves, the lighting of fires and cooking of food, when in close contact with the Confederates, were forbidden, but many a strip of bacon and occasionally a stolen chicken were fried surreptitiously in a safe hiding-place. Although a farmhouse was oftentimes available, horses and troopers were usually without shelter, and this, in rainy or freezing weather, made outpost duty an uncomfortable, if not a thrilling, experience.

The nervous period for the vedette was between midnight

[186]

CAVALRY AT SUDLEY'S FORD
BULL RUN

Not until the time this photograph was taken—March, 1862—did the Union cavalrymen revisit this little ford after the disastrous rout of the inchoate Federal army the July previous. The following March, the Confederate commander Johnston left his works at Centerville for the Peninsula, having learned that McClellan's move on Richmond would take that direction. This group of cavalrymen is advancing across the stream near the ford where they had so gallantly protected the Federal flight only a few months before. At the time this was taken, the Federal Government had already changed its first absurd decision to limit its cavalry to six regiments of regulars, and from the various States were pouring in the regiments that finally enabled the Union cavalry to outnumber and outwear the exhausted Southern horse in 1864 and 1865.

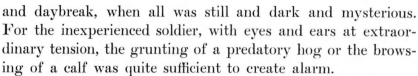

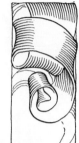

and daybreak, when all was still and dark and mysterious. For the inexperienced soldier, with eyes and ears at extraordinary tension, the grunting of a predatory hog or the browsing of a calf was quite sufficient to create alarm.

Again, when the excitement had subsided, and eyes had grown drowsy from lack of sleep, steps among the trees would bring the sharp challenge and colloquy:

"Halt! Who comes there?"

"A friend."

"Advance, friend, with the countersign."

Sometimes the "friend" was an officer, making his rounds of inspection; sometimes a countryman who had never heard of the countersign. Occasionally the answer to the countersign was a rush of feet, a blow, and the driving-in of the outpost by a force of the foe, or by guerrillas.

The tendency of the raw recruit was to see a gray uniform behind every stump, tree, or bush, and in the early period of the Civil War, the rifle-firing by opposing pickets, especially at night, was constant and uninterrupted. Many a time, too, the lone sentinel or vedette was shot down in cold blood.

A member of one of the first organized companies of Union sharpshooters tells a story of creeping with his comrades, in the early morning hours, upon a Confederate outpost. The break of a lovely day was just showing red in the eastern sky. The range to the hostile picket was considerable, but the rifles of the sharpshooters were equipped with telescopic sights.

Through the glass, a tall, soldierly-looking cavalry officer in Confederate gray could be seen through the morning mist, sitting motionless on his black charger, admiring the dawn. The rifles were leveled; the telescopic sights were adjusted on the poor fellow's chest; the triggers were pulled in unison, and although too distant to hear a sound from the outpost, the cavalryman was seen to fall dead from his horse. To the narrator, an inexperienced New England lad, such deeds were wanton murder, and he made haste to transfer to a cavalry command,

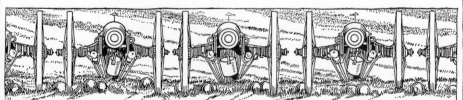

GUARDING A PONTOON-BRIDGE

These cavalrymen posted at the strategic point known as Varuna Landing, across the James River, in 1864, are engaged in no unimportant task. The Federals were by no means sure that Lee's veterans would not again make a daring move northward. However, by this time (1864) the true value of the Federal cavalry had been appreciated by the authorities; it was being used in mass on important raids, and had been given a chance to show its prowess in battle. But not until after Hooker reorganized the Army of the Potomac in 1863 was the policy definitely abandoned of splitting up the cavalry into small detachments for minor duties, and of regarding it merely as an adjunct of the infantry.

not equipped with telescopic sights and hair-trigger rifles. But as the war progressed, this constant firing by sentinels and vedettes disappeared, and opposing pickets began to comprehend that this was not war. To the guerrillas, who killed to rob and loot, it was, of course, a different matter.

The time came when the " Yankee " troopers exchanged newspapers, bacon, or hardtack with the " Johnny Rebs," for tobacco or its equivalent, or they banteringly invited each other to come out and meet half-way between the lines of outposts.

It was two years before the true rôle of cavalry was understood by the Federal commanders. During that early period, the constant use of the mounted branch as outposts for infantry divisions and army corps, was largely responsible for cavalry inefficiency, and for the tremendous breaking-down of horse-flesh. Indeed, it was not until 1864 that Sheridan impressed upon Meade the wastefulness of thus rendering thousands of cavalry mounts unserviceable through unnecessary picket duty, which could be as well performed by infantry.

But many opportunities for brave and gallant deeds occurred on outpost duty, albeit many such were performed in obscurity, and were thus never lauded to the world as heroic.

One such deed, which fortunately did not escape recognition, was that of Sergeant Martin Hagan, of the Second United States Cavalry. When the city of Fredericksburg was evacuated by the Union army on December 13, 1862, Sergeant Hagan was left behind in charge of an outpost detachment of seven troopers, with orders to remain until relieved.

For some reason or other, Hagan was not relieved, and remained at his post with his pitiably small force until the Confederate Army of Northern Virginia began entering the town. Then Hagan and his troopers succeeded in delaying the advanced troops by skirmishing. Subsequently learning that the bridges over the Rappahannock behind him had been removed, and that his outpost was the only Union force in Fredericksburg, he retired, stubbornly disputing every foot of his

A FEDERAL CAVALRY "DETAIL" GUARDING A WAGON–TRAIN, 1862

These troopers bending over their saddles in the cold autumn wind, as the wagon-train jolts along the Rappahannock bank, are one of the many "details" which dissipated the strength and impaired the efficiency of the cavalry as a distinct arm of the service during the first two years of the war.   They carried revolvers, as well as their sabers and carbines, for they had to be ready for sudden attack, an ambush, a night rush, or the dash of the swift Southern raiders who helped provision the Confederate armies from Northern wagon-trains.

way with a brigade of Confederate cavalry, until the banks of the Rappahannock were reached. Here, seeing his men and their horses well over the river, he plunged in himself under a shower of balls, and swam across without the loss of a man, horse, or article of equipment. For this gallant act of "valor and fidelity," this cavalry sergeant was awarded the Congressional Medal of Honor.

SCOUTING

At the beginning of the Civil War, what is now known as military information or intelligence was not appreciated as it was later. The organization of the scout service was not perfected; accurate military maps of the theater of operations were almost wholly lacking, and many commanders accepted the gage of battle with no very comprehensive idea of the foe's numbers, position, and *morale*, and with no accurate conception of the topography of the battlefield.

As the military organization of the Union armies was perfected, however, and the newly made officers learned their lesson in the stern school of experience, the importance of scouting became apparent, and this use of cavalry developed into a necessary preliminary to every serious encounter.

Perhaps no branch of the military operations of the Civil War gave such opportunities for individual intelligence, initiative, nerve, daring, resourcefulness, tact, and physical endurance, as the constant scouting by the cavalry of the opposing armies between the great battles of the war. It required bold riding combined with caution, keen eyesight and ready wit, undaunted courage—not recklessness—an appreciation of locality amounting to a sixth sense, and above all other things a mind able to differentiate between useful and useless information.

The increased importance given to scouting, as the cavalry of the Federal armies gained in experience and efficiency, by no means did away with the use of paid civilian spies. But the

WATCHING AT RAPPAHANNOCK STATION

A FEDERAL CAVALRY PICKET IN '62

IN DANGER AT THE TIME

THIS PHOTOGRAPH WAS TAKEN

This picture of August, 1862, shows one of the small cavalry details posted to guard the railroad at Rappahannock Station. The Confederate cavalry, operating in force, could overcome these details as easily as they could drive away an equal number of infantry, and unless it was on account of their superior facilities for flight, there was little use in using the mounted branch of the service instead of the infantry. On the other hand the Union cavalry was so constantly crippled by having its strength dissipated in such details that it was unable to pursue the Confederate raiders. Before this scene, the summer and fall of 1862, Pope and Lee had been maneuvering for position along each side of the Rappahannock River. Pope had established a *tête-de-pont* at this railroad station, and on August 22d Longstreet feinted strongly against it in order to divert Pope's attention from Jackson's efforts to turn his right flank. Longstreet and Stuart burned the railroad bridge, and drove the Federals from the *tête-de-pont*, after a contest of several hours' duration.

information furnished by soldier scouts served as a check upon untrustworthy civilians—sometimes employed as spies by both sides—and enabled the Union commanders to substantiate valuable information secured from prisoners, newspapers, and former slaves. As in a great many other things, the Confederate cavalry excelled in the use of trained officers as scouts—officers' patrols, as they are called nowadays—men whose opinion of what they observed was worth something to their commanders; while the Federal leaders were very slow to appreciate that false or faulty military information, in that it is misleading, is worse than no information at all.

In many cases loyal inhabitants of the border States were utilized as scouts, men who knew each trail and by-path, and who were more or less familiar with Confederate sentiment in their own and adjoining counties. These men were placed in a most uncomfortable position, suspected by their friends and neighbors at home, and looked upon with suspicion by their military employers. Their service to their country was oftentimes heroic, and they frequently laid down their lives in her cause.

General Sheridan was one of the first of the Union commanders who appreciated, at its true value, the importance of the information service—a part of headquarters which should be systematically organized and disciplined, and whose reports as to topography and the location of the foe could be absolutely relied upon. Indeed, this was one of the secrets of Sheridan's almost uniform success. He was always well informed as to his opponent's movements, strength, and probable intentions.

After Sheridan's engagements in the Shenandoah valley at Clifton and Berryville, he decided to dispense almost entirely with the use of civilians and alleged Confederate deserters, and to depend entirely on Union scouts. For this purpose he organized a scout battalion recruited entirely from soldiers who volunteered for this dangerous duty. These troopers were disguised in the Confederate uniform when necessary, and were paid from secret-service funds.

[194]

CAVALRY TO KEEP THE PEACE—THE "ONEIDA" COMPANY

Cavalrymen playing cards, washing, smoking pipes, whittling sticks, indolently leaning against a tree, do not fulfill the usual conception of that dashing arm of the service. These are the Oneida Cavalry, used as provost-guards and orderlies throughout the war. Not a man of them was killed in battle, and the company lost only ten by disease. This does not mean that they did not do their full share of the work, but merely that they exemplified the indifference or ignorance on the part of many military powers as to the proper rôle of the cavalry. The "Oneidas" were attached to Stoneman's cavalry command with the Army of the Potomac from the time of their organization in September, 1861, to April, 1862. They did patrol duty and took care of the prisoners during several months in the latter year. Thereafter they acted as head-quarters escort until they were mustered out, June 13, 1865, and honorably discharged from the service.

[G—13]

This assumption of the Confederate uniform, giving these soldiers the character of spies, caused Sheridan's scouts to be more or less disliked by the Cavalry Corps, and it has been stated on good authority that they were frequently fired upon deliberately by their own side, under the pretense of being taken for the foe. These scouts literally took their lives in their hands, and it required all their ready wit to escape being killed or captured by either the one side or the other. But the independence of the service, its constant risk, as well as patriotic impulses in the case of many, fascinated and appealed to a certain class of men, and they kept Sheridan well informed at all times.

The specially selected scouts of the Federal armies usually were mounted on the best available horses, and were furnished fresh remounts whenever occasion required—or they helped themselves to what the country afforded. The best scouting was done by cavalry troopers working in pairs, on the principle that two pairs of eyes are better than one pair. So in case of surprise, at least one scout might escape.

Sheridan's scouts were usually excellent pistol shots, and were encouraged to carry several revolvers in their belts or saddle holsters. They carried no sabers lest the rattle of scabbards or the gleam of bright metal attract the attention of the Southern scouts and betray their presence. The most experienced scouts traveled light. Many times they were forced to ride for their lives, and an extra pound or two made a difference in the weight-carrying speed of their horses. They usually left their grain and clothing in the headquarters' wagons, and managed to live off the country.

Sheridan's disguised scouts became expert in picking up the stragglers of the opposing army and in questioning them, and even went to the extent of riding around the Confederate columns and wagon trains. If detected, their fleet horses usually put considerable distance between them and their pursuers, but they were ever ready to shoot, and instances have been recorded of one of their number holding off four men.

BUILDING A CAVALRY CAMP

Waving sabers in battle, as the cavalryman soon learned, consumed but a small part of his time as compared with handling pickaxes and felling trees. In this photograph the cavalry detail at the headquarters of General Adelbert Ames is breaking ground to build a camp. The men have just arrived, and the horses are still saddled. A barrel is supplying draft for a temporary fireplace, and even the dog is alert and excited. The faces gazing out of the photograph below are of men who more than once have looked death in the face and have earned their comparative rest. A pleasant change from active service is this camp of Companies C and D of the First Massachusetts Cavalry. They had served at Antietam, at Kelly's Ford, at Brandy Station, at Gettysburg, in the Wilderness, at Spotsylvania, and in a host of minor operations before they were assigned to provost duty near the end of the war.

A REST IN THE WOODS

COURIERS

The risk taken by the despatch bearers of both armies, when occasion demanded, is well illustrated in the story of the fate of private William Spicer, of the Tenth Missouri Cavalry, who undertook to carry an order through the Confederate lines while Sherman was conducting his campaign in Mississippi. The cavalry of General Smith, numbering nearly seven thousand men, had been detached from the remainder of the army and sent away along the Mobile and Ohio Railroad, with orders to join the army near Meridian, on February 10, 1864.

Meanwhile, the main body had marched to Meridian, and there Sherman waited for Smith until the 18th, without receiving any tidings of the missing troopers. Then the remainder of the Federal cavalry, under Winslow, was ordered to scout twenty miles toward the direction from which Smith was expected, and to convey new orders to him. Winslow's forces reached their objective point at Lauderdale Springs, and still no news had been heard of Smith.

Scouts that traveled far into the surrounding country obtained no further news. As Winslow's orders allowed him to go no farther, he abandoned the search, but it was necessary that Smith receive Sherman's orders, and a volunteer was called for to carry the despatch through a country occupied by Forrest's cavalry, and other portions of Polk's army. The messenger would be forced to locate Smith in whatever manner he could, and then to reach him as quickly as possible.

From many volunteers, Private Spicer was finally chosen. He was an Arkansas man, and as many Confederate troops had been enlisted there, he was less likely to be suspected than a man from any of the Northern States. Spicer considered all the features of the case, and his final decision was to risk detection in the gray uniform of a Confederate. The Federals were supplied with uniforms taken from prisoners and captured wagons, which were kept for use in such an emergency

KEEPING FODDER DRY

Fodder and equipment were scarcer in the field than men. Whether the trooper slept in the open or not, he took advantage of any and every facility to keep the fodder dry and protect his horses. This photograph shows a half-ruined and deserted house utilized for these two purposes. The saddles were laid beneath the shelter; those covered with rawhide instead of leather soon split if wet, and when cracked were far from comfortable. This, like the scene below, was taken near City Point in 1864.

A HOME BECOMES A CAVALRY STABLE

QUICKLY IMPROVISED STALLS

QUARTERS FOR HORSES

The trooper's first regard was for the comfort of his horse, not only in the matter of feeding and watering, but also in respect to providing him with comfortable quarters. Along the crest of the hill stretches a row of stalls improvised with poles, to afford each horse room enough to lie down and not be walked on or kicked by his neighbor—room was essential for the hard-worked horses. The haze in the distance indicates the Virginia summer of 1864—a trying one for members of the mounted service.

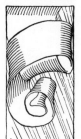

as this, and Spicer was provided with one that fitted him well. It was the evening of February 23d, when he rode northward, on his search for the missing cavalry.

With the tact of a scout well drilled in his work, he followed each little clue on his northward ride, until he had learned where Smith could be found. On the morning following his exit from his camp, he met several bodies of Confederates, who passed him with little notice.

Then another band was met. Spicer saluted; the salute was returned, and the Confederates were passing him, as the others had. But suddenly one of the party stopped and looked closely at the lone rider. The Confederates halted and Spicer was ordered to dismount. The man who had called the commander's attention to the courier stepped before Spicer. The courier recognized him as a neighbor in Arkansas.

With all the ingenuity at his command the courier fought to allay the suspicions of the Confederates, but slowly and surely the case against him was built up. Then a drumhead court-martial was held in the middle of the road. The verdict was soon reached, and Spicer was hanged to a near-by tree.

One of the swiftest and most daring courier trips of the war was made, immediately after the second battle of Bull Run, by Colonel Lafayette C. Baker, a special agent of the War Department, acting as courier for Secretary Stanton. He was sent from Washington with a message to General Banks, whose troops were at Bristoe Station, and, as was then believed, cut off from Pope's main army. Riding all night, making his way cautiously along, Baker passed through the entire Confederate army, and at daylight had reached Banks.

Waiting only for a response to the message, the despatch bearer remounted his horse and started the return trip to Washington in broad daylight. For a time he eluded the Confederates, but finally, as he attempted to pass between certain lines, he was seen, and a party of cavalrymen started in pursuit of him. In spite of the distance traveled, his horse

CAVALRY SCOUTS NEAR GETTYSBURG—1863

Nothing could illustrate better than this vivid photograph of scouts at White's house, near Gettysburg, a typical episode in the life of a cavalry scout. The young soldier and his companions are evidently stopping for directions, or for a drink of water or milk. The Pennsylvania farmers were hospitable. The man of the family has come to the front gate. His empty right sleeve seems to betoken an old soldier, greeting old friends, and asking for news from the front. The lady in her hoop-skirt remains on the porch with her little boy. His chubby legs are visible beneath his frock, and he seems to be hanging back in some awe of the troopers who are but boys themselves. The lady's hair is drawn down around her face after the fashion of the day, and the whole picture is redolent of the stirring times of '63.

raced away at a speed that soon left a number of the cavalry-men in the rear. Finally, the number of pursuers dwindled to three, and the courier, crossing the brow of a small hill, turned his horse into the woods bordering the turnpike.

The ruse was successful, and the three Confederate cav-alrymen dashed on down the hill. A short distance farther along one of the horsemen abandoned the chase and started to return. As he came abreast of Stanton's courier, a movement of Baker's horse attracted the Confederate's attention and he stopped. The cavalryman saw the courier and started to cover him with his rifle, but Baker was prepared. The Federal's revolver cracked, and the Southerner fell from his saddle.

The other Confederates had given up the chase and were returning when they heard the shot. They rushed back in time to see Baker's steed galloping across an open field to reach the road in front of them, and dashed to intercept him. The Federal was the first to reach the road, and again the pur-suit commenced. Baker turned into the fields, and with the pursuers close behind him started a last race for Bull Run.

The despatch bearer's horse was panting and exhausted, but, with the grit of a blooded racer it struggled on, holding the pursuers almost at the same distance. With a final dash Baker reached the bank, leaped into the stream and started for the opposite shore. The creek was little more than twelve yards wide at that point and the horse soon reached the other side, but there a steep bank several feet high confronted it, and it could not climb out. With revolver ready the courier waited, prepared to offer his last resistance, when a shot rang out. It was the pickets of the Federal army firing on the Confed-erates, who abandoned their pursuit at the first shot. The messenger made his way into Centreville, and mounting an-other horse dashed on toward Washington.

It was late afternoon when he delivered the messages from Banks to the Secretary. In twenty-four hours the cou-rier had ridden nearly one hundred miles.

A CHANGE OF BASE—THE CAVALRY SCREEN

This photograph of May 30, 1864, shows the Federal cavalry in actual operation of a most important func-
tion—the "screening" of the army's movements. The troopers are guarding the evacuation of Port Royal
on the Rappahannock, May 30, 1864. After the reverse to the Union arms at Spottsylvania, Grant ordered the change of base from the Rappahannock to McClellan's former starting-point, White House on
the Pamunkey. The control of the waterways, combined with Sheridan's efficient use of the cavalry, made
this an easy matter. Torbert's division encountered Gordon's brigade of Confederate cavalry at Hanovertown and drove it in the direction of Hanover Court House. Gregg's division moved up to this line; Russell's division of infantry encamped near the river-crossing in support, and behind the mask thus formed
the Army of the Potomac crossed the Pamunkey on May 28th unimpeded. Gregg was then ordered to reconnoiter towards Mechanicsville, and after a severe fight at Hawes' shop he succeeded (with the assistance of
Custer's brigade) in driving Hampton's and Fitzhugh Lee's cavalry divisions and Butler's brigade from the
field. Although the battle took place immediately in front of the Federal infantry, General Meade declined
to put the latter into action, and the battle was won by the cavalry alone. It was not to be the last time.

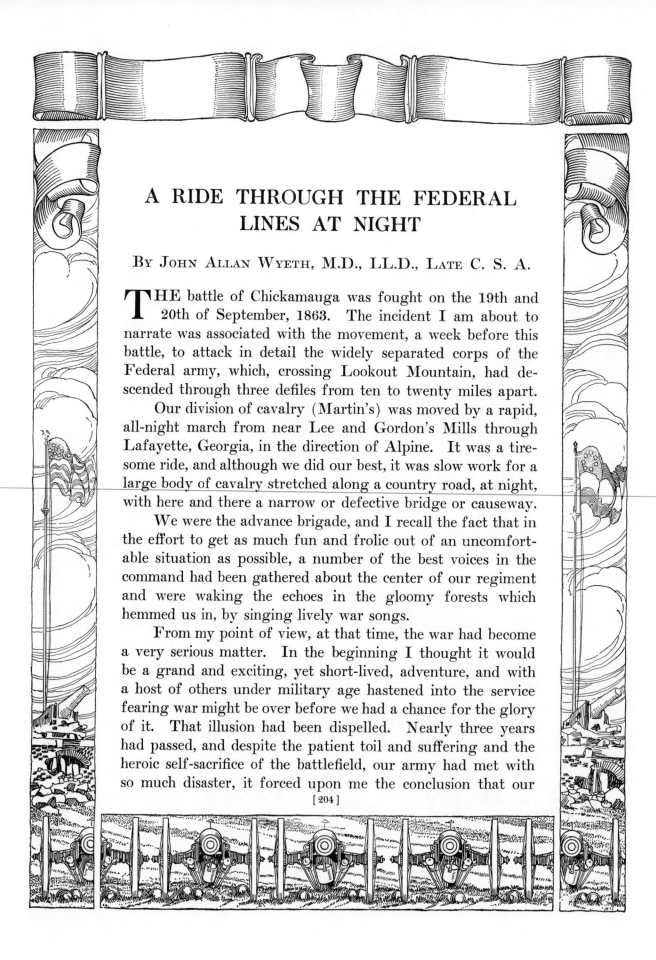

A RIDE THROUGH THE FEDERAL
LINES AT NIGHT

By John Allan Wyeth, M.D., LL.D., Late C. S. A.

THE battle of Chickamauga was fought on the 19th and 20th of September, 1863. The incident I am about to narrate was associated with the movement, a week before this battle, to attack in detail the widely separated corps of the Federal army, which, crossing Lookout Mountain, had descended through three defiles from ten to twenty miles apart.

Our division of cavalry (Martin's) was moved by a rapid, all-night march from near Lee and Gordon's Mills through Lafayette, Georgia, in the direction of Alpine. It was a tiresome ride, and although we did our best, it was slow work for a large body of cavalry stretched along a country road, at night, with here and there a narrow or defective bridge or causeway.

We were the advance brigade, and I recall the fact that in the effort to get as much fun and frolic out of an uncomfortable situation as possible, a number of the best voices in the command had been gathered about the center of our regiment and were waking the echoes in the gloomy forests which hemmed us in, by singing lively war songs.

From my point of view, at that time, the war had become a very serious matter. In the beginning I thought it would be a grand and exciting, yet short-lived, adventure, and with a host of others under military age hastened into the service fearing war might be over before we had a chance for the glory of it. That illusion had been dispelled. Nearly three years had passed, and despite the patient toil and suffering and the heroic self-sacrifice of the battlefield, our army had met with so much disaster, it forced upon me the conclusion that our

[204]

THE EVACUATION OF PORT ROYAL NEARLY COMPLETED

This photograph, taken shortly after the one preceding, witnesses how quickly an army accomplishes its movements. The pontoon-bridge leading out to the boats has been practically cleared; all but a few of the group of cavalrymen have ridden away, and the transports are whistling "all aboard," as can plainly be seen from the sharp jets of steam. A few of the cavalry remain with the headquarters wagon which stands near the head of the pontoon. Sterner work awaits the troopers after this peaceful maneuver. Grant needs every man to screen his infantry in its attempt to outflank the brilliantly maneuvered army of Lee.

struggle was hopeless, and that if we fought on as we had determined to do, death was the inevitable end. That was my conviction, and I believe it accounts for the fact that I volunteered to go on the errand which I undertook that night.

About two o'clock word was passed down from the head of the column to stop the singing, and for the entire column to move in silence. When we heard the order, we knew we were coming close to the foe. About four o'clock we were again halted, and another message was started at the head of the column and came back down the line in a low tone, for it was the custom on night marches, on account of the darkness and the crowded condition of the roadway, to transmit orders in this fashion. An aide or courier could not get through the crowded highway or ride through the thick underbrush and woods on either side. The message was, in effect, a call for a volunteer to go on a special errand.

My messmate, Lieutenant Jack Weatherley, who was killed soon after at Big Shanty, rode with me to the head of the column where, in the darkness, I made out a number of men, presumably officers and aides, some mounted and some on the ground. The general in command—Wheeler or Martin— asked if I were willing to go inside the foe's lines. I replied I would go provided I could wear my uniform, but not as a spy. He said: "You can go as you are. I want you to find a detachment of cavalry which has been sent around the right of the enemy's lines, and which by this time should be in their rear, about opposite our present position. It is important that they be found and ordered not to attack, but to rejoin this column by the route which they have already traveled. In order to reach them," he added, "you will proceed upon a road which leads through the enemy's lines, and should bring you in contact with their pickets about one mile from this point."

The message was entirely verbal. I carried nothing but one army six-shooter. Lieutenant Weatherley, Colonel Hambrick, in command of our regiment at the time, and a guide

COURIERS AT BEVERLY HOUSE—WARREN'S HEADQUARTERS AT SPOTSYLVANIA

The couriers doing duty before this farmhouse, headquarters of General G. K. Warren, are kept riding day and night at breakneck speed. The Fifth Army Corps, of which he was in command, occupied a position northwest of Spotsylvania Court House on the right of the Federal line, where it remained from May 9th to May 13th. On the evening of May 10th Warren made two assaults on the position at his front, at a loss of six thousand men. Again, on the 12th, the dogged Grant persisted in his hammering tactics and ordered heavy assaults at different points. The Federal loss on that day was approximately seven thousand men all told. For another week Grant made partial attacks all along the line, but Lee's veterans withstood every onset. In two weeks Grant lost thirty-six thousand men. The Fifth Corps bore the brunt of much of the heavy work. One can imagine with what rapidity the couriers gathered around Beverly's house wore out their horses in transmitting all-important commands.

accompanied me a few hundred yards down the road. As I started, our colonel said: "This is an important matter, and I hope you will succeed. If you do, I will see that you have a furlough for as long a period as you wish."

The officers soon left me, and the guide accompanied me half a mile further to where the road forked. He indicated the route I should travel which was to the right, as we were going, and then telling me that the Federal pickets were at a point half a mile beyond, he turned back. By this time, it must have been nearly five o'clock.

To the normal human being in times of peace and quiet, the love of life is so natural and so strong that it is difficult to appreciate, until one has passed into and through it, that strange and unusual mental condition in which the value of existence becomes a minor consideration. I look back upon this occasion as the one supreme moment when I came nearest to the elimination of every selfish consideration from the motive with which I was then actuated. I do not overstate the case in saying that death was preferable to life with failure in the accomplishment of my errand.

I had determined, if halted, to ride over every obstacle at full speed, and not to fire my pistol unless in dire extremity, although I had taken it from the holster and had it cocked and ready for quick use. I was riding a splendid horse, strong, swift, and mettlesome, and so alert that nothing escaped his quick observation.

I have no means of knowing how far I had gone, probably half a mile or more, when suddenly I felt my horse check himself as if he were about to change his gait. This movement told me that he had seen something more than the ordinary inanimate object. At the same instant he lifted his head, and in such a knowing way, that I was convinced the moment had come, and that the Federal outposts were here. Without waiting to be halted, I tightened the reins, and crouching down close to the saddle and the horse's neck, touched him with the spurs, and

[208]

A COURIER AT HEADQUARTERS

Located as they were near the Orange and Alexandria Railroad and at times between the hostile lines, the dwellings near Fairfax Court House passed time and again from the hands of one army to the other. The home in this photograph was used at different times by General Beauregard and General McClellan as headquarters. Even now a Union orderly is waiting to dash off on one of the powerful chargers. The assigning of troopers to such duties as these was part of the system which crippled the Federal cavalry till it passed under the control of efficient and aggressive Sheridan. The details of the picture indicate a hurried departure of the former occupants. The house itself is a fine example of the old Colonial Southern architecture—white columns in front of red brick. The white stucco has fallen away in places from the brick of the columns—a melancholy appearance for a home.

HORSES THAT CARRIED THE ORDERS OF THE GENERAL–IN–CHIEF

Crack horses were a first requisite for Grant's staff, escort, and couriers. This photograph shows several at Bethseda Church, the little Virginia meeting-house where the staff had halted the day before Cold Harbor. The staff consisted of fourteen officers only, and was not larger than that of some division commanders. Brigadier-General John A. Rawlins was the chief. Grant's instructions to his staff showed the value that he placed upon celerity and the overcoming of delays in communicating orders. He urged his

WAITING ON GRANT AT BETHESDA CHURCH, JUNE, 1864

officers to discuss his orders with him freely whenever it was possible in the course of an engagement or battle, to learn his views as fully as possible, and in great emergencies, where there was no time to communicate with headquarters, to act on their own initiative along the lines laid down by him without his specific orders. The result was an eager, confident, hard-riding staff that stopped at no danger, whether to horse or man. What was even more important, its members did not hesitate to assume responsibility.

[G]

AN ESCORT THAT MADE HISTORY

These men and boys formed part of the escort of General Grant during the Appomattox campaign. The same companies (B, F, and K of the Fifth United States Cavalry, under Captain Julius W. Mason) were with him at the fall of Petersburg. Perhaps they won this high distinction by their intrepid charge at Gaines' Mill, when they lost fifty-eight of the two hundred and twenty men who participated. With such gallant troopers on guard, the North felt reassured as to the safety of its general-in-chief. The little boy

MEN OF THE FIFTH "REGULAR" CAVALRY

buglers, in the very forefront of the making of American history, stand with calm and professional bearing. Although but fifteen and sixteen years old, they rode with the troopers, and not less bravely. One boy of similar age was severely wounded in one of the numerous fights between Stuart and the Second United States Cavalry near Gettysburg. His captain, whom he was faithfully following, left him for dead upon the field. Many years after the young man sent the captain his photograph to prove that he was whole and sound.

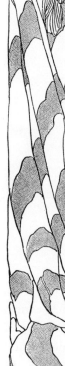

he bounded forward like the wind. His clear vision was not at fault, for as I flew by, I saw two men leap up in front of me from the edge of the roadway and jump into the shadows of the woods and undergrowth at one side. They said something to me, and I replied, but my excitement was so intense, expecting every moment the crack of their rifles, that no part of the picture which flashed through my mind remains clearly registered except the forms of two men and the swift scurry of the horse.

Fortunately they did not fire. It may be that they felt something of the excitement and fright I was experiencing, but more than likely they were drowsy or asleep, and the soft, sandy road enabled me to approach them so closely without being heard (for in the darkness they could not have seen farther than a few feet), that they were taken by surprise, and moreover, they may have thought I was a Federal picket, since I was riding into their lines. In any event, in less time than it takes to tell it, I had scurried away beyond their vision and out of range of their guns. Although I believed a large body of Federals was on either side of the road, I was riding along at such a rapid gait, that in the darkness I saw no sign of troops. I cannot even now estimate how far I went at the speed I was making—probably two or three miles. I know I had slowed up, and was riding again at a canter when daylight came, and with it I noticed in the valley below a cloud of dust not more than half a mile away. This told me of the moving cavalry, and in a few minutes more I had the great good fortune of riding into the column I was sent to intercept.

A few days after the battle of Chickamauga, all of the good mounts in the cavalry were organized to cross the Tennessee River and break up General Rosecrans' communications, and I went with this flying column. We took the great wagon train in the Sequatchie valley on the 2d of October, and on the 4th I was captured and taken to the military prison at Camp Morton, Indiana, where I remained until the latter part of February, 1865.

CHAPTER

NINE

————

CAVALRY BATTLES
AND CHARGES

————

ON THE WAY TO THE BATTLE OF GETTYSBURG
COMPANY L, SECOND "REGULARS"

The "Second" fought in the reserve brigade under General Merritt, during the second day of the battle. The leading figures in the picture are First-Sergeant Painter and First-Lieutenant Dewees. Few photographs show cavalry thus, in column.

THE WAGONS WITH THE RIGHT OF WAY

The ammunition-train had the right of way over everything else in the army, short of actual guns and soldiers, when there was any possibility of a fight. The long, cumbrous lines of commissary wagons were forced to draw off into the fields to the right and left of the road, or scatter any way they could, to make way for the ammunition-train. Its wagons were always marked, and were supposed to be kept as near the troops as possible. Soldiers could go without food for a day or two if necessary; but it might spell defeat

AMMUNITION–TRAIN OF THE THIRD DIVISION, CAVALRY CORPS

and capture to lack ammunition for an hour.   This is a photograph of the ammunition wagons of the Third
Cavalry Division commanded by General James H. Wilson.   They are going into bivouac for the night.
The wagons on the right are being formed in a semi-circle, and one of the escort has already dismounted.
A led mule is attached to the wagon on the right, for even mule power is fallible, and if one dies in the
traces he must be promptly replaced.   The men with these trains often held the fate of armies in their hands.

THE BATTLE–LINE—AN ENTIRE CAVALRY REGIMENT IN FORMATION

This stirring picture shows some of the splendid cavalry that was finally developed in the North arrayed in battle-line. Thus they looked before the bugle sounded the charge. One can almost imagine them breaking into a trot, increasing gradually to a gallop, and finally, within a score of yards of the Confederates' roaring guns, into a mad dash that carried them in clusters flashing with sabers through the struggling, writhing line. This regiment is the Thirteenth New York Cavalry, organized June 20, 1863. Two weeks after the regiment was organized these men were patroling the rear of the Army of the Potomac at Gettysburg. The following month they were quelling the draft riots in New York, and thereafter they were engaged

THE THIRTEENTH NEW YORK CAVALRY DRILLING NEAR WASHINGTON

in pursuing the redoubtable and evanescent Mosby, and keeping a watchful eye on Washington. They participated in many minor engagements in the vicinity of the Capital, and lost 128 enlisted men and officers. The photograph is proof enough that they were a well-drilled body of men. The ranks are straight and unbroken, and the company officers are keeping their proper distances. The colonel, to the extreme right in the foreground, has good reason to sit proudly erect. Note the white-horse troop in the rear, where the war chargers can be seen gracefully arching their necks. This is a triumph of wet-plate photography. Only by the highest skill could such restless animals as horses be caught with the camera of '65.

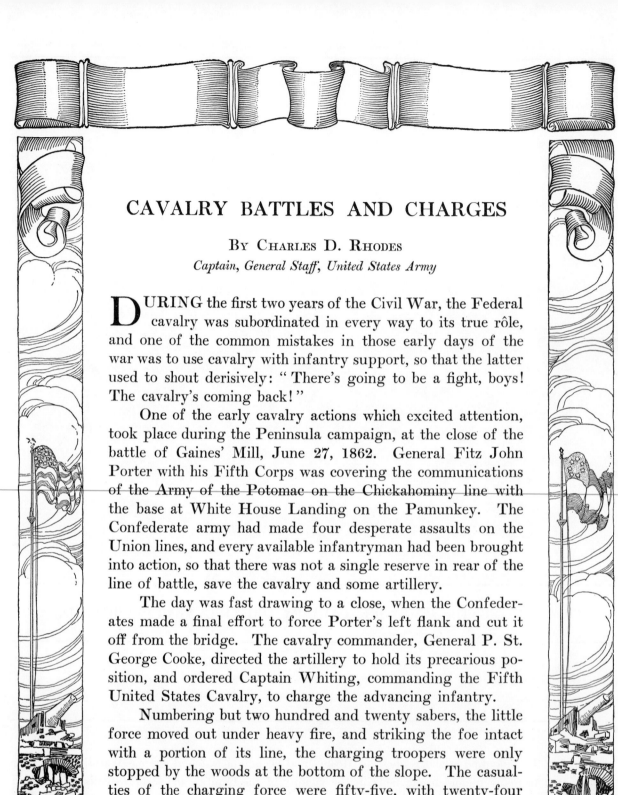

CAVALRY BATTLES AND CHARGES

By Charles D. Rhodes
Captain, General Staff, United States Army

DURING the first two years of the Civil War, the Federal cavalry was subordinated in every way to its true rôle, and one of the common mistakes in those early days of the war was to use cavalry with infantry support, so that the latter used to shout derisively: "There's going to be a fight, boys! The cavalry's coming back!"

One of the early cavalry actions which excited attention, took place during the Peninsula campaign, at the close of the battle of Gaines' Mill, June 27, 1862. General Fitz John Porter with his Fifth Corps was covering the communications of the Army of the Potomac on the Chickahominy line with the base at White House Landing on the Pamunkey. The Confederate army had made four desperate assaults on the Union lines, and every available infantryman had been brought into action, so that there was not a single reserve in rear of the line of battle, save the cavalry and some artillery.

The day was fast drawing to a close, when the Confederates made a final effort to force Porter's left flank and cut it off from the bridge. The cavalry commander, General P. St. George Cooke, directed the artillery to hold its precarious position, and ordered Captain Whiting, commanding the Fifth United States Cavalry, to charge the advancing infantry.

Numbering but two hundred and twenty sabers, the little force moved out under heavy fire, and striking the foe intact with a portion of its line, the charging troopers were only stopped by the woods at the bottom of the slope. The casualties of the charging force were fifty-five, with twenty-four

[220]

GENERAL

PHILIP ST. GEORGE

COOKE

COMMANDING

THE FIRST GREAT

FEDERAL

CAVALRY CHARGE OF THE

CIVIL WAR

Had it not been for General Philip St. George Cooke and his cavalry, Major-General Fitz-John Porter and his staff would not be enjoying the luxuries portrayed in the lower photograph, taken nineteen days after the battle of Gaines' Mill. The typical old-time Virginia cook, and the pleasant camping-ground on the banks of the river, suggest little of the deadly peril that faced the Federals June 27, 1862. The line of battle formed the arc of a circle, almost parallel to the Chickahominy. During the day the Confederate forces made four desperate assaults on the Union lines, and every available infantryman was brought into action. The only reserve on the left of the line was the cavalry and considerable artillery. As night was falling, the Confederates made a final effort to force the left flank and cut it off from the bridge across the Chickahominy. The artillery was directed to maintain its position, and General Cooke ordered Captain Whiting, commanding the Fifth United States Cavalry, to charge with his troopers. The little force of 220 sabers charged the advancing lines of Confederate infantry; a portion of the line struck the enemy intact and were stopped only by the woods at the bottom of the slope. Their casualties were fifty-five men—but under cover of the charge the artillery was safely withdrawn, and the sacrifice was well worth the results attained.

GENERAL FITZ–JOHN PORTER AND STAFF, JUNE, 1862

horses killed—a sacrifice well worth the results attained. Of this action, the Comte de Paris wrote fifteen years later: " The sacrifice of some of the bravest of the cavalry certainly saved a part of the artillery, as did, on a larger scale, the Austrian cavalry on the evening of Sadowa."

General Wesley Merritt, U. S. A., one of the ablest cavalry officers of his time, who was present at Gaines' Mill as an aide-de-camp to General Cooke, thus described this affair: *

During the early part of this battle the Union army held its ground and gained from time to time some material success. But it was only temporary. In the afternoon the writer of this, by General Cooke's direction, reported at the headquarters of the commanding general on the field, Fitz John Porter, and during his attendance there heard read a despatch from General McClellan congratulating Porter on his success. It closed with directions to drive the rebels off the field, and to take from them their artillery. At the time this despatch was being read, the enemy were forcing our troops to the rear. Hasty preparations were made for the retreat of the headquarters, and everything was in the most wretched confusion. No orders could be obtained, and I returned to my chief reporting the condition of affairs. It was apparent from movements in our front that the Confederates would make a supreme effort to force the left flank of Fitz John Porter's command, and cutting it off from the bridge over the Chickahominy, sever it from McClellan's army, and capture or disperse it.

It was growing late. Both armies were exhausted by the exertions of the day. But the prize at hand was well worth the effort, and the Confederates with renewed strength were fighting to make their victory complete. The Union cavalry commander seized the situation at a glance. The cavalry had been posted behind a plateau on the left bank of the Chickahominy, with ground to its front free of obstacles and suitable for cavalry action. To the right front of the cavalry the batteries of the reserve artillery were stationed. . . .

The events of that day at Gaines' Mill are pictured on the mind of the writer of this imperfect sketch as on a never fading photograph. The details of the battle are as vivid as if they had occurred yesterday. As

* Journal United States Cavalry Association, March, 1895.

MECHANICSVILLE, IN 1862, WHERE THE TROUBLE STARTED

At this sleepy Virginia hamlet the series of engagements that preceded the struggles along the Chickahominy in front of Richmond began. Early in June, 1862, as the Army of the Potomac extended its wings along both banks of the Chickahominy, Mechanicsville fell into its possession. There was a struggle at Beaver Dam Creek and on the neighboring fields, the defenders finally retreating in disorder down the pike and over the bridge toward Richmond, only three and a half miles away. The pickets of the opposing armies watched the bridge with jealous eyes till the Union lines were withdrawn on the 26th of June, and the Confederates retook the village.

OFFICERS OF THE FIFTH UNITED STATES CAVALRY, IN THE FAMOUS CHARGE

the Confederates came rushing across the open in front of the batteries, bent on their capture, one battery nearest our position was seen to limber up with a view to retreating. I rode hurriedly, by direction of General Cooke, to its captain, Robinson, and ordered him to unlimber and commence firing at short range, canister. He complied willingly, and said, as if in extenuation of his intended withdrawal, that he had no support. I told him the cavalry were there, and would support his and the other batteries. The rapid fire at short range of the artillery, and the daring charge of the cavalry in the face of an exhausted foe, prevented, without doubt, the enemy seizing the Chickahominy bridge and the capture or dispersion of Fitz John Porter's command. No farther advance was made by the Confederates, and the tired and beaten forces of Porter withdrew to the farther side of the Chickahominy and joined the Army of the Potomac in front of Richmond. The cavalry withdrew last as a rear guard, after having furnished torch and litter bearers to the surgeons of our army, who did what was possible to care for our wounded left on the field.

But it was not until a year later (March 17, 1863), at Kelly's Ford on the Rappahannock, that the Union cavalry first gained real confidence in itself and in its leaders.

In this engagement, following the forcing of the river crossing, two regiments of cavalry dismounted, with a section of artillery, and held the foe in front, while mounted regiments rolled up the Confederate flanks; their entire line was thrown into confusion and finally driven from the field.

The decisive cavalry battle at Brandy Station, or Beverly Ford, on June 9th, following, having for its object a reconnaissance in force of the Confederate troops on the Culpeper-Fredericksburg road, was the first great cavalry combat of the war. It virtually "made" the Union cavalry.

Buford's division of the Federal cavalry corps accompanied by Ames' infantry brigade, had been directed to cross the Rappahannock at Beverly Ford, and move by way of St. James' Church to Brandy Station. A second column composed of Gregg's and Duffié's divisions, with Russell's infantry

MAJOR CHARLES JARVIS WHITING

Major (then Captain) Whiting was the man who led the charge of the Fifth United States Cavalry upon the advancing Confederate infantry ordered by General Philip St. George Cooke at Gaines' Mill, June 27, 1862. He could entertain no hope of victory. The Confederates were already too near to allow of an effective charge. It was practically a command to die in order to check the Confederate column until infantry reenforcements could be rushed forward to save some imperiled batteries. Over twenty-five per cent. of the troopers who rode through the Confederate lines were killed, wounded, or missing.

GAINES' MILL

From this rural Virginia spot the battle of June 27th took its name. At the close of that fearful day the building fell into use as a hospital. It was later burned during a Federal raid, and nothing but the gaunt walls remain. The skull that lies in front of the mill evidently belonged to one of those brave cavalrymen who gave up their lives to save their comrades. He may have received a soldier's hasty burial, but it was by no means unusual for the heavy rains to wash away the shallow covering of soil, and to have exposed to view the remains of the men who had gone to their reward.

brigade, was to cross the river at Kelly's Ford—Gregg to push on by way of Mount Dumpling to Brandy Station, and Duffié to proceed to Stevensburg. By a strange coincidence, that brilliant cavalry leader, Stuart, planned on the same day to cross the Rappahannock at Beverly and the upper fords, for the purpose of diverting the attention of the Army of the Potomac from General Lee's northward dash into Maryland.

Under cover of a heavy fog, Buford's column crossed the river at four o'clock in the morning, surprising the Southern outposts and nearly capturing the Confederate artillery. Here, in spite of superior numbers, the Union commander, General Pleasonton, formed his cavalry in line of battle, covering the ford in less than an hour, but he could make no perceptible movement forward until Gregg's guns on the extreme left had made a general advance possible.

The Confederates fell rapidly back, and the headquarters of Stuart's chief of artillery, with all his papers and Lee's order for the intended movement, were captured. A junction was soon formed with Gregg, and with heavy losses on both sides, the foe was pushed back to Fleetwood Ridge. Of this part of the action General Stuart's biographer says:

A part of the First New Jersey Cavalry came thundering down the narrow ridge, striking McGregor's and Hart's unsupported batteries in the flank, and riding through and between guns and caissons from right to left, but were met by a determined hand-to-hand contest from the cannoneers with pistols, sponge-staffs, and whatever else came handy to fight with. The charge was repulsed by artillerists alone, not a single friendly trooper being within reach of us.

On Fleetwood Ridge the Confederate infantry rallied to the support of Stuart's cavalry, and the object of the reconnaissance having been gained, a general withdrawal of the Union cavalry was ordered, Gregg by way of the ford at Rappahannock Bridge, and Buford by Beverly Ford. But as the order was about to be executed, the Confederates fiercely

A BRIDGE OVER THE MUDDY CHICKAHOMINY—1862

This is a photograph of the insignificant stream that figured so largely in the calculations of the opposing generals before Richmond. Under the effect of the almost tropical rains, in a day luxuriant meadows would become transformed into lakes, and surging floods appear where before were stagnant pools. Thus it became doubtful in June whether the struggling Union army could depend upon the little bridges. It was said by some of the Union engineers that it was only the weight of the troops passing over them that held some in place. One was swept away immediately after a column had crossed. The muddy banks show more plainly than words what the little Chickahominy could do when it was thoroughly aroused.

[G—15]

attacked the Union right, and the most serious fighting of the day resulted. At four o'clock in the afternoon, a large Confederate infantry force being reported at Brandy Station, General Pleasonton began a general withdrawal of the Union cavalry, a movement which was executed in good order and completed by seven o'clock in the evening without molestation by the Confederates.

This great cavalry battle lasted for over ten hours, and was preeminently a mounted combat, the charges and counter-charges of the opposing horsemen being of the most desperate character. During the day, the First New Jersey Cavalry, alone, made six regimental charges, besides a number of smaller ones; the fighting and charging of the regular and Sixth Pennsylvania Cavalry was kept up for over twelve hours; and the other regiments were almost equally engaged through the eventful day.

Commenting on this defeat of the Confederate cavalry at Brandy Station, the *Richmond Examiner* of that period said:

The surprise of this occasion was the most complete that has occurred. The Confederate cavalry was carelessly strewn over the country, with the Rappahannock only between it and an enemy who has already proven his enterprise to our cost. It is said that their camp was supposed to be secure because the Rappahannock was not supposed to be fordable at the point where it actually was forded. What! Do the Yankees then know more about this river than our own soldiers, who have done nothing but ride up and down its banks for the past six months?

Brandy Station was really the turning-point in the evolution of the Federal cavalry, which had heretofore been dominated by a sense of its own inferiority to Stuart's bold horsemen. Even the Confederate writer, McClellan, has this to say of Brandy Station and its effect on the *morale* of the Union cavalry:

Up to this time, confessedly inferior to the Southern horsemen, they gained on this day that confidence in themselves and their commanders

REUNION OF OFFICERS

OF THE THIRD AND FOURTH PENNSYLVANIA

CAVALRY

The soldiers in a great war-game make merry while they can. This photograph shows the officers of the Third and Fourth Pennsylvania Cavalry picknicking on the banks of the river at Westover Landing in August, 1862. The Fourth Pennsylvania had taken part in the actions on the upper Chickahominy hardly a month before, when the Fifth United States Cavalry made their daring charge at Gaines' Mill. Both regiments had been active in the Peninsula campaign, although the Third Pennsylvania had been split up into detachments and on headquarters duty, and they were to be together on the bloody days at Antietam the middle of the following month. They have snatched a brief moment together now, and are hopefully pledging each other long lives. Neither the Union nor the Confederacy realized that the war was to stretch out over four terrible years.

which enabled them to contest so fiercely the subsequent battlefields of June, July, and October.

Passing by without comment the splendid stand of Buford's dismounted troops covering the approaches to the town of Gettysburg, in which less than three thousand cavalrymen and Calef's battery made possible the occupation by the delayed Union army of the dominating position along Cemetery Ridge and the Round Tops, the desperate battles of the cavalry on the right and left flanks at Gettysburg, are history.

On the Union left flank, Pleasonton had ordered Kilpatrick to move from Emmittsburg with his entire force to prevent a Confederate turning movement on the Round Tops, and, if practicable, to attack the Confederate flank and rear. Late on July 3, 1863, the reserve cavalry brigade under Merritt moved up and took position to the left of Kilpatrick. Custer's brigade had been detached to report to Gregg on the Union right. The fight which ensued on this third and last day of the great battle, was severe in the extreme.

Merritt's position on the left caused the Confederate general, Law, to detach a large force from his main line to protect his flank and rear. This so weakened the Confederate line in front of General Farnsworth, that Kilpatrick ordered the latter to charge the center of Law's line of infantry. The ground was most unfavorable for a mounted charge, being broken, covered with stone, and intersected by fences and stone walls.

Writing of this charge in "Battles and Leaders of the Civil War," Captain H. C. Parsons of the First Vermont Cavalry, says:

I was near Kilpatrick when he impetuously gave the order to Farnsworth to make the last charge. Farnsworth spoke with emotion: "General, do you mean it? Shall I throw my handful of men over rough ground, through timber, against a brigade of infantry? The First Vermont has already been fought half to pieces; these are too good men to kill." Kilpatrick said: "Do you refuse to obey my orders? If you are afraid to lead this charge, I will lead it."

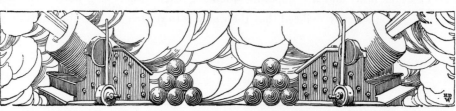

HELD BY THE CAVALRY AT ANTIETAM

The Federal cavalry bore its share of the work on the bloodiest single day of the war, September 17, 1862, at Antietam. At this bridge on the Keedysville road the gallant cavalry leader General Pleasonton had a most important part to play in the plan of attack on the Confederate positions west of Antietam Creek. In spite of galling cross-fire from the Confederate batteries, Pleasonton threw forward his mounted skirmishers, who held their ground until Tidball's batteries of the regular artillery were advanced piece by piece across the bridge. Opening with canister, the guns routed the sharpshooters, and soon four batteries were in position on the ridge beyond the creek. Here they held their ground till nightfall, at times running short of ammunition, but giving needed aid to Sumner's advance to their right and in Burnside's desperate struggle to cross the bridge below to their left. To the left of the bridge where Pleasonton's successful crossing on the morning of the 17th was accomplished stands Newcomers' Mill. On the ridge above, the cavalry and artillery held their positions, keeping open a way for reenforcements. These were much needed when the ammunition of the batteries ran low. More regular troops were sent forward, together with two more batteries from Sykes' division, under command of Captain Dryer. These reenforcements threw themselves splendidly into the fight. The cavalry had scored again.

NEWCOMERS' MILL ON ANTIETAM CREEK

Farnsworth rose in his stirrups—he looked magnificent in his passion—and cried, " Take that back ! " Kilpatrick returned his defiance, but, soon repenting, said, " I did not mean it ; forget it."

For a moment there was silence, when Farnsworth spoke calmly, " General, if you order the charge, I will lead it, but you must take the responsibility."

I did not hear the low conversation that followed, but as Farnsworth turned away, he said, " I will obey your order." Kilpatrick said earnestly, " I take the responsibility."

The charge was a daring and spectacular one. The First West Virginia, and Eighteenth Pennsylvania moved through the woods first, closely followed by the First Vermont and Fifth New York Cavalry, all mounted, and drove the foe before them until heavy stone walls and fences were reached. Two regiments cleared the obstacles, charged a second line of infantry, and were stopped by another stone wall, covering a third line of infantry. The First West Virginia was for a time entirely surrounded, but succeeded in cutting its way back with a loss of but five killed and four wounded, bringing with it a number of prisoners. When the body of Farnsworth was afterwards recovered, it was found to have received five mortal wounds.

General W. M. Graham, U. S. A. (Retired), says: *

The following is the account of Farnsworth's death as seen by a Confederate officer and by him related to me in the winter of 1876–77 at Columbia, South Carolina: I was introduced to Captain Bachman, who commanded the " Hampton Legion Battery," with which I was engaged (Battery K, First United States Artillery), at Gettysburg on July 3d. Naturally our conversation drifted to the war, and he remarked: " One of the most gallant incidents of the war witnessed by me was a cavalry charge at the battle of Gettysburg, on July 3d, made by a General Farnsworth of the Yankee army. He led his brigade, riding well ahead of his men, in a charge against my battery and the infantry supports ; we were so filled with admiration of his bravery that we were reluctant

*Journal Military Service Institution for March, 1910, p. 343.

DUFFIÉ, WHO LED THE CHARGE AT KELLY'S FORD

Led by Colonel Alfred Duffié, the dashing cavalryman whose portrait is above, Federal cavalry had its first opportunity to measure itself in a real trial of strength with the hardy horsemen of the South at Kelly's Ford on March 17, 1863. Brigadier-General William W. Averell, in command of the Second Division, Cavalry Corps, Army of the Potomac, received orders to cross the river with 3,000 cavalry and six pieces of artillery, and attack and destroy the forces of General Fitzhugh Lee, supposed to be near Culpeper Court House. Starting from Morrisville with about 2,100 men, General Averell found the crossing at Kelly's Ford obstructed by abatis and defended by sharpshooters. The First Rhode Island Cavalry effected a crossing, and the battle-line was formed on the farther side of the river. Colonel Duffié on the Federal left flank, and Colonel McIntosh on the right led almost simultaneous charges. The entire body of Confederate cavalry was driven back in confusion. The Confederates made another stand three-quarters of a mile farther back in the woods, but when the Federal cavalry finally withdrew, their killed and wounded were 78, and those of the Confederates 133.

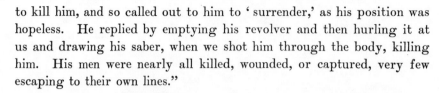

to kill him, and so called out to him to 'surrender,' as his position was hopeless. He replied by emptying his revolver and then hurling it at us and drawing his saber, when we shot him through the body, killing him. His men were nearly all killed, wounded, or captured, very few escaping to their own lines."

General Graham adds, "Bachman was a fine fellow who, like *all* those who *fought* on each side, had buried all bitterness of feeling."

All things considered, it seems wonderful that these four regiments did not suffer more severely (sixty-five casualties out of three hundred men in the charge). This fact can best be accounted for by the moral effect of the charge, the fearless troopers leaping the obstacles and sabering many of the Confederate infantry in their positions. The Confederate general, Law, said of this:

It was impossible to use our artillery to any advantage, owing to the close quarters of the attacking cavalry with our own men, the leading squadrons forcing their horses up to the very muzzles of the rifles of our infantry.

But while this was taking place on the Federal left flank, a great cavalry battle, fraught with tremendous responsibilities, was being waged on the right flank.

On July 3d, the Second Cavalry Division, under Gregg, had been ordered to the right of the line with orders to make a demonstration against the Confederates. About noon, a despatch reached Gregg that a large body of the Southern cavalry was observed from Cemetery Hill, moving against the right of the Union line. In consequence of this important information, Custer's brigade, which had been ordered back to Kilpatrick's command, was held by Gregg.

This Confederate column moving to the attack was Stuart's cavalry, which, belated by many obstacles, was advancing toward the lines of Ewell's corps. Stuart took position on a ridge, which commanded a wide area of open ground, and

[234]

COPYRIGHT, 1911, REVIEW OF REVIEWS CO.

THE HOLLOW SQUARE IN THE CIVIL WAR—A FORMATION USED AT GETTYSBURG

Many authorities doubted that the formation portrayed in this picture was used at the battle of Gettysburg. Not until the meeting of the survivors of the First Corps at Gettysburg in May, 1885, were these doubts finally dispelled. Late in the afternoon of July 1st General Buford had received orders from General Howard to go to General Doubleday's support. Buford's cavalry lay at that time a little west of the cemetery. Though vastly outnumbered by the advancing Confederate infantry, Buford formed his men for the charge. The Confederates immediately set to forming squares in echelon. This consumed time, however, and the respite materially aided in the escape of the First Corps, if it did not save the remnant from capture. Cavalry in the Civil War was not wont to charge unbroken infantry, the latter being better able to withstand a cavalry charge than cavalry itself. In such a charge the cavalry ranks become somewhat blended, and arrive in clusters on the opposing lines. The horses avoid trampling on the fallen and wounded, and jump over them if possible. Buford's threatened charge was a successful ruse.

TWO LEADERS OF THE FEDERAL CAVALRY AT GETTYSBURG

This martial photograph portrays two of the men who prevented the success of the Confederate General Stuart's charge on the third day at Gettysburg, when the tide of battle between the long lines of infantry had been wavering to and fro, and Pickett was advancing on Cemetery Ridge. Had the brilliant Stuart with his veteran cavalry gained the rear of the Federal line, the natural panic following might have been more than sufficient to win the day for the Confederate cause. About noon on July 3d, General Gregg was informed that a large body of Confederate cavalry was moving against the right of the line. General

PLEASONTON AND CUSTER, THREE MONTHS BEFORE THE BATTLE

Gregg held Custer's brigade, which had been ordered back to the left of the line, in order to help meet the attack. The Seventh Michigan Cavalry met the charge of a regiment of W. H. F. Lee's brigade, and this was followed by a charge of the First Michigan, driving back the Confederate line. Then followed counter-charges by the Confederates until a large part of both commands were fighting desperately. In this terrible cavalry combat every possible weapon was utilized. This photograph of Pleasonton on the right, who commanded all the cavalry at Gettysburg, and of the dashing Custer, was taken three months before.

SOME OF PLEASONTON'S MEN

AT GETTYSBURG

These men and mere boys stood seriously before the camera.   Without a trace of swagger they leaned upon their flashing sabers; yet they had seen all the important cavalry fighting in the East before their final supreme test at Gettysburg.   They had fought at Fair Oaks and the Seven Days around Richmond.   They had played their part at Kelly's Ford and in the great cavalry battle at Brandy Station.   They came to Gettysburg seasoned troopers, with poise and confidence in themselves.   On the first day Gregg's Second Cavalry Division, of which they formed part, fought the Second Virginia on foot with carbines.   On the second day they were deployed as dismounted skirmishers to meet Stuart's men.   The Confederate cavalry leader hoped to charge at the opportune moment when Pickett was advancing, but Pleasonton's men frus-

COMPANY D

THIRD PENNSYLVANIA CAVALRY

trated this attempt. The desperate charges and counter-charges on the Union right on that third decisive day were the fiercest of the entire war. This photograph was taken seven months later at Brandy Station, a few weeks before the Third Pennsylvania went into the Wilderness. Their time intervening since the battle of Gettysburg has been spent scouting and picketing along the Rappahannock, including many a skirmish with their active adversaries. They have had time to spruce up a bit during one of their short rests, but their quiet veteran bearing reflects the scenes they have passed through. Their swords that gleam so brilliantly are the regulation light curved cavalry sabers. With these and all other needed articles of equipment they and most of the Federal cavalry are now thoroughly equipped.

his plan of attack was to engage the Federal troops in his front with sharpshooters, while he moved the Confederate brigades of Jenkins and W. F. H. Lee secretly through the woods in an effort to reach the Union rear. Stuart hoped to strike at the psychological moment when Pickett's famous infantry charge, on the center of the Union line of battle, would engage the entire attention of the Army of the Potomac.

The cavalry combat which followed was probably as desperate and as stubbornly contested as any in which the cavalry took part during the entire period of the war. A mounted charge by a regiment of W. F. H. Lee's brigade, was met by a countercharge of the Seventh Michigan Cavalry, the two regiments meeting face to face on opposite sides of a stone wall, and discharging their carbines point blank. The First Michigan Cavalry, aided by Chester's battery made a charge which, followed by a hand-to-hand fight, drove the Confederate lines back in confusion. Then followed charges and countercharges by each opponent, until a large part of both commands was involved in a general mêlée.

In this terrible cavalry combat every possible weapon was utilized, and after it was over, men were found interlocked in each other's arms, with fingers so firmly imbedded in the flesh as to require force to remove them. The casualties were heavy for both Stuart and Gregg, but the latter was able to stop the Confederate cavalry leader's critical turning movement. Had Stuart with his veteran cavalry been able to strike the rear of the Federal army simultaneously with Pickett's infantry charge in front, the result of this decisive battle of the war might have been different.

On April 4, 1864, General Sheridan assumed command of the cavalry of the Army of the Potomac, and thereafter a new order of things was inaugurated for the Union cavalry in the Eastern theater of operations.

Sheridan insisted that his cavalry should not be separated into fragments, but should be concentrated "to fight the

CAVALRY FROM INDIANA—A FIGHTING REGIMENT AT GETTYSBURG AND ELSEWHERE

Looking at the resolute faces and confident mien of these boys from what was then the far-western State of Indiana, the reader, even of a later generation, understands instantly how it was that the Western cavalry of the Federal army earned such an enviable reputation from '61 to '65. Not only did it protect the fast-spreading Federal frontier in the West; not only did it bear the brunt of the raids conducted by the dashing leaders Grierson, Smith, Wilson, and others, whereby the more southern portions of the Confederacy were cut off from their supplies and deprived of their stores; but States like Indiana also provided several of the most conspicuously gallant regiments that served with the Eastern armies. This Third Indiana, for instance, was busy East and West. At Nashville, at Shiloh, at Stone's River, at Chattanooga, at Atlanta, and on Sherman's march to the sea, it did its duty in the West, while six companies of the regiment participated in Buford's stand at Gettysburg.

enemy's cavalry," and in deference to Sheridan's wishes, General Meade promptly relieved the cavalry from much of the arduous picket duty which it was performing at the time. But he gave little encouragement as yet to Sheridan's plans for an *independent* cavalry corps—a corps in fact as well as in name. By the end of July, the Cavalry Corps had succeeded in almost annihilating the Confederate cavalry and had accomplished the destruction of millions of dollars' worth of property useful to the Confederate Government. In all the important movements of the Army of the Potomac, the cavalry had acted as a screen, and by its hostile demonstrations against the Southern flanks and rear, had more than once forced General Lee to detach much-needed troops from his hard-pressed front.

On May 11th, at Yellow Tavern, Sheridan had fought an engagement which gave him complete control of the road to Richmond and resulted in the loss to the Confederates of Generals Stuart and James B. Gordon. Merritt's brigade first entered Yellow Tavern and secured possession of the turnpike. The other Union divisions being brought up, Custer with his own brigade, supported by Chapman's brigade of Wilson's division, made a mounted charge which was brilliantly executed, followed by a dash at the Southern line which received the charge in a stationary position. This charge resulted in the capture of two guns. Then, while Gibbs and Devin forced the Confederate right and center, Gregg charged in the rear and the battle was won.

At Deep Bottom, too, July 28th, occurred a brilliant fight which is worthy of more than passing notice.

The Second United States Cavalry led the advance on the 27th and took the New Market road in the direction of Richmond. When close to the Confederate pickets a dashing charge was made, forcing the foe back rapidly. On the afternoon of the following day the Union cavalry pickets were furiously attacked, and before the leading troops could dismount and conduct the led horses to the rear, an entire brigade of

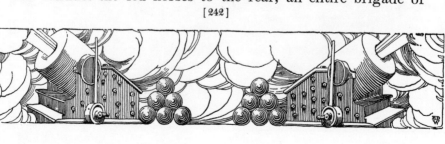

WHERE THE CAVALRY RESTED—CASTLE MURRAY, NEAR AUBURN, VIRGINIA

In the fall of 1863 the headquarters of the Army of the Potomac were pitched for some days on the Warrentown Railroad near Auburn, Virginia. Near-by lay Dr. Murray's house, called the Castle, a picturesque gray stone edifice, beautifully contrasting with the dark green ivy which had partly overgrown it, and situated in a grove on an eminence known as Rockhill. Here General Pleasonton, commanding the cavalry, had his camp, his tents forming an effective picture when silhouetted by the setting sun against the gray walls of the Castle. At night the green lamps that showed the position of the general's camp would shine mysteriously over the trees, and the band of the Sixth United States Cavalry would make the stone walls echo to its martial music. The cavalry was resting after its desperate encounters at Gettysburg and its fights along the Rappahannock. But there remained much yet for the troopers to do.

[G—16]

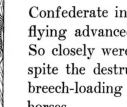

Confederate infantry broke from the woods, and with colors flying advanced in splendid alignment across an open field. So closely were the advanced Union troops pressed, that despite the destruction wrought in the Southern ranks by the breech-loading carbines, there was danger of losing the led horses.

The following is quoted from the graphic description of this fight by Lieutenant (afterwards Colonel U. S. V.) William H. Harrison, Second United States Cavalry:

With a cheer which makes our hearts bound, the First New York Dragoons, the First United States, and the Sixth Pennsylvania on the run, dismount, and form themselves on the shattered lines of the Second and Fifth. A few volleys from our carbines make the line of the enemy's infantry waver, and in an instant the cry is heard along our entire line, "Charge! Charge!" We rush forward, firing as we advance; the Confederate colors fall, and so furious is our charge that the North Carolina brigade breaks in complete rout, leaving three stands of colors, all their killed and wounded, and many prisoners in our hands. The enemy did not renew the fight, and we remained in possession of the field until relieved by our infantry.

It was, however, in the fall of the year (1864) that under Sheridan's brilliant leadership the Union cavalry won its greatest laurels. On September 19th, at Opequon Creek, Sheridan's infantry and cavalry achieved a victory which sent the Confederates under Early "whirling through Winchester," as Sheridan tersely stated in a telegram which electrified the people of the North.

While essentially a battle participated in by all arms, the brilliant part taken by Wilson's division in a mounted charge which gained possession of the ·Winchester-Berryville turnpike, and the subsequent demoralizing attack of Averell's and Merritt's cavalry divisions on the Confederate rear, had much to do with the Union victory.

The most severe fighting on the part of the cavalry took place in the afternoon. Breckinridge's Confederate corps had

[244]

BURNETT'S HOUSE, NEAR COLD HARBOR

A CLOSER VIEW

Three days before these photographs were taken Brigadier-General Alfred T. A. Torbert, with an isolated command of cavalry, was holding the breastworks at Cold Harbor in face of a magnificent attack by a brigade of Confederate infantry. The troopers busy beneath the trees are some of the very men who stood off the long gray lines blazing with fire. In the lower photograph they have moved forward, so that we can study them more closely. They seem quite nonchalant, considering their recent experience, but that is a veteran's way. Burnett's house, here pictured, stood not far from the road leading from Old Church Hotel to Old Cold Harbor. It was along this road that Torbert pursued the Confederates in the afternoon of May 30th, and it was near this house that his division of Sheridan's Cavalry Corps bivouacked that night. The following morning he continued his pursuit, first driving the Confederates into their breastworks at Cold Harbor, and then executing a flank movement to the left, which forced the Southern infantry to fall back three-quarters of a mile farther. Sheridan ordered him to withdraw from this isolated position, and he returned to the scene of his bivouac near Burnett's house.

OLD CHURCH HOTEL NEAR COLD HARBOR

The very attitude of the rough and ready cavalryman with his curved saber shows the new confidence in itself of the Federal cavalry as reorganized by Sheridan in April, 1864. Here the photographer has caught a cavalry detail at one of the typical cross-roads taverns that played so important a part in the Virginia campaigns of that year. So successful is the picture that even the rude lettering "Old Church Hotel" on the quaint, old fashioned swinging sign can be made out. The scene is typical of the times. The reorganized Federal cavalry was proving of the greatest help to Grant in locating the enemy, particularly ahead of the main column as in the case of the fight at Old Church. In Grant's advance toward Richmond from North Anna, Sheridan's cavalry corps served as an advance

FOUR DAYS AFTER THE CAVALRY CLASH OF MAY 30, 1864

guard. Torbert and Gregg with the First and Second Divisions formed the guard for the left flank. On May 27th Torbert crossed the Pamunkey at Hanover Ferry, captured Hanover Town, took part the following day in the sanguinary struggle at Hawes' Shop, and on the 29th picketed the country about Old Church Hotel seen in the picture, and toward Cold Harbor. At 4 P.M. on May 30th, the clash at Old Church took place, and it was necessary to put in General Merritt with the Reserve Brigade. The photograph was taken on June 4th, the day after the battle of Cold Harbor where the Federal loss was so severe. The horses look sleek and well-conditioned in spite of the constant marching and fighting.

fallen back on Winchester, leaving General Early's flank protected by his cavalry, which was successfully attacked by General Devin's Second Brigade and driven in confusion toward Winchester. Then within easy supporting distance of each other, the First Brigade, the Second Brigade, and the Reserve Brigade moved forward without opposition until the open fields near Winchester were reached.

What followed is well described in Lieutenant Harrison's recollections: *

While awaiting in suspense our next movement the enemy's infantry was distinctly seen attempting to change front to meet our anticipated charge. Instantly, and while in the confusion incident to their maneuver, the Second Brigade burst upon them, the enemy's infantry breaking into complete rout and falling back a confused and broken mass.

Immediately after, the Union reserve brigade under the gallant Lowell, formed to the left of the position from which the Second Brigade, under Devin, had just charged. They rode out fearlessly within five hundred yards of the Confederate line of battle, on the left of which, resting on an old earthwork was a two-gun battery. The order was given to charge the line and get the guns. Lieutenant Harrison continues:

At the sound of the bugle we took the trot, the gallop, and then the charge. As we neared their line we were welcomed by a fearful musketry fire, which temporarily confused the leading squadron, and caused the entire brigade to oblique slightly to the right. Instantly, officers cried out, "Forward! Forward!" The men raised their sabers, and responded to the command with deafening cheers. Within a hundred yards of the enemy's line we struck a blind ditch, but crossed it without breaking our front. In a moment we were face to face with the enemy. They stood as if awed by the heroism of the brigade, and in an instant broke in complete rout, our men sabering them as they vainly sought safety in flight.

* Everglade to Cañon, N. Y., 1873.

[248]

AFTER WINCHESTER—GENERAL THOMAS C. DEVIN AND STAFF

"We have just sent them whirling through Winchester, and we are after them to-morrow," was Sheridan's exultant wire of September 19, 1864, which electrified the North. Washington breathed a deep sigh of relief, and Sheridan's men started on the pursuit of Early. It was at Fisher's Hill on the 21st that the next clash occurred, and after a severe engagement of the infantry, Sheridan secured an advantageous position. On the 22d Early's rout was made complete. All that night the Federal infantry with Devin's brigade of cavalry pushed on in pursuit of the demoralized Confederates. Devin overtook them north of Mount Jackson, and had he been properly supported could doubtless have taken thousands of prisoners.

The charging force emerged from the fight with two guns, three stands of colors, and over three hundred Confederate prisoners. Altogether there had been six distinct charges by parts of the First Cavalry Division—two by the Second Brigade and one by the First Brigade; one by the Second Brigade and one by the Reserve Brigade against Early's infantry; and one, the final charge, in which all three of the brigades joined. General Custer describes the scene in graphic language:

At this time five brigades of cavalry were moving on parallel lines; most, if not all, of the brigades moved by brigade front, regiments being in parallel columns of squadrons. One continuous and heavy line of skirmishers covered the advance, using only the carbine, while the line of brigades, as they advanced across the country, the bands playing the national airs, presented in the sunlight one moving mass of glittering sabers. This, combined with the various and bright-colored banners and battle-flags, intermingled here and there with the plain blue uniforms of the troops, furnished one of the most inspiring as well as imposing scenes of martial grandeur ever witnessed upon a battlefield.

The Union victory at Opequon came at a time when its moral effect was most needed in the North, and restored the fertile Shenandoah valley to the Union armies, after a long series of humiliating reverses in that granary of the Confederacy.

A month later Custer encountered three brigades of Confederate cavalry under Rosser near Tom's Brook Crossing. Merrit at about the same time struck the cavalry of Lomax and Johnson on the Valley pike, the Federal line of battle extending across the Valley. The fighting was desperate on both sides, being essentially a saber contest. For two hours charges were given and received in solid masses, boot-to-boot, the honors being almost equally divided—the Confederates successfully holding the center while the Federal cavalry pushed back the flanks.

This finally weakened the Confederates, and as both their

GENERAL TORBERT IN THE SHENANDOAH

This photograph, made in the Shenandoah Valley in the fall of 1864, shows General Alfred T. A. Torbert, immaculately clad in a natty uniform, on the steps of a beautiful vine-clad cottage. Virginia homes such as this fared but badly in that terrible October. The black shame of war spread over the valley and rose in the smoke from burning barns. Grant had resolved that Shenandoah should no longer be allowed to act as a granary for the armies of the Confederacy. Sheridan and his men had orders ruthlessly to destroy all supplies that could not be carried away. The Confederate cavalry clung desperately to his rear, and gave so much annoyance that on October 8th Sheridan directed Torbert "to give Rosser a drubbing next morning or get whipped himself." The saber contest that ensued at Tom's Brook was the last attempt of the Confederate cavalry to reestablish their former supremacy. The sight of the devastated valley spurred the Southern troopers to the most valiant attacks, in spite of their inferior equipment. Again and again were charges made and returned on both sides. For two hours the honors were almost even, the Confederates holding the center, while the Federal cavalry pushed back the flanks. Finally Merritt and Custer ordered a charge along the whole line, and at last the Confederates broke.

flanks gave way, Merritt and Custer ordered a charge along their entire line. The retreat of Rosser's force became a panic-stricken rout, which continued for twenty-six miles up the Shenandoah valley. Eleven pieces of artillery, three hundred and thirty prisoners, ambulances, caissons, and even the headquarters' wagons of the Confederate commanders were captured by the Federal troops.

Early ascribed his defeat to Sheridan's superiority in numbers and equipment, and to the fact that Lomax's cavalry was armed entirely with rifles and had no sabers; that as a consequence they could not fight on horseback, and in open country could not successfully fight on foot with large bodies of well-trained cavalry.

In the brilliant part taken by Sheridan's cavalry in retrieving the misfortunes of the morning of October 19, 1864, when the Union camp at Cedar Creek was surprised and routed—with " Sheridan only twenty miles away "—resulting in the final defeat and pursuit of the Confederate army, the Federal cavalry alone captured 45 pieces of artillery, 32 caissons, 46 army wagons, 672 prisoners, and an enormous quantity of other property.

This battle, which Sheridan's magnetic presence turned into a great victory, was followed by a number of small but highly successful cavalry movements, culminating on March 27, 1865, in Sheridan's veteran cavalry corps joining the Army of the Potomac in front of Petersburg for the final campaign against Lee.

In the Valley campaign Sheridan's cavalry captured 2556 prisoners, 71 guns, 29 battle-flags, 52 caissons, 105 army wagons, 2557 horses, 1000 horse equipments, and 7152 beef cattle. It destroyed, among other things, 420,742 bushels of wheat, 780 barns, and over 700,000 rounds of ammunition.

Meanwhile, during the years of vicissitudes which marked the evolution of the cavalry of the East, from a multitude of weak detachments lacking organization, equipment,

CAVALRY THAT CLOSED IN ON RICHMOND

While Sheridan's troopers were distinguishing themselves in the Shenandoah, the cavalry of the Army of the James, which was closing around Richmond, were doing their part. This photograph shows the Fifth Pennsylvania Cavalry, or "Cameron Dragoons," part of the second brigade, in winter-quarters. It was taken in the fall of 1864, on the scene of the engagement at Fair Oaks and Darbytown Road, October 29th of that year. Brigadier-General August V. Kautz had led them on a raid on the Petersburg and Weldon Railroad May 5th to 11th, and on the Richmond and Danville Railroad May 12th to 17th. On June 9th they went to Petersburg and remained there during the siege operations until the Southern Capital fell. During all this time they reversed the situation of the early part of the war, and incessantly harassed the Army of Northern Virginia by constant raids, cutting its communications, and attacking its supply trains.

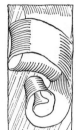

and training to a veteran army, filled with confidence in itself and in its commanders, the cavalry of the West had been equally unfortunate in its slow and discouraging development of fighting efficiency.

Under General Rosecrans, as early as 1862, the cavalry of the Army of the Cumberland was organized into three brigades under General David S. Stanley, but the mounted force actually at the disposal of its commander was but four thousand effective men. Although actively engaged, particularly in curbing the depredations of the Confederate cavalry under Forrest, its operations were not especially important. Nevertheless, at Stone's River, at Knoxville, at Chickamauga, and at other important battles, the cavalry of the West did desperate fighting and, considering its numbers, was not lacking in efficiency.

The cavalry which General Sherman assembled for his Atlanta campaign numbered about fifteen thousand sabers, organized into four divisions, and it participated with credit in all the celebrated movements and engagements of Sherman's army between May and August, 1864. Protecting the rear and preventing the destruction of the Nashville and Chattanooga Railroad by Wheeler's enterprising cavalry, some Union cavalry under Rousseau remained at Decatur until by a rapid and circuitous march around Johnston's Confederate army, in which he destroyed immense quantities of stores and damaged several railroads, Rousseau joined Sherman near Atlanta. After the fall of the latter city, a cavalry division of over five thousand men under Kilpatrick, accompanied Sherman on his famous march to the sea.

Up to this time the activities of the Union cavalry in the Southwest, while noted for boldness and celerity of movement, for endurance, and for accomplishment of results, though hampered by many drawbacks, were not yet distinguished by any of those great cavalry combats which marked the development of the cavalry of the Army of the Potomac.

[254]

RICHMOND AT LAST—APRIL, 1865

There is no need now for the troopers' carbines which can be seen projecting beside their saddles just as the cavalry rode into Richmond. The smoke still rising from the city's ruins seems to be the last great shuddering sigh of the Confederacy. The sight of the stark, blackened walls rising around them in the noonday sun brings but little joy to the hearts of the troopers. These ruined piles of brick and mortar are the homes of their brothers who fought a good fight. A few days from now, in the fullness of their hearts, the Union soldiers will be cheering their erstwhile foes at Appomattox. One more cavalry exploit, the capture of Lee's provision trains by Sheridan, which Grant in his delicacy did not reveal to the stricken commander, and the cavalry operations are over. Horses and men go back to the pursuits of peace.

Towards the close of October, 1864, however, General James H. Wilson, who had commanded a cavalry division in Sheridan's Army of the Shenandoah, and who had been instrumental in raising the efficiency of the cavalry service through the Cavalry Bureau, reported to Sherman, in Alabama, and began a thorough reorganization, a remounting and re-equipping of the cavalry corps of Sherman's army.

Wilson's cavalry corps speedily made itself felt as an integral part of the army, taking a prominent part in the battle of Franklin, scoring a decisive victory over Forrest's cavalry under Chalmers, and pressing the foe so closely that the Confederate troopers were actually driven into the Harpeth River. This decisive action of the Union cavalry prevented Forrest from turning Schofield's left flank and cutting his line of retreat.

In the battle of Nashville, which followed (December 15–16, 1864), Wilson's dismounted cavalry gallantly stormed the strong Confederate earthworks side by side with their comrades of the infantry. General Thomas mentions the part taken by this cavalry as follows:

Whilst slightly swinging to the left, [the cavalry] came upon a redoubt containing four guns, which was splendidly carried by assault, at 1 P.M., by a portion of Hatch's division, dismounted, and the captured guns turned upon the enemy. A second redoubt, stronger than the first, was next assailed and carried by the same troops that carried the first position, taking four more guns and about three hundred prisoners. The infantry, McArthur's division, on the left of the cavalry, . . . participated in both of the assaults; and, indeed, the dismounted cavalry seemed to vie with the infantry who should first gain the works; as they reached the position nearly simultaneously, both lay claim to the artillery and prisoners captured.

But the gallant part taken by Wilson's cavalry in these operations is best exemplified by the spoils of war. During and after the battle of Nashville, and including prisoners taken in the hospitals at Franklin, the Union cavalry captured 2 strong redoubts, 32 field guns, 11 caissons, 12 colors, 3232

THE FEDERAL CAVALRY AND THEIR REWARD—MAY, 1865

Shoulders squared, accouterments shining, all of the troops in perfect alignment, a unified, splendidly equipped and disciplined body, the Federal cavalry marched up Pennsylvania Avenue on that glorious sunshiny day in May when the Union armies held their grand review in Washington. What a change from the long night rides and the terrible moments of the crashing charge was this holiday parade, when not a trooper thought of sleeping in the saddle which had often proved his only bed. The battles are over now. Never again will their ears be riven by the agonized shriek of a wounded horse, said by many a cavalryman to be the most horrible sound in the field of battle. Never again will they bend over the silent body of a wounded friend. Men die more quietly than their mounts. This is an arm of the service that proved itself. From early disappointments and disasters, and dissipation of energy in useless details, it emerged a wonderfully effective fighting force that did much to hasten the surrender of the exhausted Confederacy.

prisoners (including 1 general officer), 1 bridge train of 80 pontoons, and 125 wagons. Its own losses were 122 officers and men killed, 1 field-gun, 521 wounded, and 259 missing.

The following spring, while Wilson and his horsemen were sapping the very life blood of the Confederacy, Sheridan and his cavalry of the Army of the Potomac had been playing a most important part in the grand operations of that remarkable army, now under the direction of the inexorable Grant.

After joining Grant in front of Petersburg on March 27, 1865, Sheridan received instruction from his chief to move with his three cavalry divisions of nine thousand men near or through Dinwiddie, reaching the right and rear of the Confederate army, without attempting to attack the Confederates in position. Should the latter remain entrenched, Sheridan was to destroy the Danville and South Side railroads, Lee's only avenues of supply; and then either return to the Army of the Potomac, or to join Sherman in North Carolina. History shows that two of the Confederate infantry divisions and all of Lee's cavalry failed to push back five brigades of Sheridan's cavalry, fighting dismounted, in an effort to cut off the Confederate retreat.

In the desperate fighting which took place in the days following, it was the same splendid cavalry at Five Forks, which dashed dismounted over the Southern entrenchments, carrying all before them.

And finally, on April 6th, at Sailor's Creek, after desperate and exhausting fighting by Custer's and Devin's divisions, it was Crook with his cavalry which intercepted the Confederate line of retreat, cut off three of Lee's hard-pressed infantry divisions, and made possible the surrender at Appomattox of the gallant but exhausted Army of Northern Virginia.

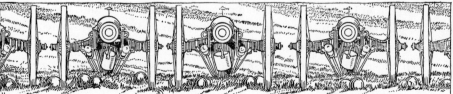

CHAPTER

TEN

CAVALRY LEADERS

NORTH AND SOUTH

CUSTER AND HIS DOG

SHERIDAN AND HIS RIGHT-HAND MEN

This photograph shows Sheridan and his leaders, who drove Early and the Confederate cavalry from the Shenandoah Valley, and brought the Federal cavalry to the zenith of its power. Sheridan stands at the extreme left of the picture. Next to him is General Forsyth, and General Merritt is seated at the table. General Devin stands with his hand on his hip, and Custer leans easily back in his chair. This is a ceremonious photograph; each leader wears the uniform of his rank. Even Custer has abandoned his favorite velvet suit. Together with the facing photograph, this offers an interesting study in the temperament of the Union cavalry leaders.

A STUDY IN TEMPERAMENT OF THE MEN WHO LED THE FEDERAL CAVALRY

The photographer has evidently requested the distinguished sitters to inspect a map, as if they were planning some actual movement such as that which "sent Early whirling through Winchester." All but Sheridan have been obliging. General Forsyth is leaning over, hand on chin, one foot on a rung of Merritt's chair. Merritt has cast down his eyes and bowed his head above the map. General Devin is leaning slightly forward in an attentive position. Custer alertly surveys his chief. But Sheridan, his hand clenched beside him, still gazes resolutely at the camera. These were the leaders who stood between the Confederate army and Washington, the capture of which might have meant foreign intervention.

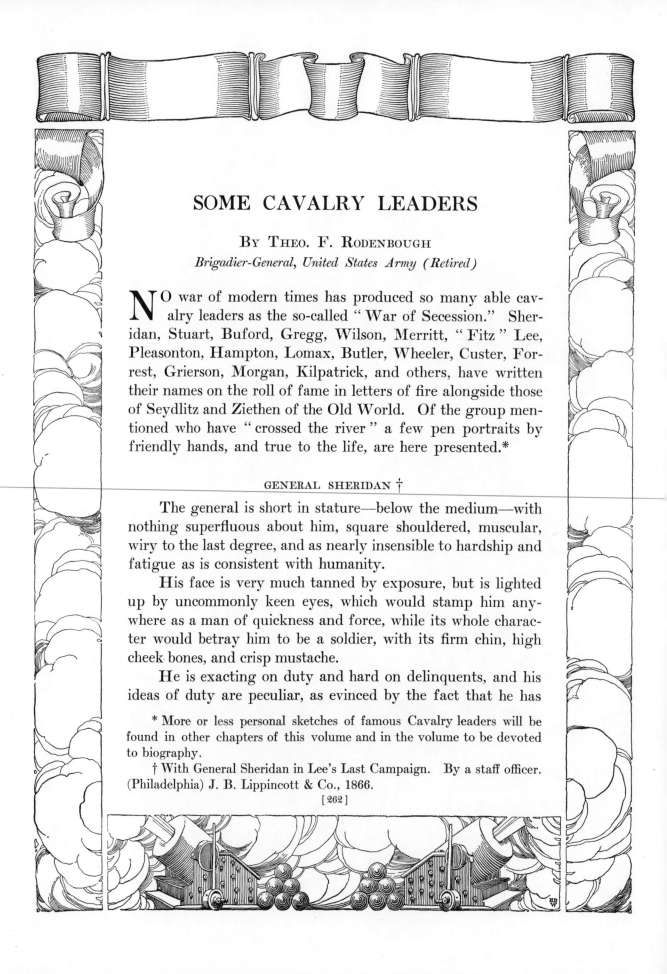

SOME CAVALRY LEADERS

By Theo. F. Rodenbough
Brigadier-General, United States Army (Retired)

NO war of modern times has produced so many able cavalry leaders as the so-called " War of Secession." Sheridan, Stuart, Buford, Gregg, Wilson, Merritt, " Fitz " Lee, Pleasonton, Hampton, Lomax, Butler, Wheeler, Custer, Forrest, Grierson, Morgan, Kilpatrick, and others, have written their names on the roll of fame in letters of fire alongside those of Seydlitz and Ziethen of the Old World. Of the group mentioned who have " crossed the river " a few pen portraits by friendly hands, and true to the life, are here presented.*

GENERAL SHERIDAN †

The general is short in stature—below the medium—with nothing superfluous about him, square shouldered, muscular, wiry to the last degree, and as nearly insensible to hardship and fatigue as is consistent with humanity.

His face is very much tanned by exposure, but is lighted up by uncommonly keen eyes, which would stamp him anywhere as a man of quickness and force, while its whole character would betray him to be a soldier, with its firm chin, high cheek bones, and crisp mustache.

He is exacting on duty and hard on delinquents, and his ideas of duty are peculiar, as evinced by the fact that he has

* More or less personal sketches of famous Cavalry leaders will be found in other chapters of this volume and in the volume to be devoted to biography.

† With General Sheridan in Lee's Last Campaign. By a staff officer. (Philadelphia) J. B. Lippincott & Co., 1866.

MAJOR–GENERAL PHILIP HENRY SHERIDAN

General Sheridan was the leader who relieved the Union cavalry from waste of energy and restored it an arm of the service as effective and terrible to the Confederacy as the Southern cavalry had been to the North at the outset of the war. He was born at Albany, N. Y., 1831, and graduated at West Point in 1853. In May, 1862, he was appointed colonel of the Second Michigan Cavalry, and served in northern Mississippi. In July he was appointed brigadier-general of volunteers and distinguished himself on October 8th at the battle of Perryville. He commanded a division of the Army of the Cumberland at Stone's River, and was appointed major-general of volunteers early in 1863. He took part in the pursuit of General Van Dorn, afterwards aided in the capture of Manchester, Tennessee, on June 27th, and was in the battle of Chickamauga. In the battles around Chattanooga he attracted the attention of General Grant. In April, 1864, he was placed in command of the cavalry corps of the Army of the Potomac, and its brilliant exploits under his leadership culminated in the death of General J. E. B. Stuart at Yellow Tavern, where the Confederates were defeated. In August, 1864, he was placed in command of the Army of the Shenandoah. He defeated General Early at Opequon Creek, Fisher's Hill, and Cedar Creek, and captured 5,000 of his men and several guns. He drove the Confederates from the valley and laid it waste. On September 10th he was made brigadier-general, and in November major-general. In July, 1865, he received the thanks of Congress for his distinguished services. He died at Nonquitt, Mass., on August 5, 1888.

THE LEADER'S EYES

never issued orders of encouragement or congratulations to his troops before or after campaigns or battles. He has apparently taken it for granted that all under his command would do as well as they could, and they did so quite as a matter of course. And to this soldierly view the troops always responded. Understanding so well what they were fighting for and the issues at stake, they would not fight harder to accomplish results simply for the satisfaction of having them recounted. . . .

Though always easy of approach, the general has little to say in busy times. Set teeth and a quick way tell when things do not go as they ought, and he has a manner on such occasions that stirs to activity all within sight, for a row seems brewing that nobody wants to be under when it bursts. Notwithstanding his handsome reputation for cursing, he is rather remarkably low-voiced, particularly on the field, where, as sometimes happens, almost everybody else is screaming. "Damn you, sir, don't yell at me," he once said to an officer who came galloping up with some bad news, and was roaring it out above the din of battle. In such moments the general leans forward on his horse's neck, and hunching his shoulders up to his ears, gives most softly spoken orders in a slow, deliberate way, as though there were niches for all the words in his hearer's memory, and they must be measured very carefully to fit exactly, that none of them be lost in the carrying. . . .

The general has a remarkable eye for topography, not only in using to the best advantage the peculiarities of the country through which he is campaigning, either for purposes of marching, assaults, or defense, but he can foresee with accuracy, by studying a map, how far the country will be available for these purposes.

He has been called ruthless and cruel because, in obedience to the orders of the officers appointed over him, he was compelled, by the stern necessities of war, to destroy property in the Shenandoah valley, and to take from the war-ridden people

MAJOR–GENERAL JAMES EWELL BROWN STUART, C.S.A.

In the hat on General Stuart's knee appears the plume which grew to symbolize the dash and gallantry of the man himself. Plume and hat were captured, and Stuart himself narrowly escaped, at Verdiersville, August 17, 1862. "I intend," he wrote, " to make the Yankees pay for that hat." Less than a week later he captured Pope's personal baggage and horses, and for many days thereafter the Federal general's uniform was on exhibition in a Richmond store window—a picturesque and characteristic reprisal. Born in Virginia in 1833, Stuart graduated at the United States Military Academy in 1854. He saw service on the Texas frontier, in Kansas, and against the Cheyenne Indians before the outbreak of the war. On April, 1861, he resigned from the United States Army and joined the Confederacy in his native State. He won distinction at Bull Run, and also the rank of brigadier-general. Stuart rode twice around the Army of the Potomac when McClellan was in command, and played a conspicuous part in the Seven Days before Richmond. At the second Bull Run, at Antietam, by a destructive raid into Pennsylvania, at Fredericksburg, and at Chancellorsville Stuart added to his laurels. He was too late for anything except the last day of Gettysburg, where the strengthened Union cavalry proved his match. He was mortally wounded at Yellow Tavern May 11, 1864, in a pitched battle with Sheridan's cavalry.

there what their friends had left them of supplies for man and beast. As he rode down the Martinsburg pike in his four-horse wagon, heels on the front seat, and smoking a cigar, while behind him his cavalry was destroying the provender that could not be carried away, the inhabitants of the Valley doubtless regarded him as history regards the emperor who fiddled while Rome was burning, and would not now believe, what is the simple truth, that this destruction was distasteful to him, and that he was moved by the distress he was obliged to multiply upon these unfortunate people, whose evil fate had left them in the ruinous track of war so long. But the Shenandoah valley was the well-worn pathway of invasion, and it became necessary that this long avenue leading to our homes should be stripped of the sustenance that rendered it possible to subsist an army there.

GENERAL STUART

Stuart was undoubtedly the most brilliant and widely known *sabreur* of his time. The term is used advisedly to describe the accomplished horseman who, while often fighting dismounted, yet by training and the influence of his environment was at his best as a leader of mounted men.

Stuart as a cadet at the Military Academy is thus described by General Fitzhugh Lee:

"I recall his distinguishing characteristics, which were a strict attention to his military duties, an erect, soldierly bearing, an immediate and almost thankful acceptance of a challenge to fight from any cadet who might in any way feel himself aggrieved, and a clear, metallic ringing voice."

In the Indian country as a subaltern in the cavalry, his commanding officer, Major Simonson, thus wrote of him:

"Lieutenant Stuart was brave and gallant, always prompt in the execution of orders, and reckless of danger or exposure. I considered him at that time one of the most promising young officers in the United States army."

[266]

MAJOR–GENERAL JOHN BUFORD

General Buford was one of the foremost cavalry leaders of the North. He is credited by many with having chosen the field on which the battle of Gettysburg was fought. He was born in 1826 in Woodford County, Kentucky, graduated at West Point in 1848, and saw service against the Indians. In November, 1861, he attained to the rank of major, and in July, 1862, he was made brigadier-general of volunteers. While in command of a cavalry brigade in 1862, Buford was wounded in the second battle of Bull Run. In McClellan's Maryland campaign, at Fredericksburg, and in the spirited cavalry engagements at Brandy Station, he played his part nobly. In Pennsylvania he displayed remarkable ability and opened the battle of Gettysburg before the arrival of Reynolds' infantry on July 1st. The Comte de Paris says in his "History of the Civil War in America": "It was Buford who selected the battlefield where the two armies were about to measure their strength." After taking part in the pursuit of Lee and subsequent operations in central Virginia, he withdrew on sick leave in November, 1863, and died in Washington on December 16th, receiving a commission as major-general only on the day of his death.

As a Confederate colonel at the first Bull Run battle, General Early reported:

"Stuart did as much toward saving the battle of First Manassas as any subordinate who participated in it; and yet he has never received any credit for it, in the official reports or otherwise. His own report is very brief and indefinite."

In a letter to President Davis, General J. E. Johnston recommended Stuart's promotion, which was made September 24, 1861:

"He is a rare man, wonderfully endowed by nature with the qualities necessary for an officer of light cavalry. Calm, firm, acute, active, and enterprising, I know of no one more competent than he to estimate the occurrences before him at their true value. If you add a real brigade of cavalry to this army, you can find no better brigadier-general to command it."

In an account of the raid into Pennsylvania (October, 1862) Colonel Alexander K. McClure speaks of the behavior of Stuart's command in passing through Chambersburg:

"General Stuart sat on his horse in the center of the town, surrounded by his staff, and his command was coming in from the country in large squads, leading their old horses and riding the new ones they had found in the stables hereabouts. General Stuart is of medium size, has a keen eye, and wears immense sandy whiskers and mustache. His demeanor to our people was that of a humane soldier. In several instances his men commenced to take private property from stores, but they were arrested by General Stuart's provost-guard. In a single instance only, that I heard of, did they enter a store by intimidating the proprietor. All of our stores and shops were closed, and with very few exceptions were not disturbed." *

General John B. Gordon, in his "Reminiscences" relates:

"An incident during the battle of Chancellorsville [illustrates] the bounding spirits of that great cavalry leader, General 'Jeb' Stuart. After Jackson's fall, Stuart was

* Campaigns of Stuart's Cavalry.

LIEUTENANT-GENERAL WADE HAMPTON, C.S.A.

General Hampton was the leader selected three months after Stuart's death to command all of Lee's cavalry. Although it had become sadly decimated, Hampton lived up to his reputation, and fought effectively to the very end of the war. His last command was the cavalry in Johnston's army, which opposed Sherman's advance from Savannah in 1865. Hampton was born in Columbia, S. C., in 1818. After graduating in law at the University of South Carolina, he gave up his time to the management of his extensive estates. At the outbreak of the war he raised and equipped from his private means the "Hampton's Legion," which did good service throughout the war. He fought at the head of his Legion at Bull Run and in the Peninsula campaign, was wounded at Fair Oaks, and soon afterward was commissioned brigadier-general. He served brilliantly at Gettysburg, where he was wounded three times, and was made major-general on August 3d following. He was engaged in opposing the advance of Sheridan toward Lynchburg in 1864, and showed such high qualities as a cavalry commander that he was commissioned lieutenant-general in August of that year, and placed in command of all of Lee's cavalry. He was Governor of South Carolina from 1876 to 1878; then United States Senator until 1891. He was United States Commissioner of Railroads, 1893 to 1897. His death occurred in 1902.

designated to lead Jackson's troops in the final charge. The soul of this brilliant cavalry commander was as full of sentiment as it was of the spirit of self-sacrifice. He was as musical as he was brave. He sang as he fought. Placing himself at the head of Jackson's advancing lines and shouting to them 'Forward,' he at once led off in that song, 'Won't you come out of the Wilderness?' He changed the words to suit the occasion. Through the dense woodland, blending in strange harmony with the rattle of rifles, could be distinctly heard that song and words, 'Now, Joe Hooker, won't you come out of the Wilderness?'"

GENERAL BUFORD *

But something more than West Point and frontier service was needed to produce a Buford. He was "no sapling chance-sown by the fountain." He had had years of training and experience in his profession, and although they were precious and indispensable, they could not have produced the same results which were realized in him, had it not been for the honorable deeds of his ancestors and the hereditary traits developed and transmitted by them. Such men as Buford are not the fruit of chance. Springing, as he did, from a sturdy Anglo-Norman family long settled in the " debatable land " on the borders of England and Scotland, he came by the virtues of the strong hand through inheritance. His kinsmen, as far back as they can be traced, were stout soldiers, rough fighters, and hard riders, accustomed to lives of vicissitude, and holding what they had under the good old rule, the simple plan, " Those to take who have the power, and those to keep who can." Men of his name were the counsellors and companions of kings, and gained renown in the War of the Roses, and in the struggle for

* Major-General John Buford. By Major-General James H. Wilson, U. S. V., Brevet Major-General, U. S. A. Oration delivered at Gettysburg on July 1, 1895.

MAJOR–GENERAL WESLEY MERRITT

General Merritt did his share toward achieving the momentous results of Gettysburg. With his reserve brigade of cavalry on the Federal left, he caused Law to detach a large force from the Confederate main line in order to protect his flank and rear. Merritt served with distinction throughout the Civil War and later in the Spanish-American War. He was born in New York City in 1836, graduated at West Point in 1860, and was assigned to the Second Dragoons. In April, 1862, he was promoted to be captain. He rode with Stoneman on his famous Richmond raid in April and May, 1863, and was in command of the cavalry reserve at Gettysburg. Merritt commanded a cavalry division in the Shenandoah Valley campaign under Sheridan from August, 1864, to March, 1865, and in the final Richmond campaign the cavalry corps. After rendering service in the Spanish-American War, and commanding the forces in the Philippines, he was retired from active service in June, 1900. He died December 3, 1910.

dominion over France. In the wars between the Stuarts and the Commonwealth they were "king's men." . . .

A distinguished officer of the same arm of the service, said of him that as a captain of dragoons "he was considered," in a regiment famed for its dashing and accomplished officers, "as the soldier *par excellence*." He adds in loving admiration, that "no man could be more popular or sincerely beloved by his fellow officers, nor could any officer be more thoroughly respected by his men, than he was. His company had no superior in the service." The same distinguished officer, writing after his career had closed in death, says, "He was a splendid cavalry officer, and one of the most successful in the service; was modest, yet brave; unostentatious, but prompt and persevering; ever ready to go where duty called him, and never shrinking from action however fraught with peril." . . .

Speaking many years after of the part taken in this great day's work * by Buford's cavalry, General F. A. Walker, in the " History of the Second Army Corps," uses the following language: " When last it was my privilege to see General Hancock in November, 1885, he pointed out to me from Cemetery Hill the position occupied by Buford at this critical juncture, and assured me that among the most inspiring sights of his military career was the splendid spectacle of that gallant cavalry as it stood there, unshaken and undaunted, in the face of the advancing Confederate infantry." No higher commendation for the cavalry can be found. Its services have been generally minimized, if not entirely ignored, by popular historians, but no competent critic can read the official reports or the Comte de Paris' " History of the Civil War in America " without giving the cavalry the highest praise for its work on this day, and throughout this campaign. " To Buford was assigned the post of danger and responsibility. He, and he alone, selected the ground," says that trustworthy historian, " upon which unforeseen circumstances were about to bring the two armies into

* The First Day, Gettysburg, July 1, 1863.

[272]

MAJOR–GENERAL NATHAN BEDFORD FORREST, C.S.A.

General Forrest was one of the born cavalry leaders. Daring and resourceful in every situation, he and his hard-riding raiders became a source of terror throughout the Mississippi Valley. He was born near the site of Chapel Hill, Tennessee, on July 31, 1821, attended school for about six months, became a horse and cattle trader, and slave trader at Memphis. He cast in his lot with the Confederacy and entered the army as a private in June, 1861. In July he organized a battalion of cavalry, of which he became lieutenant-colonel. He escaped from Fort Donelson when it surrendered to Grant, and as brigadier-general served in Kentucky under Bragg. Transferred to Northern Mississippi in November, 1863, Forrest was made major-general on December 4th of that year, and at the close of the following year was placed in command of all the cavalry with the Army of the Tennessee. On January 24, 1865, he was put in command of the cavalry in Alabama, Mississippi, and east Louisiana, and was appointed lieutenant-general on February 28th. He met defeat at the hands of General James H. Wilson at Selma, Ala., in March, 1865, and surrendered to General Canby at Gainesville the following May. He remained in business in Tennessee until he died in 1877—one of the most striking characters developed by the war.

hostile contact. Neither Meade nor Lee had any knowledge of it. . . . Buford, who, when he arrived on the evening of [June] 30th, had guessed at one glance the advantages to be derived from these positions, did not have time to give a description of them to Meade and receive his instructions. The unfailing indications to an officer of so much experience, revealed to Buford the approach of the enemy. Knowing that Reynolds was within supporting distance of him, he boldly resolved to risk everything in order to allow the latter time to reach Gettysburg in advance of the Confederate army. This first inspiration of a cavalry officer and a true soldier decided, in every respect, the fate of the campaign. It was Buford who selected the battlefield where the two armies were about to measure their strength."

GENERAL WADE HAMPTON *

Wade Hampton entered the military service of the Confederate States as colonel of the Hampton Legion, South Carolina Volunteers, June 12, 1861, said legion consisting of eight companies of infantry, four companies of cavalry, and two companies of artillery. With the infantry of his command, Colonel Hampton participated in the first battle of Bull Run, July 21, 1861, where he was wounded. He bore a part as a brigade commander in the subsequent battles on the Peninsula of Virginia, from the beginning of operations at Yorktown until the battle of Seven Pines, where he was again wounded. . . .

I have been often asked if General Hampton was a good tactician. If in a minor, technical sense, I answer to the best of my judgment, "No." I doubt if he ever read a technical book on tactics. He knew how to maneuver the units of his command so as to occupy for offensive or defensive action the strongest points of the battlefield, and that is about all there

* Butler and His Cavalry, 1861–1865. By U. R. Brooks (Columbia S. C.). The State Company, 1909.

MAJOR–GENERAL GEORGE ARMSTRONG CUSTER WITH GENERAL PLEASONTON

The *beau sabreur* of the Federal service is pictured here in his favorite velvet suit, with General Alfred Pleasonton, who commanded the cavalry at Gettysburg. This photograph was taken at Warrenton, Va., three months after that battle. At the time this picture was taken, Custer was a brigadier-general in command of the second brigade of the third division of General Pleasonton's cavalry. General Custer's impetuosity finally cost him his own life and the lives of his entire command at the hands of the Sioux Indians June 25, 1876. Custer was born in 1839 and graduated at West Point in 1861. As captain of volunteers he served with McClellan on the Peninsula. In June, 1863, he was made brigadier-general of volunteers and as the head of a brigade of cavalry distinguished himself at Gettysburg. Later he served with Sheridan in the Shenandoah, won honor at Cedar Creek, and was brevetted major-general of volunteers on October 19, 1864. Under Sheridan he participated in the battles of Five Forks, Dinwiddie Court House, and other important cavalry engagements of Grant's last campaign.

[G—18]

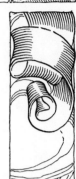
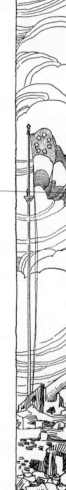

is in tactics. A successful strategist has a broader field for the employment of his military qualities. General Hampton appeared possessed of almost an instinctive topographical talent. He could take in the strong strategic points in the field of his operations with an accuracy of judgment that was surprising to his comrades. It was not necessary for him to study Jomini, Napoleon's " Campaigns," and other high authorities in the art of war. He was a law unto himself on such matters. According to the rules laid down in the books, he would do the most unmilitary things. He would hunt his antagonist as he would hunt big game in the forest. The celerity and audacity of his movements against the front, sometimes on the flank, then again in the rear, kept his enemies in a constant state of uncertainty and anxiety as to where and when they might expect him. With his wonderful powers of physical endurance, his alert, vigilant mind, his matchless horsemanship, no obstacles seemed to baffle his audacity or thwart his purpose.

GENERAL MERRITT *

Merritt was graduated in the class of 1860 at the Military Academy. He was twenty-four years of age. In scholarship he was rated at the middle of his class, and in the other soldierly qualities he was near the head. . . .

At the battle of the Opequon (Winchester), on September 19th, his division gave the most effective instance in a hundred years of war, of the use of a cavalry division in a pitched battle. He rode over Breckinridge's infantry and Fitzhugh Lee's cavalry and effectually broke the Confederate left. At this time Sheridan wrote to a friend, " I claim nothing for myself; my boys Merritt and Custer did it all.". . .

On the disastrous morning of October 19th, at Cedar

* General Wesley Merritt. By Lieutenant-Colonel Eben Swift, Eighth Cavalry. From the (March, 1911) Journal of the United States Cavalry Association.

MAJOR–GENERAL FITZHUGH LEE, C.S.A.

A nephew of the South's greatest commander, General Fitzhugh Lee did honor to his famous family. Along the Rappahannock and in the Shenandoah he measured swords with the Federal cavalry, and over thirty years later he was leading American forces in Cuba. He was born at Clermont, Va., in 1835, graduated at West Point in 1856, and from May, 1860, until the outbreak of the Civil War was instructor of cavalry at West Point. He resigned from the United States Army, and entered the Confederate service in 1861. He fought with Stuart's cavalry in almost all of the important engagements of the Army of Northern Virginia, first as colonel, from July, 1862, as brigadier-general, and from September, 1863, as major-general. He was severely wounded at Winchester, on September 19, 1864, and from March, 1865, until his surrender to General Meade at Farmville, was in command of all the cavalry of the Army of Northern Virginia. In 1896 he was sent to Cuba by President Cleveland as consul-general at Havana, and in May, 1898, when war with Spain seemed inevitable, was appointed major-general of volunteers, and placed in command of the Seventh Army Corps. He returned to Havana as Military Governor in January, 1899. He died in 1905.

Creek, Merritt's division blocked the way of Gordon's victorious Confederates, held its position north of Middletown all day, without assistance, then charged and, crossing the stream below the bridge, joined Custer in the pursuit to Fisher's Hill. In that campaign Merritt's division captured fourteen battle-flags, twenty-nine pieces of artillery, and more than three thousand prisoners. . . .

Merritt at his high prime was the embodiment of force. He was one of those rare men whose faculties are sharpened and whose view is cleared on the battlefield. His decisions were delivered with the rapidity of thought and were as clear as if they had been studied for weeks. He always said that he never found that his first judgment gained by time and reflection. In him a fiery soul was held in thrall to will. Never disturbed by doubt, or moved by fear, neither circumspect nor rash, he never missed an opportunity or made a mistake.

These were the qualities that recommended him to the confidence of that commander whose ideals were higher and more exacting than any other in our history. To his troops he was always a leader who commanded their confidence by his brave appearance, and his calmness in action, while his constant thoughtfulness and care inspired a devotion that was felt for few leaders of his rank.

GENERAL FORREST *

When the war broke out, Forrest was in the prime of his mental and physical powers. Over six feet in stature, of powerful frame, and of great activity and daring, with a personal prowess proved in many fierce encounters, he was a king among the bravest men of his time and country. He was among the first to volunteer when war broke out, and it was a matter of

* Recollections of a Virginian in the Mexican, Indian, and Civil Wars. By General Dabney Herndon Maury. (New York) Charles Scribner's Sons, 1894.

LIEUTENANT–GENERAL JOSEPH WHEELER, C.S.A.

Commander of Confederate forces in more than a hundred cavalry battles, General Wheeler well deserved the tribute of his erstwhile opponent, General Sherman, who once said: "In the event of war with a foreign country, Joe Wheeler is the man to command the cavalry of our army." He was born in 1836, and graduated at West Point in 1859. He served in the regular army until April, 1861, then entered the Confederate service. He commanded a brigade of infantry at Shiloh in April, 1862, and later in the year was transferred to the cavalry. He fought under Bragg in Kentucky at Perryville and in other engagements, and covered the retreat of Bragg's army to the southward. In January, 1863, he was commissioned major-general. In the Chattanooga campaigns Wheeler showed himself a brave and skilful officer. He harassed Sherman's flank during the march to Atlanta, and in August, 1864, led a successful raid in Sherman's rear as far north as the Kentucky line. In February, 1865, he was commissioned lieutenant-general, and continued in command of the cavalry in Johnston's army until its surrender. He served as a major-general in the Spanish-American War. He died in Brooklyn, January 25, 1906.

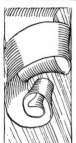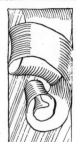

course that he should be the commander of the troops who flocked to his standard. From the very outset he evinced his extraordinary capacity for war, and in his long career of great achievement no defeat or failure was ever charged to him. . . .

When Forrest, with about twelve hundred men, set out in pursuit of Streight, he was more than a day behind him. Streight had several hundred more men in the saddle than Forrest, and being far in advance could replace a broken-down horse by a fresh one from the farms through which his route lay, while Forrest, when he lost a horse, lost a soldier, too; for no good horses were left for him. After a hot pursuit of five days and nights, during which he had lost two-thirds of his forces from broken-down horses, he overhauled his enemy and brought him to a parley. This conference took place in sight of a cut-off in the mountain road, Captain Morton and his horse artillery, which had been so long with Forrest, passing in sight along the road till they came to the cut-off, into which they would turn, reentering the road out of view, so that it seemed that a continuous stream of artillery was passing by. Forrest had so arranged that he stood with his back to the guns while Streight was facing them.

Forrest, in his characteristic way, described the scene to me. He said, " I seen him all the time he was talking, looking over my shoulder and counting the guns. Presently he said: ' Name of God! How many guns have you got? There's fifteen I've counted already!' Turning my head that way, I said, ' I reckon that's all that has kept up.' Then he said, ' I won't surrender till you tell me how many men you've got.' I said, ' I've got enough to whip you out of your boots.' To which he said, ' I won't surrender.' I turned to my bugler and said, ' Sound to mount!' Then he cried out ' I'll surrender!' I told him, ' Stack your arms right along there, Colonel, and march your men away down that hollow.'

" When this was done," continued Forrest, " I ordered my men to come forward and take possession of the arms.

MAJOR–GENERAL JAMES HARRISON WILSON AND STAFF

This brilliant cavalryman's demonstration of 1865 against Selma and Tuscaloosa, Alabama, in aid of General Canby s operations against Mobile and the center of the State, was one of the greatest cavalry raids in the West. General Wilson was born in 1837, near Shawneetown, Illinois, and graduated at West Point in 1860. He was aide-de-camp to General McClellan on the Peninsula, and served in the engineering corps in the West until after Vicksburg and Chattanooga, when he was made brigadier-general of volunteers in October, 1863. In February, 1864, he was put in charge of the cavalry bureau at Washington, and later commanded the Third Division of Sheridan's reorganized cavalry. October 5, 1864, he was brevetted major-general of volunteers for "gallant and meritorious services" during the war, and on the 24th of that month he was put in command of the cavalry corps of the Military Division of the Mississippi. He took part in the battles of Franklin and Nashville, and in March, 1865, made his famous Selma raid. In twenty-eight days Wilson had captured 288 guns and 6280 prisoners, including Jefferson Davis. Five large iron works, three factories, numerous mills and immense quantities of supplies had been destroyed. As a reward for these services, he was made major-general of volunteers on April 20, 1865. General Wilson later served with distinction in the Spanish American War, and was also in command of the British and American troops in the siege at Pekin, China.

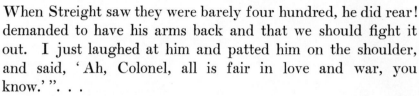

When Streight saw they were barely four hundred, he did rear! demanded to have his arms back and that we should fight it out. I just laughed at him and patted him on the shoulder, and said, 'Ah, Colonel, all is fair in love and war, you know.'". . .

Forrest knew nothing about tactics—could not drill a company. When first ordered to have his brigade ready for review, he was quite ignorant, but Armstrong told him what commands to give, and what to do with himself. . . .

Forrest will always stand as the great exponent of the power of the mounted riflemen to fight with the revolver when mounted and with the rifle on foot. His troops were not dragoons "who fought indifferently on foot or horseback," nor were they cavalry who fought only mounted and with sabers. Few of his command ever bore sabers, save some of his officers, who wore them as a badge of rank. None of Forrest's men could use the saber. He himself had no knowledge of its use, but he would encounter half a dozen expert *sabreurs* with his revolver.

GENERAL CUSTER *

It was here (Hanover, Pennsylvania, June, 1863) that the brigade first saw Custer. As the men of the Sixth, armed with their Spencer rifles, were deploying forward across the railroad into a wheat-field beyond, I heard a voice new to me, directly in rear of the portion of the line where I was, giving directions for the movement, in clear, resonant tones, and in a calm, confident manner, at once resolute and reassuring. Looking back to see whence it came, my eyes were instantly riveted upon a figure only a few feet distant, whose appearance amazed, if it did not for the moment amuse me. It was he who was giving the orders. At first, I thought he might be a staff-officer, conveying the commands of his chief. But it was at once apparent

* Personal Recollections of a Cavalryman. By J. H. Kidd, formerly Colonel, Sixth Michigan Cavalry. (Ionia, Mich.) Sentinel Printing Co.

BRIGADIER–GENERAL JOHN R. CHAMBLISS, C.S.A.

General John R. Chambliss was a Confederate cavalry leader who distinguished himself at Gettysburg. At Brandy Station, June 9, 1863, W. H. F. Lee had been wounded, and Colonel Chambliss had taken command of his brigade. On the night of June 24th Stuart left Robertson's and Jones' brigades to guard the passes of the Blue Ridge and started to move round the Army of the Potomac with the forces of Hampton, Fitzhugh Lee, and Chambliss, intending to pass between it and Centerville into Maryland and so rejoin Lee. The movements of the army forced him out of his way, so on the morning of the 30th he moved across country to Hanover, Chambliss in front and Hampton in the rear with Fitzhugh Lee well out on the flank. Chambliss attacked Kilpatrick at Hanover about 10 A.M., but was driven out before Hampton or Lee could come to his support.

MAJOR HENRY GILMOR, C.S.A.

Major Gilmor was born in Baltimore County, Maryland, in 1838. He entered the Confederate army at the outbreak of the Civil War, and was commissioned captain in 1862. In 1862–63 he was imprisoned for five months in Fort McHenry, at Baltimore, and in the latter year he raised a cavalry battalion, of which he was made major. Subsequently he commanded the First Confederate Regiment of Maryland, and in 1864 headed the advance of the forces of General Jubal A. Early into that State, and, being familiar with the country, made a successful raid north of Baltimore. He captured Frederick, Md., and created great alarm by his daring exploit so far north of the customary battlefields. In 1874 he became police commissioner of his native city. He died in 1883.

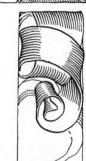

that he was *giving* orders, not transmitting them, and that he was in command of the line.

Looking at him closely, this is what I saw: An officer, superbly mounted, who sat his charger as if to the manner born. Tall, lithe, active, muscular, straight as an Indian and as quick in his movements, he had the fair complexion of a school-girl. He was clad in a suit of black velvet, elaborately trimmed with gold lace, which ran down the outer seams of his trousers, and almost covered the sleeves of his cavalry jacket. The wide collar of a navy-blue shirt was turned down over the collar of his velvet jacket, and a necktie of brilliant crimson was tied in a graceful knot at the throat, the long ends falling carelessly in front. The double rows of buttons on his breast were arranged in groups of twos, indicating the rank of brigadier-general. A soft black hat with wide brim adorned with a gilt cord, and rosette encircling a silver star, was worn turned down on one side, giving him a rakish air. His golden hair fell in graceful luxuriance nearly or quite to his shoulder, and his upper lip was garnished with a blonde mustache. A sword and belt, gilt spurs and top-boots completed his unique outfit.

A keen eye would have been slow to detect in that rider with the flowing locks and gaudy tie, in his dress of velvet and of gold, the master-spirit that he proved to be. That garb, fantastic as at first sight it appeared to be, was to be the distinguishing mark which, during all the remaining years of the war, like the white plume of Henry of Navarre, was to show us where, in the thickest of the fight, we were to seek our leader —for, where danger was, where swords were to cross, where Greek met Greek, there he was, always. Brave, but not reckless; self-confident, yet modest; ambitious, but regulating his conduct at all times by a high sense of honor and duty; eager for laurels, but scorning to wear them unworthily; ready and willing to act, but regardful of human life; quick in emergencies, cool and self-possessed, his courage was of the highest moral type, his perceptions were intuitions.

[284]

MAJOR–GENERAL HUGH JUDSON KILPATRICK

This daring cavalry leader was born in 1836 near Deckertown, New Jersey, and graduated at West Point in 1861. He entered the Federal service as captain in the Fifth New York Volunteers, generally known as Duryea's Zouaves. He was wounded at Big Bethel, June 10, 1861, and on September 25th he became lieutenant-colonel of the Second New York Cavalry. In the second battle of Bull Run, and on the left at Gettysburg, he served with conspicuous gallantry. In December, 1862, he was promoted to be colonel, and in June, 1863, to be brigadier-general of volunteers while he received the brevet of major and lieutenant-colonel in the Regular Army for repeated gallantry. In March, 1864, he made his celebrated Richmond raid and in April accompanied Sherman in his invasion of Georgia. He was wounded at Resasca, and at the close of the war he was brevetted brigadier-general in the Regular Army for "gallant and meritorious services in the capture of Fayetteville, North Carolina," and major-general for his services during the campaign under Sherman in the Carolinas. In June, 1865, he obtained the regular rank of major-general of volunteers. He died at Santiago in December, 1881.

GENERAL FITZHUGH LEE *

Major-General Fitzhugh Lee, or " Our Fitz " as he was affectionately called by his old comrades, won high distinction as a cavalryman in the Army of Northern Virginia, and since the war won higher distinction as a citizen.

After serving for a year at Carlisle Barracks as cavalry instructor of raw recruits, he reported to his regiment on the frontier of Texas, and was greatly distinguished in several fights for gallantry. In a fight with the Comanches, May 13, 1859, he was so severely wounded, being pierced through the lungs by an arrow, that the surgeons despaired of his life (especially as he had to be borne two hundred miles across the prairie in a horse litter), but he recovered and rejoined his command, and led a part of his company in January, 1860, in a very notable and successful fight with the Indians, in which he greatly distinguished himself in a single combat with a powerful Indian chief. . . .

In the campaign against Pope, and the Maryland Campaign (1862) his cavalry rendered most important service, of which General R. E. Lee said in his official report: " Its vigilance, activity, and courage were conspicuous; and to its assistance is due in a great measure some of the most important and delicate operations of the campaign." . . .

When Hampton was sent south, Lee was put in command of the entire cavalry corps of the Army of Northern Virginia, and only the break-up at Richmond prevented him from receiving his merited commission as lieutenant-general, which had been decided on by the Confederate President. . . .

When the war with Spain broke out he was made major-general of volunteers, and put in command of troops destined to capture Havana. After the close of the war he was kept

* Thirty-sixth Annual Reunion of the Association of the Graduates of the United States Military Academy, at West Point, New York, June 13, 1905.

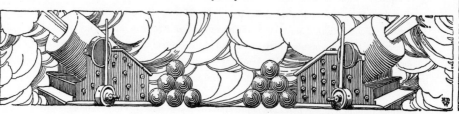

MAJOR–GENERAL LOVELL HARRISON ROUSSEAU

General Rousseau was born in Stanford, Lincoln County, Ky., in 1818. He fought in the Mexican War, distinguished himself at Buena Vista, and later settled in Louisville. In 1860 he raised the Fifth Kentucky regiment, of which he was made colonel, and in 1861 he was made brigadier-general. He served with great credit at Shiloh, and was made major-general of volunteers for gallant conduct at Perryville. He commanded the Fifth Division of the Army of the Cumberland at Stone River and at Chickamauga, and in 1864 made a cavalry raid into Alabama. In the Nashville campaign he had command of Fort Rosecrans under General Thomas, and did his share in achieving the notable results of that battle. At the time of his death in 1869 he was commander of the Department of the Gulf.

MAJOR–GENERAL GEORGE STONEMAN

General Stoneman was born at Busti, Chautauqua County, N. Y., in 1822, and graduated at West Point in 1846. Following some service in West Virginia in the early part of the war, he was appointed chief of cavalry in the Army of the Potomac. After the evacuation of Yorktown, he overtook the Confederate troops and brought on the battle of Williamsburgh in May, 1862. On November 15, 1862, he was made commander of the Third Army Corps, which he led at Fredericksburg on December 13, 1862. During Hooker's Chancellorsville campaign he led a cavalry raid toward Richmond. In April, 1864, he was made commander of a cavalry corps in the Army of the Ohio, and in the Atlanta campaign undertook a raid against Macon and Andersonville. For three months he was a prisoner.

for a time in Cuba as Commander of the District of Havana, and was made brigadier-general in the regular army, where he served with distinction until he was retired.

GENERAL WHEELER

One of the most versatile soldiers of the Civil War was Joseph Wheeler, Lieutenant-General, C. S. A., Brigadier-General, U. S. A., and in the opinion of General R. E. Lee one of " the two ablest cavalry officers which the war developed."

President Davis said that General Wheeler displayed " a dash and activity, vigilance and consummate skill, which justly entitled him to a prominent place on the roll of great cavalry leaders. By his indomitable energy he was able to keep the Government and commanders of our troops advised of the enemy's movements and by preventing foraging parties from leaving the main body, he saved from spoliation all but a narrow tract of country, and from the torch millions worth of property which would otherwise have certainly been consumed."

One of his biographers (Rev. E. S. Buford) states that: " General Wheeler has commanded in more than a hundred battles, many of which, considering the numbers engaged, were the most severe recorded in the history of cavalry. Always in the front of battle, he was wounded three times, sixteen horses were shot under him, eight of his staff-officers were killed and thirty-two wounded."

At the outbreak of the war with Spain, Wheeler was appointed a major-general, U. S. V., and during the short but sharp campaign in Cuba, displayed the same energy and ability which had distinguished him in a greater conflict. In 1899 he was ordered to the Philippines, serving there until June, 1900, when he was commissioned brigadier-general, U. S. A., and in September of the same year was retired from active service. His old opponent, General Sherman, paid this tribute to his worth: " In the event of war with a foreign country, 'Joe' Wheeler is the man to command the cavalry of our army."

[288]

CHAPTER
ELEVEN

———

FAMOUS CHARGERS

———

GRANT'S FAVORITE WAR-HORSE "CINCINNATI"

THREE CHARGERS THAT BORE A NATION'S DESTINY

These three horses can fairly be said to have borne a nation's destiny upon their backs. They are the mounts used by General Grant in his final gigantic campaign that resulted in the outwearing of the Confederacy. When photographed in June, 1864, they were "in the field" with the General-in-Chief, after the ghastly battle of Cold Harbor, and before the crossing of the James River that sealed the fate of Lee's army. On the left is "Egypt," presented to Grant by admirers in Illinois, and named for the district in

IN THE FIELD WITH GENERAL GRANT

which he was bred. The horse in the center, fully caparisoned, is "Cincinnati," also a present from a gentleman in St. Louis, who on his death-bed sent for Grant and presented him with "the finest horse in the world." The little black pony to the right is "Jeff Davis," captured in a cavalry raid on the plantation of Joe Davis, brother of the Confederate President, near Vicksburg. "Jeff Davis" looks indifferent, but "Cincinnati" and "Egypt" have pricked up their ears. Perhaps they were looking at General Grant.

[G—19]

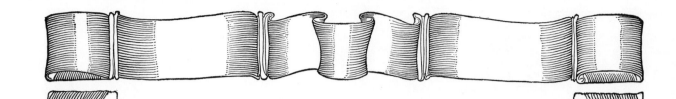

WAR–HORSES

By Theo. F. Rodenbough
Brigadier-General, United States Army (Retired)

THE battle chargers of the general officers of the Confederate and Federal armies during the American Civil War, wrote their names upon the scrolls of history by their high grade of sagacity and faithfulness. They carried their masters upon the tedious march and over the bullet-swept battlefields, and seemed to realize their importance in the conflict. The horse of the commanding officer was as well known to the rank and file as the general himself, and the soldiers were as affectionately attached to the animal as was the master.

GENERAL GRANT'S HORSES

When the Civil War broke out, my father,* General Grant, was appointed colonel of the Twenty-first Illinois Volunteer Infantry and on joining the regiment purchased a horse in Galena, Illinois. This horse, though a strong animal, proved to be unfitted for the service and, when my father was taking his regiment from Springfield, Illinois, to Missouri, he encamped on the Illinois River for several days. During the time they were there a farmer brought in a horse called "Jack." This animal was a cream-colored horse, with black eyes, mane and tail of silver white, his hair gradually becoming darker toward his feet. He was a noble animal, high spirited, very intelligent and an excellent horse in every way. He was a stallion and of considerable value. My father used him until after the battle of Chattanooga (November, 1863), as an extra horse

* This account was furnished at the author's request by General Frederick Dent Grant, U. S. A.—T. F. R.

"STONEWALL" JACKSON'S WAR–HORSE SHORTLY AFTER HIS MASTER'S DEATH

The negative of this picture, made in 1863, not long after the terrible tragedy of General Jackson's death, was destroyed in the great Richmond fire of 1865. The print is believed to be unique, and here reproduced for the first time. All day long on May 2d of 1863, "Old Sorrel," as the soldiers called him, had borne his master on the most successful flanking march of the war, which ended in the Confederate victory at Chancellorsville. There have not been many movements in military history so brilliant and decisive in their effect. At nightfall Jackson mounted "Fancy" for the last time, and rode out to reconnoiter. Gallop- ing back to avoid the Federal bullets, he and his staff were mistaken for foes and fired upon by their own men. Jackson reeled from the saddle into the arms of Captain Milburn, severely wounded. The horse bolted toward the Union lines, but was recovered and placed in the stable of Governor John Letcher at Richmond.

and for parades and ceremonial occasions. At the time of the Sanitary Fair in Chicago (1863 or '64), General Grant gave him to the fair, where he was raffled off, bringing $4,000 to the Sanitary Commission.

Soon after my father was made a brigadier-general, (August 8, 1861), he purchased a pony for me and also another horse for field service for himself. At the battle of Belmont (November 7, 1861), his horse was killed under him and he took my pony. The pony was quite small and my father, feeling that the commanding general on the field should have a larger mount, turned the pony over to one of his aides-de-camp (Captain Hyllier) and mounted the captain's horse. The pony was lost in the battle.

The next horse that my father purchased for field service was a roan called "Fox," a very powerful and spirited animal and of great endurance. This horse he rode during the siege and battles around Fort Donelson and also at Shiloh.

At the battle of Shiloh the Confederates left on the field a rawboned horse, very ugly and apparently good for nothing. As a joke, the officer who found this animal on the field, sent it with his compliments, to Colonel Lagow, one of my father's aides-de-camp, who always kept a very excellent mount and was a man of means. The other officers of the staff "jollied" the colonel about this gift. When my father saw him, he told the colonel that the animal was a thoroughbred and a valuable mount and that if he, Lagow, did not wish to keep the horse he would be glad to have him. Because of his appearance he was named "Kangaroo," and after a short period of rest and feeding and care he turned out to be a magnificent animal and was used by my father during the Vicksburg campaign.

In this campaign, General Grant had two other horses, both of them very handsome, one of which he gave away and the other he used until late in the war. During the campaign and siege of Vicksburg, a cavalry raid or scouting party arrived at Joe Davis' plantation (the brother of Jefferson Davis,

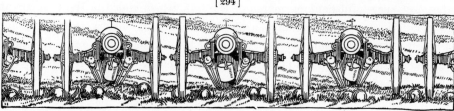

MEADE'S BATTLE–SCARRED MOUNT THREE MONTHS AFTER GETTYSBURG

"Baldy" was the horse that carried General George G. Meade from September, 1861, to the end of the war, except when "absent on sick leave." His war record is remarkable for the number of wounds from which he recovered, reporting for duty each time he was convalescent. He was wounded twice at the first battle of Bull Run, before he came into General Meade's possession. Left on the field for dead at Antietam, he was later discovered quietly grazing, with a deep wound in his neck. Again, at Gettysburg, a bullet lodged between his ribs and rendered him unable to carry his owner again until after Appomattox. "Baldy" was a bright bay horse, with white face and feet. This bullet-scarred veteran followed General Meade's hearse to his last resting-place in 1872, and survived him by a decade. The photograph was taken in October, 1863.

President of the Confederacy) and there captured a black pony which was brought to the rear of the city and presented to me. The animal was worn out when it reached headquarters but was a very easy riding horse and I used him once or twice. With care he began to pick up and soon carried himself in fine shape.

At that time my father was suffering with a carbuncle and his horse being restless caused him a great deal of pain. It was necessary for General Grant to visit the lines frequently and one day he took this pony for that purpose. The gait of the pony was so delightful that he directed that he be turned over to the quartermaster as a captured horse and a board of officers be convened to appraise the animal. This was done and my father purchased the animal and kept him until he died, which was long after the Civil War. This pony was known as "Jeff Davis."

After the battle of Chattanooga, General Grant went to St. Louis, where I was at the time, critically ill from dysentery contracted during the siege of Vicksburg. During the time of his visit to the city he received a letter from a gentleman who signed his name "S. S. Grant," the initials being the same as those of a brother of my father's, who had died in the summer of 1861. S. S. Grant wrote to the effect that he was very desirous of seeing General Grant but that he was ill and confined to his room at the Lindell Hotel and begged him to call, as he had something important to say which my father might be gratified to hear.

The name excited my father's curiosity and he called at the hotel to meet the gentleman who told him that he had, he thought, the finest horse in the world, and knowing General Grant's great liking for horses he had concluded, inasmuch as he would never be able to ride again, that he would like to give his horse to him; that he desired that the horse should have a good home and tender care and that the only condition that he would make in parting with him would be that the person receiving him would see that he was never ill-treated, and

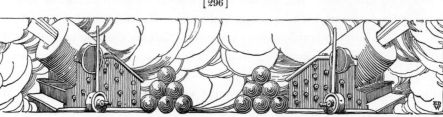

GENERAL SHERIDAN'S "WINCHESTER"

"Winchester" wore no such gaudy trappings when he sprang "up from the South, at break of day" on that famous ride of October 19, 1864, which has been immortalized in Thomas Buchanan Read's poem. The silver-mounted saddle was presented·later by admiring friends of his owner. The sleek neck then was dark with sweat, and the quivering nostrils were flecked with foam at the end of the twenty-mile dash that brought hope and courage to an army and turned defeat into the overwhelming victory of Cedar Creek. Sheridan himself was as careful of his appearance as Custer was irregular in his field dress. He was always careful of his horse, but in the field decked him in nothing more elaborate than a plain McClellan saddle and army blanket.

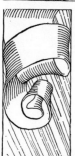

should never fall into the hands of a person that would ill-treat him. This promise was given and General Grant accepted the horse and called him "Cincinnati." This was his battle charger until the end of the war and was kept by him until the horse died at Admiral Ammen's farm in Maryland, in 1878.*

About this time (January, 1864) some people in Illinois found a horse in the southern part of that State, which they thought was remarkably beautiful. They purchased him and sent him as a present to my father. This horse was known as "Egypt" as he was raised, or at least came from southern Illinois, a district known in the State as Egypt, as the northern part was known as Canaan.

GENERAL LEE'S "TRAVELLER"

The most famous of the horses in the stables of General Lee, the Confederate commander, was "Traveller," an iron gray horse. He was raised in Greenbrier County, near Blue Sulphur Springs, and, as a colt, won first prize at a fair in Lewisburg, Virginia. When hostilities commenced between the North and the South, the horse, then known as "Jeff Davis," was owned by Major Thomas L. Broun, who had paid $175 (in gold) for him. Lee first saw the gray in the mountains of West Virginia. He instantly became attached to him, and always called him "my colt."

In the spring of 1862, this horse finally became the

* "Cincinnati" was the son of "Lexington," the fastest four-mile thoroughbred in the United States, time 7:19¾ minutes. "Cincinnati" nearly equaled the speed of his half-brother, "Kentucky," and Grant was offered $10,000 in gold or its equivalent for him, but refused. He was seventeen hands high, and in the estimation of Grant was the finest horse that he had ever seen. Grant rarely permitted anyone to mount the horse —two exceptions were Admiral Daniel Ammen and Lincoln. Ammen saved Grant's life from drowning while a school-boy. Grant says: "Lincoln spent the latter days of his life with me. He came to City Point in the last month of the war and was with me all the time. He was a fine horseman and rode my horse 'Cincinnati' every day."—T. F. R.

[298]

GENERAL ALFRED PLEASONTON AND HIS HORSE

This is the horse which General Pleasonton brought with him from Utah in 1861. This charger carried him through the Peninsular campaign when he was a major in the Second Cavalry, commanding the regiment and covering the march of the Federal army to Yorktown, August 18 and 19, 1862. It bore him at Antietam, Fredericksburg, and Chancellorsville, where Pleasonton distinguished himself by checking the flank attack of the Confederates on the Federal right, and perhaps it stepped forth a little more proudly when its owner was given command of the entire cavalry corps of the Army of the Potomac on June 7, 1863. This photograph was taken at Falmouth, Va., in the latter year. General Pleasonton is riding the same charger in the photograph of himself and Custer used to illustrate the battle of Gettysburg on page 237.

property of the general, who paid $200 in currency for him. He changed the name of his charger to "Traveller" and from the date of purchase it became almost a daily sight to see the commander astride the gray, riding about the camp.

There were a number of battle horses in Lee's stables during the war. There were "Grace Darling," "Brown Roan," "Lucy Long," "Ajax," and "Richmond," but of them all "Traveller" became the especial companion of the general. The fine proportions of this horse immediately attracted attention. He was gray in color, with black points, a long mane and long flowing tail. He stood sixteen hands high, and was five years old in the spring of 1862. His figure was muscular, with a deep chest and short back, strong haunches, flat legs, small head, quick eyes, broad forehead, and small feet. His rapid, springy step and bold carriage made him conspicuous in the camps of the Confederates. On a long and tedious march with the Army of Northern Virginia he easily carried Lee's weight at five or six miles an hour, without faltering, and at the end of the day's hard travel seemed to be as fresh as at the beginning.

The other horses broke under the strain and hardships; "Lucy Long," purchased by General "Jeb" Stuart from Stephen Dandridge and presented to Lee, served for two years in alternation with "Traveller," but in the fall of 1864 became unserviceable and was sent into the country to recuperate.* "Richmond," "Ajax," and "Brown Roan" each in turn proved unequal to the rigors of war.

* "Lucy Long," second to "Traveller" in Lee's affections, was recalled from the country just before the evacuation of Richmond; but during the confusion she was placed with the public horses and sent to Danville, and Lee lost all trace of his war-horse. A thorough search was made, and finally, in 1866, she was discovered and brought to Lexington to pass her days in leisure with General Lee and "Traveller." After a number of years the mare became feeble and seemed to lose interest in life, and when "Lucy Long" reached about thirty-three years of age a son of General Lee mercifully chloroformed the veteran war-horse of the Army of Northern Virginia.

GENERAL RUFUS INGALLS' CHARGER

Like General Grant's "Cincinnati," this horse was present at Lee's surrender at Appomattox. Major-General Rufus Ingalls was chief quartermaster of the Army of the Potomac. After the surrender he asked permission to visit the Confederate lines and renew his acquaintance with some old friends, class-mates and companions in arms. He returned with Cadmus M. Wilcox, who had been Grant's groomsman when he was married; James Longstreet, who had also been at his wedding; Heth, Gordon, Pickett, and a number of others. The American eagle is plainly visible on the major-general's saddle-cloth, which the charger is wearing. The whole outfit is spick and span, though the double bridle is not according to army regulations, and General Ingalls even enjoyed the luxury of a dog at the time this photograph was taken.

But "Traveller" sturdily accepted and withstood the hardships of the campaigns in Virginia, Maryland, and Pennsylvania. When in April, 1865, the last battle of the Army of Northern Virginia had been fought, the veteran war-horse was still on duty. When Lee rode to the McLean house at Appomattox Court House, he was astride of "Traveller," and it was this faithful four-footed companion who carried the Southern leader back to his waiting army, and then to Richmond.

When Lee became a private citizen and retired to Washington and Lee University, as its president, the veteran war-horse was still with him, and as the years passed and both master and servant neared life's ending they became more closely attached.* As the funeral cortège accompanied Lee to his last resting place, "Traveller" marched behind the hearse, his step slow and his head bowed, as if he understood the import of the occasion.

GENERAL McCLELLAN'S HORSES

While General McClellan was in command of the Army of the Potomac, in 1862, he had a number of war-horses. The favorite of them all was "Daniel Webster," soon called by the members of the general's staff "that devil Dan," because of his speed with which the staff officers had great difficulty in keeping pace. During the battle of the Antietam the great horse carried the commander safely through the day.

"Daniel Webster" was a dark bay about seventeen hands high, pure bred, with good action, never showing signs of fatigue, no matter how hard the test. He was extremely hand-

* During the life of "Traveller" after the war, he was the pet of the countryside about Lexington, Va. Many marks of affection were showered upon him. Admiring friends in England sent two sets of equipment for the veteran war-horse. Ladies in Baltimore, Md., bestowed another highly decorated set, and another came from friends at the Confederate capital, Richmond. But the set that seemed to most please "Traveller" was the one sent from St. Louis, in Missouri.

GENERAL RAWLINS' MOUNT

It is a proud little darkey boy who is exercising the horse of a general—John Aaron Rawlins, the Federal brigadier-general of volunteers, who was later promoted to the rank of major-general, U. S. A., for gallant and meritorious services during the campaign terminating with the surrender of the army under General Lee. The noble horse himself is looking around with a mildly inquiring air at the strange new instrument which the photographer is leveling at him.

some, with more than ordinary horse-sense. He was a fast walker, an important requisite in a commander's charger, but a disagreeable quality for the staff officers whose horses were kept at a slow trot. After McClellan retired to private life, "Dan" became the family horse at Orange, N. J., where he died at the age of twenty-three. McClellan said: "No soldier ever had a better horse than I had in 'Daniel Webster.'"

McClellan also had a charger named "Burns," a fiery black, named after an army friend who gave the horse to Mc-Clellan. His one failing was that at dinner time he would bolt for his oats regardless of how much depended on McClellan's presence on the battlefield at the critical moment, as in the battle of the Antietam. Running at dinner time became so much an obsession with "Burns" that McClellan was always careful not to be mounted on him at that hour of the day.*

GENERAL SHERMAN'S HORSES

General Sherman's best war-horse was killed early in the Civil War, at the battle of Shiloh, where he led the right wing of the Federal army against General A. S. Johnston's Confederate legions. Two of his other chargers were killed while being held by an orderly. Of the many horses that carried Sherman through the remaining years of the struggle, two had

* The Editor has vivid recollection of "Little Mac" in April, 1862 (then at the height of his popularity), during a ride from Fort Monroe to Big Bethel, being the first day's march of the Army of the Potomac toward Yorktown, Va. The writer commanded the escort (a squadron, Second U. S. Cavalry), and during the ten or twelve miles of the route covered at a gallop, between double lines of infantry, halted for the moment to permit the commanding general to pass, the air was literally "rent" with the cheers of the troops, filled with high hopes of an early entrance to the Confederate capital. As the brilliant staff, headed by the young chieftain of magnetic presence, with bared head, mounted on "Black Burns," swept along amid clatter of hoof, jingle of equipment, and loud hurrahs, the thought came to the writer that thus the "Little Corporal" was wont to inspire his devoted legions to loud acclaim of *Vive l'Empereur*. (T. F. R.)

GENERAL BUTTERFIELD, A WELL–MOUNTED INFANTRY GENERAL

This is a photograph of the well-mounted chief-of-staff and corps commander of the Army of the Potomac. It was the custom of generals who had been infantry officers to set their own pace, regardless of their cavalry escort. A cavalryman detailed to escort him tells the following story: "We started out with General Butterfield one day upon the Potomac to meet Confederate officers in relation to the exchange of prisoners. My regiment was ordered out to escort him. The infantry officers, accustomed to riding alone, made their way regardless of their escorts, and inside of half an hour my column was distributed over two miles of road; General Butterfield did not adapt his riding to the pace of the escort and made it very difficult for the cavalry to follow him."

a particular place in the general's affections—" Lexington "
and " Sam." The former was a Kentucky thoroughbred, and
his fine action attracted the admiration of all who saw him.
When the Federal forces finally entered and occupied Atlanta,
in 1864, Sherman was astride of " Lexington "; and after
peace was declared, in 1865, the general rode the same horse
in the final review of his army in Washington.

" Sam " was a large, half-thoroughbred bay, sixteen and a
half hands high. He possessed great speed, strength, and endurance. The horse made one of the longest and most difficult
marches ever recorded in history, from Vicksburg to Washington, through the cities of Atlanta, Savannah, Columbia, and
Richmond. He had a rapid gait, and could march five miles
an hour at a walk. While under fire " Sam " was as calm and
steady as his brave master. He was wounded several times,
while mounted, and the fault was usually due to Sherman's
disregard of the horse's anxiety to seek cover. In 1865, Sherman retired " Sam " to a well-earned rest, on an Illinois farm,
where he received every mark of affection. The gallant war-
horse died of extreme old age, in 1884.

GENERAL JACKSON'S HORSES

General Thomas J. (" Stonewall ") Jackson, the great
Southern leader, had his favorite battle charger, which at the
beginning of the war was thought to be about eleven years old.
On May 9, 1861, while Jackson was in command of the garrison at Harper's Ferry, a train load of supplies and horses,
on the way to the Federal camps, was captured. Among the
horses was one that attracted Jackson's attention. He purchased the animal from his quartermaster's department for his
own personal use. The horse, named " Old Sorrel," carried
Jackson over many of the bullet-swept battlefields and was
with Jackson when that officer fell before the volley of his
own men at the battle of Chancellorsville. During the swift
campaign through the Shenandoah, in 1862, when Jackson

[306]

AN "AIDE" OF GENERAL GRANT

A photograph of little "Jeff Davis," a pony that won General Grant's approval at the siege of Vicksburg by his easy gait. General Grant was suffering with a carbuncle and needed a horse with easy paces. A cavalry detachment had captured a suitable mount on the plantation of Joe Davis, brother of the President of the Confederacy, and that is how the little black pony came by his name. The great Union general was more apt to call him "Little Jeff." The general used him throughout the siege, but he felt that the commanding general on the battlefield should have a larger mount, and "Jeff Davis" in this photograph is apparently saddled for an orderly or aide. The little horse remained with General Grant until he died.

marched his "foot cavalry" towards the citadel at Washington, the horse was his constant companion.

In 1884, a state fair was held at Hagerstown, in Maryland, and one of the most interesting sights was that of the veteran war horse, "Old Sorrel," tethered in a corral and quietly munching choice bits of vegetables and hay. Before the fair was ended nearly all the mane and hair of his tail had disappeared, having been plucked by scores of relic hunters. For many years after the cessation of hostilities, Jackson's gallant old war-horse was held in tender esteem at the South.

When the veteran battle charger died, admirers of Jackson sent the carcass to a taxidermist and the gallant steed now rests in the Soldier's Home in Richmond, Virginia.*

GENERAL SHERIDAN'S "RIENZI"

General Sheridan's charger was foaled at or near Grand Rapids, Michigan, of the Black Hawk stock, and was brought into the Federal army by an officer of the Second Michigan Cavalry. He was presented to Sheridan, then colonel of the regiment, by the officers, in the spring of 1862, while the regiment was stationed at Rienzi, Mississippi; the horse was nearly three years old. He was over seventeen hands in height, powerfully built, with a deep chest, strong shoulders, a broad forehead, a clear eye and of great intelligence. In his prime he was one of the strongest horses Sheridan ever knew, very active, and one of the fastest walkers in the Federal army. "Rienzi" always held his head high, and by the quickness of his movements created the impression that he was exceedingly impetuous, but Sheridan was always able to control him by a firm hand and a few words. He was as cool and quiet under fire as any veteran trooper in the Cavalry Corps.

At the battle of Cedar Creek, October 19, 1864, the name of the horse was changed from "Rienzi" to "Winchester," a name derived from the town made famous by Sheridan's ride

* From the Confederate Veteran.

MOUNTS FOR ALL THE CAVALRYMEN

Behind this mixed command grouped in front of the camp stand a great number of horses. There is at least one for every cavalryman in the picture, a state of affairs that did not last long; the photograph was evidently taken before the Union armies were using up five hundred horses a day. The picture illustrates one of the few quiet hours that the Federal cavalrymen enjoyed. Infantry boys are evidently fraternizing with their comrades of the cavalry at an advanced post. The horn that shows on the cap of the second man at the left of the photograph is the insignia, adopted from European light infantry, of the infantry of the Army of the Potomac. The drummer boy also belongs to the infantry arm, and the leather scabbard of the officer kneeling near the center of the picture likewise indicates the infantry. Such photographs as these are rare. Both horses and men were resting for once.

to save his army in the Shenandoah Valley. Poets, sculptors, and painters have made the charger the subject of their works. Thomas Buchanan Read was inspired to write his immortal poem, " Sheridan's Ride," which thrilled the North.

From an account of this affair in " Scribner's Magazine," by General G. W. Forsyth, who accompanied Sheridan as aide-de-camp, the following is quoted:

The distance from Winchester to Cedar Creek, on the north bank of which the Army of the Shenandoah lay encamped, is a little less than nineteen miles. As we debouched into the fields . . . the general would wave his hat to the men and point to the front, never lessening his speed as he pressed forward. It was enough. One glance at the eager face and familiar black horse and they knew him and, starting to their feet, they swung their caps around their heads and broke into cheers as he passed beyond them; and then gathering up their belongings started after him for the front, shouting to their comrades farther out in the fields, " Sheridan! Sheridan!" waving their hats and pointing after him as he dashed onward. . . . So rapid had been our gait that nearly all of the escort save the commanding officer and a few of his best mounted men had been distanced, for they were more heavily weighted and ordinary troop horses could not live at such a pace.

In one of the closing scenes of the war—Five Forks—Sheridan was personally directing a movement against the Confederates who were protected by temporary entrenchments about two feet high. The Federal forces, both cavalry and infantry, were suffering from a sharp fire, which caused them to hesitate. "Where is my battle-flag?" cried Sheridan. Seizing it by the staff, he dashed ahead, followed by his command. The gallant steed leaped the low works and landed the Federal general fairly amid the astonished Southerners. Close behind him came Merritt's cavalrymen in a resistless charge which swept the Confederates backward in confusion. The horse passed a comfortable old age in his master's stable and died in Chicago, in 1878; the lifelike remains are now in the Museum at Governor's Island, N. Y., as a gift from his owner.

TWO FINE HORSES—THE PROVOST-MARSHAL'S MOUNTS

A couple of examples of the care given to horses at Giesboro. These two serviceable chargers belonged to Colonel George Henry Sharpe, Provost-Marshal of the Army of the Potomac. The provost-marshal of a great army must be well mounted. It is the duty of the provost-guard to arrest all criminals, take charge of deserters, follow the army and restore strag- glers to their regiments. This was no easy matter with an army of 120,000 men. Prisoners of war were also turned over to its care to be sent back to the institutions in the North. It is no wonder that the chief provided himself with powerful mounts. This photograph was taken at Brandy Station just before the strenuous campaign of the Wilderness.

GENERAL STUART'S "HIGHFLY"

The battle horse, "Highfly," carried General "Jeb" Stuart through many campaigns and had become his favored companion. The intelligence and faithfulness of the steed had many times borne the dashing cavalier through desperate perils. In the summer of 1862, at Verdiersville on the plank road between Fredericksburg and Orange, in Virginia, Stuart was stretched out upon a bench on the porch of the tavern, awaiting the arrival of General Fitzhugh Lee with whom he desired to confer on the next movement of the cavalry. "Highfly" was unbridled and grazing in the yard near the road. The clatter of horses aroused the Confederate general, and he walked to the roadway, leaving behind on the bench his hat, in which was a black plume, the pride of Stuart's heart. Suddenly, horsemen dashed around the bend in the road and Stuart was within gunshot of Federal cavalry. He was nonplussed; he had expected to see Fitzhugh Lee. Mounting his faithful and speedy bay he soon left the chagrined cavalry far behind, but the foe carried away the hat with its black plume.

GENERAL MEADE'S "BALDY"

In the first great battle of the Civil War, at Bull Run, there was a bright bay horse, with white face and feet. His rider was seriously wounded. The horse was turned back to the quartermaster to recover from his wounds received that day. Later, in September, General Meade bought the horse and named him "Baldy." Though Meade became deeply attached to the horse, his staff officers soon began to complain of the peculiar pace of "Baldy," which was hard to follow. He had a racking gait that was faster than a walk and slow for a trot and compelled the staff, alternately, to trot and then to drop into a walk, causing great discomfort.

"Baldy's" war record was remarkable. He was wounded twice at the first battle of Bull Run; he was at the battle of Drainesville; he took part in two of the seven days' fighting

THE HALT

On this and the opposite page are shown types of the horses for which the Northern States were ransacked to furnish mounts for the staff and regimental officers of the Union armies. Small wonder that this magnificent, well-groomed animal has excited the admiration of his own master who is critically looking him over. The officer is Captain Harry Page, quartermaster of the Headquarters of the Army of the Potomac, subsequently colonel and chief quartermaster of the cavalry corps under Sheridan. This was one of the most arduous posts of duty in the entire service, and one whose necessities during the severe campaigns up the Shenandoah Valley, and around Richmond, kept the young colonel always upon his mettle. He has cultivated the ability to rest and relax when the opportunity arrives. He is evidently awaiting the arrival of his wagon-train, when he will again become active at the pitching of the tents and the parking of the wagons.

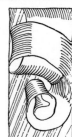

around Richmond in the summer of 1862; at Groveton, August 29th, at the second battle of Bull Run; at South Mountain and at Antietam. In the last battle the gallant horse was left on the field as dead, but in the next Federal advance "Baldy" was discovered quietly grazing on the battle-ground, with a deep wound in his neck. He was tenderly cared for and soon was again fit for duty. He bore the general at the battles of Fredericksburg and Chancellorsville. For two days "Baldy" was present at Gettysburg, where he received his most grievous wound from a bullet entering his body between the ribs, and lodging there. Meade would not part with the gallant horse, and kept him with the army until the following spring.

In the preparations of the Army of the Potomac for their last campaign, "Baldy" was sent to pasture at Downingtown, in Pennsylvania. After the surrender of Lee's army at Appomattox, Meade hurried to Philadelphia where he again met his faithful charger, fully recovered. For many years the horse and the general were inseparable companions, and when Meade died in 1872, the bullet-scarred war-horse followed the hearse. Ten years later "Baldy" died, and his head and two fore hoofs were mounted and are now cherished relics of the George G. Meade Post, Grand Army of the Republic, in Philadelphia.

GENERAL THOMAS' "BILLY"

The "Rock of Chickamauga," General George H. Thomas, possessed two intelligent war-horses, both powerful and large, and able to carry the general, who weighed nearly two hundred pounds. Both horses were bays; one named "Billy" (after Thomas' friend, General Sherman) was the darker of the two, about sixteen hands high, and stout in build. He was, like his owner, sedate in all his movements and was not easily disturbed from his habitual calm by bursting shells or the turmoil of battle. Even in retreat, the horse did not hurry his footsteps unduly, and provoked the staff by his deliberate pace.

"Billy" bore General Thomas through the campaigns in

[314]

AN OFFICER'S MOUNT

Captain Webster, whose horse this is, showed a just pride in his steed. Observe how the reins are hitched over the saddle to exhibit the arched neck to the best advantage. The equipment is regulation except for the unhooded stirrups. It has the preferable single line, curb bit, no breast strap and no martingale. The saddle is the McClellan, so-called because adopted through recommendations made by General George B. McClellan after his official European tour in 1860, although it was in reality a modification of the Mexican or Texas tree. It was an excellent saddle, and in an improved pattern remained after fifty years of trial still the standard saddle of the United States regular cavalry. In its original form it was covered with rawhide instead of leather, and when this covering split the seat became very uncomfortable to the rider. Captain Webster used a saddle cloth instead of the usual folded blanket. His horse's shiny coat shows recent thorough grooming.

middle Tennessee and northern Georgia. He was on the fields of Chickamauga and Chattanooga, and marched with the Federal host in the advance upon Atlanta. From Atlanta, he next moved to Nashville where his master engineered the crushing defeat to the Confederate arms in the winter of 1864, the last battle in which Thomas and "Billy" participated.

GENERAL HOOKER'S "LOOKOUT"

General Hooker first became acquainted with his famous charger, "Lookout," while the animal was stabled in New York, and when Louis Napoleon, the French emperor, and an English gentleman of wealth were bidding for its purchase. Napoleon repeatedly offered the owner a thousand dollars for the horse. Hooker finally obtained him and rode him in the campaigns in which he later participated.

"Lookout" was raised in Kentucky, and he was a three-quarters bred, out of a half bred mare by Mambrino. He was of a rich chestnut color, stood nearly seventeen hands high, and had long slender legs. Despite his great height, the horse was known to trot a mile in two minutes and forty-five seconds. When the battle of Chattanooga occurred, the horse was seven years old. It was here that the animal received its name of "Lookout." The grandeur of "Lookout's" stride and his height dwarfed many gallant war-horses and he has been termed the finest charger in the army.

GENERAL KEARNY'S HORSES

General Philip Kearny was a veteran of the Mexican War, with the rank of captain. It had been decided to equip Kearny's troop (First United States Dragoons) with horses all of the same color, and he went to Illinois to purchase them. He was assisted in the work by Abraham Lincoln and finally found himself in possession of one hundred gray horses. While engaged in battle before the City of Mexico, mounted upon one of the newly purchased grays, "Monmouth," Kearny was

WHEN SLEEK HORSES WERE PLENTIFUL—YORKTOWN, 1862

Confederate winter quarters near Yorktown, Virginia, which had passed into Federal hands.
When McClellan moved to the Peninsula in the spring of 1862 he had but few cavalry, but
every officer was provided with a handsome charger on which he pranced gaily up and down
the lines. "Little Mac" himself rode preferably at full speed. His appearance was the
signal for an outburst of cheering. It was to be a picnic parade of the well-equipped army
to the Confederate capital. It is presumable that the portly officer in the center of the picture
had lost some weight, and the chargers some sleekness before they were through with Lee and
Jackson. To such an extent had overwork and disease reduced the number of cavalry horses
during McClellan's retreat from the Peninsula that when General Stuart made his raid into
Pennsylvania, October 11th of the same year, only eight hundred Federal cavalry could be
mounted to follow him. Under date of October 21st, McClellan wrote to General Halleck:
"Exclusive of the cavalry force now engaged in picketing the river, I have not at present
over one thousand horses for service. Without more cavalry horses our communications
from the moment we march would be at the mercy of the large cavalry force of the enemy."

wounded in an arm, which was finally amputated. During the Civil War, Kearny had many excellent animals at his command, but his most celebrated steed was "Moscow," a high-spirited white horse. On the battlefield, "Moscow" was conspicuous because of his white coat, but Kearny was heedless of the protests of his staff against his needless exposure.

Another war-horse belonging to General Kearny was "Decatur," a light bay, which was shot through the neck in the battle of Fair Oaks or Seven Pines. "Bayard," a brown horse, was ridden by Kearny at this battle, and his fame will ever stand in history through the poem by Stedman, "Kearny at Seven Pines." At the battle of Chantilly, Kearny and "Bayard" were advancing alone near the close of the struggle, when they met with a regiment of Confederate infantry. "Bayard" instantly wheeled and dashed from danger, with Kearny laying flat upon the horse's neck. A shower of bullets fell about the general and his charger. They seemed about to escape when a fatal bullet struck the general.

The leader of the Southern legions in the West, General Albert Sidney Johnston, rode a magnificent thoroughbred bay, named "Fire-eater," on the battlefield. The steed stood patiently like a veteran when the bullets and shells hurtled about him and his master, but when the command came to charge, he was all fire and vim, like that Sunday in April, 1862, the first day of the bloody battle of Shiloh.

Among the hundreds of generals' mounts which became famous by their conspicuous bravery and sagacity on the battlefields, were General Fitzhugh Lee's little mare, "Nellie Gray," which was killed at the battle of Opequon Creek; Major-General Patrick R. Cleburne's "Dixie," killed at the battle of Perryville; General Adam R. Johnson's "Joe Smith," which was noted for its speed and endurance; and General Benjamin F. Butler's war-horse, "Almond Eye," a name derived from the peculiar formation of the eyes of the horse.

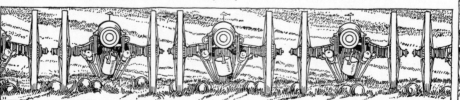

CHAPTER

TWELVE

MOUNTING THE CAVALRY
OF THE UNION ARMY

AN ORDERLY WITH AN OFFICER'S MOUNT

A THOUSAND FEDERAL CAVALRY HORSES

Lovers of horses will appreciate, in this photograph of 1864, the characteristic friendly fashion in which the cavalry "mounts" are gathering in deep communion. The numerous groups of horses in the corrals of the great depot at Giesboro, D. C., are apparently holding a series of conferences on their prospects in the coming battles. Presently all those who are in condition will resolve themselves into a committee of the whole and go off to war, whence they will return here only for hospital treatment. The corrals at Giesboro could easily contain a thousand horses, and they were never overcrowded. It was not until the true value of

"TALKING IT OVER"

cavalry was discovered, from the experience of the first two years of warfare, that this great depot was established, but it was most efficiently handled. Giesboro was a great teacher in regard to the care of horses. Cavalrymen learned what to guard against. The knowledge was acquired partly from field service, but in a great measure from the opportunity for leisurely observation, an opportunity somewhat analogous to that of a physician in a great metropolitan hospital where every kind of a physical problem has to be solved.

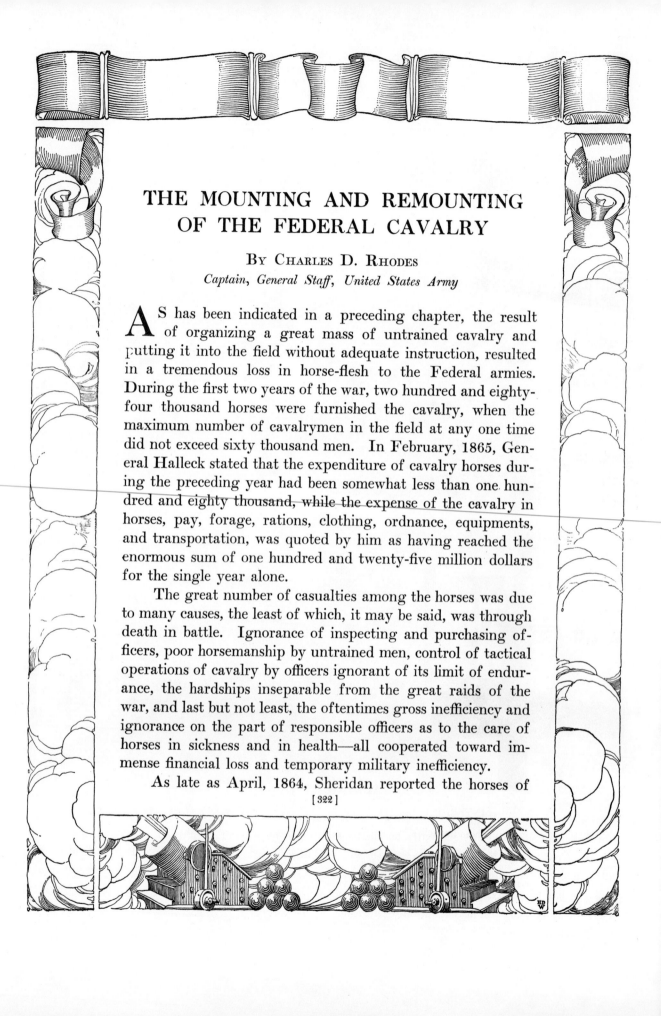

THE MOUNTING AND REMOUNTING OF THE FEDERAL CAVALRY

By Charles D. Rhodes
Captain, General Staff, United States Army

AS has been indicated in a preceding chapter, the result of organizing a great mass of untrained cavalry and putting it into the field without adequate instruction, resulted in a tremendous loss in horse-flesh to the Federal armies. During the first two years of the war, two hundred and eighty-four thousand horses were furnished the cavalry, when the maximum number of cavalrymen in the field at any one time did not exceed sixty thousand men. In February, 1865, General Halleck stated that the expenditure of cavalry horses during the preceding year had been somewhat less than one hundred and eighty thousand, while the expense of the cavalry in horses, pay, forage, rations, clothing, ordnance, equipments, and transportation, was quoted by him as having reached the enormous sum of one hundred and twenty-five million dollars for the single year alone.

The great number of casualties among the horses was due to many causes, the least of which, it may be said, was through death in battle. Ignorance of inspecting and purchasing officers, poor horsemanship by untrained men, control of tactical operations of cavalry by officers ignorant of its limit of endurance, the hardships inseparable from the great raids of the war, and last but not least, the oftentimes gross inefficiency and ignorance on the part of responsible officers as to the care of horses in sickness and in health—all cooperated toward immense financial loss and temporary military inefficiency.

As late as April, 1864, Sheridan reported the horses of

[322]

CAVALRY STABLES AT ARLINGTON—THE GREAT CORRAL IN THE DISTANCE, 3½ MILES

INTERIOR VIEW OF CAVALRY STABLES AT ARLINGTON

The streets of Washington re-echoed throughout the war with the clatter of horses' hoofs. Mounted aides, couriers, the general staff, the officers of the various regiments stationed in and about the Capital all had their chargers, and Giesboro was too far away to stable them. In the left-hand corner of the upper picture, the Giesboro corral shown on the following pages can be seen in the distance. A glance at the photograph will show that the corral was too far away to be convenient for horses in use in Washington. It is three and a half miles as the crow flies from Arlington to the corral. The photographer has written on the face of the lower photograph the date, "June 29, 1864." At this moment Grant was swinging his cavalry toward Petersburg.

[G—21]

his command worn out by the mistaken use of mounted men to protect trains—a duty which could be as well and much more economically performed by infantry; and by the unnecessary picket-duty, encircling the great infantry and cavalry camps of the Army of the Potomac on an irregular curve of nearly sixty miles.

In October, 1862, when service in the Peninsula campaign and in that of the Army of Virginia, had brought the number of mounted cavalrymen down to less than a good-sized regiment, McClellan wrote Halleck:

> It is absolutely necessary that some energetic measures be taken to supply the cavalry of this army with remount horses. The present rate of supply is 1,050 per week for the entire army here and in front of Washington. From this number the artillery draw for their batteries.

The demand for horses was so great that in many cases they were sent on active service before recovering sufficiently from the fatigue incident to a long railway journey. In one case reported, horses were left on railroad cars fifty hours without food or water, and were then taken out, issued, and used for immediate service in the field.

To such an extent had overwork and disease reduced the number of cavalry horses in the Army of the Potomac, that when the Confederate general, Stuart, made his daring raid into Pennsylvania, in October, 1862, only eight hundred Federal cavalrymen could be mounted to follow him.

Of course the original mounting of the cavalry, field-artillery, and field- and staff-officers caused a great demand for suitable chargers throughout the North. The draft animals required for transportation purposes increased the scarcity of suitable horses. Furthermore, with the unexpected losses during the first years of the war came such a dearth of animals suitable for the cavalry service, that in course of time almost any remount which conformed to the general specifications of a horse, was thankfully accepted by the Government.

[324]

SHELTER FOR SIX THOUSAND HORSES AT GIESBORO

Thirty-two immense stables, besides hospitals and other buildings, provided shelter for six thousand horses at the big cavalry depot, District of Columbia, but most of the stock was kept in open sheds or in corrals. The stockyards alone covered forty-five acres. The stables were large, well-lighted buildings with thousands of scrupulously clean stalls. The horses were divided into serviceable and unserviceable classes. About sixty per cent. of the horses received from the field for recuperation were returned to active service. Five thousand men were employed in August, 1863, to rush this cavalry depot to completion. Its maintenance was one of the costly items which aggregated an expenditure by the Union Government of $1,000,-000 a day during the entire period of the war—an expenditure running even as high as $4,000,000 a day.

THE BARRACKS AT GIESBORO

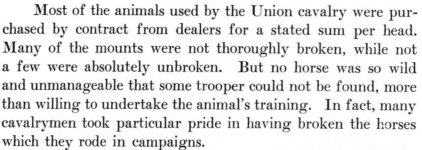

Most of the animals used by the Union cavalry were purchased by contract from dealers for a stated sum per head. Many of the mounts were not thoroughly broken, while not a few were absolutely unbroken. But no horse was so wild and unmanageable that some trooper could not be found, more than willing to undertake the animal's training. In fact, many cavalrymen took particular pride in having broken the horses which they rode in campaigns.

At the beginning of the war, when horses were being received from the West in car-load lots and shipped to the new regiments, some effort was made to organize troops of the same color—blacks, grays, bays, and sorrels—and to maintain this harmonious coloring from the remounts received from time to time. But after the regiments were fairly initiated into real campaigning and the losses in horseflesh became serious, all thought of coloring troops and regiments was abandoned, and the one idea was to secure serviceable mounts and remounts of any color, size, or description.

It is related of one cavalry colonel, whose regiment had been in several engagements and who had lost more than half his horses, that he appealed most eloquently to the quartermaster, for a supply of remounts. "Colonel," said the quartermaster in reply, "I'll tell you frankly that we haven't five pounds of horse for each man to be mounted." "That won't help much," retorted the colonel, testily; "we were thinking of riding the brutes, not of eating them."

The continual complaints as to the quality of the horses furnished, the tardiness with which remounts were supplied, and the inadequacy of conveniences for recuperating broken-down horses in the field, led to the establishment, in the year 1863, of the Cavalry Bureau, with General George Stoneman as its first chief, followed soon after by General Kenner Garrard. But it was under General James Harrison Wilson that the Cavalry Bureau reached its greatest efficiency.

This war bureau was charged with the organization and

IN BARRACKS

A COMFORTABLE SPOT

FOR THE CAVALRY TROOPER

These cavalrymen of '64 look comfortable enough in their barracks at Giesboro. When the cavalry depot was established there in '63, it was the custom to have the troopers return to the dismounted camp near Washington to be remounted and refitted. Some "coffee-coolers" purposely lost their equipments and neglected their horses in the field in order to be sent back for a time to the comfortable station. The order was finally given by General Meade to forward all horses, arms, and equipments to the soldiers in the field. While the men in this photograph are very much at ease and their lolling attitudes would seem to denote peace rather than war, they are probably none of them self-indulgent troopers who prefer this luxurious resting-place but are part of the garrison of the post charged with defending the valuable depot. There are many Civil War photographs of cattle on the hoof, but this picture contains the only representation of a sheep that has come to light.

equipment of the cavalry forces of the army, and with the providing of mounts and remounts. The inspection of horses for the latter purpose was ordered to be made by experienced cavalry officers, while the purchasing was under the direction of officers of the Quartermaster's Department of the army.

Under the general charge of the Cavalry Bureau, six principal depots were established at Giesboro, District of Columbia; St. Louis, Missouri; Greenville, Louisiana; Nashville, Tennessee; Harrisburg, Pennsylvania, and Wilmington, Delaware, for the reception, organization, and discipline of cavalry recruits, and for the collection, care, and training of horses.

The principal depot was at Giesboro, District of Columbia, on the north bank of the Potomac, below Washington, and consisted of a site of about six hundred and twenty-five acres for which the Government paid a rental of six thousand dollars per annum. Stables, stock-yards, forage-houses, storehouses, mess-houses, quarters, a grist-mill, a chapel, and wharves, were soon constructed, and within three months after taking possession (August 12, 1863) provision had been made for fifteen thousand animals; and within three months more, arrangement had been made for the care of thirty thousand animals, although twenty-one thousand was the largest number on hand at any one time. The wharves afforded facilities for three steamers of the largest class to load simultaneously; the hospitals had accommodation for two thousand six hundred and fifty horses; five thousand men were employed during the construction period, afterward reduced to fifteen hundred; while thirty-two stables, besides hospitals and other buildings, gave shelter to six thousand horses. Most of the stock was kept in open sheds or in corrals, these stock-yards alone covering forty-five acres, each yard being furnished with hay-racks and water-troughs, and having free access to the river. The estimated cost of the Giesboro Depot was $1,225,000.

The remount depot at St. Louis covered about four hundred acres, and had a force of nearly eleven hundred employees

CAVALRY TO GUARD THE DISTRICT OF COLUMBIA.

Between June and December, 1863, just at the time that the Giesboro remount depot was established, four companies of the First District of Columbia Cavalry (A, B, C, and D) were organized. These commands were assigned to special service in the District of Columbia, subject only to the orders of the War Department. The thousands of mounts at Giesboro were not many miles from the track of the Confederate raiders, and presented a tempting prize to them. But early in 1864 the "District" cavalry were ordered away to southeastern Virginia, where they served with Kautz's cavalry division in the Army of the James, during the Petersburg and Appomattox campaigns. Colonel Lafayette C. Baker, in command of this cavalry, reported an encounter with Mosby, to whose depredations their organization was chiefly due, on October 22, 1863: "Sir: This morning about ten o'clock a detachment of my battalion, under command of Major E. J. Conger, and a detachment of the California battalion, under command of Captain Eigenbrodt, encountered a squad of Mosby's men some three miles this side of Fairfax Court House and near the Little River turnpike. One of Mosby's men (named Charles Mason) was shot and instantly killed. The celebrated guerrillas, Jack Barns, Ed. Stratton, and Bill Harover, were captured and forwarded to the Old Capitol Prison. These men state that they were looking for Government horses and sutlers' wagons. None of our force were injured." Colonel Baker was in the Federal Secret Service, and used these cavalrymen as his police. Eight additional companies were subsequently organized for the First District of Columbia Cavalry at Augusta, Maine, January to March, 1864, but after some service with Kautz's cavalry, these were consolidated into two companies and merged into the First Maine Cavalry.

—blacksmiths, carpenters, wagon-makers, wheelwrights, far-riers, teamsters, and laborers in many departments.

The stables were long, well-lighted buildings with thousands of scrupulously clean stalls. From five to ten thousand horses were usually present at the depot, nearly evenly divided between serviceable and unserviceable classes—the latter class being again divided into convalescents and condemned animals. The condemned horses were those declared unfit for further military service, and unless afflicted with some incurable disability, were sold at public auction.

About fifty per cent. of the horses received from the field for recuperation were returned to active service, "fit for duty." More than half of the remainder were recuperated sufficiently to be sold as condemned animals, while less than one-fourth of the unserviceable animals received, died at the depot or were killed to prevent further suffering.

The bane of the cavalry service of the Federal armies in the field was diseases of the feet. "Hoof-rot," "grease-heel," or the "scratches" followed in the wake of days and nights spent in mud, rain, snow, and exposure to cold, and caused thousands of otherwise serviceable horses to become useless for the time being.

Sore backs became common with the hardships of campaigning, and one of the first lessons taught the inexperienced trooper was to take better care of his horse than he did of himself. The remedy against recurrence of sore backs on horses was invariably to order the trooper to walk and lead the disabled animal. With a few such lessons, cavalry soldiers of but short service became most scrupulous in smoothing out wrinkles in saddle-blankets, in dismounting to walk steep hills, in giving frequent rests to their jaded animals, and when opportunity offered, in unsaddling and cooling the backs of their mounts after hours in the saddle. Poor forage, sudden changes of forage, and overfeeding produced almost as much sickness and physical disability as no forage at all.

A RIDING COB

IN WASHINGTON, 1865

NOT THE SORT

FOR CAVALRY

This skittish little cob with the civilian saddle, photographed at the headquarters of the defense of Washington south of the Potomac, in 1865, was doubtless an excellent mount upon which to ride back to the Capital and pay calls. But experience soon taught that high-strung hunters and nervous cobs were of little or no use for either fighting or campaigning. When the battle was on and the shells began to scream a small proportion of these pedigreed animals was sufficient to stampede an entire squadron. They took fright and bolted in all directions. On the other hand, they were far too sensitive for the arduous night marches, and lost in nerves what they gained in speed. A few of them were sufficient to keep a whole column of horses who would otherwise be patiently plodding, heads down, actually stumbling along in their sleep, wide awake and restive by their nervous starts and terrors. The short-barreled, wiry Virginia horses, almost as tireless as army mules, proved to be far their superiors for active service.

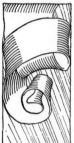
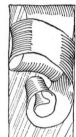

In its cantonment at Brandy Station, during the winter of 1864, the cavalry of the Army of the Potomac was nearly ruined by increasing the ration of grain to make up a deficiency in hay. During the famous Stoneman raid (March and April, 1863) an entire cavalry division was without hay for twenty-one days, in a country where but little grazing was possible. During Sheridan's last raid, in 1865, nearly three-fourths of the lameness of his horses was due to an involuntary change of forage from oats to corn.

But much of the breaking-down of cavalry horses was merely inseparable from the hardships and privations which every great war carries in its train, and which the most experienced leaders cannot foresee or prevent.

In General Sheridan's march from Winchester to Petersburg, February 27th to March 27, 1865, each trooper carried on his horse, in addition to his regular equipment, five days' rations in haversacks, seventy-five rounds of ammunition, and thirty pounds of forage. On General James H. Wilson's Selma expedition, each trooper carried, besides his ordinary kit, five days' rations, twenty-four pounds of grain, one hundred rounds of ammunition, and two extra horseshoes.

A remarkable case, illustrating the conditions surrounding the war service of cavalry regiments, was that of the Seventh Pennsylvania Cavalry. In April, 1864, this regiment started on a march from Nashville, Tennessee, to Blake's Mill, Georgia. It had nine hundred and nineteen horses fresh from the Nashville remount depot, and among its enlisted men were three hundred recruits, some of whom had never been on a horse before.

In a little over four months, the regiment marched nine hundred and two miles, not including fatiguing picket duty and troop scouting. During this period, the horses were without regular supplies of forage for twenty-six days, on scanty forage for twenty-seven days, and for seven consecutive days were without food of any kind. In one period of seventy-two

WHERE THE FEDERAL CAVALRY WAS TRAINED

Giesboro, D. C., where the cavalry of the Army of the Potomac was remounted after August, 1863, was also their drill and training camp.

A BIG RESPONSIBILITY—FORT CARROLL, GIESBORO, D. C.

Millions of dollars worth of Government property was entrusted to the men who occupied these barracks at Fort Carroll, Giesboro, D. C. The original cost of the cavalry depot was estimated at a million and a quarter dollars, and there were immense stores of fodder, medicine, cavalry equipment, and supplies at the depot, besides the value of the horses themselves. The Union Government's appropriations for the purchase of horses for the period of the war mounted to $123,864,915. The average contract price per head was $150, so that approximately 825,766 horses were used in the Union armies. Giesboro was the largest of the Government's cavalry depot and it must have been an anxious time for those responsible for the preservation of all this wealth when Early threatened Washington.

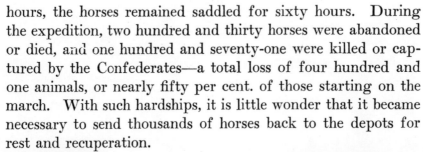

hours, the horses remained saddled for sixty hours. During the expedition, two hundred and thirty horses were abandoned or died, and one hundred and seventy-one were killed or captured by the Confederates—a total loss of four hundred and one animals, or nearly fifty per cent. of those starting on the march. With such hardships, it is little wonder that it became necessary to send thousands of horses back to the depots for rest and recuperation.

But, of course, one of the main purposes of the great horse-depots of the Civil War period, was not to recuperate horses already in the military service, but to receive, condition, and issue thousands of animals purchased throughout the country for army use.

During the fiscal year ending June 30, 1864, the Federal Government purchased 188,718 horses in addition to 20,308 captured from the Confederates and reported; while during the first eight months of the year 1864, the cavalry of the Army of the Potomac, alone, was supplied with two complete remounts or nearly forty thousand horses.

The price paid to contractors by Federal purchasing agents averaged about $150 per head, and occasionally really high-class horses found their way into the lots received at the depots. More often, however, the reverse was the case, and the inspectors of horses were usually at their wits' ends detecting the many frauds and tricks of the horse trade, which dealers attempted to perpetrate on the Government. Men otherwise known to be of the staunchest integrity seem to lose all sense of the equity of things when it comes to selling or swapping horses; and this is particularly the case when the other party to the transaction is the Government, a corporate body incapable of physical suffering and devoid of sentiment.

The Giesboro depot received between January 1, 1864, and June 30, 1866—a period of two and one-half years—an aggregate of 170,654 cavalry horses. Of this number, 96,006 were issued to troops in the field, 1574 were issued to officers,

AN ARTILLERY OFFICER'S MOUNT   A QUARTERMASTER'S MOUNT

Mounts were required by staff and regimental officers, as well as for the cavalry and mounted artillery. So great was the demand that during the second year of the war any quadruped that answered to the general specifications of a horse was seized upon. These fine animals look as if they had been obtained early in the war. The second and third show a "U. S." brand on the shoulder.

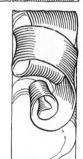

48,721 were sold, and 24,321 died. In addition to this number, over 12,000 artillery horses were handled at the depot.

While the capacity of the St. Louis depot was thirty thousand animals, it was never completely filled—the serviceable remounts being promptly forwarded to regiments in the field, and the recuperating animals being held only long enough to render them serviceable or to determine whether they would not respond to further rest or veterinary treatment. The hospitals for the accommodation and treatment of disabled animals were probably the most complete of their kind existing at that time; but after it had been demonstrated that an animal could not be nursed back to the military service, it was a matter of economy to dispose of him to some enterprising bidder for the average price of thirty dollars per head.

The depot system or caring for Government stock, receiving those newly purchased and recuperating those returning sick or disabled from the field, proved a measure of the greatest economy to the Federal Government, in addition to its marked effect on the military efficiency of the mounted service. The value of the animals returned to duty with regiments from the St. Louis depot alone, in excess of what the same animals would have been worth at public auction as condemned articles of sale, was in a single year nearly two hundred thousand dollars more than the entire operating expenses of the plant.

When it is remembered that there were six large depots, all engaged in handling the mounts and remounts of the great Federal armies, and that the depots at Giesboro and St. Louis comprised but a part of this complex system of administration and supply, the tremendous responsibilities imposed upon the Cavalry Bureau of the Federal War Department may be appreciated and understood.

AN HONOR MAN OF THE REGULARS

First-Sergeant Conrad Schmidt of the Second United States Cavalry—a fine type of the "regular" trooper. He was decorated for galloping to the assistance of his captain, whose horse had been killed in a charge, mounting the officer behind him under fire and riding off to safety, although his own horse had been wounded in five places. This was at the Opequon, September 19, 1864.